GOD
AND I
AND ELVIS

GOD
AND I
AND ELVIS

The Tried and True Elvis Hidden In Plain Sight

ILONA BAUER

(The Girl He Never Loved)

TUPELO MISSISSIPPI USA

VANTAGEPress
NEW YORK

Cover layout by Dave Riedy
Cover design by Ilona Bauer
Vantage Press and the Vantage Press colophon
are registered trademarks of Vantage Press, Inc.

FIRST EDITION
All rights reserved, including the right of
reproduction in whole or in part in any form.

Copyright © 2012 by Ilona Bauer

Published by Vantage Press, Inc.
419 Park Ave. South, New York, NY 10016

Manufactured in the United States of America
ISBN: 978-0533-164516

Library of Congress Catalog Card No: 2011913526

0 9 8 7 6 5 4 3 2 1

PREFATORY NOTE

The premise of this book, God and I and Elvis, is about the reality of the supernatural. It confirms the existence of God as He declares Himself to be in His Holy Word, the Scriptures: Omnipotent, Omniscient, Omnipresent.

It is this essential, pivotal role of the Holy Spirit, the supernatural in this story, which ties everything together.

Only with the willingness of the reader to go with me on a spiritual journey will I be able to put Elvis's life and its purpose into a more proper perspective than has been done so far. I am here to try to remedy that because it is only his spiritual quality that I have been intimately familiar with for a very, very long time.

Elvis's torment, his passion, his pain, and his joy are all audible in the huge volume of songs he left behind.

I am respectfully asking the reader to forgive me for using his songs as references to connect the reality of the Holy Spirit with the reality we live in.

    Tupelo, Mississippi 2009
    Ilona Bauer

TABLE OF CONTENTS

	Introduction: *The Way I Came To Know Elvis Presley*	ix
1	Called	1
2	Faith at Work	14
3	Falling (into my destiny) In Love	34
4	Caught In a Trap	50
5	Are You Lonesome Tonight?	72
6	So Close, Yet So Far	92
7	Confusion/Suspicion	107
8	Separate Ways	125
9	Where Do I Go From Here?	140
10	The Edge of Reality	169
11	The Power of My Love	197
12	Only the Strong Survive	217
13	Because of Love	245
14	Follow That Dream	269

15	Bridge Over Troubled Water	316
16	That's the Way it is	339
17	It's Now or Never	354
	Afterword	369

INTRODUCTION

The Way I Came to Know Elvis Presley

It was 1958 in West Germany where I was attending a public college-prep school for girls in Nuremberg. My seventeenth birthday was a few weeks away. I roomed with three girls in a student-home that was run by the Evangelical Lutheran Church. All of us were bible-believing girls as we were reared in the tradition of this church.

Serious bible-study was mandatory for an additional two years on top of the regular religious instructions, which were part and parcel of the school curriculum, all leading up to the big day of confirmation. I gave my solemn oath of obedient service to God on that very special day in May of 1955 in Wuerzburg where I was born and had lived with my mother and two sisters. In early 1956 I moved to live with my father in Nuremberg. He did not know what to do with me, which made me a complication for two aunts and a grandmother who were also quite leery of me—I looked too much like my mother for their taste. My relationship with my father and his family was complicated, to say the least, but I had a pleasant school experience. I had been elected class president for the second time and what I did not receive from school or home, I could and did call on God to provide as He had done for me many, many times before.

On that fateful morning we had math first. My friend and classmate who sat behind me, was telling me again about the guy she had mentioned to me the day before who sang so crazy on the radio. I was dreadfully preoccupied with my homework, which I was unable to finish at home as math was mostly a mystery to me. I tried to get the needed help from the class-math-genius who sat in front of me. Between worrying with my homework and having to listen to my friend's ongoing prattling about a guy I had absolutely no interest in, I was hard-pressed to remain polite, when she stuck a picture of this guy under my nose from behind. It was a small picture, only 1 x ½" but there was a young man looking straight into my eyes. A stinging pain shot through my heart (soul?), which I could feel as sharply as if someone had struck me with a switch. It took my breath away. I was transfixed. I recognized this man as someone very familiar to me and I perceived simultaneously that he was in desperate peril and that I had to help him. Just then the professor came into the classroom. We had to stand at her entering and after she had told us to be seated, I was still somewhat disconnected from my surroundings when I slowly regained consciousness and my breath. I could not help but realize that something miraculous had just happened to me. I loved this man! But who was he? There was no name on the little picture.

GOD
AND I
AND ELVIS

1

Called

It was in the year 1941 when I was born in Wuerzburg, Germany, the third child of a young mother, Annabeth and Friderich, her husband, who was sixteen years her senior.

My first memory of that time was my father coming home from where he had been stationed as a soldier in Hitler's army. We were living in what you would now call an upscale part of the city, a small distance from the Max Planck Institut on the Roentgenstrasse 6. We children had our own large room adjacent to our parents' bedroom.

I heard screaming and yelling coming from the long hallway and I was curious to see what the noise was all about, but when I opened the door I saw my father stomping on my mother with his black German soldier boots, screaming things I could not understand. The children's nurse, Liesl, quickly pushed me into the room and shut the door. The yelling continued, I could still hear it, but I knew nothing of what was going on. I was three years old at the time of that display of violence, my brother Paul was five, and my sister Anneliese was six.

The war was raging. Sirens were sounding the alarm, far away, and at night we had to put government-issued, heavy black blankets over all the windows. All too often we would huddle together listening in terror for the information being broadcast on the radio, which we all listened to, sometimes sweating as we had to cover ourselves with a blanket, followed by the humming of the enemy bombers searching for their intended targets. In retrospect, it was to our definite disadvantage to live so close to a scientific research institute.

As I recall, it was my brother who seemed most affected by the war. He had trouble sleeping and would often just bob his head up and down, up and down, onto his hands as he lay on his stomach, trying to put himself to sleep.

The building we lived in was a brownstone and my family was on the second floor. My mother's father, Otto, who also ended up in the German armed forces, lived there too.

In the winter of 1944 we were hurried down the stairs and across the courtyard into the back of the building where there was a fallout shelter. I landed on a heap of potatoes. Everybody was trying to find a place to sit and there was a confusing scramble. Voices were subdued, as the sirens were sounding very close by. We all sensed an impending disaster. And then it was quiet. Somebody said to go up the stairs to check and see what was going on. Liesl volunteered, ran quickly up the steep staircase, and opened the door. All eyes were on her when she was literally thrown down those steep stairs by the extreme force of impact of a bomb. The ensuing heat-generated fire from the explosion was clearly visible. We were hit. Our home had been destroyed. We had nothing but the clothes we were wearing and I guess whatever one put into a safe place for just such an event.

After having been bombed out we were evacuated to Heidingsfeld, a small town outside Wuerzburg, where we found shelter at the house of a medical doctor who had his office on the ground floor and lived with his family on the second floor. We had a kitchen on the fourth floor which was under the roof and had those low, angled ceilings.

In this attic kitchen there was also a bed, in which my mother slept with her boyfriend whom we children had to address as "Uncle Genoff." He was the father of my half-sister, and the reason for that tumult in the hallway back in Wuerzburg. The baby slept with them in the kitchen too and the rest of us slept in a bedroom on the second floor, where a kindly family lived.

The family structure had changed. There was no more brother and we sisters did not see him again until we were in our teens. I cannot recall an occasion when anything was explained to us but we knew better than to ask because our mother had a most volatile disposition and would scream and yell at the slightest provocation.

As we discovered from information given to us by various aunts and former employees of our grandfather, our mother lost her own mother at the age of nine. As my grandfather's only child she was the proverbial apple of his eye and he spoiled her thoroughly.

His business was in tobacco and he managed to earn himself a modest fortune; but this business kept him away from home so much, he could not make a significant contribution to a sound value structure. Consequently our mother was primarily supervised and influenced by staff.

She became willful and headstrong and always got what she set out to get. One example to illustrate this is how she got married to our father. As the story goes, my mother was looking out the window with one of her girlfriends. Some soldiers were passing by and she noticed this handsome blond-haired and blue-eyed soldier. She said to her girlfriend, "Do you see that fellow down there, the handsome one? That's the man I am going to marry!"

She was a mere sixteen and he was twice her age, but marry they did.

While she was enchanted by the idea of marriage, she had no idea what hard work and, more importantly what serious commitment it requires. Soon she was expecting her first child and the nurse that had tended to my mother now tended to her children.

Adding to these problems was the difference in my parents' backgrounds. My father came from a family of farmers. He loved and cherished his father and mother, his brothers and sisters, and all of them loved the fatherland. By contrast my mother was a spoiled city girl who was too immature yet to love anyone or anything outside herself. The world simply revolved around her.

Then our brother arrived and then there I arrived too and I know that she loved us but more like you would love a pet; if you tired of it you just walked away and did whatever else caught your fancy. But as long as she was pleased with us, her attention was what we all craved and loved. We loved our mother, but the war had ruined all her dreams, the harsh reality of raising three children soon dawned on her, and she could not escape her self-constructed dilemma. Dealing with taking care of children was not what she had signed up for. She wanted to have fun, so she started an affair with a dental student from Bulgaria while her husband was fighting at the French front and my grandfather at the Russian front. Enter our half-sister, Ivana. Our father immediately took our brother and brought him to his mother who lived in the country near Nuremberg. This left my mother with us girls—now three—and this uncle whom I learned to dislike later on but at age four, five, and six was too young yet to form any kind of opinion. As long as he did not beat us and took care of us on occasion he was all right.

We stayed in Heidingsfeld for five years, during which we had many experiences that influenced our lives for years to come.

Heidingsfeld was a small town; a remnant of the Middle Ages, replete with a stone wall surrounding it and a castle owned by a baroness who graciously loaned it to the Lutheran monastery to help the many orphaned children of the war.

My sister and I ended up there too because we got on our mother's nerves. I remember those days very well. It was there where I learned to be afraid of horses. We had a typical country outing, and as on any garden-variety country estate, there were the horses. They were far too big for me to feel comfortable around them but we all had to learn to ride those huge beasts. I objected, and screamed in fear, but to no avail. They put me on that big horse which to me looked like a Clydesdale. I was barely wrangled up on that creature when it bent down to nibble on the grass, completely bored with the whole maneuver, and I promptly slid down its neck and off its head, right before the ears. I cried and wanted to get away but one of the sisters caught me and up we went again with the same result. I think that sister had a perverse pleasure in torturing me.

I was allowed to be with my sister's age group at night because I was homesick. We were sleeping in this large rectangular room with one huge window—it was a castle, after all—and because I was the youngest and somewhat on the darling side the older children loved having me with them, which was nice, but they also had their fun with me. My bed was by that huge window and when it was thundering and lightning was flashing I was scared to death. To make matters worse, the older children told me that if I looked into the lightning I would become blind, and if I were to point at it, my finger would fall off. If I had been scared before, I was absolutely petrified then, so petrified I would put the blanket over my head and not come out from under it. Apparently I got too hot under the covers, dreamed I was on the toilet, and wet my bed. I knew what would happen at breakfast. Mother Superior would publicly shame me as I had seen her do before to someone else.

This was not the worst, however. It came after breakfast and I was not aware of what was to come when I was summoned to Sister Barbara's office. Not knowing where that was, somebody accompanied me there without saying a word and I had this sense of doom coming over me. I saw the sister standing there, holding my wet bed sheet all spread out like some wonderful work of art, and saying sternly, "You know who did this, don't you? You also know that there is punishment for this!" Little as I was I could not just let her accuse me of something I had no control over. I tried to explain but no matter. She followed procedure, motioned me to a stool, ordered me to bend over it, and she proceeded with the prescribed punishment for this kind of offense, which required three strikes with what looked like one of the legs of that stool, a quite thick wooden rod. I was outraged at this entire debacle and vowed that when I grew up I'd come back and tell this sister a few things.

For whatever reason, I was a very sexually intuitive child. I do not know how to explain it. I could move my body in a certain way and orgasm. It was like a release for me, aside from the intensely pleasurable sensation. I was not aware that this behavior, which I would engage in when I was in bed, was not acceptable. Some of the older girls told on me and I was lectured on the utter depravity of such conduct, and, moreover, told that God would punish me when I grew up and that I would not be able to have children, which was bothersome to me. I did try to abstain, though I could not quite understand why. Being so young, I had no concept of maternal instinct or of how significant the inability to have children could be someday. As I said, I tried, but was on the whole unsuccessful, despite there now being a feeling of guilt that made it a less desirable activity. This would turn out to be an ever-present problem I found myself having to deal with for a long time to come.

On many sunny days we would have wonderful field trips into the forest, which I loved. I loved the sunshine, the little bugs and butterflies, the smell of the woods, the wild flowers growing there and their sweet fragrance—it was magical. One day I was told to go to the edge of an opening in the thicket at the end of the woods, where it led to the meadow rolling down to the barns. There was a man standing there, looking intently at me and saying, "Ilona, I am your father!" I was not impressed. What was a father anyway? From my experience a father was hardly ever there. It was only years later, when I tried to envision what my father looked like, that I'd wished I had paid closer attention. Again, at five you just do not understand a whole lot about anything, which really was a blessing in disguise.

After my mother's nerves had settled we got to go home. My sister and I were often sent outside with our baby sister Ivana in tow in her buggy. We'd have our friends who either lived in the house with us or were from around the neighborhood, join us. We were just average children doing average children's things and having a good time. One thing I remember disliking was facing the force of a strong wind. It always took my breath away. I simply could not catch my breath which made me struggle for air and really scared me. I hated the smell of geraniums in the window boxes, which seemed to be everywhere, not only in the windows.

Many times on our excursions we would go to the cemetery, which I grew very fond of, and often went there alone to linger among the lovely statues of angels, figurines of the Madonna Mary and of doves and crosses. I loved it.

Our grandfather returned from the Russian front where he had been imprisoned and he shared our bedroom with us. He did love his granddaughters and he especially liked me, maybe because I resembled my mother, who resembled his late wife. When I had nightmares he would calm me. I had a particular nightmare which so terrorized me that I was afraid to go to sleep. I had this nightmare over and over again. I told my grandfather about it, explaining that in my dream I would be lying down, unable to get up, while a constantly rotating link fence was encircling me, coming ever closer, ever closer, threatening to finally constrict me; I would try desperately to scream for help but no sound would come out of my mouth. I would wake up screaming.

With the return of my grandfather our old nurse Liesl re-entered our lives. Most of the time however, my mother had young girls from Wuerzburg helping her with the housework since she had no housewife skills at anything that required strenuous work.

After my grandfather Otto's return we children were baptized into the Evangelical Lutheran Church. I entered the elementary school in Heidingsfeld where instruction in religion was part of the curriculum and I dearly loved the Bible stories. Somehow I sensed a mysterious connection between the Jesus they were telling us about in school and the lovely peaceful atmosphere at the cemetery. I also had a fascination with the dead at the funeral home nearby and I would often go there to perhaps catch a glimpse of a corpse laid out to be buried. To me it was a pleasant way to spend an hour or so. My friends did not share my interest so I mostly went alone. I would rather have been alone anyway.

As I grew older I preferred times alone. The living that went on took place in the kitchen that was a part of the apartment. It was always crowded with all sorts of folks I did not recognize from Wuerzburg. My sister was mostly bogged down with taking care of Ivana who was now old enough to be in a stroller.

More often than not when I was supposed to be with my sisters, I went off with my friends. This made it easier on my sister since she did not have to worry with me too. Sometimes she'd tell on me and I got a good talking to. I always promised to be better next time until next time came. From all accounts I was a headache to my mother. People regularly complained to her that I was running too fast up and down the stairs and that when they would caution me, I had something smart to say in reply. It was always something. They tell me I was a pretty and bubbly, outgoing girl who was just full of herself when not sick with something. I was a sickly child. I always had one sort of an ailment or another. Colds were regularly plaguing me, ugly, huge cold sores on my lips were common, I had pinworms lice, scrapes, and outright wounds from climbing up on the village wall and falling out of trees; then the wound would get infected and I had to be taken to the doctor downstairs. And there were these horrible sore throats!

It seemed that my sister had none of these things to contend with. How my poor ill-equipped mother coped with all this! I can only guess that she had to have a lot of help.

When our faithful nurse Liesl would come to help out, she would take me with her to a Catholic church to go to Mass. I was totally enraptured by the pomp and ceremony, the chants, the incense, the kneeling, and the breathtaking beauty of that cathedral. I was awestruck and felt such a love for what all this splendor transmitted to me. It was in part this overwhelming sacredness and seriousness and humble reverence for this higher power, combined with the instruction in school that made me aware that I had an ever-present source of help available to me. I felt truly special that God chose to love me and I was so fixated on the idea that I needed God to assure me that this was so indeed.

When I wanted to be alone on a rainy day I would sit on the staircase, facing a window where I could see the sky and the trees of the park across the way, and I would be brooding. Today I call it mulling. I do a lot of mulling. In those mulling-times I could perceive this indescribable presence that I readily acknowledged, and I prayed for God to please, please let me know that what I was feeling was real. But as everybody knows, God goes by a vastly different timetable from ours, certainly from mine which was, "I want it right now!"

Time passed and we entertained ourselves by staging plays where everybody was invited. The older children from outside and inside the old city wall set everything up. Whoever could perform with some skill had a part. I was a very agile girl. I loved to dance, sing, do backbends and splits, and other body-bending tricks. These stunts always got a good reception. The audience clapped in approval and I was thrilled. It is of note that although we had lost everything in the war, and we barely had enough to eat, we found a way to enjoy life. How amazingly resilient children are and what protection it is for them to be so innocent and unaware of the basic cruelty of life.

Thanks to my grandfather's business connections, we always had something to eat. He would get very angry when we'd wrinkle our noses and dared to say we did not like something. He would then tell us about all the trouble he had to go through just to get what was offered. We would apologize and eat. He insisted on saying a prayer before we started eating, an important teaching tool as far as Liesl was concerned, and it was only right as far as I was concerned. How I loved my grandfather! When I was afraid, he'd hold me and sing beautiful songs, which he loved to sing to me. I recognized them years later as staples in Enrico Caruso's and Mario Lanza's repertoires.

Time passed by. We went to the Main River, which is a tributary to the Rhine, where people would swim and play at the banks; it looked much like a beach. We children were naked—yes, all of us. I cannot remember if my mother was naked too but since I remember being stared at by the other swimmers and children, we were not at a nudist beach. My mother did not bother much with convention, which made our lives quite difficult as we grew up. She lived as she pleased and we had no sense of acceptable or unacceptable, and unless this was made clear to us we thought nothing of it. People, however, were interested in our family and when I would be asked where everybody slept, I never hesitated a moment to explain in detail who slept where and with whom. It sure would have been better if my mother had ever considered someone else other than herself.

The innocence of a child! I treasure this quality, so without guile and malice, so open; and how soon children must learn that people all too often make this world an ugly and cruel place.

Knowing deep within myself that there was someone who would be there always, I was still waiting on a sign from God.

It was the late afternoon of a day spent with my friends. I sat on the concrete base of the wrought-iron fence surrounding the stately home where we were lucky enough to have found shelter, looking at the sky with the good-byes of my friends still ringing in my ears, as they had been called in for the evening meal. The sky was looking dark and threatening but I could see the sun behind it shining brightly. It looked so beautiful and I started to pray for God to make himself known to me, when the clouds parted and this bright ray of sunshine fell right on me. I thought at once that my prayer had been answered. Yet still, like Doubting Thomas, I had to check and see if it was really true. I looked around and saw that there was darkness all around me, that only I was sitting in the light. From then on, I believed wholeheartedly. I felt a wonderful, warm feeling that seemed to have its origin within me. It enveloped me completely and I felt such a sense of peace, one that is impossible to describe. The sun disappeared as quickly as it had come and I knew I had an ally for all time.

For some reason I had the impression that it was imperative that this experience be kept secret. In fact, I was very afraid that the revealing of it would cancel everything. Though I had no concept of what "everything" consisted of, I had a very vague impression that it was important. I loved to recall this "meeting" with God and that confirmation of my innermost dreams and longing to belong.

Despite being aware of this helping presence in my life, I did not expect to have a carefree existence. To my dismay I discerned very faintly that just the opposite would be the case. I did not want to know this so I just ignored it. But way down the road the chickens would come home to roost, so to speak.

The first inkling I got of this fact happened on a regular day of playing with my sister and friends. This time we roamed around at the train station on the other side of the park. We often went behind the stationhouse where disabled freight cars would be parked off to the side. This time, however, we went inside the station. The older children would try to get candy out of the machines there. They pulled the levers and kicked the machine, ordering it to give them some candy, without success. Finally, they got tired of it and moved on while I was deciding, and even challenging myself, to prove that I was special, and that I would get some candy.

That was the last thing I remember doing. The next thing I was aware of was waking up in the hospital. I have been told that this machine apparently was no longer mounted securely onto the wall and after all the rough treatment by the gang of bigger and stronger children it was actually freestanding, and the whole thing fell on me. The children, including my sister, ran away and a lady who was waiting on the train pulled me out from under the machine and carried me to the adjoining house, and then went from door to door, trying to find out where I belonged. My sister had gone home and told our mother and I was brought to the hospital.

I was in a coma and had several holes in my head, and a broken nose. I stayed in the hospital for a long time and had to stay in bed ever so long. By the time I could go home it was required of me to walk, which I could not do without assistance. I will never forget how long and steep and impossible it seemed to tackle the stairs. It took me quite a while to do this, and once at home, I was put in my baby sister's crib during the day so I would remain safe from re-injuring the sewn-up head wounds. Never in my short life have I been so fussed over and indulged. Even my older sister was very sympathetic and sweet to me. She probably felt in part responsible since she left me there by myself. At any rate, I enjoyed all this expressed love, care, and concern.

Eventually I was well enough to resume normal activities, though at a slower pace.

Being a child, I rather quickly forgot this ordeal and continued to believe that I had this helping hand extended to me and often, motivated by desperation, I would pray for this help to come to my rescue.

One such occasion was at the dinner table. My grandfather had just finished giving his sermon on gratitude because we had "cooked horseradish" which I simply could not eat without gagging and had asked if I could forego having to eat it. It looked identical to cream of wheat, which I really loved to eat, but then I remembered that looks can be deceiving. So I prayed for God to please change the horseradish, during the transfer from the big bowl to my plate, into cream of wheat. I did not want to incite my beloved grandfather's anger.

He insisted on my having some anyway, just a little bit, so that I might learn to like it. I fully expected to have cream of wheat instead of horseradish on my plate. But it was not. I put it slowly into my mouth and tasted that horrid horseradish and promptly gagged. I swallowed it quickly and my grandfather was merciful and did not insist on my eating the rest.

Erika was one of the girls who my mother engaged more regularly to help her with the household, such as it was. I can only guess that my grandfather paid for this. Work was apparently hard to come by as Germany tried to assess the damage done by the allied forces and how to get organized to rebuild. Women who had lived comfortably before the war now found themselves having to scrub floors and do the ironing for those who could pay them for their services. This made for some strange relationships. But nobody really took notice. This was the existential fight for survival. People who would have never interacted socially before with a certain segment of society now had to swallow their pride, as beggars cannot be choosers. Erika, however, seemed different. She was inordinately concerned about her appearance, in particular her use, or I should say overuse, of makeup. Before this time, I had not seen most of the implements she used to make herself look pretty. I was curious and so I always watched her carefully when she took out her hand mirror and started her procedure. She had something else on her mind—survival was not the motivator. Her whole demeanor was so different and she certainly had a tight relationship with mother. They would whisper and giggle. I was mystified.

Since the doctor's family had been spared any material loss they still had all their nice clothes and shoes. I would always be astonished at their variety of attractive, and no doubt expensive, clothes and apparel. To me it was truly something to admire. We probably got some of the children's hand-me-downs and were very glad to get nice clothes, even if they were not new.

I can imagine how this turn of events after the war had damaged my mother personally, seriously affecting her, and therefore us children also, negatively for a long time to come.

Often we would have to go to the city, bombed out though it was. Many sections of Wuerzburg were completely flattened, with an occasional remnant of a church steeple jutting jaggedly into the gray bleakness of a war-torn country. Big steel beams, bent grotesquely, would stick out of the rubble. The main streets had been cleared but there were areas one simply could not enter.

I remember that our mother loved to go to the doctor, that in her fantasies she would be married to one and she too would have the kind of clothes, shoes, and fur coats the doctor's wife had.

Because of the divorce and the ensuing paternity issues, which arose quite naturally, our heads were measured to establish a relationship to my father. The outcome of these tests remained inconclusive. I was the child in question to my father as I preceded my half-sister by three years. At the time all this was transpiring I was not aware of this problem but it gives the reason for the many doctor visits in Wuerzburg. My mother was high-strung, nervous, and imagined herself to be sick with some incurable disease. She definitely had an affinity for Jewish doctors; our pediatrician from before the war was Jewish.

The Jews were invariably rich, part of the reason for the genocide—as I only discovered when I was in Memphis, Tennessee in 1964 and I saw a documentary on that subject on television.

The fact that I did not know anything about the Holocaust proved to be an important element in my future.

Regardless of the apparent deafness of God, as seemed to be the case when I considered myself in dire straits and he did nothing, it never affected my childlike belief in the ever-present God whom I loved. In unsettled times I could withdraw into this inner sanctum where my memory of the experience in that ray of sunshine was ever-blooming, providing a safe place to go to. I was living in a world of my own. It proved to be the golden thread that guided me through the valleys.

In 1948, the last year of our stay in Heidingsfeld, one of the children we occasionally roamed around with, who was a grade above me in school, lost his young life trying to beat an oncoming train in the train yard where the workers moved the freight cars around. Nobody saw the boy and he was decapitated. The entire school was present at his funeral and we who were his friends stood close to the bereaved mother who had lost her husband in the war. Needless to say, I had never seen such emotionally traumatic, uncontrollable pain and grief as this poor mother expressed. She tried to jump into the grave after they had lowered the casket into the ground. The people around her had to grab her to keep her from accomplishing this. Still she continued to fight them all to get to her son. It was so utterly heartrending, I am sure, to all the mothers who were in attendance who identified with her, which was impossible for us children since we could not relate to the situation. Only after living for a long time as a mother, could I somewhat grasp the intensity of this mother's anguish.

2

Faith at Work

In 1949 our family moved back to Wuerzburg into an apartment building in Grombühl, which it is still called today. Our address was Senefelder Strasse 8, a corner building with two apartments on each floor. We lived on the second floor. The entrances were close together, but one apartment would be on the Senefelder Strasse while ours was on the Grombühl-Strasse, where the streetcars ferried everyone to their destinations within the city limits. The building had three floors. We had one room with windows on both sides. It was our living room but after some time ended up a multipurpose room. Looking out the window on the address side we could see the building across the street still lying in ruins.

At first our mattresses were on the floor. We slept like this for quite a while. There was just no way for us to have regular beds. I slept with my older sister in one room, mother and my younger sister slept in another, my grandfather slept in yet another room. As one entered the apartment, there was an entry hall from which a hallway went somewhat diagonally to the right, the living room, and then there was a hallway that led to the three bedrooms, one of which was directly opposite the front door. In those days curtains were commonly used to separate spaces and after the sharp turn to the left, one went through a curtain and there was a storage closet to the left, a small bedroom that was occupied by our nurse, who seemed to follow my grandfather around. Out of devotion and loyalty or some other motive? Next to it was the

WC (the water closet), which consisted of a toilet, a tiny sink, and a small mirror. It also had a window that opened onto a porch. Then came the kitchen, which had a door that opened to that same porch where the perishables were kept during the cold months—there were no refrigerators. We also had a clothesline there and storage space for lots of things, as this porch had only a half-wall up with no windows but a clothes-rack mounted on the outside where we could hang our clothes to dry in the warm months. There were no dryers. At the very end of this hallway was a door that opened into the bathroom, which had a bathtub, a bigger sink, and another mirror. To the right of this bathroom were the three bedrooms. Going from the bathroom forward, there was our mother's room, then ours and then grandfather's bedroom.

Uncle Genoff was not there at that time. My grandfather was the head of household and he saw to it that things were run properly.

Liesl did the cooking and everything else necessary to run a household while my mother was often sick with one thing or another.

We children would climb around in the rubble across the street, always looking for buried treasure. We actually found a door which one could not easily see but was a cinch to find for curious treasure-hunters such as we were. We found perfectly preserved dishes that were much more attractive than the ones we had. While it was decided that they undoubtedly belonged to someone I had secret plans of my own. I was a very secretive girl and I always thought of a way to sneak something by the grownups, and my sister too if necessary. So I took some of those pretty dishes and smuggled them into our apartment and put them in a hidden nook in the storage room which nobody seemed to ever use.

As I lay in bed that night, however, I battled with myself. On one hand I relished that marvelous feeling of having something so pretty all to myself but on the other hand I felt so bad thinking of the people who these lovely things belonged to. I'd had enough instruction in school to know The Ten Commandments and I knew very well that I was clearly violating the Eighth Commandment. So after some back and forth I decided to take the dishes back. Taking them back was done just as secretly as taking them was. I discovered that I had a very sensitive conscience that would be a most reliable alarm system of sorts for the remainder of my life.

Wuerzburg had an American military installation and to this day I have no idea where in Wuerzburg the barracks were. That very year, after we had moved back, the American tanks came rolling down the Grombühl Strasse and the soldiers were throwing candy left and right to the children who ran out on the sidewalks and scrambled to fetch some. Of course, I liked candy every bit as much as the next child since we rarely got any in these post-war years but I must admit I was rather indignant at the idea that I should accept, let alone scramble for, this pitiful consolation prize after they had bombarded my house and we now had to play in the ruins and the rubble that were still in evidence. I stood there, with my arms crossed, and looking defiantly at the soldiers. It must be mentioned here that I had no knowledge of the details of the war, in fact, I never did find out the cause since the people around me, including teachers and later on professors, had either adopted a code of silence or I did not pay enough attention when I should have. All the children gleefully ran around while the soldiers bantered with them. A good time was had by all. The lucky children either took their candy home to share with their families, or ate it right there on the spot. I did not mind that at all. For me, it was the right thing to do given how I felt.

My sister and I, with a lot of other children from the adjoining apartment buildings up and down Grombühl Strasse and our side of the street, went to the Pestalozzi-School on top of the incline where our street ended. The incline continued a considerable distance in the opposite direction, interrupted by two streets running parallel to the Grombühl Strasse. All of these streets were lined with apartment buildings. There were many children, an average of more than forty, in each class. As strict discipline was the norm, we had relatively few behavioral problems. If one caused trouble, one would be sternly reprimanded, even subjected to corporal punishment. If that did not work the parents would be notified and corporal punishment was a certainty.

I entered the third grade and my sister entered the sixth grade. My sister jealously guarded her friends and found me to be a most unwelcome intruder. I often followed her around, which she really hated, and she would shout at me to go and find my own friends which I eventually ended up doing. There were boys and girls in each class, with the boys generally getting in more trouble than the girls. Quite normal, I should think. As I recall, I was well liked by my peers and my teachers. Since I had learned to read I spent quite a bit of free time reading about German mythology, devouring the stories of a certain prince whose name was Ironheart. He fought the good fight for honor and honesty, integrity and courage, with his love-interest Aleta, who was his equal in terms of character and her devotion to the principles her beloved espoused and defended. It was loosely based on the legend of King Arthur's Roundtable and the exploits of the knights. The center of activity in the stories about "Prince Ironheart" was concentrated at Camelot.

I asked my fourth-grade teacher if she could find Camelot for me on the map and she came back the next day and told me that she could not find it, never telling me that it was, supposedly, a mythological city in the sixth century. Maybe this wise teacher knew the state of development I was in and thought it better to let me dream of high ideals. This was an extremely important move on her part for my moral compass to grow.

Because my grandfather was still living with us we were expected to go faithfully to the "Kindergottesdienst," the children's worship service that supported the religious instruction at school. It was simply expected for the parents to make sure that their children would receive the optimum benefit of a life lived in accordance with sound Bible teaching, which in the larger sense makes for a happier individual and an orderly society.

Nobody had to tell me to go to church, since the highlight of my days in school was the hours we spent talking about this magnificent Jesus, who, over time became the epitome of perfection to me and who eventually became the ideal to fashion myself after.

By now I was ten years old. My grandfather moved out to live with his new wife over their tobacco store, still in Grombühl. This was also the end of our housekeeper/nurse as she had hoped to marry my grandfather herself. Soon after Uncle Genoff came back into the picture and our lives were turned upside down.

Since my mother had no talent for household chores and declared herself too ill to work, it was up to us children to do all the heavy work. Keeping house in those days was labor-intensive. My sister and I would take turns washing dishes and drying them. I hated to wash the dishes because due to the lack of a grease-cutting ingredient in the dish soap, I could feel that unpleasant film of grease on my hands and the dishes. Only very hot water would get rid of it.

We really hated washday. Items that had to be sterilized had to be boiled on the stove in a huge pot. The items were white, like handkerchiefs, underthings and, horror of horrors, men's long johns. After they had boiled long enough to kill the germs, we then had to carry that very hot pot with the heavy clothes carefully into the bathroom, where it was poured into the bathtub, which was already filled with soapy water with the rest of the clothes. It was even worse when it was sheet-washing day. Our hands were too small to wring out the clothes but no matter, we had to do it and do it right or else our mother would scream her head off, calling us good-for-nothings or worse. We had the washboard, and while one was using the washboard, the other was hand washing, then we would change around. We developed our own system to get the job done even if my sister took one end of the sheet and turned it one way and I took the other end and turned in the other way. We tried anything and everything to escape our mother's wrath.

Our mother didn't have an easy life. This Bulgarian whom she chose to live with did not treat her gently. They would often quarrel and scream at each other, with my mother being far louder than her boyfriend. One time he'd throw her and her things out of the room they shared, which was the corner room originally designated the living room, but after my grandfather's departure, everything seemed to go every which way; and the next time she'd throw him and his things out.

Apparently this Bulgarian was lazy and my mother was trying to persuade him to make some money some way. He did. He started a chicken farm on the immediate outskirts of Wuerzburg, near the river, and everything seemed headed in the right direction. Little did anyone guess that it is very hard work to make a business a success and hard work was simply not this man's idea of making a living. When the weather was bad and he had to go on the bicycle or the streetcar, he would be in such a bad mood that one would hardly dare to breathe for fear he'd take it out on our mother. Though she was not our favorite person, we did not want to see her getting beaten up either. Due to the inadequate care these chickens received, they caught some kind of virus and the chicken farm project was kaput, but not before we had to endure the disgusting killing of chickens, which we were supposed to de-feather. Uncle Genoff gutted them and cooked the chickens, as he was a better cook than our mother. He used the silverware from the kitchen, so I took the ones I always used and hid them. I found all of this much too disgusting. In fact, I was a very clean girl and any kind of dirt would make me unhappy. My sister was more nonchalant about dirt. It just did not bother her and my younger sister was still too young to care. To make a long story short, I was extremely unhappy at home. My older sister had it even harder since everything was always her fault. Even when I told our mother that I did it, she would not listen and continued to scream at my sister, accusing her of conspiring to drive her out of her mind and of all other kinds of outlandish behavior, none of which was true. My mother clearly did not like my sister and she would often say to me that they must have switched babies on her at the hospital because there just was no way that she could give birth to such a common person. She then would continue by saying that it must be the father's fault, since he was nothing but a criminal.

Our mother also had a talent for meanness. She would start on a Saturday morning all cheerful and good-willed, promising us two girls that we could go to the movies and watch *Robin Hood* if we cleaned the house, which meant we had to take the carpets downstairs into the common area where there were clotheslines for sheets and blankets. Those rugs were very heavy and we had to struggle to carry them down two flights of stairs and try to get them over the clothesline where we then took turns beating the dust and dirt out of them with the rug beater, a perfectly suitable name for this implement as there were no vacuum cleaners yet. Our mother used the rug beater to punish us for major offenses. My sister had always caught the brunt of our mother's anger and my mother relished using this rug beater on her, often unfairly. Even though she apparently did not think of me as such an undesirable child, I felt sorry for my poor sister and grew more and more hostile toward our mother and her sheer unfairness. After we had cleaned the house and dusted the furniture, she then tagged on that we had to clean the bathroom and the WC and other things I cannot recall. I am sure she did this deliberately so we would miss the starting time of the movie and we could not go! We were so outraged at our mother, we huddled in the corner of the bathroom and thought of some way we could kill her.

Our mother made our lives a living hell by just being a self-absorbed woman without an ounce of maternal instinct. No normal mother would treat her children the way she treated us and my sister and I would always say to each other, "When we have children we will never treat them like this. We do not want to be like our mother!"

But what forgiving creatures children are! When she would be nice to us we would practically jump through hoops for her, as we did love our mother and were willing to let bygones be bygones. She knew this and never let that interfere with her cruel ways of dealing with us.

Wuerzburg was a university town and it was very desirable to go to the Uni there. It is a most beautiful place and my sisters and I went on many excursions around town by ourselves or with the school on field trips. We saw the Residenz, a fabulously ornate building in town, many beautiful cathedrals, the castle on top of the mountain overlooking the city, and opposite, on the ridge sits the lovely Käppele, all popular tourist destinations today.

There were two students who rented rooms from us. I can only remember the female student since she had to administer first aid to my sister who got cut with a knife that I was wielding, taunting her to try to get it from me. During that play, as my sister tried to get hold of the handle, the blade slid through her four fingers and cut her deeply . The student bound her hand up and stopped the bleeding. Our mother was not at home.

Mother was very upset and I feared for my life since I was the instigator but she just gave me a serious talking-to and somehow my sister ended up being blamed for the whole debacle. Liesl, doing our mother's bidding, persecuted my poor sister much the same way, unfairly and cruelly. She was stocky and short with the big bones of a country-woman, and would box my sister on the head unaware of her own strength.

Unbeknownst to me, my sister in her desperation turned to somebody who befriended her. By the time my sister left school, after the eighth grade, she started working at a photofinishing shop which also sold other items. My sister loved photography and was dreaming of becoming a photojournalist someday. However, the owner of the shop was a former girlfriend of my father's before he married our mother and she figured she might just re-ignite his interest in her when she took care of his daughter. I am fairly certain that my sister did not know anything about these circumstances. She was just happy to find a place where she was welcome and wanted. She came home very late from her job one night and my mother had called the police, accusing my sister of streetwalking—which I did not understand at the time. It was at that point that my father was contacted to have my sister transported to this ex-girlfriend's house as he was suing our mother for custody of my sister arguing that our mother was unfit to raise this particular child.

How true! In a way I was glad that she was away from my mother but now I was alone. My little sister was fawned over because she was there with her mother and father, so I was on my own. As I recall, my misery had just begun. I was now the main cleaning person in the household. I had to do all the chores by myself. I certainly had enough experience. My mother would even rent me out to her friends who, for one reason or another, could or would not do the work themselves. I was glad to be of help to the mother of one of the girls I ran around with because she seemed so unhappy and just so helpless to get a handle on her household, quite similar to my mother. For instance, she would start with the full intention to get something done. Then her attention would be drawn to something else and she'd attend to it, then something else would pop into her head and she'd get busy with that and so on. By the time I got home from school she would be tired and the house would be in a mess with everything only half-done. Add to this the job of having a meal prepared for the family, including that Bulgarian uncle who was not shy about voicing his displeasure at her inability to take care of things. I often dreaded to go home. There was hardly ever something ready for me to eat, and a piece of bread and some cold *malzkaffee* left over from the morning had to suffice.

After the sixth grade I transferred to an all girls' school to prepare me in book-keeping, typing etc., which was on the other side of town and I always took the shortcut through the cemetery where I would often linger just to avoid going home any sooner than I absolutely had to. It always gave me comfort to sit and ponder things and I would often just think how unhappy I was and how I should really be helped out of this miserable situation. Nothing happened to improve things. Nobody went to church but me, and my mother would yell after me, always glad to see me go, to pray for her. I thought to myself, *No, I am not going to pray for you.*

On one day, and I remember it as well as if it had been yesterday, I was particularly depressed and reluctant to go home after school when I decided to go inside the chapel in the cemetery and sit down. Like the child I was, I told God all about my inability to cope and I cried bitterly, begging God to please, please help me and make that Bulgarian go away. At bedtime I would always pray for help too, and one fine day, it seemed almost the next day, the Bulgarian had left for good and gone to the United States.

As the saying goes, "Be careful what you pray for, you might just get it!" After this man left our household, my mother rented the two rooms to girls of questionable character. We now had Americans coming in the evening and often in the daytime too to visit with these girls. Though I did not understand anything about sex I could sense that that was the core of these goings-on. My mother now had an American boyfriend whom she brought home to spend the night. Mr. Denton seemed a nice man and, not really knowing anything definitive, I did not mind him being around. He seemed to stabilize my mother and make her happy. The real problem was our neighbors and I could sense the increasing displeasure of our neighbors toward us. We were always viewed negatively by them. There were many doing the same things my mother was, but they were discreet about it. My mother never bothered with convention and did not see why she should do anything different now. I could never understand why none of my girlfriends were allowed to spend the night or even just the afternoon at my house; only after I understood the whole situation much later on, did this become clear to me.

The chickens I mentioned earlier did indeed come home to roost. However, no amount of setbacks or disappointments ever affected my undying faith in this supernatural power to which I knew I had access. I remember declaring to my friend with absolute certainty that I would have a paddleboat in which we could row down the river (one of our dreams) if I prayed for it. The next morning after I had prayed for it the night before; I fully expect to find that boat under my bed. That the Bulgarian left when he did was proof to me that I was not going through all this alone. Somebody was surely concerned about my welfare.

My mother never had any money. When I needed something for school I was always the last one to bring it. Even with this God would provide. When I dusted I would find coins here and there, which enabled me to buy what I needed. I always thanked God at once because I was always under such pressure to deliver or else the teacher would call me out and make some mocking remark that would make everybody laugh at me and tease me mercilessly after school. This happened often at the Pestalozzi-School. I knew that God saw my plight.

As I grew older I developed a love for babies. I had a favorite doll, she was pretty and made of plaster but when I took her outside to play I dropped the doll and she broke. Her face had a crack across one side and I was very upset. I got a new doll for Christmas but I still loved my poor cracked doll and played mommy to it with devotion. I had to "feed" them first before I went outside to play, if this was what they needed at that time. Little did I know that I would be just that devoted to the taking care of the children I would someday have.

After my sister left and the Bulgarian too, we rearranged the rooms. I now had a room to myself. It was the room next to the WC and its window opened onto the porch just as the window of the WC did. The reason I mention this is because this situation became a problem for me: the noises which accompanied the use of the bathroom were amplified in that little echo-chamber and I could hear only too clearly every little sound. This made me self-conscious when using the bathroom and to this day I am affected by it and have what they call a shy bladder. I am only relaxed enough when I am in a strange place if I have the water running when I have to go.

My mother was a very ostentatious woman who loved attention. She would put on a fur coat, high-heeled shoes, and a used a red leash for her white spitzhund, a German small dog, and would take her for a walk, probably hoping to draw the attention of some male in the vicinity. I did not have anything to wear to school and often had to go into her wardrobe to find something I could scrunch up to make fit. Since I learned sewing in elementary school, I went to my sister's friend's house and sewed my own clothes from old things that no longer fit me. I know I must have looked like a ragamuffin but I did not mind that too much since the Bible clearly teaches that the appearance is not of the essence but what is inside, and inside I had a heart full of love for God and it kept me happy in spite of the bleakness of my life in general. My feeling of closeness to God enabled me to rise above my circumstances to be a happy-go-lucky girl who had ample opportunity to emerge and have fun with my friends and enjoy my talents for dancing and singing. I had long wished to go to ballet classes when, finally, for my birthday, I started classical ballet lessons.

This started a whole new range of experiences for me. In addition, I was generally well liked and if someone did not like me, I was just so simpleminded that I could not imagine somebody not liking me. At any rate I thoroughly enjoyed the attention and had fun with my playmates, none of whom I can remember. I also rode my sister's old bicycle around the neighborhood. Since we lived on an incline, I would frequently zoom down the street, always counting on the brakes to work. Well, one time they did not and I careened into the curb of the sidewalk as I lost control of the bike. I was hurt, but not seriously. My bike however was as good as dead. That was when I got roller-skates and, being a natural-born performer, I never let an opportunity pass to show off moves I had learned in ballet. I never wanted to go inside when called in for supper. Always one more twirl, one more pirouette with my arms moving in unison. I would frequently be late for supper and get yelled at, provided that my mother actually had something prepared, but as it was getting dark I had no choice but to go in.

One summer my mother wanted me out of the way, so she had somebody take me into the country where our nurse had her origins and I remember so well how I saw my mother disappear in the car, leaving me with people I did not know in a place that was foreign to me. It was a farmer family. Nice Catholics but their way of living and doing things seemed strange to me. They had their cows and pigs right next to the kitchen on a lowered floor and you could see them from a small window in the kitchen. Those sticky bands of flytraps were hanging everywhere as the dung heap was in close proximity to the stalls and the stench was so intense it took me a while to get used to it. I guess my mother told these people that I was a good worker and I would earn my keep this way. Hay had to be baled and transported to the hayloft of the barn and every day, weather permitting. I had to go with Liesl's brother and their mother into one field or another and help with the baling of the hay and loading it on the big wagon pulled by cows. When we got back I had to lead the cows, one after the other, to the communal fountain in the middle of the village square. These animals were quite large, with their extended middles obscuring their feet. I was so afraid that they might step on my feet but thank goodness there were no horses. Only the bigger and richer farmers could afford those. I was half scared out of my wits doing things I had never even heard of before and the country boys had themselves a high old time making fun of this city girl. I was so homesick that I would go to the place where I had last seen my mother disappearing from my sight and I would just stand there looking longingly into the distance, hoping, wishing my mother would appear. She did not. Instead I had to help getting the bales of hay way up into the hayloft with a huge pitchfork. Somebody caught the bale of hay with the pitchforks still stuck in it, which he pulled out and let slide down the "hay mountain" for me to catch. I caught it all right, right into my left knee. One of the prongs hit my knee and although we did what we could to keep it from getting infected, it got infected anyway. I was in pain for a long time and I was always afraid to remove whatever there was available to use as a bandage, because the pus from the wound would ooze out and dry overnight.

I had to soak it in water to minimize the pain as the removal of the dry bandage was ripping off the crust that was forming. I still have a scar from this misadventure. But there was something I really liked, and that was the wonderful creaminess of the milk fresh from the cows. It was delicious. Of course, the milk had to be collected and brought to another farmer who was licensed by appropriate authority to provide the pasteurization of the milk for all the dairy farmers in this village, after which, the milk was ready for the marketplace. I also liked the homemade breads and those super-delicious country hams and sausages of every variety that Germany is famous for and to this day I still dream of tasting them just one more time. All in all, as it is with everything, my time in the country was a mix of good and bad and I prefer to think of the good, while keeping the bad in the back of my mind, just so I would not repeat past failings.

Coming back to the city and back to school was a switch worth noting. My music teacher called a conference with my mother whom she had as a student when my mother was my age. When my mother came back from the conference, I asked her what the teacher said. My mother answered, "She said that you are unusual!" She did not elaborate and I got the impression that she did not want to say any more. I was somewhat perturbed by this opinion of my music teacher and I worried that she could possibly have discovered my secret. I knew from experience that adults have a way of knowing things I thought they could never find out. I was very protective of my secret—that I knew—only God and I were aware of it, and any disclosure of it I believed would result in the withdrawal of that help that was available to me and I so liberally enjoyed.

When she asked me if I would like to come with her and a few other select students to watch a performance of *Tannhauser* by Richard Wagner in Frankfurt at the old opera house, which by then had been reconstructed to its pre-war glory, I knew that my secret was safe. In her class we had theatrical performances and I was good at performing arts, good at reciting a sentence with just the correct intonation to make it understood by the audience; she thought that it would be a good learning experience for me all the way around. It was. I felt so privileged and somehow vindicated in my belief that the clothes are a negligible element in the value of the individual and I was ever-so-thankful that my music teacher knew this too.

On Sundays after church I would often go to my grandfather's apartment where his second wife always had the best food waiting for me and she was only too happy to stuff me as she knew my mother well and that cooking was not one of her favorite things to do. After the meal I would offer to wash the dishes but was always glad when she turned me down, saying nicely, "No, no, no, you go get yourself a book and read!" She did not have to tell me that twice. She had the most beautiful collection of the Nibelungen saga and I just loved to get lost in the stories of Siegfried and Brunhilde and their trials and tribulations, their requited loves and un-requited loves, their agonies of defeat and their dizzying triumphs in victory over evil. I was truly in heaven right here on earth and I got the impression that the valiant fight for the good was always worth the effort in the long run. My enthusiasm about these Germanic mythology stories spilled over into my performances of these stage plays my music teacher wrote the scripts for, which were just my style. Richard Wagner's operas were all based on German mythology. I preferred classical music and solemn church music, so I was unusual; but I also liked and listened to my mother's songs from lighthearted operettas.

Being an avid student of the Holy Bible gave me a seriousness and pensiveness that was not the norm among my peers. It proved to be the basis for my future. I was still feeling rather enamored with the idea that I would be a movie star someday, never really knowing what that would require me to do.

I had been told by someone, maybe it was our old nurse, that my mother enjoyed having friends over when we still lived in the brownstone, and she enjoyed living well, that she had me dressed in a frilly pink dress and pink socks and black patent-leather shoes, and put me on the grand piano and urged me to dance for her friends. I remember nothing of this but have formed for myself an image of this in my mind that I could at least believe I remember. The fact remains that in my mother's eyes I was more to her liking than my sister. I had a natural talent for dancing and singing and I think that my mother encouraged these tendencies as they were part and parcel of her own aspirations. She wanted to be an opera singer. Actress. Famous. Rich. Her frustration with the reality as she had fashioned it for herself and the deprivation the war brought, was immense. I imagine that her total lack of interest in the domestic area, and the consequent unwillingness to apply herself to rise to the occasion and do what must be done, only compounded her problems and she did whatever she could to escape from her self-made prison.

She would fancy herself to look like Greta Garbo, her favorite movie star. She had pictures of Greta and I have to say there was a resemblance. She would often look in the mirror and then ask us if we thought she looked like Greta Garbo, and we knew better than to say anything other than, "Yes, Mommy, you look just like her!" The day just went better.

It was to my benefit in many ways that people would always tell her that I was so pretty and that I would surely grow up to be a movie star. I had people stopping me on the street telling me how beautiful I was. One time I ran home to look in my mirror to see what they saw but I could not see it. Though it must have been true if so many people thought that I was! Having watched that girl in Heidingsfeld putting on her paint, I took my mother's lipstick and painted my lips. I then tried the eyebrow pencil and used it as I thought it to be enhancing. I thought that I looked more like a movie star! There was no tolerance for such outright gaudiness, like that girl I was imitating, who as became clear later on, was dating Americans, too. I was not allowed to go near makeup.

But I was predisposed to vanity and would secretly fret over my "beauty." To some degree I became pretty self-confident and somewhat conceited.

When I took ballet classes at the Klein-Langner Studio, I blossomed quickly into a solo performer. We tap danced at the teas of the American Ladies League and did stage performances for children modeling. I enjoyed the fussing over me and the extra attention I received from everyone connected with the Studio. Frau Klein-Langner always made sure I had nice-looking clothes on when I went anywhere with her troupe. (I think they were her children's things!) At home I was always dancing or doing acrobatics, which I really preferred. The apartment building, which had lain in ruins when we moved in, had now been rebuilt, and a quiet, handsome boy had moved in with his family. He was interested in a pretty girl from down the street whose family was more to his family's liking, but that did not prevent me from making sure that he could see me perform my acrobatic tricks. I'd open the window facing his and made sure that he could see me. I then would pretend I was totally unaware that he was looking and if I saw him looking I would close the window and draw the curtain. I am not sure how I felt about boys. I liked them but somehow I was afraid of them.

One afternoon I went window-shopping with my best girlfriend, Adelheid. We were at Woolworth's in Wuerzburg, minding our own business, when I noticed a bunch of children with their mothers making a scene, jumping up and down and pointing at us and excitedly telling their parents to look. I was puzzled and asked my friend what the matter was with these children, when she said that they must have seen me in *Hansel und Gretel* in which I danced the part of the Wicked Witch and that they must have recognized me. That was really strange to me and exceedingly uncomfortable and I urged my girlfriend to leave with me, to get away from these children—they were half my age, five or six years old.

My reputation as a ballet dancer preceded me to the new school I transferred to and I had an uneasy feeling that everybody was expecting great things from me, which I feared I could not deliver. The fact that I continuously delivered in accordance with my talent, or rather, the lack thereof, in bookkeeping and shorthand—only average—was very humiliating to me and I hated so much to let these high expectations go unfulfilled.

But I had to contend with difficult circumstances at home too. The parties at my home were becoming more frequent and the nights were often interrupted by some American mistaking my door for the door to the WC, bumbling in a half-conscious stupor into my room. One actually sat on the side of my bed, looking at me, reeking of alcohol, scaring me half to death. I could not lock my door—there was no key—maybe Liesl had taken it with her when she moved. I retreated into the farthest corner of my bed, instinctively pulling the cover up to my neck and waiting anxiously for him to go away. After a period of staring and thinking with his addled brain he finally left and I had terrifying nightmares after that, dreaming that somebody was making a big hole into my door and then sticking his arm through and it grew longer and longer so as to reach me in my bed. The sheer commotion of the constant opening and closing of doors and the noises from the WC being used would keep me awake leaving me too tired to pay attention in school.

Not only that, but I became increasingly aware that these goings-on were just not right. Since I had started very serious instruction in religion, apart from school, mandated by the Church in preparation for confirmation, I became very suspicious of my mother's conduct and the conduct of these girls she had rented rooms to, to supplement her income. I once criticized her and let her know that whatever lie she was going to tell me was just that, a lie. She angrily slapped me across the face and said, "You need to be in a correctional institution!"

Whenever they would run out of Cokes or something similar she'd try to bribe me with things the Americans could get for me at the PX if I'd go downstairs and get those items for them, as there were several shops in our building on the ground floor. I refused to comply, which absolutely drove my mother mad. But my mind was made up. According to my belief, what they were doing was wrong and I was not going to help them in that.

A girl living in our building acted as though she was my friend and I confided in her my tribulations. She took this information to her parents and it became clear to me that I had better get away from my mother because she was the opposite of everything I believed in, which were the teachings of Jesus Christ whom I dearly loved and admired and tried so hard to imitate, which was no easy task.

I had to confess my selfishness, my vanity, and my pronounced sexual proclivity and ask for forgiveness for my transgressions in these areas and then set out to teach myself to be God-pleasing which I had a lot of trouble with, but I prayed constantly for help and God always came through for me. For instance, I took great pains in cleaning our part of the stairs which we shared with one more occupant on the same floor. I made them super-clean and shiny and I was always making myself available to do things I used to try to get out of doing before. I remember how devoted I was to re-fashioning myself to become pleasing to God. It became the single most important goal in my life, and even though I liked the approval of people concerning my talent in this showy side of mine which in actuality also precipitated a certain flightiness, I treasured the intimacy with God and I became a very rooted believer in Jesus Christ and my flightiness disappeared.

In conjunction with my now-pronounced awareness of right and wrong according to the Scriptures, the increasingly more obvious lawlessness of my mother's life stood in stark contrast.

I knew that I no longer wished to stay with my mother. I was literally in danger there, particularly in the sexual area. Although I never quite understood what was actually going on, I was keenly aware that I had a weakness in this area and sooner or later I would fall victim to it in that environment and that was something I did not want, as I viewed it my God-given obligation to remain pure and holy.

I was scared of my mother but I also loved her and if there had been another way to get from her what I needed in order to develop into the person God wanted me to be, I would have remained with her. Only God Himself could have given me the courage to tell my mother that I wanted to move to my father's. I expected her to slap me in response but she was unusually calm and acted as if it did not bother her in the least.

With the help of my grandfather's wife and the former girlfriend of my father's, with whom my sister lived, the authorities were contacted and a hearing was scheduled to determine the validity of my request to have custody changed from my mother to my father.

My father did not come and I really had no idea what he looked like or whether I would like him but there was no going back. Surely things had to be better with my father.

This was in December of 1955. On the way to the courthouse my mother tried to prepare me for the questions I was going to be asked and how I was to answer them when I looked up at her towering over me in her best threatening posture, looked her straight into the eyes and said calmly, "Mommy, I will only tell the truth!" Since we were in the streetcar she could not do a thing, I guess. But in my mind I knew that my secret ally was with me and provided everything I needed for any occasion. I still have the deposition from that.

The hearing went normally, and I answered all the questions honestly. Early in 1956 I was brought to my father's house in Altenfurt, on the outskirts of Nürnberg.

However, before this I was confirmed in April 1955, an occasion which had left an indelible impression on my psyche.

The Johannes-Church was bombed out and we worshipped and studied in a makeshift church on the Martin-Luther-Strasse 1. Every Saturday we had to attend class to prepare for the examination before the actual confirmation ceremony could take place.

We went through a dry run, sitting exactly in the places we were assigned, with the boys on the right and the girls on the left side in front of the altar. On this altar were the statues of Jesus with the twelve disciples, carved of wood. Jesus was in the center, depicted washing the feet of Peter. Jesus had a golden halo around his head and was in a kneeling position.

I was looking with childlike awe at this scene when I saw my face above and between Jesus' head and slightly above Peter. It was all aglow with a light I had never seen before. I was so shocked, and in my fright turned to see whether the other children saw it too but to my relief they were completely unaware of this vision. As they were busying themselves trying to find what they needed to know for the first question, I was thinking to myself, *If this means that the important thing that I always knew I had to do, I am not going to do this, if it means I have to traipse around on earth wearing sackcloth and sandals like the original disciples were wearing*, and it looked to me like this was what my face up there was telling me. I was thinking of something more attractive and a rope for a belt was not helping. The contrast between what I had been accustomed to expect and this was just too much for me and I was ever so glad nobody saw this but me; that way I did not have to be held to account to anyone and I decided to simply put it out of my mind. But I had this feeling that I knew something, but I did not know what that something was.

The next day, Sunday, I was confirmed and I received my requested crucifix from my mother and a book of German poetry and a Lutheran hymnal from my grandmother who wrote a meaningful dedication on the third page. I have used this hymnal in my daily devotions ever since. It has been an invaluable guide and a source of comfort and joy.

As it is on this planet, joy never lasts long enough. The girl who lived in our building, to whom I had confessed the things that were going on in my family, such as it was, took the information and told her parents and they contacted the authorities before my grandmother did who advised me to try to get away from my mother. I felt so betrayed by this girl as she had found me in a most depressed state of mind and she had promised not to tell anyone.

I learned that if you wanted something to remain secret you tell no one. I have lived by this since then. Nevertheless, it was a very trying time since I never knew whether my mother was told right away and if she could make my life more miserable than ever before.

By the way, in Germany at that time I knew nothing of closets. We had *schränke*, big wooden rectangular wardrobes in which one put one's clothes on hangers. They usually had adjoining compartments for sweaters and such, and were sometimes quite fancy.

However, when this custody issue came to the forefront, my mother did not show any sign of hurt or upset or vengefulness. She dealt with me fairly and when the time came I left with a heavy heart, in part because I loved my mommy, and in part because I had to leave my remaining sister behind, and I felt responsible for her Christian upbringing, which now was in question as our mother was a Christian in name only. Living in Germany in that time you were either Catholic or Protestant (Lutheran) or Jewish.

My younger sister had no natural desire for the Word of God or the teachings of God, so I was the one cajoling her to come with me to church. Sometimes I would let her stay home since I had no mind for lengthy persuasion. One Sunday, on my way home from church some boys ambushed me and tried to kiss me. Two were holding my hands tight, so I could not defend myself and the third boy wanted the kiss. I growled and kicked and put up such a fight that they gave up. I looked at them with contempt, said nothing, and went my way home. There were four exits of the cemetery for me to get home the shortest distance and they knew the exit I normally used from my sister. When I got home I told her what had happened. I think she really did not care and was only too happy to oblige those boys. But all that did not mean a thing; I did not want to leave her with our mother by herself. Before I knew it I was in my father's house.

3

Falling

(into my destiny) In Love

Before I made the move to my father's, my mother actually bought me a new winter coat and a pair of winter shoes, something she had never done for me as far as I could recall. I thought it was downright magnificent of her, considering that I had initiated the change of custody. I realized much later on that it was because she had to make sure my father did not think her to be a non-caring mother, not so overtly anyway. Though my father never discussed my mother in any fashion, I knew that she could not fool him.

My father was a good-looking older gentleman who worked for Siemens, an electrical company in Nürnberg. He looked somewhat like George Raft and he was soft-spoken. We got along but never grew as close as we could have. I had juvenile girl-dreams of this father who would dote on his beloved daughter whom he had not seen in twelve years.

He was in actuality living with his secretary. I could tell that she was with child although that was not obvious to the casual observer but I knew just the same. Abiding by the provincial rules of conduct the wedding was imminent. After a few days of my staying with them, it became clear to me that I was not welcome there. My future stepmother, though not ever directly unkind to me, did not want me at their home, which was also the home of her mother who suffered of some kind of dementia and this complicated things.

We went into the country where I met my grandmother for the first time, my now-seventeen-year-old brother, and my cousin who loved spending time there. My Aunt Hilda, one of my father's sisters, was also there. Everybody was friendly and welcoming. My brother was a handsome young man and my cousin was nice-looking too. He was my age and went to the same kind of school that I was going to be attending; only he went to the all-boys private school.

My new school was a form of college preparatory which offered the same program as the regular prep schools, just at an accelerated pace.

I ended up staying at other relatives, often at my Aunt Mary and Uncle Robert's apartment. They had an adopted daughter, Renate, who seemed to like me. It was at their place where I got my period for the first time. My aunt explained that I was a woman now and that I was now capable of having children when I got married. I will never forget how utterly holy and privileged I felt at the very thought of becoming a mother someday. It reinforced my high ideals and I was very happy and did not mind the inconvenience associated with the monthly cycle. I felt honored and considered it part of that secret I shared only with God Himself.

The new school brought its challenges too. All these young ladies I had to learn to get along with! While I was not considered supersmart I could hold my own and my personality appeared to please the students as well as the faculty. It seemed like in no time at all that I was voted class president and I negotiated the students' concerns with the faculty. I was the oldest in the class of thirty students when I started, which dwindled to quite a few less by the time we neared graduation.

Although things were going well at school, I had to contend with a growing dis-enchantment on the home front. Renate, who was the adopted daughter, got me into more trouble than I knew how to get out of. Until I had arrived she'd been the center of the boys' attention when she would visit the country, which happened frequently as all the brothers and sisters of my father's, who lived in Nürnberg, had an interest in the property out there in the vicinity of Roth. Before the war, long before there were rumors of war, they all got together and built this house as a retreat from the city, which they knew automatically would become a target and they hoped they could then all sit it out in Bernlohe. They all made a lot of sacrifices to get everything done and they, of course, took good care of their mother who would then end up living there in her declining years. Little did they know that it would become home to my brother and in the future, also to me.

I could never figure out why Renate was against me, maybe because she had heard things said about my mother when the adults got together and discussed both the atrociousness of my mother and that I looked just like her. I would suspect that it was a unanimous assumption that since I looked like her I must be like her, as the apple does not fall far from the tree.

By all accounts I was a pleasant-to-look-at girl and the boys in Bernlohe were smitten with me right from the start. There was nothing I could have done to prevent this. Not having grown up around them from the beginning, the lines of the appropriate feelings toward me were blurry for them. This development did not remain unnoticed by Renate, who took every little thing and twisted it to suit her and her parents' and uncles' and aunts' opinion of me. It was horrible and I had no idea how to defend myself against this perceived negative and wrong opinion. People always believe what they want to. At the time I was just mystified at the animosity coming from all the adults to varying degrees.

It was a very good thing that I had no trouble in school. God always made sure I did not have more than I could stand and I often wondered why I had to leave my mother to come to this place where there was a set of problems completely foreign to me and, even just by looking at it from my perspective, it seemed that I jumped from the frying pan into the fire.

I decided the best thing to do was nothing other than be myself and hope that maybe in time they would accept that I was not the same as my mother.

I had no experience in dealing with boys. I had gone to an all-girls' school in Wuerzburg and I was in an all-girls' school in Nürnberg. I treated my brother with a genuine affection because I loved him as my brother and the same was true for my cousin.

I never knew what being in love was. I could not tell the difference with my brother Paul and cousin Wolfgang, between their being in love with me and loving me as their sister and cousin respectively.

We did a lot of things together and had a lot of fun. Our grandmother was a character and she made my brother's life quite difficult but things seemed to go better with a little humor. It loosened things up a bit and everybody was better off in the end.

We would often go into the surrounding forest and look for mushrooms, so grandmother could fix them for us. They were the most delicious mushrooms I had ever eaten and we did not mind spending considerable time trying to find those grayish delicacies. I do believe that it was the way grandmother was preparing them that made them so good and she would just love to hear the compliments we heaped on her with genuine appreciation. It made her happy.

I thought that slowly but surely she too would like me just like my brother and cousin seemed to and I always tried to be helpful and accommodating because I genuinely loved my grandmother. She ran that little domain of hers quite well. On Sundays we would go to the church in the village. Sometimes Paul would join us, I cannot remember Wolfgang ever entering the church though.

My brother left school after the eighth grade and entered into an apprentice job to learn the trade of an electrician. Since this was what our father did, it seemed only natural. My cousin, on the other hand, was still in school and spent weekends and vacations in Bernlohe/Roth where he was always building something. He simply had no time for church. He wanted to become a ship-builder. I think that after I got there he built a sailboat. We would often go off in his boat on the stream very near our property. My brother was mostly at work-school and if we had done our chores we could go sailing, down the river and we rowed back. It was fun.

As it turned out, I ended up living at my grandmother's during the warm months and then moved to Wolfgang's and his mother, Hilda's, during the cold months in Nürnberg.

The times in the country were somewhat difficult as I had to travel by train for twenty-five minutes to get to Nürnberg where I attended the Sigena-School. To get to the train station I had to walk to the next village, Unterheckenhofen, which took fifteen minutes. After arriving in Nürnberg I had to walk another ten to fifteen minutes to get to school.

I thought this was normal and never minded this except when it would rain and I'd get to school dripping wet from my shoes up.

My grandmother's place consisted of the main house (it was wired for electricity) and a small courtyard around which were two structures, one of which would become my brother's room during the warm months as it had no electricity. Adjoining it was the laundry room. In it was a huge cook pot for sheets and other whites and a wash-wringer through which one fed the wash, and the there was the bathtub that was also used to rinse the laundry. There were clotheslines too! Directly opposite the main house was an older structure dating back to the turn of the nineteenth century. It was arranged as a fairly spacious country home. Upon entering the building one would see the hallway, which was closed off as my uncle had his private getaway in the room the hallway was leading to. He entered his room in the back.

My room was on the left side in front and adjoining it was the outhouse. The room to the right was used as storage space/workroom for my father, uncles and brother and cousin. Come to think of it, I was always relegated to the toilets. When I lived at my aunt's house on the Winkler Strasse, I had my room, which was really a breezeway between the kitchen and the modern bathroom. It was probably the maid's room in times past when all well-to-do people had a maid.

Looking back, the things I had to learn to deal with were certainly not conducive to thinking of myself as special. Only God provided me with a humble disposition, yet not the oppressed and downtrodden kind, but the happy, helpful and willing to learn kind. I never minded the hardships because I was not aware of them. I had this light shining within me and it made my whole little world a fairly pleasant place.

As one can imagine, washday at my grandmother's house was an all-day affair. First I had to haul buckets of water from the well in back of the main house in big buckets to the big pot. Then the laundry had to be boiled. After that it had to be cooled off in some cold water in the aluminum bathtub and then it would be squeezed out with that wringer. Thank goodness this washroom had a drain in the center where one could get rid of the wash-and rinse waters quickly and effortlessly, but there just was no way around having to lug the water, what seemed like long-distance to me.

Of course a fire had to be made under that huge pot. My grandmother did this with the wood that was stacked in a heap, which the boys were responsible for. When we needed wood they would go into the forest and cut a suitable tree down, and drag it home where they sawed and cut it into small enough pieces that would fit into the kitchen stove as well.

My tenure at Aunt Mary's apartment was very short indeed. I feel strongly that Renate resented me, which I can understand since she considered me as an interloper. She would openly discuss her period in the presence of boys, which I would never ever do, and for this reason never told anyone when I had my period. It was just something too private to be discussed openly. I associated it with all things I held holy and sacred. In retrospect, I think it was my high-mindedness and propriety that made me so attractive to my brother and cousin. They both ended up forever dreaming of someone they could never have but could not help but love. It was really quite sad, when I think about it but there was nothing I could do to change anything.

With the male gender in such close proximity I could not help but be affected by it. I would have the most intense sexual dreams. I would wake up completely drained from the ever-so-real feelings of sexual contact that I had never had. It never entered my mind to express this strong sexual impulse as I knew it was my duty to gain control over it. I would pray and go to the cold river to swim early in the morning and wash away that sullying effect of sex upon my spirit. It was a continuous struggle and I would often backslide and engage in moving my body in a certain rhythm to achieve a climax, which was a leftover from my early childhood. But I also knew that this was cheating and time and time again I'd backslide, then resolve to do better; but on my own I would have never been able to succeed. God Himself through the Holy Spirit whom Jesus promised us as an ever-present help when we call for Him, made it possible for me to gain the upper hand over my greatest weakness, sex.

So, it is obvious to me in retrospect that this time in the country with my brother and cousin, who for all practical purposes believed as I did that one saved oneself for one's future mate, did not outright pressure me but as we all got older it became ever more difficult for them.

There is no question that I am a country girl at heart. I loved living with my grandmother. Lugging the water, carrying the heavy baskets with white and colored clothes down to the meadow where we put them straight onto the grass and had the sun dry them or hanging them up on the clothesline nearby. I loved lollygagging around in the surrounding woods and clearings that provided a view to more distant beautiful underbrush, which an occasional reindeer would nibble on. I loved the buzzing of the bees and the colorful butterflies fluttering around. It was heaven to me and it was peaceful when I was alone and I had plenty of time alone. Everything was right with the world as far as I was concerned. I'd go with my grandmother to the only store in the village, a sort of general store where they also sold country hams and sausages as the owners were butchering and processing both their own pigs and every pig farmer's in the village. I would always be stared at as some kind of oddity.

When we'd get back from the store we'd take a watering can and sprinkle the sheets one more time to get them their whitest. By the time it was afternoon snack time we got the clothes from the meadow, folded them and put beside the things that needed to be ironed. My brother knew how to iron and I'd see him ironing a shirt and a pair of pants when he would meet with some friends on Friday night. He had bought himself a moped, which I did not like. He'd go to Roth where he could get alcohol and he would come home intoxicated. We were always worried about his safety but to no avail. He had a destructive side to him that I cannot explain. My grandmother and I would sit up and wait for him to come home when he said that he'd return, but he never did and it was upsetting to both of us and he'd just fall into bed when he finally did arrive; I hated that side of him so much and I hated the friends he hung out with, as they were no good for him. I tried to explain that to him but he would say things like, "What's the use anyway, I love you and since we are brother and sister it's a hopeless situation, I may as well kill myself!" This was most distressing to me and I really could not take him seriously. Surely he was going through some type of infatuation but I guess as a very sensitive young man it felt like love to him. I had to be very careful with him.

My cousin went through the same thing except that he had secret plans for a future with me that I found out about later on.

If it had not been for all this sexual confusion I probably could have remained there. One fine day I was told that my grandmother was going around the village, saying that I had a dead embryo inside of me, that she was told by good authority that I had correspondence with my boyfriend in Wuerzburg and that he was the father. No wonder people looked at me as an oddity!

I was so shocked, distraught, hurt, and betrayed to a point that I have no words to describe. It was such an outright lie I could not get over anybody ever just coming up with, let alone that this was in clear contrast to what I had dedicated my life to, and, last but not least, that my grandmother, of all people, would be the one believing such a lie and spreading it all over the village. I was in such mental anguish, such pain of disappointment, pain of disappointment in God. I cried and cried and when there were no more tears left to cry I quietly resolved to take my life. I complained bitterly to God that I absolutely could not endure this. If this was what I got for doing His will with such dedication and focus, I did not want to live. I was standing under the mighty birch tree you could see from far off and looking out over the landscape with sorrow in my heart when I heard in my mind, *Do not do this. Time will tell*, and a most wonderful sense of well-being and utter peace flooded my whole spirit. I truly felt touched by God and I miraculously was freed from any pain or rancor. Not for a moment longer did I display or even feel ill feelings toward my grandmother and I treated her as I always had. It was as if I had taken a new lease on life and I was happier than ever before. I knew I would not, could not fail if God was in control of my life and I continued to do His will.

As I figure it, this ugly rumor was started by Renate when I asked my aunt for some stationery for a letter to my girlfriend Adelheid whom I missed and had promised that I would write to.

Being jealous and feeling pushed aside, she did what comes natural to anyone who lives life by their own rules. She very seldom came out to join us on our vacation. Her guilty feeling prevented her from remaining part of the "young ones."

While I spent the first winter from November 1956 to March 1957 at my Aunt Hilda's home, which she just had acquired in the sale of a business that was going under and which she did the bookkeeping for, I discovered first-hand how affluent families lived. The business was a tailored shirt atelier for the upper class, so to speak. This atelier was on the ground floor of an elegant brownstone of which there were quite a few in that section of town. It was a short distance from one of the main gates of the customary city wall surrounding any large town during the feudal era of Europe.

The interior was atypical of the late eighteen-hundreds with humongous tile-heaters which were very decorative. Each room had its own, ranging in colors from blue to green to gray and the kitchen had the typical layout of that time, very solid, very utilitarian. It was all updated to the modern conveniences at the time my aunt started working for the proprietor.

My aunt was an entrepreneur. She learned the business quickly and she had three and sometimes four seamstresses and a cutter working for her. Wolfgang absolutely hated to have anything to do with the business but he had to spend more and more time learning right alongside his mother every aspect of the business with the exception of the bookkeeping. He had to learn to deal with the clientele, and to oversee the running of the materials, their quality, and the cut of the garment according to the measurements he had to learn to take because this business would become his one day.

In addition to being highly skilled in her field, Hilda was also a very generous person and she gave freely and liberally, although I cannot deny that she had an ulterior motive most of the time. She had some rather strange friends who were avid believers in the occult and she would take me to their séances. I could never make any sense of what they were doing and my aunt did give up taking me with her. My cousin never had to go, he flat-out refused and she knew when not to push him too hard. She also read horoscopes which I was already used to from my mother who also read tarot cards. She and my aunt would have gotten along just fine. They could spend considerable amounts of time searching for their destiny in the stars and cards and tea-leaves. What a strange custom!

Aunt Hilda was a kind soul who could also cook those marvelous German dishes I can still taste if I put my mind to it. At Christmas she prepared a goose with potato dumplings and the best gravy ever, with a delicious green salad and wonderful dark German bread. It was truly something to remember.

She also had a piano there and I took my songbook and plinked out the melody of those beautifully spiritual lyrics accompanying the simple and oh-so-familiar tunes. I became pretty good at it and I whiled away idle time on a Sunday evening after we had come back from Bernlohe.

I cherished the times I could go to the Sebaldus Kirche (church) and just sit there, letting the ambience of these splendid depictions of the life and death of Jesus Christ surround me as if to embrace and comfort me. Every now and then the organist would practice and the sound of the organ music played by skillful hands and feet would thunder through the cathedral with its Gothic-style architecture and it would truly be an otherworldly experience. If I stayed in town with my aunt, I would always go to church on Sunday morning

I liked the anonymity. I did not have to converse and make small talk about nothing. I could just concentrate on my relationship with my Lord and Savior, uninterrupted and therefore more meaningful.

I was very serious about my faith and I knew only too well that my faith required a singlemindedness and that without it I would perish. Although my aunt never could understand my devotion, she respected it, which was also true for my father.

It was at this atelier where I got my first kiss and it was sort of a surprise move by a friend of Wolfgang's who had come home with him after school. He caught me in the foyer, which was dark at the time as business hours were over, and the lights in the atelier portion had been turned off. I was really upset about this and was horrified at the thought that I now had to marry this young man whom I did not even like. My aunt cleared that up for me, thank goodness. I am still amazed at the stunning innocence and sometimes utter naiveté with which I viewed the world around me. It is because of this worldly ineptitude that I must have had a serious protector, otherwise I would have been either dead or swallowed up by the world. I could almost feel this protection when things which would affect everybody else would leave me unaffected by their potentially destructive natures.

After I moved again to my grandmother's in March of 1957, the schedule of riding the train began again. My now-legitimate stepmother was now the proud mommy of a baby girl and pretty soon thereafter she had another girl. Paul and Wolfgang, who by then could drive, would occasionally be invited to visit with the family, which was always pleasant as my stepmother was a kind, sweet woman who knew how to get what she wanted without causing a furor (like my mother!). The children were adorable and very well taken care of by their parents and their live-in grandmother. On special holidays our grandmother would come too and tell funny stories of her life with grandfather.

At school, a classmate of mine died from some illness none of us knew she had. As the class president it was my responsibility to deliver the eulogy. The vice-president's mother wrote it as I knew very little about the girl since she was a very quiet person who did not mingle well. I felt that it would be best for the vice-president to deliver the eulogy since her mother authored it. The ceremony was brief and controlled. Only the parents showed any sign of emotion. The girl was cremated. I was perplexed by the difference between this funeral and the one in Heidingsfeld when I was eight years old.

We had a girl in class who had the most obnoxious body odor ever and she was shunned by all the other girls except me. I volunteered to have her sit next to me, trying my best to be helpful to the girl. She was a really nice girl but her odor kept the other girls at a distance and she was often teased. On this particular day a warning to the class had come down from the homeroom teacher that we were prohibited from making any disparaging remarks about this girl. He explained that it was not because of something she did not do, that this condition was beyond her control, when somebody blurted out the customary derogatory remark. The professor was so infuriated at this open display of disobedience that he demanded the responsible person to identify herself, which she did not do. He then determined that the whole class had to stay at school until the guilty party would show her hand. Nothing happened. The minutes went by. Nothing. The professor made himself comfortable, signaling that he was in this for the duration. I was getting pretty upset and looked proddingly at my classmates. Nothing happened. I was extremely disappointed at the obvious cowardice of the guilty party and the inexcusable inconsideration to have us all suffer the consequence for her mistake. From the way this looked, we'd be sitting there till the cows came home, so I said that it was I who made this disrespectful remark. I really do not think that anybody, including the professor, believed that I had done it but what could he do as I steadfastly insisted? We got to go home.

There was another feature which became part and parcel of my personality. I actively pursued letting go of my natural inclination to selfishness, vanity, sexual proclivity, and dishonesty in little things. It is ironic that in certain circumstances the welfare of the majority trumps the interest of the individual, as was the case here. I sought and received forgiveness for the transgressions that I committed, regardless of the circumstances. A lie is a lie.

It was serious business for me to become God-pleasing but every effort in that cause slowly but surely created that very solid foundation I would have need of as life brought enormous challenges my way.

Winter was approaching and I had no invitation to spend the cold months at my Aunt Hilda's. I woke up one morning and when I lit my candle my room looked like a sparkling wonderland. The moisture from my breath had clung to the ice-cold walls and had frozen into ice which sparkled in the light. At school I told my best friend, Lotte, who told her mother, and her mother looked for a place for me to move to where I would have some heat. Lotte shared her lunch with me many, many times since food was somewhat hard to come by and usually consisted of a piece of bread and an apple. Her mother was working just as hard as her father, and Lotte was a latchkey kid who lacked nothing. This family had fled from East Germany to the West under very difficult conditions and they felt sorry for me that I was living in the West in the conditions they escaped from. So my friend's mother would send extra food for me, which I enjoyed so much. It turned out that there was a home for students just like me who, for one reason or another, just had no home. I told my father about this and he arranged for me to find a place there. I shared a room with three other girls. They were all religious and were good evangelical Lutherans just like myself. It was a good solution to my problem.

During vacations this student-home operated on a reduced level but provided the basic needs for the ones who had no place to go to. If I did not visit with my grandmother for a day, I would use the vacation to sew myself some clothes. Even though my father assumed financial responsibility for me this did not mean that I had no money problems. He gave me a small allowance and I had to figure out how to get what I needed. I knew also how to knit and I bought the yarn and knitted myself a sweater which is visible in the school pictures in 1958. I did my sewing at my aunt's who had an old Singer sewing machine just like the one I used in Wuerzburg.

I have no recollection of Christmas at my father's house though I am sure they did not leave me at the student-home on Christmas day.

I could never get a sense of where my father stood on anything other than his dislike of Americans. He'd talk occasionally about metaphysics though I had no idea what that was at that time.

My relationship with my father was strange, as far as I was concerned. I could never tell whether he even liked me. I got the feeling that he just put up with me because he had no choice, but what was I to do? He resented it when I had to ask him for money and I hated to have to ask him. My brother, who was being paid for working while he was learning offered to help me out when I really needed help and he assured me that he was happy to do it because he loved me.

When I first got to Nürnberg and had started school, I was still under the impression that my father was bound to love me since I was his sweet daughter whom he had had to live without for all those years. I had the courage to ask him if I could continue with my ballet classes, but he said, "No, Ilona you do not want to do that. It's only a certain unseemly kind of woman that swings her legs on stage—you do not want to be that kind of woman!" Never before did I ever think it inappropriate in any way to study ballet. I thought of it as a beautiful discipline requiring hard work and concentration. I did not respond in defense of ballet, or show my disappointment over his negative and totally wrong opinion, as I had taken an entirely different course of focus, which had left my former enthusiasm for dancing somewhat lacking. In a way I could even guess the correlation between the atmosphere in the stage life and moral turpitude. At the student home was a girl in the next room who was dancing with the ballet for the opera house in Nürnberg and I would often see her coming home in full makeup. This reminded me of the girls at my mother's who were dating American soldiers. This only supported my easy acceptance of my father's decision as I was completely committed to being God-pleasing and ballet would just get in the way of that.

In school I was an average student. My weak subjects were math, chemistry, and physics. I fared better in languages, with English coming easily as I had started taking English in elementary school when it was offered as an elective. However, the professors were very strict about retaining the British pronunciation of the words, forbidding the influx of the American influence, which was sneaking in as American culture started to creep in through the confluence of the occupying forces and the intermingling of the perceived, and real to some, superiority of the American way of thought and life. In the public educational institutions a resistance to the Americanization of the German youth was still and in my opinion, correctly practiced. Consequently, I ended up with a British accent that I do not like to this day, as it has an annoying ring of the stiffness and stuffiness of the British bluenoses, the aristocrats, and I am certainly not that. I heard rumors from my fellow students of places they'd been and things they heard that involved American music but I never paid attention, as it did not interest me.

Math was my first class and my professor was a no-nonsense female who wore thick glasses and her hair pulled back into a bun, and on whom, my general pleasantness made absolutely no favorable impression whatsoever. I was always somewhat uncertain about the homework that would be checked for accuracy right away upon her arrival. All she was interested in was whether you could do the work she assigned to show her that you understood her instruction. That's when I always was in trouble. No matter which route she took to explain algebra, I never understood the concept. It was abstract to me and my brain was simply not able to process it. One morning—it was winter because I was wearing my green knitted sweater—I was especially nervous and very preoccupied trying to get things right for her. The girl sitting behind me, kept talking to me about some American guy she had mentioned to me the day before; the one she spoke of who sang so crazy, which I vaguely remembered her having said but was not really paying attention since I was really not interested in someone who sang crazy. Please! I was trying to avoid being chided about my inability to comprehend something that seemed so simple to everybody else. I was busy, this was important. Who cared about a crazy-singing guy and an American to boot? But she kept on and even held a picture of him under my nose. I did not want to hurt her feelings, so I looked at the very small picture of this person. He was looking straight into my eyes. A stinging pain shot through my heart area, which I felt as clearly as if someone had struck me on the arm. It took my breath away and in a paralyzed state I perceived in an instant that this person was quite familiar to me and that I loved him and I simultaneously knew that he was in imminent danger and that it was my obligation to warn him of it. I came back to consciousness as the professor arrived. I whispered to the girl behind me asking if she would let me have the picture. Of course she would, it meant nothing to her whereas to me it was my only connection to the single most important person on this earth. Not getting this picture was unthinkable. I loved this man, boy, whatever, whoever this was, and not being able to identify him for the next day was an inconceivable agony I did not want to experience; the mere thought scared me to death. I can remember nothing about how my homework stacked up against the professor's expectations. All I could think of was that I loved this person whose name I did not even know. When the professor was preoccupied with something I whispered, "What is his name?" My friend whispered back, "Elvis Presley." I had never heard the name and I certainly did not know anything else about him. The only thing I knew was that I loved him and that I had to help him stay away from this danger that he was in. That whole day was like a blur. I was so disoriented, I did not know whether I was coming or going. That little picture of Elvis Presley became my most precious possession. I put it under my pillow at night. I would take it with me wherever I went. I was completely beside myself and I prayed in my confusion for God to please help me with this because I did not understand my indescribably strong feelings of the truest love ever and did not know what I was to do about this, particularly since Elvis was all the way in America while I was this little schoolgirl in Germany who had never been anywhere.

The next day I went looking for some information on this true beloved of mine. I found an American magazine, I think it was *Photoplay*, which had an article about him. In it was an article about him being always with girls and that they were crazy about him and his rock 'n' roll which made his appearances rather unruly as he caused them to lose control. It did not sound encouraging, added to the fact that I was none too fond of Americans in general since my years in Wuerzburg left me with a negative impression of them. But I loved him regardless. From then on I cultivated a liking of everything American. I considered it my duty to familiarize myself with his culture, and in the American way of life. I was perfectly willing to overlook a lot of things but on a deeper level I noticed things I did not even want to know.

All in all this love that found me made me happy deep within and I was only too willing to talk about my love for Elvis. That was definitely not the smart thing to do. The German establishment had a very dim view of Elvis Presley and the professors were not impressed and my classmates were stunned. They apparently had thought of me as being too mature to fall into the category of an Elvis fan. I ruined that. No matter how I tried to justify my feelings for Elvis by trying to explain that Elvis was really a very good person, of which I was absolutely certain, how could he not be since I Ilona, loved him, it remained a wasted effort. Elvis Presley was bad news with the German Establishment.

4

Caught In a Trap

Still bothered by the persistent negative reaction of the adults to Elvis Presley, I took it upon myself to find out why they were taking this position. It was spring break and I took the opportunity to see what this rock 'n' roll was all about. The young people were all excited about it but I was not really convinced that it was as harmless as the strong proponents made it out to be.

The rock 'n' roll dances were fun. I, too, liked the rhythm and I could clearly feel that it was sex that provided the spring for this eruptive new way of dancing. Recognizing the nature of this enormously powerful and addictive force of the strongest natural impulse, second only to that of the instinct for survival, I understood the reaction of the budding youth on one hand and the serious opposition by the parents of these impulsive teenagers on the other.

Since I had paid my dues, so to speak, having struggled so hard to gain control over my own very strong sexual impulses, which was more like an addiction that I knew I had to control vigilantly for the rest of my life, I put on the brakes when I attended these dances and became primarily an observer.

Most of those who were unsupervised at these dances eventually found it impossible to cling to what they were taught to practice, and gave in to the heightened intensity of sexual desire that was unquestionably rock 'n' roll-induced. They reveled in it and enjoyed it and became addicted to this source of joy in lust. Quite naturally they protected that source, passionately defending the providers of such unbridled lust, which they unfortunately confused with love. They honestly thought they loved Elvis, when in reality they had inadvertently unleashed their sexual nature, but it felt like love to them and so they protected each other and Elvis, like partners in crime.

Returning to school a lot smarter than I was before spring break, I could not help but feel degraded when the math professor would say, as a response to my inability to understand her instruction, "Well, Miss Bauer, of course, if one has one's mind on Elvis Presley one cannot understand much else!" The implied reference to my own sexuality and my apparent infatuation really got under my skin, particularly because I knew for sure that sex was never in the equation. My love for Elvis was and still is of the purest kind. Though I never again spoke of my love in class and pretended it belonged to the past, my love for Elvis grew exponentially with every passing day and those whom I took into my confidence knew very well that I was seriously in love, but they could not understand what to make of it all. Neither did I. But through incessant prayer and constant pleading to God, I felt so certain that this was my destiny and that God Himself was the director of this play.

I have to admit that I had serious doubts about the whole situation myself. How in the world was anything going to work when my set of values was in such direct conflict with what Mr. Presley so openly displayed? But having this abiding faith that God could and did work everything for the good of those who loved Him and lived the Lord's Way, I made my plans to rescue Elvis from whatever he needed to be rescued from.

I had to figure out a way to get in touch with him. I saw in one of the magazines that they were looking for a girl to play the role of Anne Frank, so I sent in a picture of myself to Universal Studios in Hollywood. I had no idea who this Anne Frank was but that was not important to me. I just wanted a way to get to the United States, so I could talk to Elvis and implore him to reconsider his direction in life.

Then came the news that Elvis was going to go into the Army, which I thought was definitely in his favor as far as public opinion was concerned and to a very slight degree I felt somewhat vindicated in my insistence that he was not what he appeared to be. Shortly after that the news broke that he would be coming to Germany! Of course he had to come to Germany because it was his and my destiny to meet. I was literally on cloud nine but I could never ever get rid of this ever-present doubt that the whole thing was just not going to be one of those "...and they lived happily ever after" stories. I had this dull sense of doom hiding deep within me. One day I would be so indescribably happy and the next day I would sink into that bottomless pit of depression and the excruciating pain of separation. Oh, how I loved him. As a matter of fact, whatever selfishness was left in me after trying so hard to kill it, was instantaneously removed the moment I looked into his eyes and recognized him as part of me. Never, ever, did I have any idea that true love was so exhilarating and so deadly at the same time. I asked my father if I could go see Mr. Presley when he would come in late September 1958. My father said, "No, and if you think that you are going to get any money from me to see that American degenerate you are mistaken. If you need money, work for it." So that summer I did. My stepmother was helpful in securing me a spot in the factory where they were making these porcelain doohickeys they used to string the telephone wires around on the top of telephone poles.

I went to work at Siemens for two weeks which was all I could stand, not so much because of the work but because of the kind of girls who were working there and the loose talk I forced myself not to listen to. I saw a girl in the restroom and she was doctoring open sores on her legs which I thought were some kind of disease from loose living. But I had the money for wherever I had to travel to which turned out to be Friedberg in Hessen, pretty close to Frankfurt, where he would be stationed.

In August of that year Elvis's mother died. I found out about it in a picture which was prominently displayed at a newsstand. Elvis was shown crumpled into a pitiful crushed heap, sitting on the steps in front of his house next to his father, who was comforting the inconsolable son who had lost his beloved mother. She was known to everyone and thought to be so sweet. I experienced the most intense pain of loss that I had ever experienced before. It was as if Elvis's mother had been my mother too. This indescribable sorrow at Gladys Presley's death made me realize that I could actually feel what Elvis was feeling and I could not help but cry and cry in complete sympathy for the suffering he was going through. I knew again that we were connected in a very special way.

The next chance for a mini-vacation from school came on Reformation day when the Evangelical Lutherans observe Martin Luther's nailing the ninety-five thesis to the door of the chapel of the University of Wittenberg, defiantly declaring to the Pope his refusal to continue to be part of the lying and scheming and greedy Catholic Church, which until then was the only acceptable Christian denomination.

By the way, we had school on Saturdays too, because the material to be learned was too extensive to cover in just the five days. Our school hours were from 8 a.m. to 1 p.m., after which it was recommended that we take a nap after lunch and then study the rest of the day and do the assignments, which could take until 10 p.m. if you tarried too long after dinner. On Saturdays no assignments were given. There was an extra day off on Monday in observance of the Reformation.

My mind was far from any Reformation thoughts. I had sewn myself a navy-blue straight skirt and an off-white sleeveless blouse way back in warmer weather and I had bought an inexpensive jacket and a pair of bone pumps and I was ready to meet with the true love of my life, Elvis Presley.

I took the train to Bad Nauheim where Elvis had moved off-base into the Grunewald-Hotel on the Terrassen St. I had written to Elvis shortly after he got settled. That letter would play an important role at our meeting. It was cold and I had to wear different shoes for the travel. Upon arriving at the station in Bad Nauheim, I went to the ladies' room and changed whatever needed to be changed and did whatever I thought in those days would make me look good. A little girl, being pulled by her mother to the door, said, after she looked at me, "Mommy, when I grow up I want to look like her!" So I guessed it was mission accomplished!

When I got to the hotel, it was about 2:30 in the afternoon. The concierge was accommodating and said politely, after my inquiry on possibly meeting Mr. Presley, that Mr. Presley was not available right now but that he would be later this afternoon and that I was welcome to be seated in the hall or foyer to wait there until then.

I chose to sit in the hall because that is where I entered on the side entrance.

Doors opened and closed and hotel personnel were scurrying here and there. A girl who looked about my age came to me and said that she was the chambermaid of Mr. Presley's room and when the concierge was busy elsewhere she'd tell me things I did not ask to know. I was seated on a couch in line with the side door and to my left before me were the stairs going to the various suites. This hotel was at one time the home of a well-to-do family around the turn of the eighteenth century, dignified and tastefully furnished, so elegant that I felt I had the wrong clothes on for the privilege just to be allowed into this place. It was unsettling, to say the least, but the chambermaid's chatting got me over it. She told me that Elvis was on the second floor and that he had just returned from the base and he was taking a nap. When the door would opened slightly it was a sign that he was up from his nap. She also told me that he could not play the guitar very well and that he was rather—how shall I put it?—lewd. She continued that many times when she'd make the bed, he'd come up behind her and would open his robe under which he was wearing nothing. There was nothing worse she could have told me about him. Was he really as they said? Had I be fooling myself into thinking that he was way better, more like myself? My heart sank to the floor. I was at a loss as to what to do now. I decided that since I had come all this way, having taken all the trouble it required to come this far, I was going to go through with my original plan. And then, this girl could also have been lying for who knows what reason.

Time was going by slowly and I was so apprehensive about meeting Elvis. To talk to him about anything spiritual was like throwing pearls before swine but what would I say now? I had no idea. I was starting to get depressed when a girl with her American military father walked in the side door. The concierge was not there and the father was talking to her with a very low voice, when his daughter went into a rant about how she loved Elvis and that she would surely die if she did not get to meet him.

The father was looking for the concierge, really anybody who could help him with his hysterical daughter. That left me alone with her. She told me that she was fifteen and from Düsseldorf, where her father was stationed. I told her what I knew of the time when we could expect to see Elvis. I was still explaining when I came to the part where the door would be ajar. We looked at each other in agreement, saw that nobody was around, and up the stairs we went. The girl was behind me as we found the door ajar, so I knocked gently with trepidation when a voice from inside said matter of factly, "Come in!" I opened the door slowly and scanned the room. There were three or four men standing around. No Elvis. These men's eyes were all looking in the direction behind the door. I opened the door some more, entered the room completely and looked behind the door and there was Elvis Presley.

The girl rushed out from behind me and threw herself on Elvis who was slouched in an easy chair, his hair tousled, his feet on the ottoman. The girl repeated over and over, "Elvis, oh Elvis, I love you, I love you!" I had no idea what she thought she was going to do next. I was so shocked at her uncontrolled behavior I was shaking my head and looking rather apologetic. The girl had long blonde hair and it was falling over Elvis's face. While he was patting the girl's back he was saying that he loved her too, all the while trying to blow her hair out of his face and trying his best to get a better look at me. Finally our eyes met and in spite of my reservations I could not help but smile a smile that revealed the deep, deep love I had for him. As if stung by a bee he very unceremoniously threw the girl off him and scrambled out of the chair stood before me and apologized for his disheveled look, excused himself and went to freshen up.

At the foot of the bed was a divan and on it lounged a man who was asking the girl some questions when a little dog bounded in, barking. The man said the name of the dog was Cherry, or at any rate that is what I understood it to be, and I had just picked up this cute creature when the man said, looking at me, "I sure wish I could be the dog right now!" My enchantment with the dog vanished instantly and I put it down, looked at this man disapprovingly and walked out the door onto the landing, which was full of people and Elvis right in the middle of them, chatting and signing autographs. He was having a conversation with the crazy girl's father about military matters. He brushed by me and asked, "What do you want?" I looked undecided and shrugged my shoulders, indicating that I did not know and I really did not know why I still hung around. This circus around him, the men he surrounded himself with, were all not in Elvis's favor and I could see no way that I could make any difference in his life, let alone rescue him from some impending peril.

There is really no way to describe how insignificant and downright silly I felt. It was just good that nobody knew me there. I did not pray for help because I was mad at God for letting me walk into such an unpleasant and confusing situation.

Since I had concluded that this whole thing was a colossal mistake that the best thing for me to do was to ride it out and act like one of his fans, to save face. That would prove harder than I anticipated. To this day I cannot understand why one would want a picture or an autograph from anyone.

In all the hubbub Elvis would come by when there seemed to be a lull because people were readying their cameras or digging for something or because so-and-so wanted him to sign a picture, and he'd ask again what I wanted. This time however I knew what I wanted. I wanted the letter back I wrote to him some weeks earlier. He said that he could not do that since he had received letters by the boxful. But I was insistent, so he called, "Red, go get the boxes with all the letters I got since I came here, she wants hers back!" While this Red person went to get the boxes with the letters he proceeded to tell me that I would never find my letter. I looked at him and said with conviction, "Oh yes, I will."

Red returned with two big boxes, put them on the table which was a part of one of those old-time constructions with a mirror in the center, a low table one could sit on to remove shoes, with places on either side to accommodate hats and umbrellas.

I immediately went to work on finding the letter. I surely did not want any evidence of my silliness in Elvis's possession—the very thought would make me blush with embarrassment. It took me all of thirty seconds and there it was! I took it out and waved it gleefully at Elvis when he said in utter disbelief, "This is your letter?" The fifteen-year-old asked me if I wanted a picture with Elvis, saying that she would mail me a print. I said that I did not want to have a picture with Elvis when he intervened and said, "Oh yes you do!" and with that he put me on one side of him and the crazy girl on the other side. Of course I had a problem with that, as I had this letter in my hand and I surely did not want a record of this, so I busied myself to hide it between Elvis's body and mine. If this picture should ever surface, it will show me with my right arm crossing over my front hiding the letter. Elvis was wondering what I was doing there under his arm with my hand.

After this girl told her dad to bend over so she could write down my address on his back, to be able to send me the picture, I told her my address, which was the student-home on the Glockenhofstrasse 14 Nürnberg. She and her dad started to leave, but when she was halfway down the stairs she remembered that her mother had told her to invite Elvis to their house for Christmas, to which Elvis replied, "Thank you, honey, but I'll have my family here. But I'll remember you!"

I was standing with my back against the railing of the landing and I heard this exchange when I said casually to Elvis, "Mr. Presley, you are the Army's greatest lover and—" I made a pause for effect—"liar!" It really galled me to have to call him anything great, but those words were a headline in *Photoplay*. I was playing the role of an Elvis fan and as such I could afford being generous. Elvis jumped up the stairs, stood in front of me and said somewhat threateningly, "What did you say?" Unperturbed and ever-so-deliberately, I repeated, "Mr. Presley, you are the Army's greatest lover and"—an even longer pause than before—"liar!" Elvis growled and turned his head disapprovingly. Just as suddenly as all these people had come they disappeared and there was only Elvis and me. He asked me if I wanted a picture or an autograph. I said no to both but then, remembering that I was this Elvis fan, I thought that maybe they would typically ask him to sing their favorite tune for them, so I asked him if he could sing "Love Me Tender" for me, which he said that he could not without music. That was just as well with me since I did not really care anyway.

He brought up the letter which he said was really lawfully his and therefore he would like to read it. At first I objected but then I thought what difference does it make, the whole thing is a lost cause and Elvis will never remember, there was just too much competition for his attention from all sides, including his personal entourage working to make him feel at home away from home in a foreign country. So I agreed. He opened the letter and started to read, "Dear Elvis... something about that I love him be he devil or angel etc," when I jerked it out of his hand and insisted that he could not read and then proceeded to finish reading the letter to him while he was looking at this strange girl and this new development. He offered to autograph it and he simply did not pay any attention to my continuing objections.

He then sat back down on that low table and I sat down beside him. Red opened the bedroom door and made sure that Elvis was not in any kind of trouble. Elvis motioned him that he was okay and to close the door.

I then proceeded to tell him of my reaction upon hearing of his mother's death and as I was talking, remembering, I started crying and he turned to me and said softly, "But she wasn't your mother!" and ever so gently touched my hair as if to comfort me. I had been forgetting my fan status for a moment and thought that Elvis must surely think that I am some kind of deranged, strange girl. So, being angry at myself, I jumped up and asked him whether he thought that rock 'n' roll was art and whether he thought it was good to move the way he does on stage and I parodied him, swiveling mildly. He was getting serious again and said thoughtfully that he did not think it was art. He got up too and we were standing in the center of the landing.

I then said to him, and I have no idea where it came from, "Mr. Presley, for some people fame and fortune are a curse!" Then I declared myself ready to leave when he asked me if I wanted to kiss him.

I was indignant. Was sex all these men thought about? I said sternly, "No." He then asked me to please hug him. I had no idea what hug meant and what I had to do but I figured that surely it would not be as bad as kissing. The British English word is "embrace"—that was all I knew. So I stood there, with my hands stiffly folded behind my back waiting for whatever this hug was. Elvis was waiting too for me to hug him when I got tired of waiting and walked toward the stairs to leave. He cut me off just as I was taking the first step down. He stood two steps below me which put us on even level. He took my hands from behind me and wrapped them around himself and my right cheek touched his right cheek and we remained like this for longer than it took me to retrieve my letter. He then asked me to come back, which

I said I could not do. He asked me why. Could I tell him of my disappointment at the things and people he surrounded himself with, would it make any sense to him for me to explain that I could not stand the environment he had chosen for himself? There was really nothing he could have said that would have changed anything, my teeth were set on edge and there was nothing I could do. So I said that I was still in school and that I lived too far away to just go whenever I please. He then said that he was in the army and he could not go whenever or wherever he pleased either.

"That leaves us nowhere," he said, and I shrugged my shoulders in agreement with that statement. I got away as fast as my feet could carry me for I was so upset at the whole turn of events and I was afraid I would faint. It was a most emotionally draining experience, particularly in that I had to play-act my way through without losing my composure and dignity. He was standing on the landing watching me and waving until I was out of sight.

I cannot remember how I got back to the train station. Once I was in my compartment by myself I got so furious with God, complaining that I just could not believe that He had set me up for this crushing blow to my faith. I was devastated. To think that I had trusted my whole life in His hands, blithely overcoming every obstacle to get so far as to finally meet this man whom I cherished deep within my heart and had expected something different, certainly not such an obviously unacceptable state of affairs in Elvis's life. I took the letter and that little picture which had started it all and tore them to smithereens and tossed them in the trash, telling myself if God wanted to have a sucker whom He can send on a wild goose-chase He'd have to find somebody else. I was no longer available.

I was completely emotionally, mentally, and spiritually disoriented. How could I continue to live without God, on whom my whole existence found its bearings? What was I going to say to my friends, who knew that I was going to meet E.P.? I mulled it over and decided the best way to deal with it was to say the least controversial and certainly least unpleasant things about it, make light of it and treat it as some kind of an adventure that was now over. It worked. I became more available to my friends who had been in my ears for the longest time to go on dates with boys they knew. I always felt that I did not do the things every teenager enjoyed doing since my mind was preoccupied with this love I had for Elvis. I had no eye for anyone, and that nobody liked. So, for the first time I went out on a date, but I found no joy in it. I was content that my friends liked the change but imperceptibly I slid right back into where I had tried so hard to get out of. By the time Easter came around I was ready to see Elvis again. This time my brother had to pay for almost everything and I promised to pay him back which he did not want me to do. This time I did not tell anyone. I was almost ashamed of my inability to get hold of my feelings. It was infuriating in a way to be so controlled by true love. I wore a pretty pink dress and I carried the same ivory jacket I was wearing on my first visit. The chambermaid and I stayed in touch and she invited me to the house where Elvis had moved to on the Goethestrasse 14. I bought some flowers for Elvis's grandmother as she and Elvis's dad were living there too. Come to think of it they were at the hotel because she wanted chickens out back. I think they joined him at Christmastime, just like he had told the fifteen-year-old from Düsseldorf back in November of 1958. I wore the same shoes and there I stood, ringing the doorbell. Vernon, Elvis's father, answered the door and I explained to him that I came by invitation of the chambermaid and that these flowers were for Minnie, Elvis's grandmother. He called for her and in the meantime he was looking me up and down like I was some kind of piece of meat to be inspected which did aggravate me right from the start. He was trying to make up for his disrespect and complimented me on my ability to speak English so well when I reminded him that such things are actually learned in school for some people. He was so annoying, an older man ogling women so soon after his wife's death. Then came Minnie. The poor dear had no teeth but she had a toothpick stuck firmly between her thin lips. I gave her the flowers and she seemed genuinely delighted to receive them and she asked me in. We ended up in her room which was on the ground floor. Those stucco houses all have basements, so the ground floor was actually in between the first and the underground floor as you must climb a few stairs to get to the front door to the first floor. Usually the basement serves as another living space, with the windows being half on top of the ground and half under.

    I was seated with my back against the door, facing the window, and the chambermaid and Minnie were on either side of me with a full view of the door. Minnie had put the flowers I'd brought into a vase, which was standing in the middle of the round table. The chambermaid whispered that Elvis was coming downstairs and I thought to myself, "I am not going to turn around." But this increasing hum of activity and a sense of excitement was building so high that I could not help but turn around. Just as I caught a glimpse of the door, there was Elvis walking by. It could not have been more than a split second or less when he did a double take and stepped into the room. It quickly filled up with people. I got up as the chambermaid jumped up and proceeded to introduce me to Elvis. He interrupted her and said to me, "We know each other, don't we?" I sort of smiled in agreement, thinking briefly of the debacle of our initial meeting. He then asked if I wanted to come to the movies at the base with them. I really did not want to see a movie, so I stalled by saying, "What are they playing?" to which he said that he did not know. I did not say anything to that, so he called this trusted friend, Red, and ordered him to call the base to find out what was playing. People kept talking to Elvis on every side and then Red came back and yelled over the general noise, "Elvis, they are showing *The Hound of the Baskervilles!*" Elvis looked at me and repeated it and I was still at a loss as to whether or not I wanted to go. Elvis left to get the trip for the show going and I was literally swooshed out with the throng of bodies going outside and piling into the cars. The lead car was a BMW and Elvis was driving. A girl was between him and the man who was on that divan back in November, whose name was Charlie Hodge, as I found out, and in the back was Red and who knows which females. I was still standing undecided and really annoyed on the sidewalk. I just could not accept that there was not more interest in me from Elvis. I was still laboring under the impression that he and I had some unfinished business and he was not cooperating as I had hoped he would.

    Charlie kept the door open and urged me to come along and I kept on resisting when he reached out, grabbed my hand and pulled me into the car, and all the while I was protesting that there was no more room in the car. He just got me into the car and put me on his lap, closed the door and off we went. Elvis had one arm out the open window, tapping out the rhythm as he was singing, "Now and Then There's a Fool Such as I" on the roof of the car. I was very uncomfortable and I had to hold on to the sun visors to keep from falling every which way because the road to Friedberg was full of curves. I made sure I sat on Charlie's knees and I was pretty embarrassed at the whole situation. I had never been that close to any man before and I found it downright indecent.

I would try not to look at Elvis and he was trying not to look at me but when we thought the other was not looking we got caught looking at each other. It was funny and we both smiled amused.

When we got to the theater my hands were black from the dust on the visors, so I told Charlie that I had to wash my hands. By the time I was out of the restroom everybody was seated. Elvis was sitting in the center of a row in the center of the theater and there was one more place at the very end for me next to Charlie. I sat down and Charlie asked if everything was okay. I nodded "'yes" and tried to catch up with what was going on onscreen.

As my luck would have it, this movie was in black and white. I think it was with Basil Rathbone as Sherlock Holmes and it had English subtitles. Those really fascinated me as I had never seen that before and I challenged myself to see if I could read and understand the contents of the movie. I was completely into translating and Charlie was constantly talking, which was irritating, so I told him to be quiet and he did not say another word. Every now and then I would lean forward to check on Elvis when he leaned forward to check on me and we did that same peep and hide game just as in the car and we were satisfied with that.

After the movie was over we all stood around in small groups waiting for the cars to be brought around. Elvis came strolling by and asked me if I liked the movie and I, in all honesty could not say that I did, so I said no. He then said that he liked it and started to look at the sky that was just covered with stars. He commented how pretty they looked. The cars came, we piled in and I have no recollection of that trip back to Bad Nauheim.

When we got there, Elvis was leading the way and he stood up there at his front door and I was being swooshed again by the crowd, but

I did not want to go inside. Even though I did not know what was coming next, I had the feeling that there was going to be some kind of loosely planned orgy. I was utterly turned off and said to Charlie, "I am not going in, I am going to catch the train and go home," to which he replied that I should not do that as I could sleep with him in his bed. I said to him, "No, thank you!" and started to shake hands when Elvis came down to where I stood as I had made my way with the crowd up the stairs to say good-bye. He stood in front of me and I thanked him for the movie, we shook hands and I left, never turning back and seething inside with an uncontrollable mix of intense pain and anger. Pain because I loved him so deeply inside and angry because I had once again put myself in all kinds of humiliating circumstances with absolutely nothing to show for it but the fact that I was incapable of controlling my emotions and that I must be some kind of fool to continue with what appeared to be a ridiculous one-sided love affair. Then my intellect would continue reasoning that I was in control of my destiny, the captain of my ship and I could and would determine my own destiny. Period.

I caught the train back home and promised myself that I would do whatever it took to kill this love of mine for Elvis Presley. And who was he anyway? Some crazy, immoral, unprincipled American, whose primary goal in life seemed to be to see how many women he could have sex with. What business would I have with someone like that?

However, there were all these roadblocks to my strangling my love for him, as I had this inexplicable knowledge that there was more to this than met the eye. Sometime after I had fallen so hard for Elvis, back in early 1958, I had two dreams which sort of outlined the general direction of this, whatever it was, which I could never determine.

In one dream I was on my way to a prison and I was looking for my true love, Elvis. I got to the prison where there were huge throngs of people. In my dream I was thinking, *How on earth am I going to get through this sea of humanity?* when the people simply parted to let me through. Once inside the jail, the warden accompanied me to the jail cell where Elvis was. I stepped in, we exchanged a few words. I do not know what they were but he walked out of the cell with me but when we stepped out into freedom the crowds simply swallowed him up and I lost him. This was very unsettling since it was my dream to be married to him and the mother of his children. Of course, I do what everybody has a tendency to do when they know good and well that the reality was anything but rosy, I ignored it and went into "denial overdrive."

Then came this other dream that was more mysterious and I had all kinds of trouble trying to figure out what it meant.

A pair of big hands threw me into a violent body of water with heaving waves. I went down into it, down where the currents were the strongest. I was tossed about, to and fro, up and down, around and around, and I could feel myself getting nauseated from all this circular motion when I was spewed out by this angry sea onto the shore. I lifted my head as best I could and looked around to see where I was when I recognized the landscape as the Sea of Galilee (from pictures in my Bible). I tried to get up but I was too weak, so I dragged myself farther inland. I tried again to get up but I simply could not find the strength and continued crawling in the direction of something, but I did not know what it was. After crawling some more, I tried again to get up and I was finally able to stand on my feet. I looked in a direction that took me to the right and kept going and going, all the while looking for something, when I came upon a group of men all wearing white robes. I approached this group and as I came closer they were all towering over me and I was walking among them, looking for somebody I could not find. At that point I woke up and realized that there was a serious meaning to this dream. But what was it?

I thought this and that and I even thought that it could mean that I had to go to the U.S., which I rejected outright as I was in no mood to go to a foreign country, certainly not to America where they apparently were breeding these oversexed red-blooded boys en masse. I asked my aunt because she believed like I did that dreams have meaning. I told her of this very clear dream that was just like I was watching a movie and she said that this meant that I would be well liked by both men and women (which I was already aware of—tell me something I didn't know!) and that the water meant the spirit but that was all she could come up with. I completely disregarded her interpretation and concluded that in time I would understand but it just did not help me at that time, except to leave me with a nagging feeling of a difficult and generally unpleasant road ahead. I did not want to know that! Depressing, depressing.

When I came back from my second attempt to get this situation resolved, once again having nothing accomplished, I was ever so determined to get hold of my emotions but it was hopeless. It seemed the more I struggled to get loose the tighter I became enmeshed till I could do nothing other than to present God with an ultimatum. It was, "All right, I am going one more time, if you do not do anything then to settle this thing one way or the other I am through with this. No more." I have got to make some sense especially to myself since I was in a constant state of confusion with all the mixed signals. One day I was confident that it will all be happiness and the next day I was certain that I will surely perish in doom and gloom.

I was now fast approaching the end of my school years and my preoccupation with this love of mine for Elvis. I had no mind for school. I did not graduate, which did not bother me much because I already had four more years of school than my sister and my brother and that was fine with me. I had to decide where to go from here. I loved children, and through the student home I got the necessary recommendations to the Red Cross Hospital in Frankfurt to register there for training as a baby-nurse, which required me to spend a year with a family, learning how to take care of children. Yes, I chose to move away to Frankfurt because it was closer to Elvis since Bad Nauheim was just a very short train ride from there and it afforded me a safe distance from my brother and cousin at the same time.

Whenever I spent time in Bernlohe with my grandmother, brother and cousin, I got involved in their drama of being in love with me. My brother would tell me that he was in love with me but not to tell my cousin and my cousin would tell me that he loved me and but not to tell my brother. Of course I never did but the trouble I had with this ridiculous scenario was getting more complicated by the week. My brother resigned himself to the fact that this was an ill-fated love and that it could never be, but my cousin had schemes in his head to emigrate to Australia where we could marry, as it was against the law in Germany from what I understood. It behooves me to say here that

I never gave any indication to either one of them that my affection for them was more than purely on a sister-brother level and a cousin-cousin level respectively, and to this day I cannot figure out what it was that made them so emotionally involved. I can only guess that it was the time for them to emerge into fully sexual men and they were naturally attracted to me because of that. Whatever the reason for their infatuation, it was extremely important that I did not go over the line with either one of them which was made much easier for me to accomplish because I had set my cap for Elvis and therefore did not, under any circumstances, put a blemish on my established track record of vowed chastity.

Of course they knew of my fascination with Elvis but apparently chose to ignore it. Be that as it may, it was a good thing for all concerned that I left for Frankfurt. And both of them were so good to me; they defended me against accusations that were falsely leveled against me and their instinctive chivalrous protection of the proverbial "damsel in distress" had gotten them at odds with their uncles and aunts with whom they had never had trouble before. They made up in large part for the animosity that continued to plague my adult relatives and the endless suspicion that I was just like my mother. I loved Paul and Wolfgang for all their helpfulness and kindness and I hated in a way to leave them without ever being able to do anything for them in return to show my gratitude. I thanked them often as developments called for but I believed they deserved more.

In June of 1959 I left for Frankfurt. I had only the bare necessities and I left things I valued like presents from various people for my confirmation and little trinkets that I had cherished growing up, in Bernlohe in a chest of drawers in "my" room.

Upon arriving at my future employers', Dr. and Mrs. Kreuzfelder's, house, and after I was introduced to the newborn girl, Elise, and their four-year-old boy Reinholt, I asked permission to take care of a personal matter, saying that I would be back at 8 p.m.

The personal matter, of course, was the Elvis problem. I was ever-so-determined to bring it to a conclusion, no matter what. I truly was tired of hanging between heaven and earth, so to speak, never knowing which way to go.

I got to Elvis's house around 12:30 p.m. and went straight to his door. Charlie came outside and we chatted for a while. He asked me my name as he could never grasp it before and he would call me Eleanor, which always irritated me. So I told him that it was i-l-o-n-a, but he still had trouble saying it. He told me that Elvis would be coming back from the base but that he would come in through the back entrance because there were fans gathering out front and Elvis was too tired to deal with them right then. I chatted with him and the ever-growing crowd of fans.

After a while I went to the back of the house on the Goethestrasse 14 and, lo and behold, Elvis drove up in a fire-engine-red car.

I cannot recall who was driving but Elvis sat on the passenger side and rolled his window down when he saw me. He looked rather unhappy and I asked him what was wrong. He said that he had an upset stomach and just did not feel well. I said that he should go inside, take something to soothe his stomach ache and then lie down for a while. He said that this is what he was going to do and asked if I would be there when he felt better. He looked just miserable. I said that I could not do that since I was obligated to return to Frankfurt to keep an engagement at 8 p.m. with my new employer. He looked straight ahead, forlornly into the distance. I said good-bye and I walked off and that was the last time I saw Elvis on German soil.

I hitchhiked to Frankfurt and considered the matter completely finished. I considered it the decision with the agreement of God that this is the way it had to be but not without an indignant rant about how unreasonable the whole proposition seemed right from the start and that from now on I was going to live like a normal person. I did view myself as different from anyone else and I so wanted to be normal and do normal things. I was pretty excited at the prospect of not having to worry about Elvis anymore.

Dr. and Mrs. Kreuzfeld were the nicest people ever and I felt a part of the family in no time at all. For the first few months I slept in the room with the newborn and when she woke up crying the mother would come in and take care of the baby and then leave to go back to her and her husband's bedroom.

Soon they decided that they could have a room for me in the basement. They hired an architect—I think he was one of their friends—they were a lawyer-family, and before I knew it the workmen came and prepared the ground to afford me a separate entrance. It did not change my lifestyle at all at first and the children's mother accused me of being snooty because I did not want to go out with one of the workers who apparently had told her of his interest in me. That really hurt my feelings because I never thought of myself as a snob. Just because I am selective does not mean that I am a snob. But to prove to her that she was wrong I agreed to go on a date with said worker but I could have saved him and myself embarrassment because I had to turn him down cold when he thought that since he had invested money in dinner and dancing he was now entitled to sex with me. Well, at least I proved her wrong. I just knew more about what I liked than she did.

We went to a small place called Arnoldshain in Hessen, where Dr. and Mrs. K. had an apartment and where they spent the summer with the children because it was away from the city and there was a safe, wonderful, pastoral landscape with a gurgling brook close by and lots of trees and lovely meadows. I liked it very much out there and, one day when the fair came to town, I went on my day off to have some fun at the fair. I met the nicest young man, Max, there and we spent time together from then on. He was the only child of an elderly, stodgy couple who were related to the prominent family in the spa town next to Arnoldshain. My new boyfriend was so proud of his uncle, who lived in a luxurious home up on the ridge overlooking the surrounding villages. There was some farming going on but the primary source of income was the tourism traffic from people looking for a lovely respite from the city. They owned a leather-goods manufacturing enterprise that was highly profitable. His parents were the proprietors of a bed-and-breakfast that kept them pretty busy year around.

I really thought I had a handle on this—my life and my ability to determine for myself which direction I wanted to go in. I was glad that I looked and acted like everyone else and I never mentioned the Elvis debacle to my employers in any form or fashion because it now seemed so juvenile and silly; I was perfectly content to admit to myself that I must have had some kind of mental breakdown and I had finally recuperated.

Of course the fact that I now had this wonderfully attentive and ever-so-accommodating boyfriend, who seemed to be genuinely smitten with me made it a lot easier to forget and if this deep love of mine for Elvis tried to rear its head, I simply muzzled it by making myself available to all sorts of activities with my newfound love-interest who enjoyed nothing more than to please me. It was ever so nice and easy.

Christmas 1959 was coming closer and my cousin came to get me to spend a few days with my family in Nürnberg and Bernlohe. He met my employers and they were impressed by his nice manners and they recognized too that he was infatuated with me. Thank goodness I now had a boyfriend and could avoid any awkward replays of the past. I never knew whether or not it bothered him.

After I got back from my visit home, Max asked me to go for a weekend to Garmisch on the Tegernsee close to Switzerland and I agreed to join him. I asked him to please rent two rooms as I still believed in the sanctity of sex and he was not disappointed. In fact he seemed pleased at my request, as he wanted to marry me, and in Germany at the time the good men respected the purity of their intendeds. After we got there and had dinner, we retreated to our respective rooms and I was already in bed doing my nightly devotions, reading the solemn prayers of Martin Luther in the hymnal my grandfather's second wife gave me, when Max knocked on my door

I asked him in and thought for a moment that he would try to seduce me but he saw that I was busy with matters of faith which seemed to have the effect of a cold shower on him and he never let on that he was disappointed. I even think he liked my staunch resolve to remain untouched, so to speak.

Meanwhile I had concluded that I must keep God at arm's length as far as my decisions for myself and what I wanted out of life were concerned, which was a very simple thing. I just wanted to be like everyone else who seemed to be able to enjoy things that normal people enjoy like friends and love and marriage and children—simple stuff, but I did not want to live outside His protection or his commandments.

I was ever so content to finally feel like I belonged to the human race and my employers could not have been happier for me because they liked my young man and thought us to be a good match. I read in the paper that Elvis was looking forward to going back to the States and I thought to myself, *They ought to put a muzzle on his mouth, put weights on his legs and drown him for all the furor he unleashes wherever he goes.*

My boyfriend knew nothing of Elvis and me, and I was too ashamed to admit to my quasi-insane affection for him. Besides he did not like anything American, so the subject of Elvis never came up in any context. Thank goodness.

Max was only too proud to show me off to his extended family but his parents had their reservations since I did not grow up in their community and reasoned that there is no telling where I came from or what kind of a family or background I had, they remained cool to my presence in their house when I came to spend time with their son at his home.

Life was good. We planned to marry in June or July 1960 when my year with this nice family would be officially over, and although I had never given serious thought to what would be required of me as a wife, I figured if everybody else could do it, so could I.

It was my boyfriend's birthday and he said to me, "Dearest, since we are going to get married soon it is important that we find out if we are sexually compatible, so tonight for my birthday we are going to find out." It seemed a reasonable request and I agreed. I was so anxious about it all that I cannot remember a thing about it. I guess I blocked it out of my mind. What I do remember, however was that we were in his parent's bed and that he told his parents and that they were beside themselves. They had been away visiting relatives. It was understood that this would be the only time to engage in sexual activity and so we looked forward after that, he more than me, to our wedding day.

Elvis, meanwhile, departed for the U.S. and I thought, deliberately, *Good-bye to bad rubbish,* and I did not give him another thought.

One fine morning at the breakfast table I sat down and skimmed over the contents of the newspaper that Dr. K. customarily read before breakfast with his wife and then during breakfast they would reflect on some of the events. This day they both left together as she sometimes helped out at the office when his secretary was ill. The children were still asleep and there it was, a relatively small notice but it might as well have had the headline read, "Ilona, this is for you!" It said that Elvis went immediately to Nashville upon his return home to record some songs, and in one in particular he would be talking. It gave specifics on when to expect the record to be available and where. I knew at once that this song was for me and me alone. I just could not, dared not, really believe it, partly because I wanted so to be normal and get married to my boyfriend and partly because I did not want to go on chasing a dream without a shred of possibility of its coming true except in my imagination. Besides it was an agonizing condition to have to live knowing that you were meant to be together and yet you could not make it happen for one reason or another, which then meant that you really did not know a thing as far as the here and now was concerned and that, after all, was what we were living in, the here and now. I never mentioned anything about any of these developments, very upsetting though they were, and even pondered the possibility that I could be out of my mind and I would definitely be better off not telling anyone.

With enough anticipation to cover two people, I found out that the record was available in town and it was a strain to act as if I were just going to town as usual to go window-shopping and to control even my voice as it revealed an excitement. I had a time not to give anything away in part for fear it would then all be ruined.

5

Are You Lonesome Tonight?

So, here I was, tempting fate once again. I went into the music shop in the middle of the town center and I asked for the newly released Elvis Presley record. The salesman handed it to me and I asked if I could use one of their turntables to listen to it right then and there because I did not even have a turntable of my own and I could surely not wait to secretly use my employers'. There just was no way that I could bear that suspense for that long without giving everything away.

I read the title and it was "Are You Lonesome Tonight?" I heard my beloved's velvety voice, filled with sadness, singing the refrain and then pensively going into the now world famous:

> I wonder if you are lonesome tonight.
> You know someone said that the world is a stage and each must play a part.
> Fate had me playing in love with you as my sweetheart.
> Act One was when we met. I loved you at first glance.
> You read your lines so cleverly and never missed a cue.
> Then came Act Two. You seemed to change, you acted strange and why I've never known.
> Honey, you lied when you said you love me and I have no cause to doubt you.
> But I'd rather go on hearing your lies than to go on living without you.

> Now the stage is bare and I'm standing there with
> emptiness all around
> And if you won't come back to me then they can bring the
> curtain down.

There are hardly words to describe my reaction to this confession of love for me by him and the impact of the finality of the last sentence!

I experienced a nauseating feeling in my stomach and a pain that was so intense that it caused me to double over and it felt like Elvis had taken my heart, pulled it out, ripped it in two and taking, one half with him, left me with the other half standing there profusely bleeding, as I felt myself being on the verge of fainting.

I was mortally wounded.

Once again my whole world was turned upside down as I knew that I had to go to the United States of America to continue this overwhelmingly powerful feeling of love I had for this man and only this man. There just could not ever be a substitute.

On one hand I was so deliriously happy I could burst and then there was this gloom and doom feeling I could never shake.

Incidentally, the melody to "Are you Lonesome Tonight?" is the same as "Fascination" from the forties, which is the theme score in "Love in the Afternoon" with Gary Cooper and Audrey Hepburn and Maurice Chevalier. Another song of Elvis' coming out of this same batch recorded in March 1960 is "Fame and Fortune," which is a direct answer to my prophetical: "Mr. Presley, for some people fame and fortune are a curse!"

I had purchased the record and listened to it when my employers were not home. Dr. K. had an old recording machine he used at work as he had to tape depositions and the like. Since he updated his equipment he let me use the old one. Needless to say that I immediately disengaged myself from my fiancé, trying to explain the unexplainable by saying that I had to go and finish some unfinished business over there and when that was done I would return to him. He did not want to believe any of it but since I had already told the family of my decision to emigrate to the U.S., and why, he knew that this was as serious as cancer, so to speak.

Of course I was ready to go as soon as my contractual obligation to this nice family was completed but that was not possible as neither of my parents was willing to give me permission to leave the country since I was only nineteen years old and my father in particular refused to even accept that I would go where the degenerates lived and I had no choice but to wait until I was twenty-one years old, which would be in February of 1962.

I did not mind it all that much because the oh-so-familiar doubt would creep in and hold me in a sort of twilight zone. Was all this real, does he really love me or was I indeed as mad as a hatter, which could be the case as I always knew my mother to be rather more unhinged than selfish, mean, cruel and vindictive. I could have inherited her tilt to madness. Unsettling train of thought.

As I have always been accustomed to, my only refuge was the good Lord whom I was trying so hard to serve and I just knew that he would not steer me wrong, no matter how bad it looked to the carnal eye. And it looked bad to the average, normal person. The only thing that I could say was that I felt that I must do this no matter what. But I was so intent about my decision that Max's offer to remain friends and do things together simply would not do as I had to remain alone and prepare myself mentally and emotionally for the task ahead, and besides, it simply would not be fair to him. It would surely feel like I was using him.

It was a very hard time and yet it was also a wonderful time when I would become so intimate with God, sitting in the one of gothic cathedrals in Frankfurt and simply repeating the lonely journey I was on in Nürnberg when I did the very same thing while contemplating a meeting with Elvis who was then still in the U.S. and no one knew that he was coming to Germany.

When people who knew me found out that I was going to go to the U.S. I got all kinds of reactions, most of them discouraging if not downright alarming. True, I did not know a soul there except Elvis and Charlie and Red and it was highly unlikely that anyone would facilitate a connection to Elvis for me. But that did not keep me from trying. As a heartfelt response to "Are You Lonesome Tonight?" I taped my acknowledgement of his confession of love and I spoke of a higher plane that always came into my mind. I had Beethoven's *Ninth*

Symphony playing in the background, the soft adagio which has a melancholy quality to it and I mailed it to him. Whether he ever got it, is anyone's guess. Nobody at Elvis's home was really interested in what was good for him as that would or could interfere with their agendas and they all had them. No amount of discouragement could change any of that. Sometimes I thought that if I was really crazy, this waiting could tell the tale but there was no change in attitude.

I had to make sure I had people who would sponsor me, so I applied at an agency connecting jobseekers with employers looking for workers. I was put in touch with a Jewish family, the Newmans, who lived on Wynmore Road in Scarsdale, in Westchester County, New York State.

This family consisted of a father, mother and two boys, ages five and seven; the writing style of the woman appealed to me, as it was friendly and accommodating, assuring me that I would be treated as a member of the family and that suited me very well as this was the way it was with the current family.

When everything was signed and sealed, I had obligated myself for one year starting on April 7, 1962 and ending April 7, 1963. There were several other requirements that needed to be met to satisfy the German authorities and the American Consulate, which was in Frankfurt, thank goodness.

As all my plans had changed so drastically, I had to ask this wonderful family if they would permit me to remain with them after the contractual one year is over. They said that I could; I was fairly certain that they would not mind, as we often recognized how well-suited to each other we were and, of course I loved their children, who loved me right back. Since I was more like a family member than an employee, these lovely people were sincerely concerned about me and they ever-so-sensitively suggested to me that it might be high time to consult a psychiatrist since one can get just as sick in the mind as in the body and that I would not hesitate to go to the doctor if I had a broken leg, for instance. I knew very well where they were coming from, however I also knew that I was operating on a very different level than the average person and that I was therefore listening to a different drummer. But the assertion that I might have a mental illness of some kind was only true insofar as it concerned extreme lovesickness and for that there is no cure the doctor can offer, other than to help you drug yourself out of feeling the euphoria of love and the so very debilitating plummeting into the abyss of unrequited or unfulfilled true love. Whenever they hinted at my possible mental maladjustment I smiled and assured them that I was all right and that I appreciated their concern.

I volunteered at the Red Cross Hospital where I was registered to begin in July of 1960 to study to become a pediatric nurse. They had already given me the standard issue nametags which they provided for every student to sew into their clothes and later on into the uniforms. I still have them. I have always liked them because they had my name on them and I liked my name, "Ilona." Nobody else did because no one knew how to pronounce it correctly, as it is an Hungarian name.

The flipside to "Are You Lonesome Tonight?" was "I Gotta Know," which was right in line with my sending the aforementioned tape. It was my answer. Every song he sang from then on which had LOVE as the dominant theme I considered to be communication from Elvis.

I did not notice it then but the different style of singing a song had surely changed dramatically after his days in the Army. He knew I hated rock 'n' roll and he searched my culture, at least the musical heritage of the Germans, and in a larger sense, the European musical background, which is so noticeable in songs like "It's Now Or Never," and "Surrender," just to name two.

Then he made *G.I. Blues* and I could hardly wait to go see it and I immediately recognized the similarity in the story of the film to what Elvis experienced in Germany. The main characters were the reverse from the story as it happened in reality. The scene where Lily is in her dressing-room and Cookie comes in (and she had just gotten the brush-off from Tulsa minutes before) and the ensuing exchange between those two reflects, in a general but important way, how Elvis recognized the true from the false that he encountered each and every day in his life. He had a very hard life to live indeed.

Though Elvis and I were thousands of miles apart, we were always connected. I found the physical distance that separation, that "cut-off condition'" to be unbearable, which was the primary reason for me to be so focused on at least getting onto the same continent.

This connection was never more evident to me than at the time when the family went for two weeks to Langeoog, an island in the North Sea where the affluent whiled away the summer days playing in the sand by the seashore. We lived in a cottage that was in close proximity to the sea and one evening when we ate at one of the restaurants, the radio was playing a love song of Elvis's and as I listened to it I felt my heartstrings strummed so strongly. Even though I cannot recall the song, the words were coming directly into my soul, and I was receptive to whatever it was that was tying us so closely together. It became a palpable quality I could catch by looking over the sea and thinking of him as he was at that time, in the Pacific Ocean and I am sure that he was doing that very same thing thinking of me as he was filming *Blue Hawaii*. "No More" is my favorite song in that movie. By the way, the soundtrack in *G.I. Blues* is a direct reference to his experiences with me. Just consider "Doing the Best I Can," "Did You Ever?" and, of course, "Wooden Heart," in which he sings in German, which is so endearing as far as I am concerned. "What's She Really Like?" stands alone as Elvis's recognition of the true immensity that he had come upon which gave me hope that he was kind of like me.

The problem, however was the ever-present, never-ceasing onslaught of the real world and the knowledge of another where we belonged together. We could not escape the problems that continuously kept driving us apart, nor did either one of us understand the purpose of all this protracted misery. It was simply not for us to know. Exasperating. Confusing. Aggravating. Frustrating. There was no end in sight and even if happiness would be there for us when I got to America, I could live with it and wait if only I did not have that nagging feeling that this love of ours had no future happiness here on earth.

At any rate I did my part. I was always trying but nothing worked. After the family and I came back from the North Sea and everyday life resumed, which meant that Reinholt now was in first grade and had homework, the parents had a social where the children's parents got together to get to know each other. Mrs. K. was wearing an expensive fur coat and she looked ever so classy. I knew from experience that she always valued expensive things as she would often show me the fabulous jewelry her husband presented her with when the first child was born and then when the second one arrived. While I thought that this was very nice for her husband to do this, it only showed me that these people, like most, valued things I did not particularly care for. I mused to myself that I did not need these things to be happy. When I complimented her sincerely on the attractiveness of her appearance in those fancy things she replied, "Well, Ilona, when you marry Elvis Presley you can have all these kinds of things and more!" I truly felt insulted but I quickly realized that with her mindset this was a normal conclusion to arrive at, and I surely did not want to irritate her, so I said nothing in my defense. But it did annoy me—her implication that I loved his wealth. I have never ever felt poor, though by human calculation I was, but I just never felt it. On the contrary, I felt rich somehow and it was the reward God had in store for those who value the things of the Spirit more than the things of this world that are really nothing more than built-in obstacles we need to diligently aim to overcome. Our salvation lies in the striving for pleasing God and God takes care of the rest which is a thriving relationship here on earth with Him and a place with Him in the heavenly spheres in eternity.

The hardest part for me in trying to occupy my time with things that would reassure me that I was on the right track was that I had to flee from people as they simply could not understand and I could not and would not blame them. It was just that I could not maintain an emotional equilibrium constantly having to defend my position without sounding unhinged. As a result I was whispered about as a disturbed person by those who knew me. So I would go on my days off to the American band concerts the military put on as part of their public-relations effort for the German communities. I also took a bus and rode to Friedberg where I knew that Elvis had been just two years ago and a sense of longing came into my soul and it reminded me of the time my mother left me in the country with strangers and how I was just standing there and imagining her coming down the road to get me. I treasured every gesture of Elvis's when we had our first meeting. He looked so average and inconspicuous and normal. Handsome, yes, he was that too, but I hardly gave it any thought because I was on a serious mission. I had to rescue him and nothing I found made any sense to me as it was happening, taking this original goal into focus.

Finally the day of my departure came. It was the twenty-eighth of March, 1962, and I left Germany, my beloved home country. I was pretty upset about this as I was a German who felt connected to the land, not so much to my family and friends but I was comfortable there and now I was going where? To something foreign and uncomfortable, but go I must. We flew against the sun and even though I got on the plane at noon I arrived in the New York skies at two or three o'clock. As we were approaching LaGuardia Airport we had to circle several times since we were not permitted to land just yet. I looked out the window and saw a stunning view of the island of Manhattan, as I was told by my fellow passengers. It was truly a memorable sight and that sun was reflecting off the wing of the plane which was at a sharp angle as it was coming in for the landing. For a moment it seemed as if Manhattan was opposite of me and the sky was under me as it was reflected from the Long Island Sound. It was a scary confusing moment when I had trouble finding my balance, as everything seemed out of kilter. I was ever so glad to finally get off that plane and onto firm ground. That was my first time flying and I could have just as easily done without it ever again.

My future employers came to meet me and they were welcoming me, treating me like a valuable guest. I guess I was at that time. We drove to their home in Scarsdale where they lived. The father was a successful textile merchant and the mother was a stay-at-home mother with an active social life.

My time there was a learning experience that would serve me well and it provided some funny occurrences. I am still chuckling when I think about them, though at the time they were not all that amusing.

I was shown to my room which was behind the kitchen. I had my own small bathroom, of course, but I could not help but think of Cinderella living in the kitchen cinders. Add to this that I found uniforms in my closet and I had a sinking feeling that Mrs. Newman, who fashioned these nice letters was actually misrepresenting herself and her intentions.

On the mirror was a schedule outlining my duties for every day. A Mr. Clean was mentioned and I asked her who this Mr. Clean is and why does he clean the windows. The Kreuzfelders had a cleaning lady coming once a month for windows, floors and other things—I was puzzled about it being a man. She cleared that up for me, saying that she would show me everything. We were speaking German because she wanted her sons to learn to speak German as her parents were from Germany and still spoke German at home.

The first thing I remembered to check out, of course, was the distance from where I was to where Elvis was. To my surprise, unpleasant as it turned out to be, the distance was too great for a little German girl to ever have been able to imagine! I inquired about the mode of transportation and the time involved and it was enough to make me wonder if God was in this at all. I could not just hop on a train and get to where I was going in an hour's time as it was in Germany. I was caught completely unaware of this and I had to re-arrange my thinking and planning. Meanwhile I had to fulfill my obligation to the Newmans who had put up my fare to come to the United States and a fair wage for my service and the fare back to Germany after the completion of the year.

There were quite a few things I had to get accustomed to. At first I did not notice much of anything, as things in a household are fairly similar in the industrialized countries. I had never seen a television before. I was mesmerized. The children were allowed to watch cartoons which I also found enjoyable but I really liked *I Love Lucy*. I was not too crazy about *The Three Stooges* but I always looked forward to TV time with the children.

The lady of the house indeed informed me on all the details of that schedule on the mirror in my room. She introduced me to all the mentioned cleaning products, including Mr. Clean, and I followed her instructions.

My entrance to the house was the same as for all the service personnel and delivery people, the kitchen door in the back. I wore my assigned uniform, which I did not like. I never was required to wear a uniform and I would have found it outrageous to be required to wear one as a house-daughter which my job-description was in Germany, although I understood from the correspondence during the negotiations that I would be a house-daughter there as well. It really angered me and after a month or two and disrespectful conduct from the children who apparently were accustomed to treat the maid, which is what I ended up being, with the same condescending attitude they had shown their previous maid who, from what I understood, was black. I had some repair work to do on those children as I cannot and will not tolerate disrespect from children, and I don't care whose they are.

We had a few scenes and I complained to the mother about it and it seemed to get better for a while. Of course they went on their outings and vacations by themselves. I was only the maid. She gave fancy dinner parties where I had to serve the food and I really hated those because she was making it a point to show off her German maid. I had no idea about the Holocaust, so I could not appreciate the importance of this as her Jewish, nouveau-riche friends were the focus of this woman's social life. I would hear her talking on the telephone about what Jackie Kennedy wore where and then the "look-alike original" at Bergdorf's was discussed. I got together with maids from other rich Americans who were German and we exchanged information and helped each other out.

We took train rides to New York City and went sightseeing and made fun of Americans as we thought they were weird. Entirely too rich for their own good and far too spoiled.

More than anything this woman tried to please and impress her husband and he absolutely fawned over her accordingly. It was nice to see that work the way she wanted it, and she worked hard at it (and it required serious work).

The children had a turntable that they were no longer interested in and they let me use it for my recordings, which I had brought from Germany. Much of the music was classical recordings I had gotten from my family in Frankfurt, as the mother was an avid listener and an admirer of all the classical greats. I loved this music more than any other kind because it could so easily transport me into the presence of God. But I also brought Elvis recordings which kept me in touch, so to speak, and they were indeed my prized possessions. It was essential that I stayed emotionally connected to Elvis, to do what I had to do.

After gathering information about the ins and outs of getting things done, I decided to visit Memphis, Tennessee on the Fourth of July in

1962. As the time for the trip came nearer and nearer I had the bright idea that I should inquire whether Elvis would be in town. It was actually Mrs. Newman's suggestion, even though my mind was made up to go, regardless. Sure enough, the reply was that Elvis was currently in Hollywood filming some movie and there was no certainty of his being there when I arrived. For whatever reason I never paid any attention to Elvis's movies after *Blue Hawaii* and therefore never knew any particulars.

I was not discouraged, as I was relying on God to arrange things. It was, after all, His Plan. I thought to myself, *Surely God would not let me fly all the way to Memphis and Elvis not be there*, and I even determined in my heart that if indeed Elvis was not available, I was getting off this nonsensical merry-go-round once again.

When I ordered the tickets for a return flight to Memphis over the phone, the person on the other end asked me if I was Zsa Zsa Gabor. I said no and that I did not even know of a Zsa Zsa Gabor. After this incident I heard it so often and when I discovered who this Zsa Zsa was I did not like to be compared to her in any way. After *Green Acres* I could always say, "I know but you really mean Eva Gabor," as Zsa Zsa was always in the news for some outrageous thing or another, but people did not care about that difference and I just had to learn to get used to it. Zsa Zsa it was.

It was a sunny day and my girlfriends joined me and we went by bus to White Plains where I got on the train to go to New York City and from there to the airport. I enjoyed looking out the window and marveling at the enormous expanse of land that is the United States of America. After two hours flying time we arrived in Memphis, and when I got off the plane it felt to me like somebody had taken all the oxygen out of the air. It was so hot and sticky that I had to adjust to this change. I believe it was ninety-nine degrees and the humidity was seventy percent. It was unreal and I was wondering how people could or even would want to live here. But the South has a lot of things going for it that you simply cannot find in the North as I found out.

The airport at that time was surely a quaint thing. We had to pick up our baggage outside where they had some kind of awnings, under which we would eventually find our luggage. The only way to get from the airport to where you needed to go was by taxi. As I was waiting for mine, I saw the taxi ahead of me driving down a dirt road, leaving a thick dust cloud behind it. I could hardly make sense of any of this backwardness but then I remembered Mr. Newman saying in total astonishment after I disclosed my intention to visit Memphis, "What in the world do you want to do in Memphis, it's nothing but a dirty river town with a bunch of hillbillies!" It looked to me that he was right.

I had the taxi driver advise me where to go to be closest to Elvis's house. He drove me to the Howard Johnson on the corner of Brooks Road and Highway 51 South. I absolutely loved swimming-pools then and always thought that anyone with their own swimming pool must be rich! The sun was so intense but my mind was not on the ever-so-inviting swimming-pool at that motel. My mind was on my mission as I perceived it to be. Seriously. I walked up Highway 51 South, sometimes I hitched a ride which was offered to me, and everybody local knew Elvis's place.

When I got there it was Vester Presley, Elvis's uncle, on duty as the guard. He'd go in and out of the guard shack and as I was the only one there, we sat in the shack, which had a fan, and chatted. It was of major interest to him to meet somebody from Germany and we talked a lot about this and that. Every now and then a group of young fans would come by and he'd patiently answer their questions. He was a kindly man who discharged his duties as a guard/public relations person with dignity, overall, and I never got the feeling that he was anything but what he appeared to be, which is something I cannot say about a cousin of Elvis's on his mother's side of the family. But that comes later. Apparently Vester was chewing tobacco which I had never heard of before. He'd spit every now and then and I could not stand it. As I later found out this habit was widespread and perfectly acceptable in certain social strata. Another habit I found strange was the inevitable toothpick sticking out between the lips and the constant poking of the teeth in public. I thought to myself that this must be part and parcel of the poverty-stricken background Elvis was born into and reasoned that this was really not his fault and that he could develop into a person of note in bringing people to Christ with the right influence and support.

The next day I met Harold Lloyd, a nephew of the late Gladys Presley. His wife Marcelle was there too and she and I got along just fine. She gave me her address, so we could stay in touch, and I thought how nice of her to be so kind to me, a perfect stranger. I cannot remember whether or not I told them of my dealings with Elvis in Germany. Marcelle had some of her children with her and she and I spent a good part of the time trying to keep them out of trouble.

All in all it was a pleasant trip, acquainting myself a little bit with the cultural pecularities of Southern folks. But the main reason for my going there remained unaddressed, as Mr. Presley was a no-show. I was dumbfounded but to a certain degree I was almost accustomed to things not going the way I thought they should. I wearily resigned myself to having to accept what appeared to be obvious by now. I must have been out of my mind to think that there was something between Elvis and me, which he was also aware of. Really?

I spoke very little about my trip to the Newmans and stayed on the funny side of things, making fun of the river town aspect of Memphis which amused them since it played right along their line of thinking.

I was told that the former maids would go out with the milkman or the postman or the man from the cleaner's, who delivered the clean clothes and picked up the soiled ones, all expensive things, of course, and that they never had a maid who did not date. *Here we go again!* I thought.

It was a good thing that we German girls met this very nice man who happened to be cruising in White Plains as we were trying to buy things we needed for our beauty care. One of the girls waved at him, more as a joke, and he said hello. He was driving a slate blue Bonneville convertible and he had the top down, as it was a sunny day and very warm. He pulled over and we all introduced ourselves. He said his name was Sal. He invited us to a soda shop and we had a nice time chatting with him. He was on the mature side and I liked that. There was something so conservative, steady, and reliable about him which I liked. It turned out that he wanted my phone number, which I gladly gave him, and this was the beginning of the Americanization of us girls in general and of myself in particular.

This kind and educated man took a liking to me and it got my mind on other things, which provided a distraction from the discouraging results of my fourth attempt to get it right with Elvis, as I thought right to be, which was that we belonged together and that we therefore were meant to be a couple. Even though I had a lot of fun with this man and my girlfriends, whom he generously invited along, insisting that my friends were his friends too, I could never escape that dull ache within my soul that kept a veil of sorrow blanketed over me and that no amount of distractions could ever dispel.

I fought hard to have some kind of life, always trying to be sensible and realistic and practical and on some level I seemed to make gains and I could even fool myself that I had this love for Elvis licked and I could do things just like everybody else.

I did. I enjoyed many different experiences that my relationship with this gentleman afforded me. He was of Italian descent and very much old-school. Sal lived in Mamaroneck with his mother. I believe he had a sister, Penelope. Professionally, he belonged to a group of accountants and he appeared to be good at what he did and his self-confidence was definitely rooted in the arduous process of hard work and sacrifice. He did not have to pretend to be something that he was not. It was very easy for me to get along with him. I have never thought it necessary or even right to pretend to be something other than what I am, like it or not.

Sal introduced me to his mother and sister who lived close by. I introduced him to my employers and that made it easier for me overall. He was forty-one years old and I was twenty-one. The age difference did not interfere, as I was pretty well matched to his old-fashioned ideas of how things should be.

He was Catholic and I was Lutheran but the difference was never seriously discussed as I did not really have any thoughts of marriage, though he might have had. After all, my tentative plans were to return to Germany. There was no point as far as I could see to keep on chasing that dream of mine with Elvis. It was a backup plan, though, to be sure.

We went to see *My Fair Lady* on Broadway and we also saw *West Side Story*. We went to nightclubs in the City, which is what the suburbanites called New York City. He took us on scenic drives into the Catskill Mountains and explained the cultural differences in various areas where the customs and feel were determined by the ethnic origin of the larger part of the population.

I even learned to drive in New York State. This nice man took the time to patiently teach me how to drive and on the day I had to take the driving test, he took my employer's car to work so I could use his car to take the test in. Mrs. Newman took me to the test site and I passed the test and she let me drive us home. I had all but forgotten all the nice things people did for me but I do want to take the opportunity to say that, for all their shortcomings, the American people as a whole are unequivocally the most generous, giving, and forgiving people on the face of this earth!

I had blonded my hair with "Miss Clairol" and cut it short to be in vogue with the current popular Kim Novak hairdo, as it was a no-muss, no-fuss kind of style. I never went for high maintenance things anyway. I am just a simple girl with simple tastes. For some reason though I evoked the opposite response from people. Generally I was viewed as a snooty person who had to have things just so. How appearances can be deceiving!

On a Sunday morning I ventured to a Baptist church which my employers recommended. It was within walking distance of their home. I went thinking I was going to just simply go in, take my seat and join the congregation in the worship-service. However, this was not to be.

Upon entering the church building I was greeted by a nice lady who asked me this and that and before I knew it I was surrounded by a bevy of women who were all talking at once. They all seemed to say the same thing like how nice it was of me to visit their church and how they would be here to help me in faith issues and others. I was so taken aback by all that attention I did not expect or even like. I somehow felt I had to reciprocate their friendliness with something but I did not know with what. It was a rather awkward situation for me. I was just a "maid" from Germany, doing my year in the U.S., as I normally said when asked what prompted me to venture abroad. I would say that I was curious about America and that I wanted to widen my horizons. Who, indeed, would accept the truth? Never mind widening my horizons, I was in the country to marry none other than Elvis Presley! Wouldn't they have turned away from me as if I had had leprosy?!

It was much later that I understood that the set-up of the church and state were separate and churches had to supply their own living and operating expenses. The more members, the more money. So that friendliness and undue attention actually, and by necessity, had its root in an ulterior motive. As my employer had given me one of her suits that she no longer wore, I wore it to church, and I guess I looked richer than I was. I never returned to that church as I was put off by the whole concept.

There was an incident earlier on in my employment where I was merrily singing all manner of folksongs from my German repertoire and I happened to sing the German anthem as well. Mrs. Newman took me aside and said very seriously to me, "You may not sing that song in this house." I was utterly puzzled at this command and could not make heads or tails of it. I thought that they were really strange to go through all the trouble and expense to bring a German national to their home to teach and primarily talk to their children in German, so they would learn to speak the language but then they did not want me to sing or even hum the German anthem. They were just quirky, I thought. Even though they were Jewish they put up a Christmas tree and exchanged gifts exchange and visited with family. Not that I was looking for differences but it was sort of a mish-mash of faiths. They told me that they were Reformed Jews. I had no idea what this meant then but I lived to learn.

I did never know how to thank my boyfriend for all his help and guidance, not to mention all the money he spent in that process. He would occasionally mention that it was highly unusual for a man to go along with everything as he had and not ask for sexual favors in return. He made me feel so bad. What could I do?

It seems that sex was being used as payment for services rendered and that was what I was looking at in the end. If ever there was a man in my life who deserved to be recompensed in this manner, it was he. I had already given myself to my fiancé in preparation of the planned marriage, so what difference did it make to be kind to this nice man? So I did begin a sexual relationship with him but I cannot remember anything about it. If one is not emotionally involved, and by emotional I mean the spark of love activates things, then it just becomes forgettable as far as I am concerned. I liked my boyfriend and I respected him but that just was not enough for me to respond as I wished I could have. Not knowing where he stood on this I assumed I had done my part to even things out and he probably had been through a few relationships of this kind before.

I am not saying that I did not enjoy sex with this man. I was sensitive to any sexual pleasure by nature. I think the reason I cannot remember anything about it was an effort to assuage my guilt at having transgressed against God's Law. It continued to be a sore spot for me but if I have learned anything it is that I love a forgiving God who loves me just because. He calls me His own because I try so hard please Him and do things His way. Even though I failed many times, I could go to Him with a contrite heart and He would remember my sin no more. As always, once that was done I resolved in my heart to cling to what I had always believed and tried to be true to that. I was starting anew with a clean slate. It was a cleansing and uplifting experience and encouraged me to continue striving to live a God-pleasing life.

I am sure I did not share my personal affair with my girlfriends because they were by all appearances more moral than I and had been brought up in religious homes. They were interested in seeing the sights of New York so Sal let me have his car on one or two occasions, and I took my girlfriends to wherever we agreed on going, and I felt like an important person, being the driver and all, but I confess I would have never found my way home had it not been for my girlfriends' astute senses of direction. To this day I prefer to just drive where I must and where I know my way around—other than that I'd rather let someone else do the driving.

We went to all the museums, the Statue of Liberty, the Empire State Building, and we even spent an afternoon at Jones Beach. The masses of people were impressive as they were crowding around the edge of the Atlantic Ocean, which was a scary sight as it seemed so vast and mysterious in its darkness off on the horizon.

It was such a fun time with friends, and one in particular who was the one who determined pretty much where we were going, as she was the smartest and most studious. The rest of us trusted her decisions. We also took along a girl from Sweden and she was different from us, not because she was Swedish, necessarily, but her worldview differed from ours in that she was much more open to the prevailing moral attitudes in flux as they were. To my way of thinking the Americans at the time were far too live-and-let-live for me, as everybody pretty much did as they pleased, which I considered to be very scary. I felt like I was a bird let out of the cage and as exciting as that might have been it proved to be immensely scary to me, as there were no warning signs anywhere and nobody to advise you on how to conduct yourself. If you wanted to, you could always say that everybody was doing it and move on. I felt a lot safer in my cage, thank you. It is because I felt uprooted in many ways that I thought that I would return to Germany at the conclusion of my contract with this Jewish family—if this Elvis situation did not do a complete turn-around.

The money I earned, I put away, as I have always believed in saving and I am by nature quite frugal. I grew up having only the bare necessities; it was second nature to me to be frugal; to do otherwise would probably be painful for me.

We went to a performance of Anna Plisetskaya at the Metropolitan Opera at Lincoln Center where Adlai Stevenson, a political heavyweight at the time, was also in attendance. Needless to say I was still enamored with the art of ballet. We were all just blown away as Miss Plisetskaya did her famous "Dance of the Dying Swan." How anyone could have such superior control and grace is beyond me. And then there was Nureyev. He appeared to have no weight at all as he flung himself into the air, zoomed in a split halfway across the stage and twirled around, never loosing his orientation. I never did like the tights on the male ballet-dancers but it was in the name of art that I was able to endure it.

All these things were fairly routine ways to entertain yourself and it was pretty much what I was used to in Germany.

Once I went shopping by myself in White Plains and there was a man on the sidewalk selling American flags. I thought I'd be nice and buy one for myself from him. I asked him how much it was and as soon as he heard my accent he went into a tirade about how he was in prison in Germany and he kept on cursing me and huffed and puffed as he was taking my money grudgingly. This had never happened to me before in New York but I could not imagine people in the South showing this animosity, just because I was a "foreigner." Oh, yes?

As the end of my tenure in Scarsdale slowly came closer and closer, I had a decision to make. A very important decision. Was I going to return to Germany or not? I could not decide and so I opted for a last try at getting in touch with my eternal love, Elvis, in Memphis and then take a sightseeing trip from there to New Mexico, then California, from there back to New York and then back to Frankfurt. It sounded like a perfectly reasonable plan and there was no criticism from anyone and it sounded practical to me too.

I gave God another chance to get things right and I had only a lukewarm feeling of a better outcome with Elvis than had been the case so far.

But while I was going through the period of indecision and was probably easily agitated I yelled at the children too much and the lady of the house informed me that if I yelled at the children one more time she'd rather see me leave tomorrow than to wait another week, which was all that was left according to my contract.

I took her up on it, as I was miffed that she never really saw to it that the children respected me as an authority figure. She just made half-hearted attempts to accommodate her husband, to whom I had taken my complaints when she was not forthcoming in correcting this situation. I was accustomed to children who respected those in authority as they should be taught to do and I simply could not make my peace with the belligerent attitude just because they were rich and I was the hired help.

We parted cordially and I thanked them for everything they had done to help me become accustomed to the American way of doing things.

I went to Grand Central Station, where I took the train to Memphis via Pittsburgh and that was an experience in itself, the milling crowds of people going to their intended destinations, carrying luggage, and looking anxiously to the listed schedules for the trains and the respective tracks. It was truly nerve-racking and exhausting and I was ever so glad to finally get on the train and sit down. Then came the transfer to the train to Memphis and it was then that I could actually enjoy the ride as the train forged its way through Pennsylvania, Ohio, Kentucky, and Tennessee. It was incredibly pretty in Kentucky. The people on the train were so accommodating. We could walk around and look out from different points of view. It was just great! I could not help but admire this big beautiful country that is the United States of America.

6

So Close, Yet So Far

I arrived in Memphis, Tennessee, on the twenty-fourth of March, 1963, at the now-abandoned main train station, with all my worldly goods in a big suitcase and a matching hatbox.

I had the cabdriver take me to what was then the Tennessee Hotel in downtown Memphis and I ventured out from there the next day to find out what was what in my new surroundings. I rented a car and drove out to Highway 51 South to see if Elvis was home. He was not.

But there was this ever-so-cute young man who resembled Elvis. I found out soon after we exchanged a few introductory remarks that he was an avid Elvis fan; more than that he literally lived to be as much like Elvis as he could manage. He took an immediate shine to me and I was kind of amused. He was only eighteen years old, a baby, as far as I was concerned, but he was so engaging and sweet I could not help but like him. He followed me around and I did not really mind. His name was Marvin and he was like a lost puppy which had found a kind soul he could latch onto. I did not care because he reminded me so much of Elvis and he was very nice and attentive to me.

He told me his sad story of a father who had to be institutionalized because of encephalitis, which made him a danger to himself and others, including his family. I felt heartily sorry for the poor child and spent most of the time conveying my sympathy for his situation. It sort of glued us together as I had an extremely strong maternal instinct which went into overdrive. Before I knew it I was thinking of extending my stay in Memphis, but I had to find other lodgings. There was the YWCA on Monroe Street, just around the corner, and I moved in there. I had six weeks to find a job and then other accommodations. I looked in the paper for advertised available jobs and I went on several interviews but the men were in some cases rather dubious in their intentions.

Before I returned the rented car I visited Marcelle, the guard's wife, and found her somewhere on Poplar Avenue, living in poor conditions, with too many children for her to take care of by herself. I guess they lived in the vicinity of the area where Gladys and Vernon had lived with Elvis in the housing projects and just had not had the money to move themselves closer to where Harold worked since Elvis had bought the Graceland property and needed protection. That came later on, as I discovered as I could always get the information from Marvin, who knew everything that was going on there, inside and outside of Elvis's house.

I liked living at the "Y" and went to the Bon Ton Cafe up the street. I went shopping at Woolworth's at the corner of Monroe and Second Streets. There was not much to see at that time in Memphis. Beale Street was abandoned, with the exception of Lansky Brothers, where Elvis had bought his outlandish clothes in the early years of success, I was told.

It is worth mentioning here that Marvin imitated Elvis at the stage of Elvis's development after he came back from Germany. He did not go back to his long sideburns, as he was trying so hard to be what he thought I would approve of, clean-cut and conservative. I did approve but he was never there for me to tell him. In the meantime I developed a sincere affection for this Elvis look-alike and he fell head over heels in love with me. He introduced me to his mother, Hortense, who liked me, and before I knew it I was living with his mother and him in their duplex-apartment on 2297 Elzey Avenue, across from the Fairgrounds, also referred to as Libertyland.

His mother was the owner and operator of a daycare on Lamar Avenue, and I started working there from then on. I slept in the second bedroom and Marvin and his mother slept in the other bedroom in twin beds; it had the bathroom. There was another bedroom in which

Marvin slept when his father, Edward, Sr., came home for the weekend on occasion.

We'd leave together, all of us to work at the nursery, as we always called it, as Marvin was the only driver of the only car. It did not take me long to know my way around with the system she had going. In those days we had only white children. Women were just realizing that they did not have to rely on their husbands for appreciation for a well-done job, as that was hard to come by then because men were the rulers of their homes and pretty much took for granted all the work that was involved in running a household with children successfully. The women went to work and discovered pretty soon that there was a better life than domestic servitude out there for them. Without noticing the changes we changed.

Marvin had a car, a 1955 Ford, because his Daddy was a Ford man, I guess. After getting us to work, he'd return home. Often he would show up at work late because he had to have his hair look just so and it took him longer to get ready. I was very busy at the nursery with all that needed to be done there to meet with the requirements of the licensing bureau. This involved periodic spot-checks from the health department.

We had to sterilize everything and the children all had their own cots with their names on them and there was cooking to be done and pre-school instruction as well. During naptime Hortense and I and another worker would eat our lunch in the kitchen, and as she was a smoker, I started smoking too. I had tried it some in New York with my girlfriends, just to be cool, so this was not new. I really liked Marvin's mother and she appeared to genuinely like me and we got along splendidly and I was always trying to please her. We would then watch the soap operas which I found so interesting and we would always look forward to the next day to see what happened to the various characters who found themselves in trouble of all kinds.

There was always plenty of fodder for discussions and lively debate as we had different opinions on what was right and wrong. It became more difficult as time wore on as the soaps actually made themselves into vehicles for social commentary. They faithfully portrayed what was happening in the society at large.

Marvin had had another girlfriend whom he saw as well, which did not bother me in the least. I was not involved with him, and he could do what he wanted. But as time went on he insisted that he really loved me and that he wanted to marry me.

I explained to him about my time with Elvis in Germany and that I was here in Memphis to re-connect with Elvis and that I could not marry him for this very reason.

On weekends we would go fishing at some lake or we'd meet up with some of his friends and their girlfriends and we would go to Moon Lake and party. They'd have the car radio blaring the popular rock tunes and drink beer and act crazy. The girls would have picnic food prepared and it was fun. Strange but fun. They had their own way of joking and if they ran out of something to laugh about, Marvin would ask me to say a certain word which I did and they would just bust out laughing at my accent. I always went along with this good-natured fun as they seemed like yokels to me, albeit cute yokels, and I did not want to be uppity in any way. Besides, I found their slow way of talking and swallowing entire syllables quite amusing and charming.

The most fun these loveable rubes derived from my accent at that time was my pronunciation of words with the beginning letter "w." Marvin and I went fishing one time—I think we went to Reelfoot Lake—where we fished among some tree stumps and I said that I could not put those "viggly vorms" on the hook. Forever after this it turned into hilarious fun to hear me say that and I am certain that Marvin went to "the gate" and made ample fun of my way of talking when he used his time off as the spoiled son of the proprietor. He always got her to let him go, if he bugged her long enough, to keep company with the guards at the gate of Elvis's house and whoever came by and he wanted to entertain them. I had to stay and work, of course.

The lives of some of his friends changed as they had married and held down jobs to support their growing families. (There had been those rock 'n' roll parties!) It became rarer and rarer for us to get together for parties as responsibilities encroached on this fun-time with friends.

We are now in May 1963 and I had met Marvin's sister, Sue, and her three children and his brother, Edward, Jr., who also had three children.

Edward, Jr.'s wife and Sue were good friends and helped each other out.

These people were in an entirely different age group than Marvin but certainly closer to mine. I was told that Marvin really was not planned for because having had a boy, Edward, Jr., and Sue, she the mother said she did not want anymore but . . . then there was Marvin!

These two siblings were muttering things like, "Mother spoils this kid rotten, not only does she employ an attractive girl to work for her but she puts her shoes under his bed!" Jealousy was running rampant and at first I did not understand what they meant by this.

Edward, Jr. was always very nice to me, to my face, and loved to share his stories of the time he was in the service and how he was briefly stationed in Germany; how beautiful a country Germany was and how he wished he could have stayed longer and how he hoped to be able to go back and show his family what he was talking about. Sue also seemed nice to my face, but what they said behind my back apparently was another story.

Hortense was put into an awkward position because their allegations and innuendos clearly had some basis in fact. I was working at her place of business and I was living at her residence but that was all.

Whenever Marvin and I went to the gate Elvis was not there. I was told that he was working on yet another movie. We hung around the gate and I was friendly to whoever was friendly to me and if I felt particularly good, I could entertain the fans with my Elvis stories. They went crazy over them and Marvin got jealous, especially when I was talking to a male fan. Marvin would accuse me of flirting and I can honestly say I did not know what flirting was. I have never flirted in my life. I was merely nice back to those who were nice to me. I really resented this as it was just not true. Not that it was any of his business since we were not involved. I should have been able to talk to whomever I chose! Some things about him began to bother me.

But I liked what I was doing and I liked the quaintness of the Southern folks. I liked their slow-as-molasses-in-the-winter way of talking, and last but not least, I liked that there was an abundance of churches, which surely was a good thing. I went to church on Sunday with Hortense but Marvin would never go. We went to Temple Baptist church where her family, as it then was, were members and as I was with her I did not experience the kind of attention since it was a much larger church than the one in Scarsdale, N.Y. I liked going to church with her and she seemed to like it that I was "religious." All in all it was a good place to be.

I loved the South. It had a slower pace and people were by and large more conservative in their attitudes toward important issues like the traditions of their forefathers which were still practiced by the majority and it is this respect for tradition that made me feel more like I can remember things being in Germany and so it was that I felt more at home here in the southern region of the country than I ever had in New York.

But there was an inherent danger in feeling so at home away from home. I got completely confused in terms of how I felt about anything. Elvis remained a no-show, The Elvis look-alike was after me full force to convince me to marry him, all the while feeling safe and secure in this comfortable setting in a pleasant environment with a woman who was to me the mother I never had and really needed at this time and thoroughly enjoyed working for. I knew I was fond of her son but I could not see myself marrying him. He was too young, he was too this and too that and besides I loved Elvis.

The pressure became too great and I felt I had to leave in order to sort out my feelings. I went back to New York and decided to stay there until I knew what I wanted and which way to go. I had to find a job and I contacted an employment agency that put me in touch with a lady who lived in Manhattan and needed somebody to take care of her only daughter, as she had to work. She lived in an apartment and to get to it I had to go down Lexington Avenue, which was not easy since it was lunchtime and everybody was going one way but I had to go the other to keep this appointment with this lady. It was like swimming against the current and I had to step off the sidewalk into the street in order to be able to get to where I needed to go.

When I got there I was greeted by a very elegantly dressed woman who appeared to be accustomed to interviewing prospective caretakers of her daughter. I quickly saw why. This woman had absolutely no control of this four-year-old girl. She called the girl's name and entreated her to come and meet the new nanny. The girl threw her doll out of the door of the room she was in and screamed that she was not coming out. The silly mother tried some more coaxing and promised her some favor if the girl would come out. The child liked that prospect and came out but just as soon as she saw me, she threw herself on the floor and kicked and screamed as the woman was trying to inform me that she does not believe in corporal punishment and so she continued to demonstrate to me how she dealt with her child, who was threatening that she would throw the doll down the stairs. The mother remained stoic throughout the whole scene of uncalled-for disobedience and disrespect. I flat out told the woman that there was no way that I would ever consider working for her because I did not share her ideas on child-rearing at all. The poor child could probably sense that I would be as tough as nails on her and she would be quite right. I think this was one example of how Dr. Spock's ideas were heralded as the new and more intelligent way of raising children with talk and reasoning. I agree but only after they had first been taught the rudimentary things when they were one, two and three and that requires the setting up of reasonable rules that must be consistently enforced, even with a spanking if necessary. The child feels better and it is better for the parents and the people at large who come in contact with the child. I could not get over that display of how to make it hard on the child and yourself while trying to do things a better way. Some old-fashioned ideas are still best as they have proven themselves to work as they should.

I ended up getting a job with a family in Brooklyn, N.Y. They were a young family with two little children. The mother had MS and I had to take over, as she was incapacitated. It was a sad situation and they could not really afford me and they certainly did not have the necessary accommodations for a live-in help. I had a futon in the basement in a game room of sorts, where family members from both sides would congregate and play. I had no privacy to speak of and I was very depressed. Here I was, away from things I liked and so close to returning to Germany, as I had written to my ex-fiancé of my plan to travel some through the country and then come back to him. Yet I could not bring myself to take that final step and book a flight back to

Germany. I remembered only too well how painful it was to have this big ocean between Elvis and me way back when.

I loved Elvis and that was that.

I called Hortense to find out how things are and she told me that Marvin was not doing well. He could not sleep and he could not eat and that I should come back, if for no other reason but to help him get better.

So I returned but I kept things on a rather cool level because I did want to help him but I did not want to marry him.

I loved Elvis and I was going to do my level best to settle things once and for all.

Going back to the "Y" and rooming there, I met two girls who were looking to rent an apartment together and so we rented a place on Peabody Street. I applied for the position of household help with a family in Parkway Village and rode the bus every day to and from there to where I lived.

This family was of Polish origin and there were four boys who were used to being responsible, especially the eldest. He was such a help to me to deal with everything.

Soon they moved to a bigger place in a more country-like setting and I moved in with them as they now had more room. I now lived on Weaver Road but it might as well have been on the other side of the moon since I did not have a car and there were no bus lines out there. The only way I could ever go anywhere is when somebody took me. I never mentioned anything about Elvis to them for fear they would think I suffered from arrested development which surely would not reflect well on my character.

Yes, I went with Marvin but we did not go to "the gate." He mostly brought me to visit with his mother and I just spent time with them and even went to Western State Hospital to visit with his father there. Was Elvis in town and had Marvin deliberately avoided taking me there?

Marvin came out to visit me on Weaver Road and I remember the night very well. The parents were out at a party, the children were asleep and we walked outside where the stars were shining brightly and Marvin was charming and before I knew what had happened we had sexual intercourse and I felt amazingly good. I cannot explain it. He did love me and I simply did what was highly overdue.

In the back of my mind I still held onto Elvis but he became so remote. Life just happens.

This was August 1963. I started to feel just awful. I could not stand the smell of food and I was so very tired. I kept on going thinking I'd get to feeling better after a while but things only got worse. I felt so bad. Not only physically but also because I was utterly discouraged about this whole Elvis-thing and I sulked, defending myself against the surfacing charge of disobedience and defiance against God. By now I was truly tired of trying to figure out why that was and just did what came naturally and lived. Besides, I reasoned, it was not fair to put me into this impossible situation. So there!

Dragging myself through the days and taking every chance I could find to lie down, I felt I was losing myself. I finally told the Mrs. Slovensky, who was an assistant nurse in the operating room at Baptist Memorial Hospital, a very competent and capable woman, in total charge of her household and indeed her life, as she and her husband worked in this perfect unison to tackle life on its terms and to do their level best to raise their offspring the way they believed was the right way, which included private Catholic school as they were faithful members of the Catholic Church. I told her of my aversion to smells of food and she told me that I needed to see a doctor at once. She told me that I was pregnant. In a way I could not believe it because I was still under the spell of the girl at the orphanage who said that if I continued in my sexual ways I would not be able to have children and heaven only knows how hard I had to try to bring my sexual urges under my control to become God-pleasing which was the desire of my heart because I loved God.

In a way I was also resigned to the apparent impossibility of my dream to marry Elvis to come true.

The mother took me to the doctor who confirmed what she already knew. After that everything sort of happened as if I were in a trance and I hardly knew what I was saying or doing. Hortense found out and before I knew it we had the blood test done and within days we stood before the Pastor of Temple Baptist Church on Cooper Street in his office and said our vows, which I took very seriously and the finality of those words put me further into a mental fog. I tried to be upbeat and it was necessary that I tried because it would surely not be good for my husband to think that I resented being married to him. But I was under total management of my now mother-in-law as I could not think clearly. She told me what to do and I did it. We, her son and I, moved into the bedroom I once occupied when I was just living there which was only six short months ago and how ironic it was that the day of our marriage ceremony was the same date Elvis and I had met five years earlier—November 2, in Bad Nauheim, Germany.

My husband was happy and he did what he could to make me feel better as I put the focus of my misery on the effects of my condition and he was very sympathetic. His mother was also very helpful and I really think she was glad in a way because it settled her son down and he now had a direction rather than living aimlessly through the days.

I went back to the daycare to work, which was probably just fine with Hortense because I was a good worker and lots of fun for the children and it suited me perfectly since I loved children.

Shortly thereafter the President was assassinated, which left the entire country in a state of confusion. I remember I was getting the cots down while the children were eating when the news came on the television, and all the adults simply stopped doing what they were doing and congregated in front of the TV while only the children kept on munching, not grasping the enormity of this event.

We just could not believe it and the whole day and the whole week was dominated by the unbelievable reality that the President of the United States was dead. Killed by a bullet. It was surreal. Who can forget the scenes of the funeral when a whole nation grieved the loss and the images of Jackie and the now fatherless children? Who can forget the riderless horse, the cortege? We all cried. It was truly the darkest time in modern American history.

I remember very little about the time between our marriage ceremony and the birth of our daughter. The duplex next door to my mother-in-law became available and we moved ourselves in there. This was like a new lease on life for me because I did then what every expectant woman does and enjoys doing, I was building a nest. The nesting was so wonderful and I felt much better physically. I did not feel pregnant at all and did everything as I did before and the warnings for me not to overdo things simply fell on deaf ears.

I came to grips with the reality of things and accepted the responsibility of having gone against God's commandment and asked with a contrite heart for forgiveness and promised as an atonement that I would be the best mother and wife I could be.

That was a good promise but the living out of it day after day was not so easy. I could not help but be sensitive to all the little irritations that come along, particularly as far as my husband was concerned. Being German did not help. The effects of culture-shock made themselves so very noticeable. Where I could shrug them off before, since they did not affect me on a personal level, they now became part of my everyday life. It was very trying and my poor husband could not understand much of anything. He was wrestling with trying to find a job which he really hated as it was seriously curtailing his freewheeling excursions to the gate where he was at home.

Trouble, trouble, trouble.

But there was no feasible way out of it. One particular day, after arguing constantly about one thing or the other, I was so furious I went upstairs at the daycare and took my heavy suitcases down, crying and screaming that I was not going to stay in this crazy country where they throw God out of the schools (Madelyn O'Hare had just succeeded in banning schools from referring to or teaching about the God of the Scriptures), and kill their presidents etc., etc. and I was going back to Germany! The children had not arrived yet, and we had to be there at least an hour earlier to get things prepared for the day. My mother-in-law sent me home with my husband as I was far too upset to be any good around the children and so I went home with my suitcases and sat there by myself because my husband had other things to do, like finding a job.

After some more crying and screaming and throwing things in a fit of rage I threw myself on my bed and then there was this silence.

I guess I had no more tears left to cry and my throat was sore from screaming and I was plumb tuckered out. I realized with such clarity that I was truly caught and I had another life within me and I had to act like a mature mother-to-be who takes care of the defenseless young.

After this, that kind of outburst became very, very rare. I collected myself and called my mother-in-law and asked if I could come back and finish the day at work. When my husband came back he found a very apologetic wife with the most sincere promise never to act like this again and he drove me to the daycare and I apologized to my mother-in-law who was kind enough to minimize my terrible conduct by saying that she acted just as crazy when she was expecting her youngest son, my husband. But we all must do what we have to do and do it well. She was such a help to me and I could not have asked for a better friend who was also my mother-in-law. I was devoted to her which came so naturally in response to her generous and forgiving ways. Sometimes I even thought that I put up with everything for her. She was very important to me.

As far as returning to Germany was concerned, this was a dead, dead, issue. I cannot remember if I even wrote to my ex-fiancé. I felt too guilty!

I had been drafted to a whole new way of life I never intended to sign up for. I never could mention Elvis Presley in a serious way since I had come back from Brooklyn because it was a sore subject with many people and it was certainly something I could never address in terms of emotional attachment because I now loved my husband. With all his shortcomings he was as good as anyone else, but he had one thing going for him that made a difference to me, he looked like Elvis, tried to sound like him which he really did and to a degree it was that resemblance that carried me over the possible resentment of having been caught by him. There simply was no point in crying over spilled milk and I did my level best to reassure him that I loved him which I did. He was the father of my child and that meant everything to me. It truly gave our union a very strong foundation. I was fully committed to him and our family.

There was never a chance that I could forget Elvis and my love for him but I had a job to do. What was strange was that my husband brought the latest recordings of Elvis home and he played them on the turntable we had purchased. I was treading on thin ice emotionally. I was forever torn between what I HAD to do and what I wanted to do. It was grueling. My husband liked Elvis's rocking music, which I did not like at all but I cannot imagine what I would have done if he'd listened to the romantic ones. I am not sure how he felt about my love for Elvis except for his asking me every so often, "Do you love me or Elvis?" What could I possibly answer him? Since I promised to be faithful to him there was no other answer possible but what I always answered and meant, "I love you!" and he believed me as he should.

Our daughter was born prematurely. I guess I had been overdoing it after all. The Beatles were due to arrive in the U.S. and the nation was transfixed awaiting their arrival when I told my husband to call the doctor again and tell him that I was in unbearable pain. This pain actually started while I was at work. I called the doctor myself and complained and he just said that this was normal for a woman who had not had a child before and to relax. Well, the pain did not subside and I did not know what was going on but I called again and he was quite impatient with me, so I just suffered but by the end of the day I was in such severe pain, I could not stand it anymore. After my husband called again the doctor said for him to take me to the hospital and that he would be there. I had barely gotten there and after the doctor examined me he said that the baby was on the way to be born and that there was no time to do anything but to let nature take its course. He summoned interns and said to me that he hoped that I did not mind if they observed. I was in such excruciating pain that I was too preoccupied to protest and I gave birth to a girl who weighed only two pounds and eleven ounces. I was horrified and so angry with this doctor. I was in labor for a long time and had he taken my complaints seriously from the start, all this could have possibly been avoided. Doctors, well, they don't really know what they are dealing with talking on the telephone. I guess I should have gone to his office. They put me in a room with a girl who had just delivered a boy who was brought to her periodically. I only got to see the attending pediatrician who advised me not to see my child as the next three days were crucial and it could be that she would not make it. So there I was in the hospital with a girl in the room who was beaming with pride at her healthy baby and I could not even see mine.

Life. It is not a beach. I was released from the hospital a day later and I called a cab to take me home. When I got there our apartment was dark. The curtains had been drawn and I was pretty depressed.

My husband had gotten a job with Kimco. I think they were making car parts of some sort. Hortense had bought herself her own car and got her driver's license and drove herself where she needed to go. Her mother, Mary, my husband's grandmother, was staying with her at that time and I guess it was a good thing for me to live in a dark house, according to her. She knew I was coming home from the hospital and she had access to our apartment because they were connected by a door that had made this dwelling a single-family home at one time. But she had her own ideas about me. She was a suspicious type and carried herself with the idea that I was some kind of spy, "Just listen to her talk!" I overheard her say to somebody.

The baby, we called her Rachel, was in an incubator for two months. She had lungs that were developed enough for her to live with the proper care. We went to the hospital to see her and we could finally take her home after she was over four pounds. She was so small, I had trouble getting hold of her especially during the burping procedure. She was somewhere there on my shoulder. I had to be very careful. She kept on gaining weight and becoming stronger every day. By the time she was eight months old she drove us completely crazy with her screaming jags. Of course I thought something was wrong with her and I took her to her doctor. He examined her head to toe and could not find anything wrong with her and he raised the possibility that she had been spoiled, understandably so because she was premature and needed to be "spoiled" but it was now time to teach her that she was not going to be picked up at the first cry, which she had become accustomed to expect. This child had a set of lungs that would not ever let you think she had been on the verge of death at one time. Yes, she had strong lungs! If there is one thing I will not have it's a spoiled child. But the screaming continued, and she got so mad when you did not come running, she was having herself fits of anger. After a while, however, she accepted that no amount of screaming was going to get her what she wanted and she became a happy and contented baby we could actually live with. There were times when I was not at all sure.

It was expected of me to go to work at the daycare center and our daughter was going to be looked after by a former co-worker who lived close to the center and babysat for four babies at her house. I did not like this setup at all. I missed my child something terrible and I was convinced that nobody could take care of her as I could and it almost killed me to have to hand her over early in the morning to someone else who certainly did not love her as much as I did. No amount of telling me that this what people did in this day and time could make me feel better about it. I was not "people" and I did not want to do what people did this day and time either. To me it was the most horrendous thing to farm out your children to be taken care of by strangers. I absolutely hated it. On my lunch hour I would walk to the babysitter and visit with my baby. Sometime she'd be sleeping and I would just gaze at her and wish I did not have to leave but instead be there when she woke up. I was so unhappy about this. Granted, I made a little bit of money to help but by the time I paid the babysitter there was too little left to compensate me for the sacrifice I was forced to make and it was a sacrifice.

7

Confusion/Suspicion

Needless to say my preoccupation with the cares of being a mother crowded out my attachment to Elvis. However, when I heard "Indescribably Blue" for the first time, it completely caught me off guard and I could not defend myself against this powerful emotional onslaught. Elvis had a direct line to my heart and there was nothing I could do about it. But I was married now and so very obligated to fulfill my promise to God that I would be the best mother and wife. That had not changed.

In the fall of 1964 when my husband and I went to the Graceland gate because Elvis was home. I was in the guard shack talking to somebody. The number of people hanging around had increased and there were always girls, girls alone, girls with their boyfriends and then there were us married folk, too. As I was talking, Charlie Hodge walked in. He heard my voice and looked at me and then burst out with glee and excitement in his demeanor and said, "It is you!" The emphasis was on "is." I tried my level best to cool his delight and replied, "Yes it is, but I am married!" He shrugged his shoulder as if to say that that did not matter, to which I found myself forced to say, very seriously, "But I am very married," with the emphasis on "very." His whole countenance fell into this worried look and we did not talk after that, as he was busy with other things and I did not give the incident much thought as I considered the case closed.

Elvis went to the Memphian that night. He rented the theater after regular business hours and he and his buddies and hangers-on, which is what my husband and I were, joined him there. I cannot remember much about that night except that Elvis and I acknowledged each other's presence. That was it. I cannot say whether Priscilla was there with him then or not. There would be many more nights at the Memphian with Elvis and Priscilla and without Priscilla.

I was faced with the troubles of my life as a mother of the sweetest baby in the world and I was trying to figure out a way to correct this unreasonable request by society at large that I should surrender my right and privilege to take care of my own child myself. There was a solution to this problem and I decided that I was going to have another baby which would make it hardly worth it for me to work at the daycare and then have to pay for two babies to be taken care of. Even Hortense would have to agree whether she liked it or not.

Of course I did not speak of my intentions to anyone and I surely did not know if it would even happen. But happen it did and I was expecting our second child.

I am not sure if I can describe the life I was living. I was married to a man who looked like Elvis but wasn't Elvis and the real Elvis for whom I had cared for so long was just down the street, so to speak. His songs of longing and loving and aching were enough to send me over the edge. There was this constant back and forth in my mind of going off to chase the old dream and the determination to live up to what I had promised. Add to this that I was also bothered by the fact that Elvis could have taken the initiative and let me at least confirm what I already knew but as it stood on an intellectual level, there was nothing tangibly apparent.

I lived in a tailspin of conflicting emotions and I had enormous amounts of trouble of which no one was aware or even cared about. Though the pregnancy was normal, I had severe sleeping problems. My doctor, and yes, I changed doctors, not because of what happened the first time around but because I did not want to return to Baptist Memorial Hospital and the new doctor was affiliated with the Methodist Hospital, prescribed the best medicine I have ever taken. It was Placidyl and I can hardly describe the euphoria this drug provided and lulled me to sleep with. It was extraordinary. I can certainly understand the addiction aspect of such a drug. You have problems, you hurt, just take a pill and you will feel better. It was great! I was looking forward to bedtime just so I could drift off in the drug-induced, ever-so-pleasant feeling. Of course, the doctor did not give me enough to be able to take one every night, so I had to be conservative and keep them handy if I experienced serious trouble sleeping. I had to be up early in the morning to take care of our daughter and to see my husband off to work. I was in the last weeks of the third trimester and I had to get the necessary sleep to handle everything. At night I just could not get comfortable enough to be able to sleep, not to mention the anguish I was living with.

Between 1965 and 1966 I seriously considered suicide. I just could not take it anymore. Anyone who has ever been on the brink of madness knows what I am saying. My poor husband did not know what to make of it. I tried to kill myself three times and each time it was the thought of my beloved children and who would be taking care of them that gave me the will to continue to live. I was only too thankful that the doctor did not report it to the police. I do not know of the extent of the discussions between him and my husband.

Once having overcome this hurdle I vowed to myself that I would stay strong to be that best mother and wife, as I had promised God. I was thoroughly ashamed of myself for being so weak and I can only say, "Walk a mile in my shoes!" and then tell me what you would contemplate of doing. This is why it is important for us not to judge. No one can really ever know what goes on in another person's life.

However, I tried to remedy the situation with Elvis in my own way. I called Charlie Hodge and we met at the Old Hickory Log, a greasy spoon eatery on Elvis Presley Boulevard, right across from Elvis's house. We exchanged how-do-you-dos, and then he said, "You know that you are married to the wrong man!" which I was acutely aware of, of course, but I felt somewhat irritated at the implied casualness of "just get a divorce and everything will be fine." I found myself saying that I loved my husband, the father of my children. He then tried to build Elvis up by saying what an honor it was to have a street named after him. I did agree with him, only to a degree, about that, thinking to myself that many streets have been named after outlaws and other scalawags, so this was not entirely an endorsement as far as I was concerned. It just did not impress me and besides, I loved Elvis regardless.

It was several months later when I felt compelled to write a note to Elvis for Charlie to give to him. The handing over of the note took place at the customary late-night visits to the Memphian. In it I explained to Elvis that he should marry Priscilla as I was obligated to my husband and our two children. I did not mention my promise to God and I said something about "on another plane" which I cannot remember the context for. Scripturally speaking I was not allowed to divorce one man to marry another, so the whole thing was moot in my way of thinking. This was late 1966 or early 1967 and we all know the rest of the story.

Once he married Priscilla, devastating as this was for me, I had to deal with it the best I knew how. At least the uncertainty factor was gone and I could concentrate on my marriage and hope that Elvis would find some happiness as he undoubtedly loved Priscilla as I loved Marvin.

When Elvis and Priscilla came back from their Las Vegas wedding they rented the Fairgrounds and we all were there to hang out with them and ride the rides. We were on the Tilt-a-Whirl and Elvis and Priscilla were in the car in front of us. Elvis turned around and looked through the grill straight into my eyes and said, without saying a word, "Now are you happy?" He was directly in front of me. There was nothing that needed to be said and I certainly did not congratulate them on their wedding. To tell the truth, I knew with certainty that he had always wanted a church wedding with the woman of his dreams, with the whole hometown celebrating the nuptials, just as I had always dreamed of the same thing with him.

In 1965-1966 I had the strangest experience to date in the U.S. I had a dream in which Elvis and I were flying in the sky. He was some way ahead of me and he called me for help. I tried so hard to get to him to help him, I sped up and flew as fast as I knew how to catch up with him, but just as I almost touched his hand, he plummeted down into what looked like Manhattan, a group of tall buildings just as I had seen on my arrival on the Lufthansa in 1962, out of my reach. Only after Elvis's death did this dream reveal its meaning to me.

I had this dream three consecutive nights and it really made me wonder what all this meant as I knew there had to be a precedent for this phenomenon and I had to find out what I was supposed to learn from it. On the face of it, the negative value of this connection I had with Elvis was discouraging, to be sure, as it matched my sense of doom about the future of our relationship. I did not want to believe it but it somehow prepared me for the whole ordeal I was destined to have to go through.

I went to the library on Peabody and took out books on the following topics: religion, philosophy, psychology and various other related themes like psychic phenomena. I read so much and it was an eye-opener. I had plenty of time to read in the evenings as my husband had changed jobs and went on the third shift which afforded me quiet-time after the children were put to bed by 8:00 p.m. and before he would come home at 11:30 p.m.

I learned that indeed there are things that cannot be explained by scientific methods because they are not of this world but another—just as real and relevant as the one we live in—for a short, very short span of time.

It is so strange to have an inkling of things so spectacularly mysterious and spellbinding and then have to deal with the mundane existence here, doing ordinary things to keep on living when in fact the whole potentially could be marvelously beautiful and enriching if we could combine the two realities into one. Is this what the Holy Bible speaks of?

All this exploration into the existing knowledge brought me so very near to God and I determined that I had to find a church for us. My husband had always promised to go to church with me but he never did. It became a serious contributing factor in the unraveling of our relationship as husband and wife.

Soon the news came that Priscilla was expecting, which really hit me hard. Just to solidify my standing with my husband who complained that I failed to give him a son, I was going to expand our little family and hopefully give him that boy he was wishing for. We had our son, Jeremy, in June of 1968 and it was a happy time. In fact I don't think I could have been happier. I had my lovely children that I could take care of myself and I felt utterly rich in spite of being poor actually. But then material wealth was never important to me.

That reminds me of an incident with Elvis and Priscilla. It was New Year's Eve and Elvis had rented Hernando's Hideaway on Brooks Road, and we were all invited. I remember that it was brutally cold that night. There was a black band playing and Elvis and Priscilla were presiding. I paid no attention to them and only concerned myself with my husband. I could hardly afford to do otherwise because he'd make trouble for me accusing me of this and that, all imaginary, of course. I have lived to learn, among other things, that it is always the ones that are guilty of the things they accuse the innocent ones of because they apply their own low standard in measuring. My husband and I were talking about how Elvis had it made and my husband was feeling sorry for himself because he did not have the money that Elvis had and after the party, as we were going into the car, I was just happy to get some heat on my feet and I was so looking forward to my little home with my precious children and I was even glad that I did not have to deal with all the craziness that was Elvis's life. I would have had no control over anything and I could never abide by that. I knew what I liked and I had it and I was content in my situation.

Marvin still found the time to go to the gate. I did not keep up with him as I was very busy. I was a very good mother and I taught my children early on about Jesus Christ and read to them the Bible stories from a ten-volume edition for children, often found in doctor's offices at that time.

I would often be informed about the goings-on at Elvis's. Most of it was just normal stuff like Elvis and Priscilla took some private time which meant that the guys were not included. There were some worrisome signs but they were expecting the arrival of Lisa Marie and Elvis appeared to be happy.

Elvis and Priscilla hired a German nurse for Lisa Marie. I called her once and she told me of Elvis' undisciplined way when it came to seeing the baby—waking her up whenever he felt like it. I had no time to concern myself with her troubles in her employment as I had troubles aplenty of my own. I had always clung to the notion that Elvis was an unusually good person, so if something ugly came out about him I simply would not believe it. That actually was the trigger for my telling him to marry Pris. The talk in Memphis was that he had been living with this girl since she was seventeen and had known her since she was fourteen, which cast him into the category of Jerry Lee Lewis, who married his teenage cousin and ruined his career, as we were in the Bible Belt. Not only that, but I felt Elvis should be a role model for his young fans, as they will imitate their idols, like it or not. He was clearly sending the wrong message. While he was having her stashed in his mansion he was cavorting around with who knows what in Hollywood, which did not change after they were married, much to my dismay. Like I said I put it out of my mind because this was not the Elvis I knew. In fact I had no knowledge of this showbiz persona nor did I like it. It forced him to be something that he was not and he was definitely serious when he said that the image is one thing but the man is quite another and after all he was a normal man, and to live up to an unreal image is very difficult, if not impossible.

Then add to this the downside of having money. You have lots of friends who aren't really friends, a lot of people who tell you every lie in the book if it gets them what they want and they always want something.

One time, it was still before Elvis was married, I think it was 1965, and my husband and I were getting into the car after seeing a movie at the Memphian when he removed a packet of prophylactics from under his windshield wiper and I asked him why somebody would do this to his car and what does it mean. He said that it was just the way "the guys" (Elvis's entourage) were joking around and I thought nothing of it.

There was another time when I was there at the Memphian by myself. They were showing a film I did not like and I said, "I don't like this movie. I am going home!" I went into the lobby to call a cab and Red West came after me and said, "You don't need to call a cab, I'll be glad to take you home!" I said, "What do you want to do that for?" He said something like "Maybe we could talk or something." I got really angry at him and told him that I would tell Elvis about this. I called the cab and left. When I got home I told my husband that Red propositioned me and for him to do something about this, but he told me that

that was nothing; the guys always did that. *Oh really*, I thought and I had made up my mind right then and there that I was going to set that Red West straight the very next night at the Memphian.

I caught up with him in the lobby and asked him if I ever have given him any reason to think I was into that sort of thing and that he knew that I was married and that he was married too. He apologized profusely and began buttering me up by saying that I was such a beautiful woman. I looked at him with disgust and said, "That is no excuse!" and left him standing there.

It was only many years later that I remembered in a flashback that Elvis whispered something to Red after I announced that I was leaving and it was that whispered something that Red was following. I can only speculate with the reader what it was that Elvis had on his mind.

Since Red knows the answer to this we must wait till he decides to tell the truth which he would be proving to be very good at.

In 1967 Elvis had just finished *Paradise, Hawaiian Style* and he had the dog thing going of which I was not aware at the time. He got on all fours and came over to where my husband and I were sitting and barked and howled like a dog and I had to lift my feet to let him by and he kept on barking at me. Everybody was laughing—they were always laughing at everything Elvis did if that was what Elvis wanted, regardless if it was funny or not. I found this too annoying. I asked my husband what to make of this after Elvis got back to his seat. He only said that Elvis did crazy things. I had no idea that he was high on something because the Elvis I knew would never do such a thing as he was far too shy. Rumors swirled that Elvis used drugs but I did not believe it, could not believe it.

By the way, the seating-arrangement at the Memphian was the same as they had in the theater on the base in Friedberg, Germany. At the Memphian were more people who were scattered out behind Elvis. There was no one permitted to sit anywhere in front of him!

I was expecting our fourth child. We had decided to give our little boy a playmate just as the older girls had each other. For several nights in a row my husband had not come home when he said he would and he said each time that he was going to the movies with Elvis. It had not been too long ago that my mother-in-law had asked me if I did not think that her son was being unfaithful to me and I indignantly said that he would never do such a thing, fully believing that he would do just like me and keep the vows he made when we got married. I even asked my husband outright if he was unfaithful to me, when he looked me in the eye and said that he would never do such a thing. The words of my mother-in-law still ringing in my ears, I walked to the Memphian at 3 o'clock in the morning. I was already six or seven months along. I went inside to get him to come home but he was not there and nobody had seen him. I cannot remember what he said to explain this, I was too glad he was home and I simply did not think anything was wrong.

My husband was rarely at home and when he was, it was mostly spent watching football or the bathroom since he still took a very long time to fix his hair. He usually slept till 10 a.m. and it was a challenge for me to keep the children quiet in the only other room, the living room, but with diligence I managed. We just had to creep around so not to wake him and it was not easy. For a while my mother-in-law let us use the room connecting the apartments, so we could spread out some and even use her bathroom when she was not home which made it a little easier.

But it was like some unwritten rule that she expected to be compensated for her generosity by telling me how I had to raise my children which I did not want her to do. She had spoiled her son, my husband, to such a degree that I had trouble with him just going to work regularly. He went to the doctor and had him tell the employer that he could not come in for work as he was suffering from depression and had to be on medication. He never had any trouble fixing his hair and tomcatting around. I had no sympathy for him because in my way of thinking he had to do what was required of him as the father and husband just as I had to do my part as the mother and wife. Simple. Of course, when he was not working we had nothing coming in and he would go begging to his mother who would always come through for him, which in turn put me on the hot seat when I insisted on dealing with my children my way, which was basically based on what the Holy Bible admonished me to do. This meant an age-appropriate form of discipline and rules to live by.

One day Rachel wanted a pencil and a paper so she could write like mommy, I gave her the paper and the pencil and I started her off by writing the letters to the word "Mommy" and she sat down and started to copy them. I was busy ironing and all seemed well and under control when she decided to take the pencil and run through the apartment with it. I told her to stop and she would not listen. I warned her that it is dangerous to run with the pencil in her hand because she could trip and fall and injure her eyes or something. She did not mind me. I did not warn her a third time because the situation was too dangerous, so I took the pencil from her and told her to stop running in the house as running was something we only do outside. She had herself a conniption fit, threw herself on the floor, kicked her feet and screamed at the top of her lungs. I held her legs and told her if she did not stop screaming I'd put her in the bathroom where she could scream as long as she liked. She continued to kick her feet, screaming at the top of her lungs and throwing herself around in a total rage. Well, I was not going to have this kind of behavior. I lifted her off the floor, gave her a good spanking and dragged her into the bathroom and closed the door. Not only did she not stop screaming but she continued to throw herself around, kicking the bathtub, with tears of extreme anger streaming down her face, I could not believe it! My mother-in-law meanwhile called the police and they came and checked the situation out. I explained to them the whole thing in great detail and they just left because they did not see anything wrong other than routine problems with a headstrong child which were being dealt with as I saw fit, and I had that right as a parent. The fact that my mother-in-law called the police on me made me very angry and I told her that I would deal with my children my way and that she had had her turn to deal with her children her way. This made her mad at me and she withdrew the use of the room and several other things that ended up hurting the children too. It was a mess and I was caught between a rock and a hard place, but as is always the case when you are dependent on the kindness of someone you have to pay the piper eventually. I did not like the animosity between us and I reached out to her and did my level best to please her in spite of many misgivings on my part. It was hard, and the inability or unwillingness of my husband to support me against his mother was just another problem, as he relied on her to fix whatever he managed to mess up for him, which she always did,

We had our fourth child in October of 1969. We had hoped that it would be another boy but it was a little girl instead, Susan. I was very busy indeed trying to take care of everything. I do not think that I went back to the Memphian ever again which would have made it the last time that I had seen Elvis when I was looking for my husband that time.

But just because I had made my choice to do everything I could to build a life without my true love, did not mean that this was a done deal on an emotional level. No amount of talking to myself could sever this deep, deep emotional-spiritual bond Elvis and I shared. Even though I forced myself to discard many of the records of his songs which tied me to him with a power I cannot describe or explain, I could not bring myself to get rid of all of them and I retained the ones in which he confessed in a variety of ways how he loved me. It was identically the very same way I felt about him. To destroy them would have been like cutting off a vital part of me. It was impossible. The pain of separation was painful enough. I missed him so and I simply could not get around having to go to the center of myself, which was only with him and I literally sneaked a listen, like an addict. I would indulge my poor soul in the soothing assurance of our love which I could hear so clearly in songs from 1969. Priscilla wanted to come with him to Nashville where he recorded these LPs, *From Elvis in Memphis* and *Elvis Back in Memphis* and *Love Letters from Elvis*. The songs "Do You Know Who I Am?" "A Little Bit of Green," and "And the Grass Won't Pay No Mind," in which I can hear him saying "von't pay no mind," which would always make me smile. He would not allow Priscilla to accompany him to these recordings. Then there is "I'll Hold You in My Heart" and so many, many more.

That I did not go insane during that time I attribute to the providence and protection God has always enveloped me with. I certainly cannot take credit for being strong enough to adhere to my convictions with such tenacity when at the same time I was being torn into a thousand pieces by being so in love and yet to have to live without it and my soul was screaming in desperation for Elvis's.

The reality that I was living in did not afford me much time to linger in the warmth of his love. I hid the recordings, even from myself, and became immersed in my busy, busy life, taking care of my four children whom I loved and cherished. It was a natural role for me to be the mommy to these four angels. I adored them and I lived for them. It was only through them that my love for my husband found its roots. It has always been a dream of mine to be a mother who took care of the children and the home and to have that devoted husband who would make the living to take care of his family.

Little did I know that this was not everybody's dream, certainly not the man's. I could never fathom how anyone could think otherwise. It completely threw me for a loop when Marvin did not exhibit the same devotion to his family as came so natural to me. He was happy to have just enough money to jump into his car and go and do whatever pleased him, which was usually hanging out at "the gate."

I still am of the opinion that it is essential to have one's mind "made over" through faith in Jesus Christ and the sincere striving toward pleasing God, which means to adhere to His commandments and guidance as is given to us in his Holy Word, the Scriptures. It then follows that one's goals and dreams do not focus on one's selfish concerns but rather on the happiness of others in this case, the family.

I have cried so many tears over this love Elvis and I shared but had to live without. However I also "knew" that there was a purpose to all this misery and that I was following a script I did not know in detail but could only sense ever so vaguely and that I was on a certain track, one I did not know where it would lead but was incapable of deviating from.

Literally fighting for survival, I was certain that if I just kept my mind on the things of God and worked to do what I must, which was to rear the children in the admonition of the Lord, He would do the rest and this knowledge gave me enormous peace of mind and the strength to go on keeping on, never really knowing where all this would lead. It is a good thing though that we do not know the future. We could not do what is required of us out of utter fear and would remain incapacitated.

The children and I joined a Lutheran church which became a stabilizing factor in my life and the lives of my children. The Lutheran traditions gave me a feel of my homeland and the spiritual capital I had accumulated during my growing-up years in Germany was a perfect basis to build on and be supported by these wonderful people at Christ the King Lutheran Church on Parkway in East Memphis. Most of the members at that time had German roots and it was ever so nice to be in touch with your own kind, so to speak, when living in a foreign country. I loved my church and I was an avid churchgoer and my children blossomed too into these wonderful children who believed in Our Redeemer and it did my heart so good.

The more the children and I got involved in church activities the deeper the gulf between my husband and me grew, and no amount of pleading for him to join us made him get involved. I could not let that influence my life and the children's lives as my responsibility to myself and my children was crystal clear to me. My life was well-organized and the Lord was with me, no doubt.

I had a splash pool out back for the children and I did my ironing outside so I could get a suntan at the same time and supervise the children too. My mother-in-law commented, with amusement in her voice, that I was as contented as a cow. I was. I had my children with me.

I took my children with me to go to the Brooks Museum of Art and to the Zoo. We went on walks around the neighborhood. In the off-season we went across the street, Parkway that is, to the Fairgrounds and the children could swing on the swings there and climb around on a locomotive there, too.

The older children loved their little siblings and played mommy to them. It was just too cute.

However, somebody must have reported us to the authorities for living with four children in a duplex with only one bedroom which was no problem for me. I had a set of bunk beds and a third single for the bigger children in the dinette and when the baby got too big for her crib, I added the fourth bunk on top of the single one. It was truly a wall-to-wall bed situation. I had a curtain to separate the children's area from our bedroom and there was a door closing off the small kitchen so I could fix my husband something to eat when he came home in the middle of the night. I managed. I was perfectly willing to live like this and be in charge of my children's lives rather than going to work at some job and farming my children out.

It was simply unnatural to me to do anything else but what I was doing. I guess it was the Department of Human Services who came to inspect. The man looked around. Everything was clean, the children were happy, and he left, saying that he could not find anything wrong.

At the time I had no idea what it was all about. I just thought that was another one of those weird things they did in this crazy country and I told my mother-in-law who knew very well what this was all about but she never clued me in. I suspect, looking back, that my sister-in-law could have been the one who called these people. She was so very jealous of me, of which I was not aware at the time either. She'd make fun of me and my accent and she would always cause some trouble. She was a working girl because she bought into the emerging thought at the time that women could do what men could do and do it better and be mothers at the same time. But she was not a happy woman. She drank too much and smoked too much and worked overtime trying to convince herself that she had the world on a string. Her mother had not made it a secret that she loved me and she often said that she thought God had brought me into her life. Over the years that attitude apparently changed some as she had to reckon with her own daughter who just would not have "some foreigner muscle in on her territory."

I've been made fun of because of my accent. My cooking. My everything. Sometime in 1964 I inadvertently was watching a documentary on the Second World War. I had never heard of the Holocaust, so I was curious what this was all about and I cannot tell in any way how absolutely horrified I was when I found out what we Germans did to the Jewish people. I was devastated at man's inhumanity to man and also that I was part of a people who did such deplorable, indescribably horrific cruelties to another group. I was so ashamed of being German. It was terrible. It became clear to me then why the Jewish family in Scarsdale acted so strange. No wonder many Americans, Jewish or not, did not like the Germans; I could not even blame them as I did not like myself for being German, even though I was completely innocent, but that collective guilt was unavoidable for me. I was very ashamed of being German for the longest time but as time went by I resolved that this was a troubling past and I could not change that but I could change my own attitude toward anybody Jewish and be extra nice to them. I have always preferred the Jewish professionals as I always felt an affinity for them and I admired their intelligence.

It has not escaped my attention that this country is favored by God and it has a pivotal role in the coming of the Lord's Day at the conclusion of this world system.

As I read a lot I discovered that the Americans had their own troubles in their treatment of fellow humans because of the color of their skin. I remember an incident when I was riding the bus to Parkway Village back when I was working for this Polish family. I was sitting behind the driver. The bus stopped and this old black man got on board. He was fumbling for the fare and a coin fell into the ticket/garbage-bag hanging of the driver's chair. The man tried to explain this to the driver who snarled at him with contempt and told him to find it. The old man busied himself trying to find it and he could not, so the driver ordered him to throw everything on the floor, that this was the only way that he could find it.

The man did as he was told and had to get on his hands and knees to find that missing coin. I could not stand it anymore and I got on the floor to help him look for it and I found it. I had younger eyes! The old black man thanked me heartily and went all the way to the back which at that time I did not understand as there were plenty empty seats right behind me.

But I lived to learn that there was such a thing as segregation, as I experienced the garbage strike and all the associated upheaval that followed.

The only explanation for my unawareness of things around me as far as I am concerned is that this was a necessary feature in my ability to cope with things. Apparently there was a deficit in my overall capacity to pay attention to too many things at once without losing the ability to focus and deal with things successfully.

I am not even sure that Marvin noticed the inherent immensity of the civil rights struggle as it unfolded. I merely concur with the basic rights of equality for every human being. I felt heartily sorry for the

Negro and his demeaning status in this country. However it was risky to come right out and be pro-black in some segments of society.

Hortense had a hard time adjusting to the sweeping changes that required her to integrate her student body which was closely monitored by the Department of Human Services, which issued the necessary information to qualify for licensing a business involving the care of children. She grew up in a segregated South and it just is not easy to go against something you have adhered to for a lifetime. Only the passing of time could help ease the change of thinking. She reasoned that their money was as green as that of white people. And it did, but I must admit that it was a sort of a shock to see black faces where there were none before.

Before we knew it we saw no color whatever. They were all just precious children with the same abilities and typical behaviors.

The only deviating thing I remember was that the black mommies did not want their children in the sun as it would make them darker! In those days they wanted their children more like the white ones.

I was expecting our son at the time and we were instructed to carry our garbage cans to the curb ourselves if we expected to have our garbage removed. I was four-and-a-half months along and I asked my husband early in the morning to please carry the can to the curbside, as it was full and heavy and we had five inches of snow on the ground, when he told me that he could not do this because his hair wasn't fixed! He did put a high premium on his hair. I never could understand it and I surely couldn't change it.

Marvin lived for himself only and he dealt with his family in a detached sort of way which made it unavoidable that all the decisions ended up being made by me which put me, like it or not, in a position of authority of sorts. Because he did not fulfill his required and necessary involvement in the decision-making process he felt disconnected. That became more and more apparent when the children started school and I determined that they should be educated—in reading, writing and arithmetic, for sure—but much more important to me in the ways of the Lord, which I believed makes for a happier person all the way around. This then involved regular church attendance and related activities that he never participated in or even just showed any interest in for the sake of the children if for no other reason.

I did the best I could in making him feel important and shifted the positive outcome to his credit in a general way as I realized that in spite of his shortcomings he was still the breadwinner, which gave me the opportunity to be a full-time mother which was absolutely imperative for my sanity. I did not want to jeopardize our relationship as this too was a very important component to my personal happiness. And then he was the children's father, which in my way of thinking automatically put him in a position requiring respect. Yes, on that alone.

However it was for naught that I did my part. Because of his feeling of inferiority precipitated by his unwillingness to step up to the plate, and the unavoidable guilt, he was subject to find acceptance and approval wherever he could find it and he did find it as easily as falling of a log. All that was asked of him was to be what he really wanted to be and that was an Elvis look-alike and reap the benefits without doing much of anything except to just indulge himself and enjoy.

I do not want anyone thinking I was this innocent victim of circumstance as I did my share of complaining, criticizing and mocking, if for no other reason than to vent my frustration with him. Though he was generally mild-mannered, he would also reach his limit of endurance and once threw the gravy-bowl at me. It ended up on the wall. I remember one time, after he had spent hours in the bathroom fixing his hair to go out, when I decided to foil his plan and hid the keys from him. Maybe then he would see how much I would like for him to stay home with me since I had been more than understanding as far as his need to have a change of scenery was concerned and generously let him go. He had taken full advantage of this largesse and it was the third night in a row that he was going out by himself. He got so angry he lost control and short of hitting me, which he had never done, he was so desperate to get where he was going that he pulled me by my hair and bent my head back so hard I was afraid that my neck would get broken at which point I relented and gave him the keys to his car.

I was a busy mother with a hundred things to do and I simply did not have the time to brood over things I could not even conceive of, let alone want to, and the tell-tale signs of my husband's unfaithfulness never came into my conscious mind. I called Vernon, Elvis' dad in my exasperation asking him to send Marvin home, thinking of course that he was just hanging around at "the gate."

As any good mother knows it is a time-consuming and very hard job to rear children and I took my job as a mother very seriously and devoted my waking hours to the care of my home and children.

In my opinion it would have been of enormous benefit for my husband to put himself under the love of God and follow the precepts of a successful life proscribed by God Himself and he could have had this abundant life the Bible speaks of. This is available to anyone who believes in the Triune God of the Scriptures.

One night after he came home from one of his outings he was saying something in his sleep and I was awake and I tried to listen to what he was saying. He was mumbling and the only thing I could understand was "Maureen." I wondered if this could be the name of one of the girls at the gate and went to sleep.

I had the most revealing dream:

In it I was going to my husband's car and I opened the door on the passenger-side. I bent down to open the glove compartment where I found a letter. When I took it out and started to read it, I experienced a sick feeling in my stomach which was very pronounced, so much so that it woke me up. I recalled the dream and told myself that I would do just as I had done in the dream, after I had put the children in my car and had everybody in their seats before I would leave to take the two older ones to school on Parkway the next morning since it was part of Christ the King Lutheran Church.

And so I did.

8

Separate Ways

I got the children ready for school, put them in the car and went over to my husband's car, which was a gold Mercury Montego with a black roof. He had left the car unlocked, which was a common practice in 1971, and I went through the same motions as I had made in my dream but there was nothing in the glove compartment of any note. I looked in the binocular case with the binoculars in them when I saw letters slid between the binoculars and the case. I took them out, not one but three letters in all. One was pastel blue, one was pastel green and the other was pastel pink. I took them with me into the car and I could hardly control my nerves as I knew that all this was going to impact my life in the most unpleasant way. I removed one letter out of its envelope and started to read and I read in the most excruciating intimate detail the nature of my husband's relationship with this "Maureen," who was also married. I was so upset that I became sick to my stomach—just like in that dream! I had to pull the car over to collect myself as I could hardly see straight with tears welling up. The children asked what was wrong and what does one say in situations like this but, "Nothing children, it is something Daddy and Mommy have to work out!" After the children were in school, I got into the car and cried and cried.

I just could not get over that my husband did such a thing. Just could not get over it.

When I got home and put the little ones in their respective safe places, I woke up my husband and confronted him with these letters.

He was very contrite and docile and said that he assumed that we are now getting a divorce which was the last thing I wanted and I asked him what he wanted and he said, without batting an eye, the he would like to have both of us women because he loved us both. This, of course was not acceptable to me and so I looked in the Yellow Pages for a local lawyer and made an appointment for a consultation. My mother-in-law was also very upset and I do not know what transpired between her and Marvin or what was said but when I came back from the consultation with that lawyer I was ever-so-sure that I did not want this blasted divorce. My husband said that he was very sorry that he had hurt me this way and that he was not going to stay in touch with Maureen and that he was going to be a faithful husband who would spend more time with the children. I was so relieved. The very idea of having to put my children into a daycare made me ill.

His mother had bought him a house for us to move into and at that point I really did not care who paid for what as long as it would make him happy and he'd forget about his wayward ways.

Elvis by then was getting divorce papers served on him by Priscilla and a lot of the goings-on in his household became fodder for the Memphis rumor mill. On the surface it was the same trash I had to contend with as Priscilla.

Now we lived in a three-bedroom house with a laundry room, a den, a dining-area, a living room, a small kitchen, and a bathroom. The house was close to Orange Mound and over the years it became a racially mixed neighborhood. We had a nice backyard which my husband mowed and he actually seemed to enjoy it. By the time our son was four he took him fishing and my husband seemed to take to this husband-father thing. However, we still had problems with his hair and the long time he took to get it to do just right. As I am writing this it occurs to me that he could have been doing who knows what while he let the hairdryer run—no, he wouldn't, would he? Men without God at the center of their lives are disgusting creatures just as are women who do not have God at the center of their lives. In fact, I have discovered for myself that a life spent living without God at the center is a wasted life.

We had moved to this house sometime in 1972 and Elvis and Priscilla were getting their divorce. My husband would come home telling me how upset Elvis was and how he was using drugs and getting crazier by the minute. While these developments were disappointing on one hand, they were also a sign to me that Elvis was incapable of having a mature rewarding relationship with a woman who had respect for herself, for a variety of reasons. Being such a famous person makes it very difficult to be happy with just the simple requirements for happiness that are available to anyone, but hard to come by for a person so admired and fawned over and spoiled and deceived as he was and it is testimony to the trap he was caught in and could not get out of. This was his destiny and he was aware of it.

My husband enjoyed telling me of Elvis's misery as he considered himself better than Elvis because he was not getting a divorce from me. He squeaked by that one. He even said occasionally that he thought Elvis was jealous of him and he attributed this jealousy to the fact that he was ten years younger and better looking. I never responded to these kinds of musings as I knew the true reason of Elvis's jealousy of my husband . . . and it was not for those reasons.

Being totally full of himself and his imagined irresistibility, he had to find an appreciative audience to feed this delusion to make it seem real and I just did not count. I was just the mother of his children and I required him to do something other than primp and preen. He also had the opinion that women were inferior to men and that in fact they were nothing more than incubators and that was the undoing of our marriage. He took me and everything I did for our family for granted, and just to underscore his contempt for the female he felt entitled to do just as his idol had.

After about a year of domestic bliss he veered back into his old ways but there was this difference: he no longer cared if I knew that he was being unfaithful. He came home whenever he felt like it, left when he felt like it and even had the flavor-of-the-month call at our home to ask to speak to him. He literally acted as though it was his God-given right to do this. I was so upset at this development and I did not know what to do.

I went to the pastor at my church and I told him the tawdry story that was my life and he said, "Ilona, knowing what you know about your husband's conduct, if you were to stay with him you would be condoning what he does and since he has already been found guilty of adultery before, he is not likely to change. According to the Scriptures adultery is mentioned as the only valid reason for a divorce."

This was a very difficult decision I had to make as I truly hate divorce, basically because God hates it, and generally because my mother was divorced and had four children and if there was one thing I fought like crazy not to ever be, it was like my mother. Had I not promised myself that way back when, as a young person, knowing full well that the children end up suffering? I absolutely did not want that for my beloved children and my heart was near breaking at the mere thought of it. But I could also not in clear conscience remain in a marriage that was being violated in the worst way by my unfaithful husband. I believe in the sanctity of marriage and there was no way on this green earth that I could condone his actions in principle or in any other way.

I prayed for God to show me how to deal with this and it occurred to me that this might, just might, open the way for me to get together with Elvis, after all. This thought gave me the strength and courage to ask my husband for a divorce. He did not care one iota and he actually cooperated on every point of the negotiations that followed. He had accused me of having a boyfriend who was the lawyer I had gone to for consultation two years earlier, which was a lie, but so as not to be accused of this again I selected a female lawyer.

He moved into an apartment practically across the street from Elvis. My children were kind of glad that he moved out because they seemed to just get in his way when he was trying to live as though he had no family and he was unfair and unkind and inattentive and he was all these things and more to me. Since his problem with his hair took up most of his waking hours and kept him in the bathroom, I knew I had better make sure he had the right kind of hairspray available for him. (One time I bought another kind and he got so mad he threw the can at me.) It was just that he became an aggravation and an imposition to us to have him around as there was no peace when he was home.

I helped him get settled in his place and it felt to me like I was helping an older child get out on his own.

I loved the peace and quiet we could now enjoy. The children were content, as they had their mommy who had always taken care of them.

It was Hortense who offered me a job at her daycare which was ideal for me because I could take the two older children to school and bring the two younger ones with me to the daycare where they would be in their respective classes but I would always be nearby.

At 2:30 p.m. I would leave the daycare while the children were still napping and I'd pick up the girls from school and go back to the daycare and finish my hours there. We'd usually get home around 6:30 p.m. and do whatever was necessary to prepare for the next day.

I have always felt safe and secure in a home setting and at the daycare with the children's grandmother being there and my many children it felt like home to me and I found coping with the divorce not as traumatic as I had feared it would be. My mother-in-law's reaction to my intention of divorcing her son was, "I would have divorced him a long time ago!" I was deeply hurt by my husband and I told myself that I would never marry again unless it was to Elvis.

That ever-so-vague sense of doom was there still and I had to force myself to fashion my life in a way where it would go on independently of Elvis's which was difficult, to say the least. Nothing I had dreamed of in connection with Elvis had shown any sign of turning around.

The day when our divorce would become final had arrived. My now ex-husband-to-be chose not to come to court as this was no longer necessary since they had passed the no-fault divorce legislation and we had agreed on the terms. The only request my husband had of me was not to cite the specific reasons for the divorce, true as they were, so we settled for those "irreconcilable differences." When the judge listened to my lawyer presenting my cut-and-dried case he pronounced this our marriage dissolved. The lawyer stepped over to me, handed me the final decree, shook my hand and congratulated me on now being a free woman. Congratulations indeed! I did not want to be a free woman. I did not want to lose my husband, the father of my children, to a disgusting thing like a divorce. I was taken aback by the way this all happened but I tried so hard to tell myself that many people get divorced and they all continue to function and recuperate. Oftentimes they even have a better quality of life even though the financial aspect made it extremely difficult in many ways. I took comfort in the fact that I had peace and I no longer had to be humiliated and disrespected and, most of all, I could now pursue my interests concerning my church and my children's school without having to be made to feel as if I was doing something wrong. We could have unfettered conversations about Jesus Christ and in a way it tied me ever closer to my church. We'd have daily devotions and the children learned to tithe and give offerings just as the Holy Word of God admonishes us to do and the children knew nothing else and I was confident that God would keep his promise and guide them through their lives as I was doing what he commanded me as the mother to do, which was to teach them His ways. There was never any thought of any other possibility.

I went into hibernation, so to speak. Since I had my children to take care of I had no intention of dating. The very idea of another man being around my children was totally unbearable. Their father would come by faithfully on Thursday evenings after work and pay his child support, and, when it fit into his busy schedule, he would come on Sunday evenings, around six o'clock, to visit with his children, which they did enjoy. They would tell him of things that happened in school and he seemed to enjoy the visits too. They did not require him to give anything he was really not willing to give, since what he was willing to give was already spoken for, so to speak, by his devotion to himself.

As was the custom in the sixties and seventies, most everyone who felt depressed or anxious or whatever took Valium and Hortense was no exception and it was just one of those things we did in those days. Whenever I would feel bad at work and I would mention it to my, I should now say, ex-mother-in-law, she would offer me one of her Valiums and it would always make me feel better and I never thought anything of it. I knew Marvin's mother to be nothing but a law-abiding, responsible person I had trusted for a long time and she was in good standing in the business community and well-respected by the authorities and I was now just an alien who had to report to the postmaster of my immigration status every year. So I had every reason to be confident that nothing bad could happen to me by sticking close to her. I had my own prescription for Valium but I never took it to work with me.

The women who brought their children to our daycare were now more and more divorced women and I got to talking to one in particular because she had just gone through something similar to what I had and she was always making it a point to tell me that I needed to get out of my house and meet other people, "that life goes on" and I would find that being divorced does not have to be the end of the world but rather the beginning of something new and exciting, which she could attest to. This went on for a while and sometimes her bugging me would stop and I would be relieved because in a way she pressured me to at least consider something that I did not want to consider and which was just something unpleasant. Then all of a sudden she started again; only this time she would not just be talking but she was talking me into meeting with her and some friends at the Admiral Benbow Inn on Brooks Road and Airways Boulevard.

It had been a bad day for me and I was still trying to get out of it by explaining to her that I had not eaten etc., etc. but she insisted. So I gave in, thinking to myself that I'd do this and get her off my back and be done with it. It was a Friday and I had taken one of Hortense's Valiums to make me feel better as I still felt under the weather by 4 p.m. That seemed to help and I took my ex-mother-in-law's sister, who was somewhat slow and was working and living at the daycare, home with us so she could watch the children while I was out and everybody knew where I was going with the mother of a well-liked handsome boy we took care of every day.

After I had made sure that the children were taken care of and I had put on my war paint and changed clothes, I left for the Admiral Benbow Inn. When I got there I found this mother with several men who were busy talking. She introduced me to everybody and then told me that she was leaving with her married boyfriend and his friends to fly to somewhere on his small plane and that I was going to have a good time with this man whom they left behind. I was so disgusted at the whole setup and I was definitely not in the mood to be nice to some man I did not know nor did I even remotely like him. He seemed excited as he had been led to believe that "fun was in store for him tonight"!

He ordered me a drink which he explained to me ahead of time and I agreed that a Tom Collins sounded good to me. It tasted refreshing as it had a fruity taste I could appreciate and I sipped on it for a while and we did the small-talk bit. After a while he casually mentioned that he had a room at the Inn and I got the message loud and clear. I told him that I was not interested in that sort of thing and that I would prefer to go home. He disappeared without saying anything to me and I politely waited and waited so I could thank him for the drink but he never returned. I asked the waiter if I needed to pay for the drink and he informed me that it was taken care of. So I left. I got into my car and drove home. It was about 10:30 p.m. when I made a left turn on Pendleton to go onto Ketchum when I lost consciousness after hitting a woman in the side of her car as she had proceeded to make a right turn coming from the opposite direction. The next thing I remember was that I was in a police car and I could barely comprehend what was happening. They took me downtown and put me in a cell. I fell asleep right away and the next morning my ex-husband bailed me out of jail and brought me home. I was so ashamed of myself I did not want to live. To me this was too much to deal with adding onto the unhappiness over this ugly divorce with which I was desperately trying to come to terms with. I simply found it all so problematic and overwhelming I wanted to die and I remember being completely hysterical. They called my pastor and he came and talked to me and although I cannot remember what he said or prayed it must have given me courage and hope to keep on going. A brighter tomorrow would surely come.

This was a most horrifying ordeal for me. I had to get a lawyer, not to mention that "my car" was totaled—it was really Hortense's. She took care of all my expenses connected with that DUI and I subsequently was put on a suspended license which restricted my driving to places where I had to go to take care of my responsibilities. After six months, I got a car on my own and I remember so very well how marvelously independent I felt to be able to buy something that big; it was a Plymouth Fury and it had air-conditioning and a working radio which the Falcon Sprint I totaled did not have! Through all the legal wrangling I had to ask myself why I was under the influence when I only had one Tom Collins. The mother of my eldest daughter's best friend was a nurse and she urged me to think of every little thing I did that day and we discovered together that this seemingly innocuous Valium, in conjunction with no food and the Tom Collins was the cause of my loss of control. It also explained why my mother-in-law was so unusually helpful considering that I was no longer married to her son. I never said anything about this discovery and in this case it was best to let sleeping dogs lie. I thanked her profusely for all her help and I was feeling ever more indebted to her and I was only too happy to do what ever she asked me to do.

It took me a while before I felt redeemed after this serious accident which could have resulted in my killing someone.

Nobody at work ever mentioned it as they could easily see that it had hit me hard to recuperate from it.

Marvin was now more concerned about the children and he took them to buy ice cream at the old place on Airways that we had occasionally gone to as a family.

Time heals a lot of things and this was no exception. I did not go out again and planned on just taking care of my children. It was perfectly fine with me.

I had a German friend from church and school and she was taking classes at the university to get the credits she needed to be able to teach high school and she invited me to go with her and her husband to the Oktoberfest there. I had joined the German Club through her as well and they had events too. So I did go out in a controlled environment, so to speak, as this couple always picked me up and brought me home, too. At the university, however, there was a young man who made my acquaintance and I could not get rid of him as he was convinced that I was just what he needed. He absolutely threw me for a loop with his constant dropping by and making plans to go here and there. It was crazy. He had studied music and taken voice lessons, as he wanted to sing opera, so we and the children often went to the recitals of the different master classes. I was twelve years older than this German-American. His parents had immigrated shortly after the war and he was born in this country but he found himself at odds with the culture and what his parents brought him up to believe and I think he thought he found in me the perfect blending of Old World and New World. It was strange, as I knew he was off-kilter in many ways. But he was good for my son, who was at the age of getting interested in snakes, fixing things and concocting chemical mixtures, which this student specialized in. He was an inventor of sorts. His father owned a tiling company which did a lot of the city projects and they were constantly working on developing new ways of doing old things—or discovering new ones.

Of course he thought we would get married but I knew that I could not contend with him. But he was ever so persistent and really drove me crazy. He was also driving my older girls crazy who simply did not like him which I could never understand because he was always nice to them. He really cared for all my children and went out of his way to make sure that they would be included whenever possible.

He and his mother had a problematic relationship, the nature of which I can only guess at, and one time she chased him out of the house with a butcher knife and he ended up at my doorstep without any money or a place to go to. He begged me to let him spend the night while he could figure out what to do about his situation.

I really, really, did not want him in my house but I could also not send him away with no place to sleep. So I let him sleep in my den and the next day he asked if he could spend a few days at my house. He said he'd re-tile my (actually Hortense's) bathroom, which was in dire need of help. We discussed it with her and she agreed to pay for the material and he would do the labor as payment for staying there. That is what he ended up doing. I then took the opportunity go out on a date with an older man whom he also knew; and he worked on the bathroom and the children were supervised all at the same time.

But I was so glad when he was finished with the bathroom—which he really did a very good job on. The idea of a man in my house overnight just did not sit well with me.

In between various boyfriends there seemed to be all the children I once knew as children but they were now grown-up and had heard that I was divorced and they came by to tell me of their dreams of me when they were in their early teens and younger. I have never been so shocked to discover that this sexual energy develops so early and I realized I was not alone when I was struggling to harness it and bring it under my control, do or die!

Now they came to make their dream come true! It was weird. The dating game was not for me. I found that the only interest men had in me was to go to bed with me and I absolutely resented the then-predominant notion as the result of the sixties—the Kinsey Report (Sigmund Freud adherents!), the Pill, National Organization for Women, etc., and the acceptance of promiscuity as a way of life and I found out from experience that the one-night stands are demeaning to a woman and ultimately damaging to her in many important ways.

Elvis had a song come out titled, "Love Me, Love the Life I Lead," which irritated me to no end. I thought that I could have been wrong about him after all and he was just what he was and his reputation indicated and that I must have been out of my mind to think that he shared my ideals of womanhood and the sacredness of a relationship between a man and a woman. It threw me again into this unsettledness as far as my faith was concerned as these were so closely connected.

I had scheduled my older children to go to summer camp with the church, thinking it would be a good experience for them, and I was glad that I had the money to let them go. I saw them off on Friday morning in June of 1975 and the younger ones and I went home. All at once I decided that I could ask their grandmother if she would mind keeping the two overnight, as I was planning to see her son who lived up the street from her since she moved into a condo on Raines Road. She said yes, she'd be happy to have them. I never had my children spend the night anywhere away from me and I really hated having asked her to do this but I said what I said and I had to do what I had to do, which was to bring to a close once and for all, for ill or good. I had to give this Elvis drama one more try. So I went to my ex-husband's apartment and we chatted for a while and I had a Coke with some Old Charter and he showed me a picture of an extremely sexy-looking "Wonder Woman," which he had put on the inside of his entertainment unit which was at the foot of his bed. I have no idea why he showed me this but after having had a Valium to brace myself for what I had to do, very little registered. Somehow we ended up having sex, it was sort of expected by him that we do this since we were once married and many times I just did not want to hurt his feelings and besides, it was something that was familiar and somehow seemed not as wrong as sex with a stranger. (Don't we always find a way to justify our sins?)

I called Charlie from my ex-husband's place and he agreed to meet me at his room at the Howard Johnson's. I had not seen him since 1969 when I was looking for my husband at the Memphian. I had tried very hard since then to keep Elvis's show biz moves at arm's length as that whole scene did not interest me. When I got there he was just getting ready to step out and buy some beer. So I was in this room and I looked out the sliding door and I could see my reflection in the glass and for just a split-second I saw someone hurrying by and I thought that I must have been seeing things. I closed the curtain and, being bored and feeling rather good I did a back bend which I always loved to do, when Charlie entered the room catching me with my face upside down looking at him from that position. I got myself into an upright position and he offered me a bottle of beer which I accepted and he was smoking a cigarette and offered me one. So here we were sitting, smoking cigarettes and drinking beer when he asked me whether I would consider marrying a man in whose life I would not be the only woman, to which I responded by saying that I just had gotten out of a situation like that and "No, I would not." I am not sure whether we had sex before I said that or after. I can remember little about the experience but in a way I had become accustomed that it was expected to have sex and I had known him for seventeen years and he was the go-between for me and Elvis and I thought at the time why not? This may be good for Elvis to find out that what he is requiring for himself I can require too. See how he likes it. Charlie then told me that even married women wanted to be with Elvis and I was not sure why he was telling me this. I did not care to know what Elvis made women do. I had a dim enough view of it already. I remember telling him that I cared for my ex-husband as he was the father of my children. I asked him if I could use his phone to call a friend of mine with whom I arranged a time to meet with as I was now certain. And that was that. One more one-night stand and I became more disgusted with myself, men, and Elvis and the only thing to do was to chat with this friend and round out the evening. When I arrived at home, this student, Gunther, was in my driveway, waiting on me to come home, then I had to wrestle with him because he was bent on having sex too. What is the matter with men? Do they think of nothing else? I was so depressed after that Friday night it was unreal. I had told Elvis in effect that I was not going to marry him. Did I really say that? I could not believe it! But I did, and in a strange way it became clear to me that I had to follow that line of thinking the same way it was when I did not give in to admitting in so many words that I loved Elvis and needed him desperately when I met with Charlie at the Old Hickory Log some years earlier.

The only solace I ever had was in the taking care of my children and I missed them so, I went as early as was polite to pick them up from their grandmother's house and brought them home and I spent the day with them and went to church the next morning where I repented of my wayward ways and was forgiven. I promised that I would keep to myself and with God's help be the woman I had always dreamed of being.

I was so desperate to retreat from men, I seriously considered joining the Quakers or the Mennonites, where I could feel safe and protected. I hated to be divorced and I could never get away from the attention of one man or the other. It was terrible.

Meanwhile Elvis went from bad to worse. Marvin told me of Elvis's addiction to drugs and his excursions on his Harley. He would run into Elvis and some of his buddies who were following him and Elvis was conversing with them with slurred speech. Had I not already been disgusted enough with Elvis's conduct since he had been living with Linda Thompson after his divorce from Priscilla? Then Linda left him also and then his last attempt at marriage with that Ginger who was entirely too immature to deal with someone with his giant-size problems. He had a constant battle with his weight and then, adding insult to injury, there came this book by his former friends and confidants Red West and Red's cousin Sonny West, which promised to reveal everything that had been going on in Elvis's life. It truly made Elvis sick to death because it would tear off the mask he was wearing, certainly reminiscent of my emphasizing "liar" at Elvis's and my first meeting in Bad Nauheim. I had already heard enough disturbing things through the rumor mill and I did not care one bit to know any more of something I hated.

I was just sick of the whole ugly thing.

In my life, working for the children's grandmother, some things had changed for the worse. I personally think that my employer, Hortense, got addicted to Valium and she started to drink alcohol more often than I could remember her doing before. She preferred Bacardi rum and I would not doubt that her daughter had something to do with all this. She acted increasingly strange as it pertained to me. She was downright insulting and disrespectful to me in front of the other workers. She'd go on vacation with her daughter and grandchildren and leave me in charge since she had promoted me to assistant manager in addition to being the kindergarten teacher. I found out later on that she would tell the workers that they did not need to listen to me, as everybody knew what they were expected to do. This made me very angry and I told her that I was leaving, which I did but I can not describe how horrified I was at the prospect of actually having to interact with the world at large. I felt protected at the daycare and was at home there. I was so scared I ran back to her and begged her to take me back but things got ever worse.

I had gone to the house of the church secretary where we were having a meeting about something concerning the altar guild, of which I was a member, and when I came home I found my eldest child talking to her grandmother. I took the receiver from her and talked to Hortense when she told me that she was going to take my children away from me since I was an alien and she had the right to take them from me since I was an unfit mother and that she knew what I was doing. I told her that I had been at a meeting for the church and that I think she had too much to drink and that she needed to sleep it off and then I hung up. She was obviously on a drunken rant. My daughter told me of the things her grandmother told her about me, scandalous things, and I told her to forget it because Mimi was not in her right mind. But it was definitely the beginning of the end. She invited us to luncheon at the Piccadilly's in Whitehaven and we pretended that nothing happened. But there was a breach of trust. I became a naturalized citizen of the United States of America as soon as was possible, in 1976, all the while working at the daycare and enjoying that safe, familiar atmosphere. I had to celebrate any holidays with my children because Sue did not want me at the family gatherings. She was forever fighting with her husband who also drank too much. She divorced him, then re-married him, then divorced him again. He'd become violent and so on and so on. So she was a troubled woman too. The children and I had our own celebrations and they were excited to be able to help with the preparations as it was fun for all of us. We made it fun. Their father would come and join us sometimes and he was always welcome.

One year at Easter, I was as busy as a bee trying to prepare for this special celebration of the resurrection of Jesus Christ. I had cut my yard, front and back, and the children were doing the indoor things and everything was running as smooth as silk when I noticed a yard two houses down from ours that was looking awful and I decided to ask the person living there, who I knew was a very old lady, if she wanted me to cut her grass. She said that this would be so nice since her yard boy did not show up and so I merrily cut her front and back yards. I was happy to have been able to do something for somebody just to make them happy and I felt good.

It was some weeks later that I was told that Hortense went around saying that I was crazy, that I would go around and cut other people's yards even if they did not want it. I could not believe it. Apparently she was working on a dossier at that time to substantiate her assertion that I was an unfit mother.

9

Where Do I Go From Here?

In the early months of 1977 Elvis recorded what turned out be his last LP, called Moody Blue and on it is a song that describes his Baby Moody Blue, which is revelatory but "Little Darling" really drives his sincere, deeply felt desperation home.

The whole album is a testimony of his love for me and I must confess that I got that message but there was just nothing I could do or wanted to do. We were on opposite sides as far as our value systems were concerned and there was no way that I could deal with any of the problems he had. He was so ensnared in the ways of the world, mouthing words of faith in his beautiful renditions of gospel songs, but he did not exhibit the slightest adherence to what these wonderful songs expressed. For some reason he missed the fact that faith in Jesus and the blessings that we can derive from it are dependent upon practicing the teachings of Jesus as they are laid out on in the Bible. These two components are inseparable and must work together to be able to live the promised "abundant life" here on earth, while at the same time laying up treasure for the world to come. He did not seem to have the capacity to grasp this. Even if he had grasped this fact and he would have tried to change his circumstances accordingly, it would have required a fundamental and drastic overhaul of in his life. The world simply would have not permitted that, which put him between heaven and hell, having to pay homage to both. These conflicting entities are in fact the presence of good and evil in each one of us. Ultimately we must make a choice, one or the other, but to play it both ways as he had was certain destruction for himself and regrettably, on a larger scale, a whole world which had became addicted to, "If it feels good, do it and if you can make money doing it, sell it."

It is with these kinds of deliberations that I had to take the position that I took. It did not get me around wondering why I had to do all this, as I have had to spend my life trying to kill my love for him, which was a futile effort as this kind of love cannot be destroyed.

As anyone who is a serious student of Scripture knows, it is not possible to be perfect here on earth. If that were the case we would have no need for the saving grace of faith in Christ. But we are commanded to keep striving toward perfection, and it is in this striving to be God-pleasing that our salvation is assured. Perfection is God's business.

Elvis, at the time I had to decide our future, was at the top of his game and therefore far too strong and influential for me to deal with him on a personal level. I was not any too strong myself yet and would have been sucked into his way of life by the sheer dynamic force that he was—the force of this world. The other possibility was that Elvis would have bowed out of show biz in which case the second phenomenal success after his stint in the Army would never have happened.

Without knowing it I followed the script as it is written in the Bible—to save myself I had to flee the force of temptation and walk alone the other way.

I was leading a complicated life, to be sure, as I was struggling to cope with work and children, school and church. I had to let go of my duties as a member of the Altar Guild because I was weighed down under my obligations and responsibilities. Then there were the seemingly never-ending troubles with Hortense and the grief she caused me at work. I was doing good to just keep going. It is not easy to work with children all day and come home and deal with more children, and since they were my own it required every bit of strength I could muster. Then the ever-present problems with men in general and Marvin in particular.

On Sunday evening, it was the fourteenth of August 1977, the children's father came by as was customary, and he brought that aforementioned book which was titled, *Elvis, What Happened?* He put it on the chair by the kitchen door and said that I needed to read it and that, "Once you start reading it you will not be able to put it down." I thought to myself that this would not be a problem for me because I was not even going to waste my time reading it in the first place. He chatted with the children and we did some small talk and when he left he reminded me to remember what he said, that the book was a must-read for me.

The evening progressed as normal for a Sunday evening and I would pass by the book many times while going about my business and each time I took mental notice of it. It became a magnet and I was itching to get the children to bed so I could get started reading.

But I pretended to myself that I really did not care and when the children were in bed at their regular bedtime, I made it a point to drag my preparations for bed out as long as possible, taking a leisurely bath and whatnot. Finally I picked up the book, checked on my sweet children—they always looked so sweet when they were sleeping—and I settled in my bed and started to read. As much as it galls me to have to admit that my ex-husband was right—he was right! I couldn't have put the book down if I tried. I was completely riveted to the minute detail of the total lawlessness that surrounded Elvis on a daily basis. There was not a shred of a hint of a bare minimum of decency anywhere. I was aghast, so much so that I bolted up in my bed and exclaimed, "My God, this man cannot live!" I finished reading the book that night and I cannot remember how I had the courage to read the entire account of Elvis's debauchery and the perverseness of his entire conduct on every level. I was positively horrified. I cannot in so many words describe the utter desolation of spirit; and a heaviness settled over me that made it hard for me to move the following day. It was as if I had lead in my arms and legs and the crushing heavy feeling of nothingness enveloped me. It was an extraordinary sensation of indescribable doom. I tried to explain to my ex-mother-in-law about what I had read and she did not believe a thing I tried to convey to her. She has always irritated me with her blind worship of Elvis, so it did really not surprise me that she would put the blame on Red who, as she insisted, wrote that book out of revenge, for Elvis having fired him and not having invited him to the wedding back in 1967. She may have had a point as she knew more about that part of it because she was friends with the mother of Sonny West (Ruby) who was the co-author and also was a former employee of the Presleys. Ruby actually worked at the daycare and if there was ever a screaming mimi, she was it. That woman had the shrillest voice I'd ever heard and she was also the one who babysat my daughter after she got up to six pounds and I had to go to work at the daycare. Hortense was absolutely not of any help to me and I would almost agree if someone were to suggest that it was she who was annoyed with me for trying to ruin her "love" for Elvis. This unspoken standoff continued into the next day and the heaviness I experienced was still hanging on. I was so devastated at the disclosure of the Elvis I did not know and did not want to know, in such excruciating detail—in black and white—irrefutable evidence. I knew it was the truth because the rumors I'd heard for a long time, and tried so hard not to believe, lined up perfectly with what was printed in that book. I was in emotional freefall, I did not know how to feel, where to go from here or what to do. It was unequivocally the most horrifying feeling of disconnectness with myself as I could not tell anymore who this "myself" was.

I was exhausted and working as if on automatic pilot. Lunch was over and we got the children calmed down with a cartoon on the television while we were putting down the cots and covered them with the sheets inside of them and I was just about to get ready to lie down on the table in the kindergarten room when the phone rang. I answered the phone and it was Hortense's sister, Ella Pearl. She said, "Did you know that Elvis is dead?" I said, "No, I did not know," and she went on to tell me this and that and all I can remember was that I felt such a feeling of relief, it was unreal. For just a split-second I thought that maybe now I could have a normal life. The two sisters talked at length since I called Hortense to the phone. Ella Pearl also operated a daycare.

The outpouring of expressions of grief over the death of Elvis are testimony to the emotional attachment the world had with its king, and he was the king of the world, with countless servants and followers who were ready to do his bidding at the drop of a hat as they became as addicted to his brand of rebellion disguised in the cloak of harmless fun. At its roots, however, it had the vice of self-indulgence which we are by nature susceptible to and Elvis, without even trying, led the way to destruction like a Pied Piper.

I could not get over this overt and very real pain of loss that his followers displayed and I had to ask myself how was it possible that everybody talks of this wretch of a man in the most glowing terms, to the point in some cases where they could not even find words to express the "marvelousness" of Elvis. I was nonplussed and I thought I must have gotten stuck in some time warp.

Then I reasoned that it could just be me because I did not make any headway with him and it was a clear case of sour grapes. I could not make any sense of the developments whatsoever as this theory could not explain this acute sense of relief I felt at the news of Elvis's death.

One good thing came out of this as his death did not really catch me unprepared. Having suffered from this bottomless sense of depression after having read this book two nights earlier I was released from that heavy weight of nothingness that had paralyzed me and made me feel as if I were a dead person walking.

But now I had to re-construct my bearings as the reason for my living was gone. I was so furious with God for having duped me into this nonsensical scheme and, to top it all off, all of this for such a disgusting individual as Elvis to boot! I went from fits of rage to whimpering, pleading to Him to show me where to go from here and what to do or what to think. The reason for my being in the U.S. was because of love by God's direction, I truly believed. I had married whom I married because I believed what the Bible teaches on the subject of immorality and repented of my transgressions over and over as was necessary as I kept on messing up. I now had four children and I was in a foreign country, surrounded by people who were trying to derail my faith in Jesus Christ and my devotion to His teachings.

The constant haggling over one thing or another Elvis was like a monotonous droning in my brain. One simply could not get away from it. It was everywhere, all the time.

After a long time even the enormous impact that Elvis's death had on this world subsided and it was definitely best for me to keep my opinion on that subject to myself. Besides, now that it had become common knowledge that Elvis was a disaster, I had no desire to admit that I ever loved him. My lips were sealed.

Maybe it was my ex-mother-in-law's hope that her son and I would re-marry and she would put me under pressure to make me desperate enough to run to him, or rather invite him to re-consider. I do not know, but since the divorce in 1974, we had still been invited to the family gatherings for a year, as if nothing had changed and we would meet at the daycare where there was enough room for everybody. It is ironic that this very same building at 2011 Lamar Avenue was the first home to Vernon and Gladys Presley and their thirteen-year-old son, Elvis, after they arrived in Memphis having left their rural home in Tupelo, Mississippi. According to the people who ran an upholstery shop for cars next door, the Presleys would often come over and ask to use the phone. I would always say to one or the other co-worker, "Just think, Elvis took a shower in here," mockingly, of course. The building over the years got an updated addition to enlarge the place and to have a more appealing facade.

My ex-husband and I would go with the children on vacation to Gatlinburg and Chattanooga and it was a pleasant event for everybody involved.

I think my ex-husband felt guilty for not having done that before because the children and I went to Eureka Springs with a nineteen-year-old boy as the driver. I was far too scared to drive by myself as I was not accustomed to drive on the Interstate. Be that as it may, we enjoyed both vacations, through I felt safer with my ex-husband. I must admit that having come all the way from Germany and then being afraid of everything did not make any sense to me either but I never ever was a "Modern Millie" and I could not change that.

What made my relationship with the children's grandmother so confounding was that she could be so generous one time and so very stingy the next. I never found out, or took the trouble to find out, whether she was paying me enough for working for her. I took for granted that she would pay me according to the pay scale, and commensurate with the responsibility I shouldered, but when I told my friends what I made, they could not believe it. I did not worry too much about this since

I could make ends meet with the contribution from the children's father in the form of child support and I would faithfully save a certain amount, which I kept in the Missouri Synod Exchange Fund of my church.

Hortense would often brag about how much she was contributing to the Billy Graham Association. I always thought that this was so good of her since it was only seeing Billy Graham on TV that made America somewhat comfortable to me in my first years in this country.

It had come to my attention that as she became more familiar with the ins and outs of the business she was in, she devised every conceivable way to make more money, even at the expense of the children who were woefully underfed. She considered ketchup a vegetable and the portions became smaller and smaller but the number of children she enrolled became larger and larger even though she was licensed for a whole lot less and we had children sleeping wherever we could find a little spot to put a cot in and it made it a lot harder on all of us as she did not hire another person.

She succumbed to that old greed and she knew it, hence the increased reliance on Valium and alcohol to numb the conscience. But her shortchanging me to such a degree that I could neither live or die, in view of her making money hand over fist, really hurt my feelings.

As usual I could not afford to be too hurt as I depended on my children's grandmother for a job, but it was becoming harder and harder. She would think nothing of it to offer the children and me little hard biscuits no one else would want to eat and in fact had not been eaten by the other grandchildren who were there that morning. My children did not want to eat them either and they asked me if they had to. I told them no and then I joked with their grandmother, asking if she planned to play golf with them. Edward, Sr., had been released from Western State Mental Hospital into her care and lived there and he was always good for comic relief and I was joking around with him. His memory was stuck in the past and we got to hear the same stories over and over.

It was just the contemptuous attitude toward my children and me that had taken her over and maybe I was in a way inviting it by being so dependent on her. I do not know what happened. I had come to believe that it was true when she said she loved me and she was a perfect substitute for the kind of mother I'd always wished I could have had. When my first child was born I remember wishing I had my mother with me but then I recalled all the miserable things she was capable of doing and I was sorry that I even had such a crazy thought. In fact, my mother had sent the sheriff to my house requesting him to make sure that I was not a streetwalker.

I do think that my mother was mentally ill to some degree because of the war and her fragile psyche.

It was rather pitiful on my part to put up with those obvious attacks on my self-respect by Hortense, yet I could not face the scary world out there. I would rather continue to swallow my pride. I'd cut the grass at the daycare with my lawnmower, which I had to haul into the trunk of my car and out of it. I could definitely not do that today.

The children and I would go to the swimming pool their grandmother's condominium had there to be used by the renters and their guests. We went there often without telling their grandmother because I did not want to be a nuisance but we took full advantage of it and we all had beautiful suntans and all my children learned to swim there. We got permission from the management through Hortense and that was giving us this lovely chance to enjoy summer fun that cost next to nothing.

As far as I was concerned I had a good life with my children and they just blossomed. The eldest daughter would soon be confirmed, a ritual I had undergone when I was fourteen and remembered so well. She had to write an essay about what her faith meant to her in which she wrote, rather she chose, the First Commandment to explain:

> "To me the first commandment means that God has made the promise to be my God forever. It also means that He does not want us to make anything or anyone more important in our lives than God. God first made His promise to me when I was baptized, I can be sure God will keep His promise but since there is the Old Adam in me, I cannot keep this or any commandment without being saved by Christ's forgiveness and the faith given to me by God through the Bible.
>
> "By promising to be our God, He promises to take care of us at all

times, give us everything we need to live, protect us, and give us the great future we have with God because of His love for us."

She got an award of some kind and she was so happy and I was gratified as things developed as I had hoped so much and worked so hard for. Truly, I considered myself blessed.

We even went to a fancy restaurant to celebrate my eldest daughter's confirmation, which her grandmother attended and then treated all of us, including Marvin, who joined us for the festivities. I am sure it cost Hortense a pretty penny because we went to The Windjammer in Saddle Creek, a shopping haven for the very well-heeled. Of course, I could not stop mentioning to anyone who would listen, how accomplished a confirmand my daughter was which was very important to me. Maybe it made her envious because she did not avail her children of the kind of spiritual education every child deserves. I got clothes from her that she no longer wore and I never minded wearing someone else's clothes. If they looked good on me and I liked them, I wore them and would never give it another thought. For this occasion, however, I was treated to a shopping spree of sorts by my ex-mother-in-law and I could buy an outfit for several occasions. That is how she was. On one hand so very generous and thoughtful and then on the other hand exceedingly stingy and downright insulting or indifferent.

To make a long story short, we did not get back to that relationship as it was before the threat to take my children from me. It is true, of course that I had male friends, and I have never claimed to be perfect, but, I was always trying to be a good mother to my children because it was something that simply came naturally to me. Besides, I had made a promise to God way back when. I am sure I made mistakes and for that I am sorry. But God forgives and I did not have to carry the burden of guilt through my life.

I cannot remember the exact circumstances that brought about the final break between my ex-mother-in-law and myself, which resulted my quitting my employment with her. As best as I remember, it was the fairly constant criticism by my friends who had no personal advantage riding on this situation with my employer and the way she was treating me.

For some reason, probably in conducting his business as the accountant for the daycare, the CPA came by and, having been alerted by my friends to the possible violations of this or that law, I asked him about the specifics. I was not familiar with these kinds of issues but he was and he told me in a blanket statement that my employer was laughing her way to the bank as she treated us, me and her slow sister, as indentured servants and paid us accordingly.

This was something I could not overlook, no matter how hard I tried. This was serious enough to force me to realize that if ever there was a time to cut professional ties, this was it. I understood this clearly but that did not get me around to being practically scared stiff at the very thought of having to face this big ugly cutthroat world, up close and personal. I prayed my heart out to God for help and I took every conceivable step that I thought I must do in order to train myself for this grueling task ahead. I resolved that I would absolutely not take any more Valium. I changed my diet to include natural supplements and a stringent restriction to food guaranteed to be healthy, consisting mainly of vegetables, a little meat, and some bread. I started jogging and I practiced Transcendental Meditation. I have never felt that there was a correlation between this practice and the abandonment of my devotion to the Triune God whom I have loved forever. I found however that it indeed relaxes and prepares the mind for good thinking, the thoughts being one's choice. I chose to talk to God, having prepared myself every which way to do what I had to do if I wanted to save any respect for myself at all and to save face in front of my friends.

To save face was very important to me, as was the fact that I had to demonstrate to my children too that there were times when one must take a stand against all odds because it is the right thing to do. I fully believed that, but the necessary courage for the execution of this difficult position did not come by itself for me, but I was certain that I had an advocate who would help when help was needed. I will never forget the feeling of dread I had when I quit and explained to Hortense that it was just time to move on. She did not react in any way and probably thought that I would return again just as I had done several times before. But for me, in spite of the feeling of dread, I was determined never to return into this slavery, based almost entirely on my fear of the world and my perceived inability to cope—it was really more this acute distaste for the world as I saw it.

There is no denying it— simultaneously with the harrowing feeling of insecurity was this encouraging feeling that comes when one has accomplished something, and my leaving the accustomed security that came with my job was an enormous accomplishment for me.

It was vitally important that I took this important step in my overall development.

I now had to look for a job. I took a position with a fitness center. I liked fitness and I was all for self-improvement the natural way. My hours were split, some in the morning, then again in the afternoon until the center closed for the day. This made me very unhappy because I could not spend any meaningful time with my children, who were all in school then. So I quit there. It needs to be mentioned that I did not qualify for unemployment compensation, which made it very stressful for me, but I kept up my regimen of discipline and I managed. Time went by and I got no responses from anywhere I applied for a job. I went to the unemployment office which was at that time on Madison Avenue, downtown. Nothing. I was subsisting on the child support from my ex-husband and I could meet the monthly bills with that, but there was no money left to feed the children or myself with. Thanks to Gunther, the friend I could not get rid of, I was able to apply for food stamps, which is something I would not have known to do, and that helped us survive. I cannot understand people who get on food stamps and then remain on them for whatever reason. It is a stopgap measure to enable people like myself who find themselves in a difficult situation and need assistance. I was really feeling strange but I was grateful to have been extended this help. It did nothing for my self-esteem and I was getting increasingly concerned about our future but I was never tempted, for even a split-second, to go back to my former employer and mother-in-law. We were not enemies by any standard and I always accommodated her wanting to see the children. After all they were still her grandchildren.

The encouragement I received from my friends was helpful, but as time dragged on and there was no positive result, these friendships became frayed and I understood. The only one who was always there unfailingly with words of encouragement was Gunther, whom my daughters, really only the older ones, did not like. The youngest one was too happy-go-lucky to scrutinize everything and then judge and Jeremy liked this other male—no problem there.

If it had not been for him just being there when I felt like crying because I was afraid, I do not know what I would have done. He'd comfort me by reciting Scripture he had been taught by his parents and it always made me feel better. I knew what he said was true and I just could not think of it myself as I was too upset. He may have been a little off kilter but his affection for me and my children was genuine. The woman who called the house when I was still married to him was a serious love for Marvin and they continued their relationship until she tragically died in a fiery car explosion in 1975. She had been on a drive to town on Democrat Road when she stopped at a service station to get gas. The attendant filled the gas tank and she was on her way, having locked the doors. Soon after she had left the station, her car caught on fire and she could not get out of the car because the doors were locked and the metal of the handle to open it was too hot. She was transported to the burn unit at the MED and lingered there in pain. My ex-husband was devastated and he spent as much time as his work schedule permitted to be with her. Having to come all the way from Whitehaven was difficult and time-consuming, so he asked me if he could spend nights at our house, which I could hardly deny him even though I was completely revolted at this, at the very thought of having to be nice to him when he was so obviously lawless as to engage in a love affair with a married woman while he was still married. It was too much, but the nature of the terrible circumstances superseded my grievances. He'd come back from the hospital and describe the serious condition of his lover, how her skin was burnt to a crisp and black and how she was so swollen because of all the fluid build-up.

Finally, after too long a time of suffering, this woman succumbed. I was told that the woman's husband had had an extra tank put in that car to allow for added capacity for pulling of their boat and that the attendant put the gas into the wrong tank. How that worked I shall never know but that is what I've been told.

Now, in 1977, Marvin had this pretty woman with her two children sharing his apartment.

This girlfriend was in Memphis to get a glimpse of Elvis and so she took a vacation from her husband in California and took a trip down south with their two children. Of course this caused problems with my letting the children visit to play with her children as they were not married and living together. I pointed out to them that I am trying to teach the children the way to live in accordance with Scripture and therefore their arrangement was not conducive to that and I caught a lot of flak over that. She apparently told her husband in California that she was not coming back. She got a job with an insurance company and did very well. She was a very pretty woman who took her prettiness to market, so to speak, and took advantage wherever she could. This time it was my ex-husband whom she fancied and loved. Before that involvement he was just going from one to the other or, if there was no desirable other, he'd come to me.

It was Marvin who actually gave me the idea that I could do what his girlfriend was doing and become an insurance agent. I liked the sound of that and from what I had been told it was not beyond my abilities. I found out all the ins and outs and wherefores and had the girlfriend set up an appointment with her branch manager and he and I met at a restaurant for lunch and discussed the possibility of my working for his company. He pointed out to me that the closest office to my home was in easy walking-distance and it was clearly visible from the window of the restaurant and this was definitely a selling point as far as I was concerned. I was enthusiastic and so hopeful that at long last I could be as modern and independent as I needed to be in order to succeed according to the world standard. After all, I was living in this very same world and I had had to learn everything the hard way. The income potential was there and if this girl could do it, so can I.

Being primed and ready to charge on a brand-new course was exhilarating and scary at the same time. I had to meet with what I feared the most, the world, one on one.

I interviewed with the manager at the branch I would be working at and he thought that I would make a good insurance representative/agent and he introduced me to the twenty-four other all-male agents.

This was 1978 and women were still venturing slowly into male-dominated fields. There were two female secretaries to process the daily transactions and who kept the agents on alert for possible problems with this or that customer.

Every morning I had to gather up my courage, hold my breath, and step into this new world, pretending that I felt just as at home there as they did and they looked to me like this was as easy for them as falling of a log.

I was aspiring to become as comfortable as that and I worked hard to get that done which required a lot of my time when I was not out working. There was a lot of material with which I had to familiarize myself and a lot of terminology that I did not understand, and the whole concept in general and how it all worked together was a bit confusing. It was challenging but I liked it. I had a very nice sales manager who was patient and understanding. He was happily married and he never hesitated to let everybody know that he loved his wife and their two children. Perfect. I was way too serious about learning my new vocation to look for a relationship, and the desire to provide for my children gave me the impetus. I was a debit agent and I had my debit in the Cooper-Young area where I had to collect monthly premiums on existing policies, mostly burial policies for the primarily elderly people living in that old neighborhood. For this I was compensated with a base pay that was more than what I had earned at my former employer after taxes, but I was expected to sell insurance on my debit, add on to the existing policies or wherever I could find a prospective customer. It was even mandatory to sell as much as possible, as the base pay would decrease drastically after a certain time.

I did pretty well and I increased my income which was so wonderful. I had no free time.

Gunther would complain that he no longer got any of my attention and that was surely true. Between work and taking care of my children and studying, there was no time for anything else. I explained to him the seriousness of the situation and that making a living for my children had to come first and it took the time it took. If he wanted to come over and look at me while I was studying after the children were in bed he could come but he couldn't distract me. He promised that he would not distract me and so he came over and watched TV.

On my debit I would encounter some strange things. For instance, there were these two old women living in this old house, looking as drab and depressing as possible. When I first went there and they asked me in, I was greeted by the most intense stench of cat urine I had ever smelled before. It literally took my breath away and I had to brace myself each month I went there to collect. Cats were slinking around and several were on their favorite chair or sofa or windowsill. Some of them would get scared by the presence of a stranger. I didn't want to sit down anywhere as there was cat hair everywhere. I tried to be friendly, considering that I had a hard time not grimacing at having to inhale this nauseating odor. There were too many cats and these old ladies were incapable of looking after them, because they were suffering from dementia. It was sad.

There was another situation where this woman lived by herself on Cox Street in a large house, certainly too large for this lonely old woman. She was pleased to see me and was glad that I was young and pretty and she asked me in. There were only a few sticks of furniture, just the very bare essentials. A bed in the bedroom, a couch in the living room and barrels of some kind here and there which doubled as makeshift tables. I conducted the business standing when I heard this gnawing noise coming from the couch. I asked her what kind of noise that was and she told me matter-of-factly that that were the rats and that they were everywhere and that she had to keep her food in these barrels to keep it away from the rats as they would be eating everything before she got to it. Her kitchen was bare, too, and thank goodness the rats could not get into the refrigerator. It was just too much for me. I told my manager and asked him to call the proper authorities to alert them to this rat-infested house that was also a hazard to the people around her.

The poor woman suffered from some type of senility and didn't grasp that this was no way to live. She must have been eighty-plus years old. The next month the house was empty and condemned and months after that it was razed to the ground.

I actually was more of a social worker, as I got caught up in the various miseries of people's lives and I did the best I could to give comfort wherever and whenever I could. I'd come home, having spent most of my time listening to people who were just waiting for someone to listen to their problems and feel properly sorry for them, and I did but I did not sell a dime's worth of insurance.

My manager was not pleased and he told me that it was imperative to keep in mind that you are in this business to make money, nothing else. I had to keep myself focused on that and that alone and conduct business as a professional agent.

With his keeping me on track I sold some new policies on my debit and even got some brand-new business. It was getting more like I could control my natural tendency for compassion for the poor and helpless. But it was always an effort.

I also noticed women who were literally held captive by their husbands, through the same kind of fear I had when I was working for my mother-in-law. They lacked confidence in themselves because their husbands kept them jailed mentally by berating them and telling them that they could never survive if they had to fend for themselves out in the world, hence they must obey and serve the king of the house in whatever manner he decided. Some of them were so scared of their husbands it was frightening. I was ever so glad I did not have a husband!

On my debit was a street named Oliver Street and my sales manager just got so tickled whenever I had to say "Oliver." At the sales meetings that took place on a weekly basis he would ask me to say "Oliver" for him, which of course I did and then they all would laugh heartily at the funny way I would pronounce it and I just could not get over why they would think that was so funny.

There were three different staffs and each had its own manager at their respective tables in proximity to their offices and mine was at the far end of the large room. My back was turned to the rest of the staffs. Every month the top producer would be identified according to his sales and then recognized and complimented and congratulated on this accomplishment at which time I got to see all the other agents. There were men of all ages and shapes and it was interesting for me to ponder their family lives as most of them were married. I think there were only two or three who were divorced and then of course there was lonely me, the only female in the bunch.

I so enjoyed the sense of independence and self-reliance that was mine to experience for the first time in my life. It was an intoxicating kind of feeling and it certainly made me understand the eagerness of women in general, to abandon their dependence on their husbands, forced upon them by society and tradition, and thereby putting them at risk of being exploited, intentionally or not. The result was the same: the husbands, having been conditioned by centuries of being taught that men were superior to women, felt that therefore they must be in control of the functioning of the family and other affairs. This notion, quite possibly has its origin in Genesis 3 and had been the guiding principle for the early Jews and later on for the Christians, even though Jesus Christ, the Son of God, had already leveled the playing field by making no distinction between men and women in his immediate circle. I leave it up to readers to figure out for themselves who the source of the continuing discrimination against the woman is, and the marginalizing of her strengths and abilities which has remained under-reported over the millennia. This is not to say that we are free of the divine order of things. The difference is that the woman, given a choice, should, of her own volition, choose that which is God-pleasing, thereby ensuring a safe harbor for the children and the husband to thrive in and so being able to cope with the stresses of daily life. She does this because of love for God first and for her family second. This of course allows the same kind of choice to the man, who is prompted by love for God first and for his family second and not because he has been erroneously taught that he is entitled to the superior status. However, these are the things dreams are made of, you say. Not so. God has given us the recipe for such a near-utopian harmony in this world; but the perfection of it lies entirely in the hearts of men and women equally.

But simultaneously with the intoxicating feeling of freedom and self-determination came this inexplicable feeling of emptiness, senselessness and the strange, vague sense of danger lurking, like a trap, in the seemingly wonderful euphoria without any downside. This caused panic inside my heart and I could not figure out why this was so. I knew that I never ever cared for being independent as a goal in itself hence it was distressing for me to have to confess that this whole scenario was foreign to me and certainly not worthy enough a goal to be pursued for its own sake. I was scared once again, as I could not understand anything. Add to this the experience with Elvis and the "mission impossible" it appeared to have been, and the constant feeling of being some sort of prey in this dog-eat-dog world where the hunter was always a man with nefarious intentions. I prayed and cried to God and lamented that I just could not deal with all this and that I surely could not live the single life as there would always be one man or another and I just could not bear the promiscuous lifestyle that had been gaining ground steadily because of my own predilection for sex. I prayed that if it would be in His will to have me marry again, to please show me the man I was to marry as I did not do such a good job the first time. I was dead serious.

My children did not think that there was anything the matter, of course, as children care mostly about themselves and their immediate wants and needs. If they are met, all is right with their world and this is good. All too soon comes the time when they also know that things are not always as they seem and that there can be a whole lot of trouble brewing.

Gunther had to pick my children up from school because my car was being repaired and I had walked to the office and done some work from there. On his way back from school he swung by the office to pick me up. They saw an agent standing at the door and after the children looked at him they said that this guy was weird. Gunther agreed with them and I had to agree with all of them, even though he was the one who offered to help me in the event I needed help. I do not know why I thought that he was weird, but I did.

It had just been a few days before when this agent and I were making small talk in the outer office after he had settled accounts with the secretaries and I just happened to be leaving and had to pass by him. He told me that he was divorced, had one child and that he would probably spend Thanksgiving with his parents in Brownsville. I told him that I was having Thanksgiving as usual at my house for my four children and that was all that was said. Thanksgiving came and went. I knew an elderly gentleman whom I had met some time ago at "Parents Without Partners," which was having its weekly dances a short distance from where I lived and where I had gone dancing occasionally some years earlier. This man had no one to ask him over for the holiday as he was persona non grata with his ex-wife and his adult children.

My children were never opposed to the idea to have someone celebrate with us because I had been teaching them the importance of sharing one's blessings with those who did not have any and since this man had just come out of hospital from some type of heart surgery, he definitely qualified. It was that same kind of adhering to the teachings of Scripture that prompted me to teach my children early on that we must visit the shut-ins, the elderly and the imprisoned, which I did while I was still married. We then visited my husband's grandmother who ended up in a nursing home after a short stint of living on her own when she moved out from my mother-in-law's home.

So it was nothing unusual for my children to have someone join and it was a blessed Thanksgiving. Of course there was always the church service and related activities sanctioned by the church which gave me comfort and security and a connectedness to God to whom I owed everything.

I am sure that Gunther came visiting that day too, because he loved my household and being around as some kind of mentor to my son who found in this friend just what he needed, somebody to be interested in the things he was. It was a very nice day. Conspicuously absent was the children's father but he was preoccupied with his pretty girlfriend—we are now in 1978—and her demand for his attention to her and her children. The children were used to his indifference and really did not seem to care but I was hurting plenty for them and bemoaning their father's disinterest. It was not because he did not love them but rather that he loved himself more.

On December seventh, a Thursday, I went on a work appointment with this weird agent, having approached him to give me the help I now found myself in need of. I was driving, as he explained what he was going to show me and how to do it efficiently. He was also telling me of how hurt he was when he had to leave his daughter and the house he and his ex lived in, where he drew the mural on the wall of the nursery, and how his wife just told him to leave because he would not buy her a car. She stayed home with the baby and felt trapped after she had begun making her own living as a technician at a hospital.

He went to great lengths to explain to me how devastating it was for him to not being able to see his child every day. I felt so very sorry for him. I then talked some about my ex-husband's misconduct and the resulting divorce and the problems with my ex-mother-in-law as my employer. Then we discussed our ideas about what we wanted for our children and it was as if he could read my mind and he said the things to me before I could tell them to him. We exchanged approving glances, somewhat amused at the whole conversation, when it came over me as if someone had switched on a light and said, "Eureka! This is the man for you!"

I was not so sure about this and I leaned back to get a better look at him and thought to myself that he was too ugly, if compared to Elvis, that is, and besides he is weird when, as if I were programmed, I heard myself saying to him, "Do you want to marry me?" He looked at me with shock in his expression and said cautiously, "Let me think about this and I will give you my answer in the morning." That was fine with me as I already knew the answer and we continued on our drive to a particular neighborhood where young marrieds lived. I explained to him the practical advantages and the possibility of his getting custody of his daughter, which I was all for. He was his most charming self and he could charm the socks off you if he set his mind on it. When we were at one of his prospects which he x-dated from the office, he went through the presentation, showed the appropriate product line for the needs of the customer and then in a low-key fashion, did the closing, got the signatures and the first premium and case closed. He was good at this. He'd engage the person in some pleasant chatter about seemingly nothing but on closer inspection it yielded information he would then use to gain the confidence necessary for a stranger to buy from him and not from somebody else. It was fun to watch him. I think we went to three homes in that neighborhood, of which he closed two, with the third one being a call-back. He was definitely in good form and as we had been exchanging friendly glances during the proceedings we decided to continue the evening by going to dinner and we had a very good time chatting about this and that, completely avoiding the topic of marriage. That was already taken care of as far as I was concerned and certainly for him, as he was going to make a decision overnight.

I drove him to the office where he did some office stuff and then he followed me home, which was just around the corner, across the street. The children were now old enough to be left by themselves as the eldest was going on fifteen. I introduced the children to him and him to the children. They did not think anything of it since I introduced them to quite a few men as I did not have anyone to take care of my children properly. They were always there and life did go on. He kissed me goodnight and I remember thinking, *"Hmm, this could really work,"* as his kiss was very pleasant to me. I went to bed calm and collected and certain of his "yes" in the morning at the office. When I got there I asked him immediately what his answer was and he said, "Yes, I will marry you." No surprise there. I was now setting the date when he suggested June of 1979, which was unacceptable to me. Then he suggested Valentine's Day which did not suit me either, when he said, "Can I call my mother first?" I said, "Of course," and handed him one of the many phones in the office. He called his mother and told her that he was getting married to a woman who has four children and he told me that she said, "Well, son, do you know what you are doing?" to which I heard him say yes, he thought so. We decided on the 28th of December 1978. Not once did I wonder how my children would feel about this and that was always on my mind when I thought of another man being around them in place of their father, even in his role and living with us. Not one iota of questioning. I simply took for granted that the way this happened was God-ordained and as such could not be anything but right and therefore good for my beloved children.

I told my future husband at that point that he needed to talk to my pastor which he eagerly agreed to and he was just the most accommodating, kind, fun-loving nice man who simply cemented the conviction that he was indeed the right man with every passing day in my mind. We had to outline a plan for the immediate future which included informing our friends of the upcoming nuptials, the moving of his furniture into my rented house and several other things I cannot remember. We were very busy with preparations for the consolidation of two households, when Gunther from the not-so-distant past showed up and was so shocked to hear that I was getting married to somebody I hardly knew. By then it had only been a week and a half since he had informed me that because he was just like a fifth wheel, hanging around, that he was not coming over for a while, which was fine with me. I could not do any more for him than what I had already done, and no, there was no future in a permanent way in my life for him. I could not believe how very upset he was when he came over and there was my future husband. Gunther tried to reason that if anyone had the right to marry me it was him because he had known me far longer than anyone. My fiancé tried to explain to him ever so nicely that the length of time did not really matter here but my decision to marry him rather than the old friend alone was what mattered. He was inconsolable and told me that he was going to talk to my pastor. We had already been to a conference with my pastor by then, at which time my future-intended gave a stellar performance of the tried and true Christian with the most honorable intentions of taking care of his responsibilities. I was impressed once again and completely certain that this was going to be a very good thing. My fiancé was a Baptist of sorts and that was familiar to me from my first husband. When I questioned him why he was not going to church regularly, he said that all the upset with his ex-wife just turned him away from church but that he would mend his ways and come with us to the Lutheran church, which was also what he promised my pastor who was concerned about my and my children's spiritual welfare. I simply could not see a problem anywhere. My pastor called me and told me to come to his office before I left with the children after school. I did, and he asked me if there were any more men who could possibly make similar claims on me as this Gunther, who had indeed threatened to attend the ceremony and object to the whole thing. The pastor assured me that there would be enough man-power to have him removed but that he could not assure me a peaceful ceremony if there were more than one man and if there were, he needed to know to prepare for the eventuality of more objections. I was totally embarrassed and I had to explain to him the nature of this ongoing friendship with this good friend. I assured him that this was the only one and it really brought home to me the fact that as a single female I was in danger and had indeed to some degree not only become a divorcee with four children, just like my mother, but also a fast-living, promiscuous woman as well, just like my mother! I found out firsthand how detrimental it is for a woman to run these risks with men outside of the sanctity of marriage. It is destructive, dehumanizing, humiliating and diminishes all that woman was created for by God Himself. I was so thankful that I was getting married and would be protected from other predatory males and that my sexuality could be given the expression within the God-sanctioned confines of a church wedding. I made sure that my intended knew that in the event of other children I would stay home to take care of them which he said he was in agreement with and I had no reason to doubt him in the slightest. He also said that we should not have sex but once (compatability factor!) before the wedding which really impressed me and I thought that this man was tailor-made for me.

Needless to say, everybody who knew me and about me, was up in arms about the insanity of marrying a man whom one hardly knew but all the caution was thrown into the wind by me. I could not explain to anyone why I felt that he was right for me. Because God had let me know that this man was the man for me? They would have laughed me off the planet!

There was one occasion, however, that clearly gave me a preview of my future with this man. I just did not want to know it!

We were on our way to Jack's apartment for him to meet with his roommate to sign some necessary papers to adjust the lease agreement. On the way there he confessed that he was living with a woman—the roommate—who was a topless dancer and had had her child taken by the Department of Human Services. For a split second I was struck by a sense of horror going through me from the top of my head to the soles of my feet! I looked at him as he was promising that this was simply going to be his past and that our future would be far better because he realized that he needed to change and I was ever so certain that he meant every word of this at that moment. Add to this that this was on a Monday and our church ceremony was scheduled for that following Thursday. Family and friends had been invited and the Polish couple from my past were giving us the reception in the church basement. It was entirely too embarrassing to have to cancel all this and confess that I had been suffering from a delusion. Jack worked overtime to dispel my misgivings that had reared their unsettling heads. It worked beautifully and we married on the 28th of December 1978 at Christ the King Lutheran Church.

Three days later we went to a New Year's Eve party at my German friend's house. We drank a little wine and welcomed the new year and things seemed fine. On the way home though, my husband launched into a tirade of accusations of all kinds and cussing and cursing at me using profanities of such caliber I had never even heard before and any effort on my part to calm him down by trying to assure him that I was absolutely innocent of the charges he was leveling against me, was useless and made him all the more furious. I was scared of him ever since then and I really could never be certain whether or not he truly cared for me or if his motive to marry me had a more sinister origin.

The unfortunate circumstance that my eldest daughter Rachel was awakened by the noise of his disgusting rantings, which he continued even after we got home, having no regard that he could wake up the children, never mind the filth he was spewing, contributed to the outright hatred my daughter felt for this man and she told me that she had thought all along that he was no good. I was devastated!

This was the introduction to my future!

The following morning he disappeared without letting me know where he was going or when he would be back. In order to understand any of this I figured that he was trying to adjust to his new life which was drastically different from the life he lived before and that he was doubting too whether he had not made a mistake, however sincere his decision to be a better person and father to his own daughter, whom we could possibly get custody of, may have been and probably still was, every now and then. It was not easy for any of us to adjust to all the changes. So I reasoned that we were in the adjustment period and I acted as if nothing had happened at all when he came back. I do think that it was easiest for me to make peace with the strangeness of our situation as I was sincerely laboring under the conviction that God was still in control of my life and I was still trying to do His will and this gave me whatever I needed in order to cope. At that time this was easy to say and believe. I can only say that it is a good thing that we do not know the future. We simply could not deal with it. In my case the saying that ignorance is bliss definitely revealed itself to be ever so true.

As far as my daughter was concerned the damage done was irrevocable. There simply was no way to convince her that this incident was a one-time thing. She knew. This made everything more difficult because she did not hide her contempt for him and her open hostility toward him complicated my relationship with him from then on.

We struck some sort of makeshift truce at the basis of which lay the undeniable sexual compatibility that was extraordinary considering the huge discrepancies of our basic characters. It definitely helped conceal a lot of the ugliness that was at the root of his lapse in common decency, to say the very least.

He attended church with us and made nice with the people there and nobody was any the wiser. I thought that he would eventually adapt graciously to a more rewarding way of life by going through the motions at first and then eventually feel the reward in doing the right thing for the sake of it because it is the Lord's way and surely he wanted to be God-pleasing as well as myself.

We went house-hunting since we were asked to leave the premises by Hortense who had set a time-limit for us to move. This came after Marvin all at once decided to get married to this pretty girl with her two children. It almost seemed as though my ex had been taking his sweet time to enjoy all he could and then at his convenience would marry me again. This completely out-of-left-field marriage of mine caught him off guard and he then was open to the pressure from this girl to marry her. So the time Jack and I had was three months to find other accommodations. This was an exciting time for all of us, particularly for my second daughter, Judy, who was embarrassed by the zip code we lived in and I remember dancing around in the house with her at the prospect of maybe living in a beautiful big house and it felt so good to me to be able to make her happy. She was confirmed that same year and we made it a nice festive celebration at the old domicile and we moved soon after that to our new house.

But before all that could take place, we had to endure my husband's behavior which was mystifying to me. One day would be wonderful and all seemed right with the world and the next he would be inexplicably morose, distant and in a withdrawal mode, withdrawing from me, the children, the house—everything. I had no idea what was going on.

After tax-time he settled the debts which he had accrued over the year after his divorce, which included a tax-debt on the house he and his second wife had been living in. His ex-wife moved into an apartment and they split the furniture from what I understood. I cannot remember at what point he confessed that our marriage was his third. We were already married, that I am sure of, and he went into considerable detail of the reason for this divorce from his first wife. He was too young when he married his high school sweetheart and did not keep his marriage vow to remain faithful. Common enough, but disturbing for me since I had been on the receiving end of that kind of a deal, which he was very aware of as I had always underscored that adultery was the only acceptable reason for divorce according to the Scriptures. He paid off an account with a big retailer I used for me and my children, where I could by on credit. I never once doubted that he was dealing honestly with the money we got from the IRS that year which was considerable as he could claim the children as dependents. It was, of course, to my disadvantage not to ever ask him about his financial dealings but I knew that he was very skillful in protecting his monetary advantage no matter what was going on in his life. He could be so focused on the immediate requirements of any given situation without an ounce of emotion which is something I was never capable of doing myself. It was so foreign to me which was the reason for my giving him authority of everything financial. I had an irrational fear of the finances, contracts, etc. and I was consequently agreeable to his taking control. The whole thing scared me to death. Why I could never understand.

After all the financial dealings were over with, my husband simply moved out and lived with his cousin who lived in Raleigh, a neighborhood where we did insurance business, or rather he did.

I was dumbfounded. As I recall the usual drill was that he picked on something, anything, unpredictable and zeroed in on it, making it into a bone of contention and then he would just up and leave in a huff. The children were as confused as I was but I did not let my husband's erratic behavior interfere with taking care of my children's welfare and carried on as if nothing was wrong. What else could I do? He was gone for two or three weeks and one fine day he called and wanted to meet with me to discuss our future. I was for that and we met at Shoney's on Summer Avenue. He was conciliatory and he decided to come back home and try again. It is entirely possible that he felt disillusioned about what he had expected this marriage could yield him in the sexual arena. For him smoking pot was part and parcel of sex. We were in the aftermath of Woodstock and an unprecedented wave of general lawlessness had permeated the entire society and pot was a very big part of this rebellion against established social norms. My husband was a hippie masquerading in a business suit as a conservative.

I had tried smoking pot and I liked the good mood it put me in. I hated the inhaling and having to hold it in the lungs as it was burning and I just did not like it enough to put myself through this undoubtedly dangerous procedure. I could easily do without the giggling. I voiced my displeasure with his using the toxic plant and tried to impress on him the fact that as a parent it was my responsibility to set an example for my children and smoking pot was not a fitting part of that. He did agree and tried to be discreet but children are no dummies and in this case they had good noses that could recognize that peculiar sweet aroma of pot, even when he smoked it in his car as it permeated his clothes.

He knew from the beginning that I was conservative to the core—after all, I was eight years older than he was and I had a longer period of living by long-established rules which had their origins in the accepted use of Scripture's statutes of God. It was probably well within the realm of possibility that he wanted a conservative life as far as financial success was concerned and all the trappings that signified that success but secretly was hoping that he could have kinky goings-on in his personal, i.e., sexual life. He repeatedly rebelled against my conventional view of things and my determination to keep on teaching my children these values. It is worth noting that with his continuing smoking pot the moodiness which he displayed so often was a result of that. In addition he liked to drink beer. I was more a wine person. Culturally I was conditioned to prefer wine and I saw nothing wrong with having an occasional glass of wine which I had always made sure I had on hand. Likewise I had no trouble accepting his preference for beer and we made sure we had some of it on hand. The Lutheran Church does not forbid the ingesting of alcohol, they only warned about overindulgence and strongly preached against losing control over one's ability to think and act responsibly. It was a problem for many people, to be sure. Life is hard and everybody is looking for relief. I can understand this very well. It is very hard to refrain from such an easily available legal "sedative."

We cobbled together some type of fairly peaceful co-existence of opposites and it made life bearable, as it was at times very exciting. My husband was a charmer and I was like putty in his hands as he was very chivalrous and instinctually protective of the one he focused his attention on. It made up for the negatives in our relationship. My strong sexuality came in handy to keep him satisfied in this area, I assumed, and it did bring us closer together. Before I knew it I was pregnant with our child but all the stress and strain of our marriage and the impending move to a new house, the children, and work caused me to lose it in a miscarriage.

My husband had a desire to live in midtown so we had looked for a home there. We had found one that we all liked, but for some reason we ended up in the Blue Ridge Park area. But we were still in the Memphis proper.

In May of 1979 we moved and it was a move filled with expectations of a bright future for everyone, including my husband's daughter, Beth, who was barely two years old and a most delightful little girl whom we all grew to love. She was just such a cutie and such a happy little camper you could not help but love her.

We settled into our house. There were three bedrooms, a living room, dining room, kitchen with washer and dryer in a closet in the breakfast room area, and a roomy den. It was a ranch-style house and had a fenced-in backyard with an Esther Williams swimming pool, which was partially in-ground where the deep end was and the shallow end was above ground. We loved it. A swimming pool of our very own! We really must be doing well! We all thought we were and my husband appeared to enjoy the admiration that came his way from my children, except the eldest. She simply did not like anything and just played nice if there was no way she could not get out of it. We'd all be playing board games which my husband liked to indulge in with the children and which was an enjoyable time for all participants but this eldest child of mine preferred to stay in her room and read instead. It was a constant balancing act for me to keep these two warring forces living in a standoff. It was a do-able condition for me as I was given the necessary wisdom by God Himself to deal with everything to assure the happiness of the whole family unit without going insane myself in the process.

My husband convinced me that we could not allow my eldest daughter to hide in her room with a book because at some point we as parents must exercise our authority to force, if necessary, her to join in the family activities, as this separateness of hers could possibly grow into all kinds of trouble down the line. So we moved her and her sister into the living room, where the youngest and the middle daughter were sleeping. Now the youngest, Susan, was sleeping in the room by herself, the two older girls shared the converted living room and the son, Jeremy, had his own room from the start. The youngest girl, Susan, was outgoing and always happy to join in any family fun, so there was no problem with her isolating herself in her room which was at the end of the hall. Now the eldest had to contend with being close to the center of activity, which she did not like. She was going to a public high school, as the Lutheran school only went up to the eighth grade. The conventional wisdom at the time was that by the time the child reached the age of fourteen, the value system was in place, and I felt comfortable at her being tested, so to speak, if she had indeed learned to cope in a Christian fashion in a public school. The next in line for this adventure was the second daughter, Judy. The son, Jeremy, and youngest daughter, Susan, had to be driven to school and picked every day as they were still going to the church-school. I have to add here that I paid a very small amount; the Lutheran Church paid for the rest.

We were in dire financial straits as the monthly expenses had increased substantially and there was no other solution than to have them all go to public school after the eighth grade. The older girl had to ride public transportation as we had placed her in a school outside our district because the local school did not offer German, which Rachel wanted to study.

10

The Edge of Reality

My husband had changed from where we had been working together to another insurance company in hopes of making more money. I remained working at the same place and it was convenient since my office was on the same street as the grade school, only in different part of town. I had to work some evenings and my husband was gone too and I just assumed he was working too. He had outlined the budget and I was to pay the bills. I had no trouble doing this as I was accustomed to this ever since I was married for the first time and it had always been important to me to pay my bills on time, which was not the case with my husband. There was never enough money for incidentals which my husband absolutely refused to acknowledge were indeed an actual necessity. If I called his attention to this he would get so horrifyingly ugly to me, call me names, berate me in front of my children and simply pretend that he did not hear the facts as they were. I cannot describe how this affected me. Never in my life had I been accused of mishandling money or of being stupid or incompetent. I was so afraid of these humiliating outbursts of his as I could feel the confusion this type of behavior engendered in my children. While Rachel was only saying, with her gestures and glances, "I told you so!" the younger one, Judy, quietly used this turn of events to lay a solid foundation of rebellion toward me, completely unnoticeable in the beginning.

My ex-husband did not pay his child support anymore, claiming that the children now were my new husband's problem. There could not have been anything worse than him saying that to me which I foolishly related to my husband who went into a drunken tirade after he had come home very late "from work" one night. Even though he was very much aware this kind of language was unbearable to me he used the most vulgar expressions and it felt to me as if I was being beaten with a club. Of course the children could not help but hear and I am sure they wondered what I would do about all this. I was aghast! At the time it did not occur to me that my children were puzzled about my marrying a man who did things they were taught all their lives not to do. I did what I could in the way of explaining Jack's behavior, and since he always came up with some impressive move to cover up his serious transgressions or at least make us forget about them which always worked for me, and since I was hopelessly optimistic, we sort of muddled through. I never felt free of the fear of the next horrendous display of disrespect toward me. Sometimes there would be a break and he would lull me into a state of relaxation. I would let my guard down and act as though things were normal. It was one of those nice times when I got pregnant with our first son. There was simply nothing worse for me that could have happened. He was not glad to say the very least.

Things deteriorated at a fast clip. We had no money and I had to contact Hortense and ask her to help me taking care of the children because her son did not do what he was supposed to and had been so good and faithful in doing before I re-married. She said that she would call her son and see what she could do. She also told me on one of our visits that she had serious doubts about the girl he married and that she thought that she was a lying so-and-so. Her efforts resulted in one single payment and he was already far behind and I had the trouble with the bouncing checks his wife mailed. It was a very trying time. I had to sell my gold jewelry which had been given to me by the Kreuzfelders in Germany.

This money tided us over, but some more consistent source of added funds had to come or we would end up in the poorhouse.

I called Hortense again and she agreed to meet with me Monday morning. That never happened. Her daughter, Sue, had taken her to her house for the weekend and the blood-pressure medicine had been left behind. Hortense had gotten herself so upset over this child-support issue and not being able to keep our appointment because she had been whisked to her daughter's house which left her without transportation that she had a heart attack and was rushed to the hospital where she had to watch a fight between Edward, Jr., and Marvin over his irresponsibility. She went into cardiac arrest soon thereafter and died. My ex-husband called me in tears and accused me of killing his mother.

I was extremely sorry at her demise but the blame for her death was not on me. It was a confluence of different circumstances that killed her and all of her children contributed to it just by being themselves. Besides when your time is up, it's up and there is nothing you can do about it.

I sought legal help to force Marvin to do what he must by law for his children. As these things always take a long time, I went through hell and back many times over with this husband of mine.

In the settlement of Hortense's estate she had left her car to my eldest daughter. Marvin bought this car from us and we bought a used car with that money for the eldest who had to learn to drive. I was so glad that Jack took it upon himself to teach her and she took the test and passed it the first time, got her driver's license and could now drive herself and Judy to school and back. Both the girls had jobs babysitting a woman's children, alternating, and then it became a job for only Judy, as the older one got a job at Wendy's. I had to be the driver for all the children's needs in addition to working, cooking, cleaning and being with child. I know God was with me, I could not have lived through this without His help, but at the time I was often wondering whether He even knew of all the trouble I was in.

Jack had this elaborate sound-system that consisted of the stereo-unit and big speakers which he suspended from the ceiling and he enjoyed his music which I really hated. Bob Dylan, Elton John, David Bowie, The Beatles and so on, the music of the sixties and early seventies. To me this was music coming straight from hell. The lyrics were glamorizing evil in various forms and I detested it. He had built a structure of wood which he painted black and he stored all his records there.

I treasured my classical music and had held on to the Elvis records just as keepsakes and besides, I had spent money on them, so I figured that I might as well keep them.

As far as my connection to Elvis was concerned, I only told my husband of the essential things which were that I had loved the man and as he was now dead this was a dead issue. However I could not help but wonder what all this Elvis drama was about but it just never made any sense, no matter from which point I looked at it. I concluded that this was obviously over since he was gone. My life at that time was as dangerous to me as walking in a minefield. I never knew when something was going to wreak havoc in my daily life as there was much ammunition just waiting for a careless step and bam, hell was here again. In fact to compare our household and my relationship with Jack to a war zone would not be an exaggeration. When my husband played his devil-music, as I termed it, I left the house. As my son, Jeremy, grew older he learned to like this type music, only that he preferred the hellish sounds of his generation which was heavy metal and I hated that too and warned him not to listen to this kind of music. He was not allowed to play it in our house.

When I was about four months along my ob-gyn took the required amnio since I was now thirty-nine years old and the result was that I was urged to have an abortion as there was something wrong with the baby. I thought this to be strange and I simply did not believe the findings and so I did nothing. Several weeks later the doctor's nurse called me and told me that they ran another culture and I could go ahead and go for full term. I had never thought of anything else.

Who can remember the reasons for all the fights? We fought constantly over one thing or the other. The older children's working helped some as they could provide for their own private needs themselves and I took some other children to school for money as the single mother needed transportation for her children who were going to the same school as mine. Other than that I economized everywhere I could, bought the cheapest everything and day-old bread at the discount bread store. I hung the clothes on the clothesline outside.

When I was in my sixth month we had a fight and I was just indignant at my husband's total lack of concern for me. He said, among other things that I should have gone ahead and had the abortion since it was the mailman's child anyway for all he knew. I thought I had heard every conceivable insult, every derogatory utterance there was but he always came up with another perverted thing which put me in a tailspin of desperation and acute pain deep within.

After a lot of crying I would tell myself that I needed to get away from this monster of a man. He was like Dr. Jekyll and Mr. Hyde and I just could not take it. Just before the baby was due we had another confrontation and I was in a constant state of upset. I went to the doctor for my weekly visit when he put me in the hospital as the baby was on the way to be born. My husband was not aware that I had a doctor's appointment as he simply did not care. He was really surprised when they summoned him to the hospital. I had nothing for the baby yet. I just did not have any money and he did absolutely nothing for his child. Nothing. Though he was always quick to keep up appearances when somebody was around. I had mentioned to his mother several times how deplorable her son was and what she thought I should do about it. She did the same thing he did when he did not want to deal with something, she just ignored it. And besides, she had told me some time ago that her son's first wife was really the only girl he really ever loved.

There was no help coming from her. She was going through her own problems with her husband who was an alcoholic, according to her. He was my husband's stepfather. His biological father had been killed.

Our baby's was jaundiced, so he had to stay in the hospital. We took him home three days later. By then I had rounded up some baby things from a thrift store and somebody gave us a baby bed.

The baby slept with us in our bedroom, where I had emptied a big drawer of the hutch and put the baby in there for the first few weeks which worked well. My husband found his Dr. Jekyll-side and at least was not a hazard to my health and welfare which was something for him. On Saturdays and Sundays it was nonstop football and beer-drinking. It was always the same noise coming from the TV and the continuous, "Ilona can you get me another beer?" I was married to an all-out American moron! I have never understood this national obsession with sports. Granted, sports are a good thing in and of themselves as they promote teamwork, discipline and physical fitness but this fever-pitched competition is just ridiculous. On occasion I would join him in watching an important game and I can only say that it surely would raise my blood pressure with all the suspense as to who was going to do what in order to have the favorite team to win. It was entirely too much excitement for my high-strung personality, but I liked the fun everybody seemed to have watching these games, and lucky me if Jack's favorite team won. No ugly outbursts of displeasure and the following bad mood that could hang on for quite a while as all the details would be discussed over the phone with somebody.

When football season was over, we had basketball and then baseball. But I'd rather have my husband be at home and annoy me with his endless ballgame watching than having him away from home. I needed him there and I was determined to make it as pleasant as I knew how. He did take advantage of this, which, when it did not suit him, did not make any difference and he went off to who knows where. I found his behavior extremely taxing and I said "hello" to Valium again. I needed some relief from that pressure which was making me nervous. Our son, Richard, was a very crying baby and I had to devote a lot of time just trying to calm him down. At night I would camp out in the den on the couch and keep him on my chest which was the only place that would relax him enough to go to sleep. It did nothing for my beauty sleep. I had to be fully alert the next day as I had so many responsibilities to tackle. Everybody got a good night's sleep and that was very important to me. I now was on paid maternity leave and I took my job as wife and mother very seriously and I told my husband that things pertaining to the running of the house and taking care of the children were my duty. In the afternoon, when the baby took a nap, I took a nap too and it carried me through the rest of the day. Wherever I went, the baby went with me. That is how I liked it and besides there was no other way most of the time and when I would have to leave him, which happened very rarely, I could not wait to come back and take care of him. I just did not trust anyone to do as good a job as I, his loving mother.

When I had to go to court for the hearing on the child-support case against my ex-husband I had to take baby with me. I know that it was definitely influencing the judge to practically throw the book at Marvin because it looked as though he was leaving me high and dry with an infant, having to struggle to get him to pay for all the other children too! I could not help but feel sorry for Marvin because it was not true but I was in no shape to correct the judge.

My husband would, for whatever reason, bring his little daughter, Beth, outside of the scheduled every-other-weekend visits which was putting more pressure on me but I managed. He had a bracelet made for himself with the name of his daughter on it. He had a small boat which he also gave the name of his daughter. In other words, he was crazy about his daughter but I put my foot down when he, under the influence of some type of drug (most likely pot) wanted to have her sleep with him. He fought me like mad and kicked me in the shin while he was holding her in his arms. He then left with her. I had to go to the emergency-room and have my injury looked at by a doctor. It was only a superficial wound from the impact of his shoe and nothing was broken, though it felt like it and I limped for a few days. He had smacked me around numerous times but I fought back and hurt him, too. The very idea to strike a woman was too much for me to take quietly. After he got back with the cutie, Beth, he was very apologetic and he did no longer insist on having the child sleep with him.

We had had another confrontation about something that he chose to make a bone of contention for no apparent reason as far as I could see and he left in an agitated state for who knows where and, as was a regular occurrence, would come home completely drunk. If I knew what was good for me I would lie down beside him until he would go to sleep, otherwise he would accuse me the next day of not loving him. If he was only mildly buzzed he would take the liberty of indulging in lambasting my eldest daughter in the most vicious and totally unfair way. This cut me to the quick, and when he was finally through with his disgusting, ever-so-hurtful rantings, I would just lie there, crying softly, thinking that this just could not be real. There just weren't men like this and I was so deeply hurt at this outright assault on me as a woman in general and as a mother in particular and I truly hated him from the bottom of my heart. I never mentioned this uncontrolled display of utter disregard for my feelings on any level, but I was devastated and realized that I could not handle this situation. So I took an overdose of Valium and went to sleep in the hope that I would not wake up.

My husband took care of all he could as I discovered when I woke up and I resigned myself to the fact that I had to do whatever it took to keep on going and think of my children which gave me renewed strength.

The warfare between us continued and it was grueling, with no sign of change for the better. Considering everything and by talking to people about my situation, I became convinced that a divorce was inevitable. Of course I could not square this with the certainty that this was God's plan for me, as God hated divorce as much as I did, but at that point I just thought that it must have been the devil himself who got permission from God to ensnare me in this diabolical relationship and I wasn't able to deal with it and hope to survive.

I contacted the lawyer I used in my first divorce from the habitually unfaithful husband of ten years and I told Jack of my plans to divorce him. He warned me that I did not know what I was up against and he was right. I got a front-row seat to the true nature of this man as he was displaying an incredible nastiness of character. He was so calculating, treacherous, merciless, conniving, and totally ruthless and unscrupulous. In his defense against my allegations of mental and physical cruelty he took the most generic, completely innocent occurrences and twisted them in a way only an evil person is capable of doing, as he knew very well that this was nothing but lies, lies and some more lies. By the time he got through he had painted me as an unbalanced woman who was quite possibly unfaithful, out of control, and only interested in his money. I quickly realized that I could not successfully defend myself in court or anywhere else against such blatant dishonesty. I could not fathom any of this and I was absolutely horrified! This was truly a daunting task which was way outside my capability to tackle as I was already so emotionally drained and scared of this devil. He held all the trump cards. I had lost everything in this short marriage, everything. My financial independence, such as it was, was gone. My furniture had been sold at a yard sale and the money used for common property over which he was fighting me. I had no job but I had an infant whom I would have to leave with somebody to be able to go to work which I had never been able to do—I just was never a modern woman. It was too, too much and when he made overtures for reconciliation, I did not hesitate long to take a deep breath and mustered the hope for a better tomorrow which he told me we were going to have from now on.

Little did I know, or even could have ever be able to think, that he would then go and get a lawyer and file for divorce against me.

At the same time, he was qualifying for a trip to Germany and he asked me if I wanted to come along as it would give me an opportunity to see my family. I did not care to see my family or my country as I was far too upset about the impending divorce, for which the papers had been finished and needed to be signed by me to go forward.

At practically the last minute, I decided to go along to Germany. Preparations for the wives of the winners had already been done weeks before, so there was no problem, and I had a current passport, as I had at one time even thought of returning to Germany with the baby—well he was a year old by then—and I thought I could give the older children into the custody of their biological father as they were too old to acclimate to foreign surroundings and another language. This only shows my acute desperation. I had done the same thing in my first marriage. I was going to take my children (then 2, 3, 7, and 8) with me to Germany.

My husband's mother was called to take care of the household and the children.

Off we went to Germany. I cannot remember much about this trip. We went to see my mother and my sister and my father, brother, cousin and my aunt and, of course their wives and children.

While this was nice I must have seemed to them that I was like out of my mind because the circumstances in my personal life were at the point of doing me in and yet it just was not the time to let anyone know! It was unreal.

The only thing I remember vividly was the horror of being so far away from where my heart was and it was not in Germany. The feeling of hanging between heaven and hell and being in free-fall into hell was ever so real, and I was desperately trying to gain a foothold on something so I could regain some sense of balance. I realized that I had no other choice but to continue the dance with the devil which

I had termed my relationship with this man. And so it was. He was telling me how he would love to have a daughter who would look like me when we were making love. The sugar-lies came like salve on my wounded spirit and I willingly believed every word he was saying. As the trip continued to its conclusion it was as if we had been on our honeymoon, which we never had after the wedding, when we went to an inexpensive hotel somewhere in the countryside, not far from home, for a weekend.

It was a renewed dedication of doing everything and then some to keep this marriage going and the times of harmony in the household were longer lasting. Rachel was looking forward to graduating from high school and Judy was making her own plans, of which I knew nothing. I remember her saying, with contempt for me in her voice, that she was going to marry somebody who would give her everything. By everything she meant the big, fancy house, servants, etc., etc.—her idea of happiness at any rate. She was working at Wendy's too and came to know all kinds of people but she never told me anything and her sister did not either. They must have had an agreement between themselves not to let me know anything, as they both were disappointed that I did not sign the papers to agree to the divorce. Not only did I not get rid of this horrid man but I became pregnant with our second child which I sincerely hoped would be the daughter he longed for, since his girl with his former wife had moved to Chicago with her mother. Rachel and Judy really did not care to be around me and my husband and I could certainly understand this. Add to this the fact that Jack convinced me that in order for him to be the head of the household, which I wanted him to be in keeping with the divine order of family life, he should have authority over the children, all of them. I saw that this request was reasonable for someone who was going to be a good father and husband from then on and I agreed. I did not know that he was going to be unreasonable at times and make life unnecessarily difficult, especially for Jeremy.

The trip to Germany was in 1981 and I had settled into life with this extraordinarily problematic man whom I hated so much one moment and was so attracted to and loved the next. When they say that a child is a tie that binds, they are certainly speaking the truth. The presence of a child, a sweet combination of both people who had promised to love one another till death do them part, is indeed a very strong tie that binds, but it applies more to the woman than the man. It was through this boy we had together that I, his mother, out of love extended love to his father.

In early 1982 my cousin announced his visit with us here in Memphis. I was excited to have him come and meet all my children and he wanted to do some sightseeing and relax as his doctor had prescribed rest and relaxation. I had to tell him that we did not have the means to afford much in that way and he assured me that he would take care of these things himself. He was a successful businessman who was looking to expand his business to the U.S. He brought each of us a present and he bunked with us for a few days. He wanted to visit New York City and wanted me to come along, as I knew more about it than he did, having lived in New York for a while. I absolutely did not want to leave my family. My son, who was just starting to walk, and ever so cute, was pulling on my heartstrings but I had to accommodate Wolfgang. I thought nothing of it as my husband was all for it. He and my cousin seemed to get along well. So my cousin and I went via airplane to New York City and back. We stayed in separate rooms. It was very cold and riding the subway and walking down Fifth Avenue to see the high-end stores in which he was interested, made me so cold, I felt like an icicle and literally had to take a hot bath to thaw. I was miserable and yet I had to be pleasant and cheerful and make him think I had fun. It was grueling.

After our return from New York, Wolfgang insisted on visiting the house Elvis lived in. He knew of my fascination with Elvis, of course, and I had no choice but to accommodate him. When I said that I had put this Elvis-mess, as I called it to myself, behind me, I was very serious and I did not like to be reminded of it.

At that time Graceland just sat there. I had hoped that after a certain length of time this interest in Elvis would die a natural death and I would be home-free. Every now and then I heard rumblings of turning the house into a tourist attraction and I will never forget how agitated I became at the thought of having a visible reminder of Elvis staring me in the face, so to speak, and have his life and his affairs regurgitated ad nauseum. I was asking myself why they can't let the dead man rest in peace and shut up about him and his miserable life as I would then be better off by far.

My cousin and I drove there and I looked around trying to connect on an emotional level to my experience in the past but there was nothing there. It was just some house and some gravesite and I went through the motions of a tour guide and matter of factly explained little details I could remember from personal experience.

My cousin was impressed and assured me that this was an important thing for him to have done as everybody in Germany was crazy about Elvis and would never forgive him if he did not come back with descriptions of Elvis's house. Go figure!

I could not help, however, being puzzled at my strange, un-emotional reaction. Granted, I had never liked the house and never had the desire to go inside although I could have, but to me this house was like the pit of hell with all sorts of unholy goings-on that I did not want any part of. It was rather odd, I have to admit, but in a way it made sense. The Elvis the world knew and loved had lived here in the ways of the world and I just had no connection to that as I only knew the spiritual man.

I had not learned yet that Jack was the treacherous devil that he rarely displayed himself to be. I could in no wise ever be able to imagine the degree of his diabolically manipulative, opportunistic, calculating, evil scheming. I had no knowledge of such things and never in a million years would have believed that I would find myself yoked together with such a man, had somebody told me of my fate.

After Wolfgang had left to return to Germany all hell broke loose. Jack accused me of having an affair with my cousin, saying that I could not wait to go off with him to New York. The fact that Wolfgang gave me earrings and a necklace showed that he still loved me. True, my cousin still carried the torch for me but it takes two to tango and I never had reciprocated in a romantic way. Besides, I had explained all this before and the jewelry was from my aunt whom he had met the year before in Germany. It was unbelievable that he hounded me mercilessly and then, to top it off, act as the injured party and go off with his friends and come home drunk out of his mind. I was beside myself. Here I was, having done nothing to warrant this punitive conduct of my husband's and yet there was nothing I could do. I was hurt at his tasteless insinuations and his low-life accusations and I can honestly say that I was just too dumb to get away from him or I was in some kind of state of mind that allows such abusive behavior to go on.

My father died that year and my cousin took over his property to tend to it, as it was adjoining my cousin's property, which he had developed into a sort of miniature country estate, with stables and paddocks and a beautiful huge swimming pool in a natural setting of shrubs, bushes, flowers and trees which made it a visual treat. The house was an A-shaped structure with windows everywhere and an open fireplace of huge dimensions that was actually used as the cooking stove in the winter. He also had an indoor pool that he could jump into for an early morning swim before he went off to work. He lived in Bernlohe but he also had an apartment over his atelier. If he felt like it he and his wife would stay there and then go to their fancy digs in the country. My cousin's wife was a good horsewoman and she appeared to be a very nice person. They never had any children and after some years of trying unsuccessfully to become parents they decided to go their separate ways.

Money was always in very short supply and I literally subsisted on the bare essentials. I bought some winter clothes for our son from a person in a low-income neighborhood, where we should have lived. Another poor mother sold the clothes of her youngest child for next to nothing, which was all I could afford, and it was heaven-sent because he simply had nothing to wear to protect him from the cold. Since I had to take him with me wherever I went, it was an unavoidable necessity which simply fell under the heading of incidentals and my husband did not acknowledge them as real. It is ever so true that we lived as if we had money but all the while we were poorer than the people who lived in trailers. Well, it was more that I lived in poverty with my children. It did not apply to my husband who bought what he took a fancy to.

After a while the agreement I had made to let him have authority over my children felt to me as if I was delivering them up to be sacrificed and it was then that I could understand to some degree what Abraham must have felt like when he was told to kill his son Isaac. But way down deep I had the sense that everything would be all right in the end, no matter how impossible it seemed to be. So I followed through, but it was most troubling to me since I had no idea how this would play itself out. It was indescribably horrifying. Naturally, as I was too much of a mother, I would always run interference and argue in defense of Jeremy. It only made it quite clear to me that my husband had a dislike for my son and took it out on him, and my protective measures would make him so angry at me that he would fall back into these tirades about me and my inabilities and all this in the most vulgar way. It was terrible. Then at other times he would be so helpful to Jeremy. He would sign for a dirt bike my son wanted so badly. I did not like dirt bikes and motorcycles, as I thought them to be dangerous. I would not put it past my husband to make sure that the boy got what he wanted and so take care of two things at the same time, which were to show Jeremy that he loved him, after all, and to upset me and let me know that he really did not care if I wanted or didn't want him to have a dirt bike. It was understood that Jeremy had to pay for it with the money he earned from a part-time job, cleaning an office and cutting grass in the summer to which I had to drive him until he learned to drive.

We were all constantly caught in this trap of never knowing which way to think or feel. It changed practically overnight from being so sure that he loved us to thinking that he could not care less what we thought or felt.

One time my son wanted to go somewhere and I told him no. He went to my husband and asked him and Jack said yes, which made me quite angry and I told him never to undercut my authority just because he now had been given equal authority over the children. This made him furious and he started to hit me. Judy, who had had just about enough of him, blocked his striking me and she got hit by him instead. She called the police and when they came, my husband was in complete control and very reasonably explained that I was overwrought because I was high-strung and that nothing really happened that was worth bothering them with and they took his word for it and left.

This was shortly after we had returned from Germany. One afternoon all of us were in the backyard, busy with something, and our baby son, Richard, was there too, just playing. All of a sudden Jack noticed that the boy had practically disappeared, in a split-second, and he asked everybody whether they had seen him. Nobody had and all of us knew nothing of where the boy was. He had fallen into the pool at the deep end and he was at the bottom, just lying there. Jack jumped right in and went to the bottom to fish him out and I was hysterical and all this boy did was cough once or twice, bat his eyes and act as if he had just been on an interesting adventure. We were so relieved and I was so gratified that I had such an alert and capable husband after all. It is those kinds of things I would have never been able to handle and he was so good at so many things. It was truly confusing how to feel about him. He bought himself a motorcycle, even though we did not have enough money for me to have any insurance to pay for the delivery of our second child, who was on the way, but that simply did not concern him. He did not have any coverage for pregnancy in his insurance plan as he did not want any more children at the time he signed on with this other agency a year earlier. I was no longer working and that just did not matter to him. I ended up going to a clinic for the indigent and we had to pay a minimal amount which covered the care during the pregnancy, the delivery, and the after-care.

Against my wishes he purchased this motorcycle and rode it whenever he wanted to indulge in his bachelor fantasies, complete with pot-smoking and who knows what. There were many times that I wished that he would get killed on that thing—many, many times.

Judy became very resentful toward me and I could never tell her anything that she did not take the wrong way. She had it in her head that I did not want her to be happy because I had asked her one time why she was wearing so much makeup and starving herself into a skinny, raily shadow of herself and implied that she would attract the attention of boys who cannot be trusted. I tried to explain that the opposite sex responds to the wrapping, so to speak, and if she did not want to look like a prostitute why put all the war-paint on? Our relationship became more strained and she cut herself off from me emotionally. In the mornings, when she would make her way to the bathroom at the end of the hall, she would give me a contemptuous glance and turn her nose up at me and shuffle herself off down the hall to the bathroom. It was irritating and I had no idea how to reach her.

One fine day she came to me and asked me if she could get married. She was only seventeen at that time and I said that she could not since she had another year of school ahead of her. She then asked me if I would give my permission to marry if she had her high school diploma to which I said yes, thinking that would take another year and by then she would think herself out of love and she would opt for college after all, even though she had never shown any interest in college. Quite the opposite, as she loathed her older sister striving to go to college and become a teacher which I wholeheartedly encouraged. I also was aware that college was not for everybody and there was nothing wrong with that either. Just because one does not have a college degree does not make a person worth any less as long as they earn their keep in an honest way. She was aware of this. Well, this girl decided to go to summer school that year, got her diploma and came to me and said, "You told me that you would give me your permission to get married if I had my high school diploma. I have it now and I want to go with this sailor to Seattle where we will get married." I was completely caught off guard but I figured that with the kind of determination she had shown, she was going to do just what she set out to do. There was little chance that I could keep her from making this mistake no matter what and I had said that I would give my permission. I signed the paper she handed me which was probably drawn up with the help of her intended and it was a very short time after that, that she was gone. She was so excited to finally be rid of me, my husband and everything that had bothered her and she had a head full of happy dreams of a much better life for herself. Of course I wished her everything she dreamed of. Had I not given my permission she would have run away with this sailor and I would not have known where she was or how to reach her. I was left out in the cold either way.

If I had been completely unprepared to deal with a man like my husband and I had had no idea that such men existed, I was just as completely unprepared to deal with my growing children. I had simply no idea that they would not do as they had been taught all their lives, at home, in Sunday school, elementary school and church. I took it for granted that they would be like me when I was a young person growing up in Germany under trying conditions. I was very disappointed and on some level angry with them for not obeying God's directives, as given to us in the Scriptures. I took the only position I could and let things alone and have LIFE teach them that it is for our benefit to do things God's way.

Judy called after she arrived in Seattle and they were married which I never doubted and she seemed happy and I was happy for her.

I was getting close to the delivery date of what I had prayed from the beginning would be a daughter. I did not have the amnio because this hospital, a charity hospital run by nuns, did not insist on one and I did not want one as my experience with amnio was not so good the first time. I was now forty-one years old and should have had one. I was miserable being so big and it was such a relief to go in the pool and have the water buoy the weight but as this was a particularly hot summer, the utility bill was higher, too, with running the air conditioner more. My husband gave me the choice: I could either have the pool and no air-conditioning during the day or no pool and all day air-conditioning. I thought he had lost his mind but I did the best I could to economize and still have it comfortable for him when he came home in the evening. It just showed that he simply did not care which meant that he did not love me. An unpleasant thought indeed when I was just about to give birth to his dream-daughter! We now had the child-support issue solved and the money was coming in regularly through the court. Beth, from his second marriage, was with us too and she enjoyed the pool just like everybody else.

In a way I had ended up in the same situation I was in when I worked for my ex-mother-in-law, Hortense—in total dependence, the only difference being the taskmaster. The system was the same, only that this was at an accelerated degree and the torment was so intense and on an intimate level and a continuous presence and there was no way out other than to hope and pray that God would help me through this—and I needed some serious help.

It was about one or two Saturdays before the birth of the baby and the younger children were with my husband, as was Beth, Jack's daughter.

The eldest was out too, running errands to prepare for moving to St. Louis where she had earned a scholarship to attend Washington University to study German.

Our son was napping and so was I and since I was quite big I was on my back sleeping when I could feel something on my cheek, it felt like a breath, but I thought it could have been an insect of some kind and I sleepily brushed it away trying not to have this wake me up completely when I felt it again, only that this time it was unmistakable—it was a breath on my right cheek. I was startled and got up thinking that there had to be somebody in the house and I was going to find out who and let them have it because I was not amused at being awakened from my nap, which I sorely needed. I got up and looked in the kitchen. If it had been in the closed-off part of the house, separating the front rooms from the bedrooms by a door, I would have heard that since I am a light sleeper, so I did not look there. I went into the front section, through the French doors, and there I saw a figure clothed in white, without any shoes. I was sort of transfixed at this spectacle. I wanted to see who this was and as I was scanning slowly upwards to see the figure dissipated and I was perplexed as I realized that this had something to do with Elvis. However, because I had spent years trying to make sense of this ordeal I had to endure I was in no wise eager to go down that road again, particularly now that he was dead, which should have been the end of it. But I also had the feeling that this was just a way to prepare me for things to come. I thought it was an outright imposition because I had so much to deal with and did well just to keep up with everything and trying to stay out of the traps that were at every turn, just waiting for me to fall into them.

I mentioned this apparition to my eldest daughter and she said, "Mommy, this is weird." I agreed and put it out of my mind.

A short time later, Rachel was to move on campus and Beth was to be brought back to her mother in Chicago. I was busy as a bee getting everything ready when my water broke. It was then decided that all the children were going with my husband on that trip and that I was going to be brought to the hospital on their way out of town. I helped them pack their things too and made sure in Mother Hubbard-fashion that everything was done, so fun could be had by all. On the way to the hospital I was in excruciating pain and the examining doctor said that the baby was on its way to be born. I had no idea that they did not use any drugs to lessen the birth pains and as I was still in agony and they kept on telling me to keep on pushing and nothing happened when I told them that I did not want that baby and they said that it was too late for that now, when my daughter Tracy finally made her grand entrance into this world. My family saw the baby and they left to go on this scheduled necessary trip. I spent the most peaceful time in that hospital.

The baby stayed with me in the room and I took care of her by myself and the nurse just came every now and then to check on me and the baby. It was the most rewarding time I had ever spent with any of my children after they were born. I was not groggy from drugs and so able to care for my baby's needs myself which I enjoyed immensely. Nobody knew that I was in the hospital and it was heaven. After two days my family came by on their way back from the trip, picked the baby and me up and home we went. I had no time or opportunity to rest from then on. My husband was tired from all the driving but he still wanted his beer. I did all the washing and sorting and putting away of stuff. The children helped me, of course, and told me of the horrific conduct and bad language of their stepfather but there was nothing I could do about it. Tracy had to be cared for too, and dinner had to be made and it was a constant running my legs off from then on. Richard was so happy to see his mommy and I was ever so happy to have them all back with me where I could take care of them and I never brought up the children's complaints to my husband. It did not serve any purpose other than to make him angry with the children for telling on him and besides he never changed his ways that I could see on any enduring basis.

The baby was worked into the daily schedule and life went on. The money problems continued, however and it got pretty rocky around our house. Jeremy was now getting ready to learn to drive and I was looking forward to have him get his license as that would free me from all that driving them to their school and picking them up. I carpooled with the mother of one of his friends and this cut down some of the driving. I had to pack up the baby and our little son and it was just so cumbersome. I had to take my son to his part-time job and pick him up from there too later in the evening. It was a hassle. It was much better when Jeremy learned to drive!

But there is a price to be paid for the convenience of having the children drive themselves and that was they did not always say where they were going or with whom, no matter how we impressed on them how easy it is to stray from doing what one is supposed to and that we would trust them as long as they would not give us a reason not to. This was understood and once again I could not believe that my wonderful son would do any of the things that I was told much later that he did. It was always a jolt to my faith in the established order of things.

Tracy was a good baby, thank goodness, and she was no trouble at night. My husband was really not that impressed with her, in fact when I asked him to get me something that I needed for her he looked at me in total disgust and said that would be the last time that he would do this. He brought what I needed for her, packed a bag and moved in with his cousin. He was gone for two or three weeks. I did not know what to think. I know he did not care much for our son but I was really dumbfounded over his lack of love for his daughter. I was just puzzled and really did not know what to do. I just carried on as normally as I could. He always made sure that he covered all the bases in case of a legal action against him, so he made sure that his investment, the house, was current in the payments and he left it up to me to handle the rest somehow. The how was of no interest to him. Thank goodness for credit cards! I had to get one of those and I used it only if I absolutely could do nothing else. After three weeks he returned and decided that he wanted to rent his own office and start to go into business for himself.

My husband again changed to another insurance agency; this time it was with an insurance broker whom he contracted with to get started in business for himself. He had a secretary who probably worked also for this broker. One time I came unannounced to see for myself the office he was responsible for and I noticed that this secretary was dressed in a completely inappropriate fashion for business. I pointed this out to him after she made a hasty retreat, which I found unsettling. I did not want to dwell on yet another facet of my husband's shabby character as I had plenty to deal with as it was, and I put it out of my mind.

I am sure the pressure to make it on his own in the insurance business was quite relentless and I gave him extra leeway and tried to overlook most affronts to my dignity as a woman and a mother because I knew that I could never, and certainly would never want to, do what he set his mind to do as he was ambitious and driven to succeed. Since my interest was solely on providing a home for my children, which required my presence in the home, I had made a bargain with the devil, to take whatever he dished out if only I could stay home with the children.

Judy asked me if she could come back to move in with us because her husband abused her much the same way as mine did me. I said yes, because I owed her another year of at-home time since she left my home prematurely in hopes to find all her wishes and dreams fulfilled with this sailor. The description of her ugly experiences during her one-year marriage was the same horrid tale I lived through and was still living through in my own life and I really hated to have to listen to a detailed rendition of hell, particularly because it was my child. She discovered that beauty in and of itself is no guarantee for red-carpet treatment by the opposite sex as they mean something entirely different when they tell you that they love you. They mean that they love the way you look and they desire you; they have no concept of love. Love requires sacrifice.

I explained to her the house rules but she did in no wise respect them. I warned her repeatedly but she would not listen. I caught her in several indelicate situations which I simply could not allow to go unchallenged. We had a big discussion and I then told her that she had to find some other place to do these things as I still had younger children, for whom she was setting a bad example and I myself hated this kind of conduct, particularly since she had been taught the Lord's way of living and she was outrageously brazen in her defiance of those rules.

She left and took up with somebody who shared her interests and they rented an apartment together. These two women were both working and just did as they pleased in their private lives which I didn't dare to dwell on.

She got very ill on one occasion and she could not go to work and did not have the money to pay for the prescription she needed to get filled.

It was the middle of the night when she called me, as she was burning up with fever and she was in a panic. She told me of an all-night pharmacy on the way to her apartment. I could ill afford this expense but she needed it. I had been to her apartment one time before so I did not have to search for it in the middle of the night and it was a pitiful existence that she was living. She had pneumonia and she looked terrible. I felt so sorry for her and kept on checking on her but as soon as she was well, she had things once again under her own control!

I now had a sixteen-year-old boy and a fifteen-year-old girl, a three-year-old and a one-year-old. Rachel had her own hellish experiences as she was getting caught up in the college atmosphere. There were no safeguards for young persons in place. I was so naive!

I could not believe that these centers for higher learning did not find it necessary to make sure that these young lives were spiritually protected and encouraged to follow the teachings of their respective homes and churches. I defended my faith and the teachings of the Christian doctrine. I had tried to adhere to and instill these values in my children, against my own daughter who had taken on the thinking of the intelligentsia, the progressives who asserted that there was no God, and that if there were a God, He indeed would have better things to do, than to spend his time worrying about the sex lives of the people. I was really angry, at the institution first and my daughter second, for placing so little value on the faith of her growing-up years and just accepting whatever thought was prevailing at the university. I took it quite personally and I was angry with my rebellious children for respecting me so little and most of all, to have no respect for, and faith in the teachings of Jesus Christ. I found that it was futile to counter her intellectual suppositions about God with the simple declarations of faith that were at my disposal at the time and, I must admit, made me sound like an ignorant, simple-minded provincial dunce by comparison. It was very unnerving for me and I really did not like having to deal with my now-unbelieving children. I did not know how. The mistakes they made, blinded by new ideas, were in actuality serious transgressions against God's laws but they did not see it this way. I asked my pastor about what to do and voiced my displeasure at the notion that children would do all the wrong things for the wrong reasons and that it was then the parent's duty to do damage control and hope the children would eventually find their way back to the faith of their, in my case, mother. I was not happy with that explanation and remained resentful toward my modern children. The only comfort I could retain was always the next child. Maybe he or she would do the right thing and continue to believe. What a pipe dream that proved to be all the way down the line. Once again, isn't it a blessing that we do not know the future? It allowed me to hope and keep on fighting for what I believed.

I cannot possibly explain why my children turned out the way they did but ultimately it was and is their responsibility to choose the right thing, having had the proper instructions. I am sure that there are scientific explanations that sound eminently educated and therefore must be right, which is simply not true.

Our home life had so much strain coming from so many sides, I never knew which way I was going just trying to keep up with the rapid and unavoidable changes. I was losing control over practically everything pertaining to my children from my previous marriage. They were getting too old to confine them to the restrictions of the natural family structure now that they had their own transportation and kept company with whomever they chose and there was very little I could do about it. Church attendance became spotty, as they always had one excuse or another, and I now had little ones to teach and make sure that they would get the right spiritual foundation in keeping with my faith.

A very nice black couple—he was from Chicago and she was from Jamaica—and their four children had moved into our cove and the youngest of theirs became good friends with my Richard. The woman, Merle, was an outstanding Christian and she became an important part in my life. We soon found that we had something very important in common: we loved Jesus Christ. But she had the support of an equally sincere believer who lived what he preached, which I thought must be the most beneficial thing in structuring family life. The husband, Russel, was the kind and God-pleasing head of household and the mother was at home tending to the needs and wants of her husband and their children and in that order.

I am profoundly thankful for every truly Christian father who fulfills his God-given responsibility to his wife and children and this includes highly educated men whose eyes have been opened to the truth—no dummies there—only wise men.

None of this was the case in my marriage. My husband and I were still fighting for supremacy, with me laboring under the assumption that I was the more experienced one, the older one and he for just simply being male and hiding conveniently behind the divine order to exercise and demand superior status. Having always had the responsibility for my children and everything pertaining to the household and family life in my first marriage, and then truly for everything during those years as a divorced person, made it very difficult for me to let go of that leader instinct I had developed and was really not aware of. So we were always warring over one thing or the other and I deeply resented him for not being responsive in the slightest to the position he forced me into by being so despotic when it came to money. He simply ignored my complaints and for this I fought back the best way I knew how. There were times when I hated to have my things from my past lovely life (comparatively speaking) in the same room where he would watch his ballgames and drink his beer. I would remove all the things that made a house a home and it looked shockingly bare. I had moved into Jeremy's room as I was warring. It was always like this. I had to fight for every little thing one way or the other. It was a constant tit-for-tat and I am sure I did not rate high on the sanity scale as far as Jeremy and Susan were concerned.

Marvin, my ex-husband was now married to yet another woman with whom he had another daughter. My son would obligate himself to spend time in the summer to babysit that child and maybe go fishing with his father, which they both liked. It was during one of those absences of my son's when I took the opportunity to play out my resentment toward my husband by moving into his room. It never cured a thing. We'd make up and he'd make promises but he never had any serious intention to change.

The inability on my part to accept this outright emotional abuse from my husband by deliberately withholding necessary monies to run the household just because he could, provided the ever-present secret wish to divorce him, right or wrong, to get away from the sheer indignity of my position. No matter how often I intellectually reasoned with myself that I could take anything as long as I could stay home and take care of my children, it was extremely hard to live it out. The fact that I did not go back to work and put the children in danger, as millions of women did every day, really angered him to no end. His idea was that a woman should be self-supporting and do whatever is required of her as well. This to me was simply perverse.

This good Christian lady came often with her youngest daughter to my house to play with our son and we got to talking and it became clear in a very short time that I had a very good advisor in her as she was very proficient in Scripture.

Although out of desperation I actually looked up what the Bible said on the subject of how the wife was to conduct herself, which I had taken for granted I did, and had to discover to my dismay that I had had no idea how to deal with my husband in accordance with Bible teaching and I finally recognized the old saying "You can catch more flies with honey than with vinegar." I still had the undercurrent of resentment. Just when I would think I had made progress and things were improving, he'd do something vile and I'd be set back and resort to my secret wish (and in my eyes my right) to get rid of this poor excuse for a husband.

It was a most taxing time and as I was praying for God to please help me because I simply could not do this by myself, this lovely mother of four came into my life and she proved to be of valuable assistance in my effort to go in the right direction.

One time when she came over and we were in the den studying Scripture and praying for understanding, the two buddies who were both two-and-a-half, going on three, had taken the baby powder for my baby daughter and shaken the powder all over the place in the front room which I had transformed into the German room. This was really just a sitting-room with a daybed, with pictures of the most beautiful German scenery. We were nonplussed as they told us that they were making it snow! We had to laugh and we cleaned up with the vacuum but it was so amusing. Without close supervision these little ones can get into all kinds of mischief. I had no clue that I had left the baby powder in that room.

As I was seeking a solution and was preoccupied with the myriad of problems that were mine to solve, I had the strangest experience after the apparition I saw before my daughter was born. I was awakened by my crying in my sleep around two o'clock in the morning by just a tiny snippet of one of Elvis's mournful love songs from a long time ago. I got up and went into the living room/den and sat there trying to remember which song this was but no matter how hard I tried I could not figure it out. I had that vague feeling that it was very important that I find out which song this was and so I dug up the secret stash of records that I had put away. It took me some time to remember in which section and among which other records I had hidden them.

I listened to the ones from the sixties, but I had only a few of them because I destroyed some after Elvis married Priscilla, and I had to do something to underscore that this was definitely the end of my having to occupy myself with the life of Elvis Presley.

What I was reminded of during that search for this one song was Charlie Hodge, who had accompanied Elvis on several of his recordings, singing harmony or picking up the slack if Elvis got too stressed vocally, that is. He sang with Elvis on "The Heart of Rome" and it brought back memories I thought I had all but forgotten. It was, for me, like going into forbidden territory and I felt extremely guilty and I was afraid someone might wake up and catch me listening to Elvis whom I had "buried," or rather tried to bury, so many times. What would I say? What could I say? That I had been crying in my sleep, which woke me up and then there was this tiny unidentifiable tune in my head which I was now trying to identify? I was so scared of this possibility that I left things undiscovered for now. I just did not have the wherewithal to continue my search and I was also afraid to get started on that one-way track of chasing a dream, never mind that the principal character in that dream was dead. I had spent enough time chasing that rabbit when he was alive and I'd be hornswoggled if I'd go down that road again!

I had been told by a nurse who assisted during the birth of my son that there was something wrong with the boy and that she felt sorry for me. She also was the mother of one of Jeremy's friends and I pressed her for more information when she was implying that my son was born with the genitalia of both sexes. At that time this condition was not thought of as commonplace as it is today and I was very concerned about the welfare of our precious son. I called the doctor who had advised me to get an abortion as this was obviously connected to what I now had been told.

The doctor was pretty irritated at this nurse and said that she did not know what she was talking about and should in no wise have talked out of school. He did, however tell me that our son had Klinefelter's syndrome, which is a chromosomal abnormality. Boys would normally have XY, but our son had an additional X-chromosome which put him at risk for infertility, decreased production of testosterone and the occurrence of breast cancer. There is no cure for this disorder but the testosterone deficit could be corrected with oral doses of testosterone at the onset of puberty. He suggested that I get in touch with a geneticist and he gave me the name of the doctor. This was disconcerting news, to be sure, but I could deal with it. I took our son to the geneticist who went into great detail to make me understand the nature of this disorder and he used graphs and pictures to educate a lay person such as myself. He measured the head, the chest, the legs and arms and pronounced him to appear normal so far. On the next visit I had asked the doctor if this condition is a predisposition to homosexuality, as I had noticed certain behaviors generally ascribed to girls. The boy had had a very strong desire to dress himself in Judy's uniforms and he had a peculiar way of running. He showed no interest in the conventional boy's toys like trucks and trains and football—he'd rather play with gender-neutral things like puzzles, cute little buggies or ABC building blocks but his favorite was to dress up in the girl's clothes and he would insist on playing in them and it was difficult for me to force him out of them.

This put my husband at odds with this child as we both suspected that there was the distinct possibility that this child would be a homosexual. The geneticist informed me that there was no scientific evidence that these two components were related.

Now came the battle of nature versus nurture and it was interesting to see the outcome develop.

We treated our son as a full male child and did all the things with him that normal boys do. The doctor told us that is what we needed to do and it was pretty easy, even if the boy did not enjoy some of the things that fell into this range, like baseball, for instance. It was at the ballgames later on that we noticed his decidedly effeminate gait when he was running to catch a ball. We all know men who are somewhat effeminate in their demeanor but they are not practicing homosexuals, as most of them have families and live good happy lives and raise their children with love and care.

Our own daughter, Tracy, was growing into a sweet angelic creature and I made sure that after she could say "da-da" I made her "Daddy's girl" and so she replaced the daughter he had access to only every now and then, while another man played daddy for her. He seemed to like his little girl more and more and he brought her little toys from trips he had to take and he preferred to buy the girl-things but he also brought something for the boy as I would have been all over him if he had been that overtly displaying favoritism and he would not want to be that obvious. His method was that of an utterly disorienting, passive-aggressive kind. Lethal.

Shortly after Jeremy got the dirt-bike I did not want him to have, something malfunctioned and it was up to me to see that the bike got fixed, which was an inordinate ordeal for me, as I hated everything about motorcycles. I had to take him to the motorcycle shops and talk about things I had no understanding of. When Jack and I were on good terms, he would take care of it with my son but if we were at odds, which was more often than I care to remember, I was on my own.

11

THE POWER OF MY LOVE

It was easy for my husband to mete out punishment to my children for their various offenses, but it was I who was the enforcer, which was the hard part. He did not have to deal with the constant moaning and complaining when they were grounded for the day, for instance. He did not have to look at the unhappy faces and the pitiful contrite demeanors and sincere apologies and still have to maintain the tough stance when I was willing to forget the whole darn thing myself and just let them be happy. It was tougher on me than it was on them, I am sure. At the same time I had to deal with the crankiness of the younger children and worry about how to pay for everything that was needed to keep things going so that my husband would feel comfortable and welcome at his castle.

I'd spend a lot of sleepless nights agonizing over my husband's mystifying penchant for torturing me and at the same time swearing that he loved me. I would cry myself to sleep many a night and get up in the morning with a pleasant, positive composure, hoping against all odds that today could be different. This hope for the "pie in the sky" made me feel foolish at times and it was in those times that I felt I had to ban him from my life.

However, my friend who came over to share matters of faith with me kept on insisting that with God there is no such thing as an impossible thing and that I am obligated to employ all spiritual resources to fight what I recognized as combat fatigue. I did not want to hear this as I knew intuitively that she was ever so right, but I felt much better pursuing a divorce. After all, he was an abuser and I just did not want to have to suffer anymore just because I was trying to live by a set of rules I had signed onto come hell or high water. I needed some relief and also a degree of "I'll show him!" It made me feel a whole lot better than having to continue to be this man's slave and be thankful for it to boot. I even thought of a plan of not being home at our customary time and day for our meeting as I did not want her to ruin my plans for doing it my way! But that posed another problem, albeit a minor one on the surface; I would have to come up with lies and that was simply not part of my nature. So she came over and again I had to listen to what I did not want to hear!

In all this conflict of emotions I had to deal with dreams of Elvis that were giving me reason to search for answers. I dreamed that Priscilla and I were standing beside a coffin and we were both looking into the coffin when she turned to me and said accusingly, "You could have helped him!" I turned to her and said something which I, the dreamer, could not hear. There were a series of dreams concerning Elvis, one in particular where I woke up with the admonition in my mind, "Think about the past! Think about the past!" I did not want to think about the past! The man was dead. Leave me alone! Besides, even when I thought of the past with him I could only come up with "then I said this and then he said that and that's that." I was no wiser after that. The dreams kept coming and I thought that maybe I would find a clue in his music and so I was sneaking out of bed and starting to listen to all the songs I still had.

I am not sure that I can adequately describe what happened to me during those times. The songs I listened to then were, "Love Letters," "And the Grass Won't Pay No Mind," "From a Jack to a King," "Without Love," "This Is Our Dance," "When I'm Over You," "If I Were You," "Heart of Rome," "I'll Never Know," "Surrender," "I Just Can't Help Believin'," "Kentucky Rain," "My Babe," "It's Midnight," "It's a Matter of Time," "It's a Long Lonely Highway," "After Loving You," and many more.

As I was listening to Elvis's voice with its velvet quality singing in a most sincerely felt, deepest-love, emotional way, giving each verbal expression that inimitable revealing glimpse into his soul by the nuances of timbre, fashioning a shining jewel of the purest love there is, I was mesmerized as it felt to me as if a huge wave of this love rolled over me, making me as weak as a kitten, piercing me as with a very sharp instrument deep within my soul and at the same time enveloping me with a most soothing and comforting balm. I was shaken to the very core of my being and I was trembling in my heart and I could not help but cry and cry and cry and it was to me as if I would never be able to keep from crying. I was awestruck at this experience as I could clearly feel God's presence. I felt extremely privileged to have been granted such an exquisite experience and I kept it to myself as I did not yet understand why this happened to me. In my mind I was transported into another world where I wanted to be but couldn't. I was like an ill person, except that I did not feel ill, but quite the contrary. However, I could not keep from crying every time I would remember that love of Elvis's and it became a problem for my husband as he was just perplexed at my strange behavior. Without noticing, a transformation had taken place in me. I had been trying so hard to live in accordance with what the Scriptures teach about the wife's responsibility regarding her husband but I could not circumvent the resentment I was harboring against my oppressor. A miracle happened—and it was a miracle. I no longer felt any resentment against anyone; only love, a kind of which I have heard all my life and could never understand. It was and is that divine love. AGAPE.

I had to explain to Jack the best I could that this was all spiritual and it was then I told him of the apparition before the birth of our daughter and the dreams throughout my life and in the recent past in particular. I had already told him at the time of our marriage plans that I was "told" by God to marry him. (I never wasted any time thinking about how odd that must have sounded to him.) He looked at me and said, "You know, that figure you saw could have been Jesus!" I had not been able to come to that conclusion as the figure was barefoot and the white garment could have been the type of bellbottom pants Elvis was wearing in his last years here on earth. I was just glad that Jack reacted this way, as there was now a chance that we together could remedy what was so wrong between us. But deep inside I was in an agonizing dilemma. Dealing with my husband and my wayward children just was not what I wanted to do. Just let God fix all that and let me get out of here and go where I want to be. I could not eat or sleep and I was forever crying but I was ever so nice and kind to everyone, my husband in particular. Now he was the one who was disoriented, as all his efforts to show me that he was indeed the king of his castle and I had to do his bidding whether I liked it or not no longer yielded the conflict he was looking for, and over time he seemed to change for the better. But that did not change my deep longing to join Elvis and I was secretly working toward that goal as I truly felt that God could take care of my beloved children if He chose to take me home.

My husband had applied for a contract with a big insurance company, which at that time required their representatives/agents to be of good moral character, married, and established in their communities, preferably with children. He had a good chance to land this contract and he was ever so upset about the possibility of not getting it as he had just hung all his hopes and dreams on working under the big umbrella of this company which was licensed to sell insurance in many states, including Tennessee. Jack would come home all upset, asking me if I thought that he would get that contract. I told him that I was confident that he would indeed get it if we maybe could pray together about it. He became this docile, friendly fellow who would speak of the things of God quite often and I was so sure that we had turned the corner, so to speak. He would come to church with us and he would help me with the little ones. We had them baptized in "my" church and we kept on praying for my husband's bright future with this very good company. He did get the contract and it was a very good time for his ego. Now came the next hard part. He had to prove that he could make it on his own and he took advantage of the offered advice of the regional representative who monitored all the agents and gave support when needed. It was a Godsend for him and he took to the whole independent businessman routine like a duck to water. He was making more and more money, which I did not know. He, in effect, only played nice when he was in trouble and he shared that freely but when he was rolling in dough and happy as a clam and proud of his wonderfulness, he was mum.

I did not let that deter me from being this supportive, understanding, ever-forgiving wife I had turned into by the sheer grace of God and I wanted to show my gratitude in some tangible way, so I volunteered to teach Sunday school at the Lutheran church, which I enjoyed doing. I had rediscovered the musical version of "The Lord's Prayer" sung by Mario Lanza in my stash of music, and it connected me so directly with God that was impossible for me to describe. My enthusiasm over this prompted me to have everybody listen to it, just once, for me, and I was hoping that they too could hear and feel what I was hearing and feeling but that never happened. I brought it to my second-graders in my Sunday school class and played it for them but I discovered that I was the only one who could appreciate the exquisite beauty and wisdom contained in the words themselves and in the beautiful, harmonious music, underscoring this perfect prayer. I am just as thrilled by it today if not more so.

As my husband grew more successful he distanced himself from God. The first time I noticed that he was drifting away was when he resumed his excessive drinking. His condescending attitude toward me, a mere woman, showed me that all was not well with him. Even though he came to church with us, on the way home he would start to criticize the church and I had to try to defend what we believed in which would always end up in a stand-off. It only confused Jeremy and Susan more and more. I even dreaded going to church, even being extremely apprehensive about the value of going to church at all under these conditions, as his criticism affected me too. I could feel myself being challenged on that which was the heart and soul of me, my faith, and yet I could not make him understand that, while churches are not perfect, as they consist of imperfect people, the reason for them being in existence is to transmit to us the perfect wisdom of God through His son Jesus Christ and the Holy Spirit. I simply did not have the ability to enlighten him and it made me very uncertain about where to go from there, particularly now that my husband was in a drifting mode.

In the process of being guided by the strong Christian advisor God had seen fit to send my way, I learned that relying on the ever-present help of God would bear fruit eventually. We should be patient and persistent in our faith and hope and the needed help would come. Since I could not think of anything else I could do, I accepted to just give it time, as I know from experience that God works in mysterious ways but He works.

Feeling somewhat confused at the continuing difficulties with my husband, as he saw nothing wrong with acting as though he was somehow entitled to be just as he was by nature, but could at the same time claim himself to be a Christian and count on the blessings available as promised by God. His business endeavor was quite successful which, I think, gave him the idea that he deserved that just because he obediently spouted Biblical phrases, deceiving himself into thinking that this was all there was to being a believer.

Through this miraculous transformation I experienced, I was given the ability to protect myself from his ever-so-deadly, simmering, deep-seated hatred of women, but especially of me, which he expressed in a hundred little ways. I could, without pretending respond as though I did not hear his mental, emotional, and spiritual attacks against me. It was a truly God-given ability and I give God all the credit. On my own I would not have been wise enough or strong enough to endure what seemed like hell to me.

My friend would look at me with an empty look in her eyes, thereby telling me that she had no ability to understand any of what I was saying, as she had no experience like this herself. There was no sign of sympathy in her demeanor ever. She was hammering instead at the help that I was sure to receive if I gave it time. But I was running out of time as far as I was concerned and I would have rather died as I had wished in the first place. I mentioned this to her and she said that Christ had already died and this sealed the salvation of the believer. To be perfectly honest, I just did not want to do the hard stuff. Dying was easy by comparison.

My good friend was generous enough to share with me the source of her never-changing, peaceful ways, which she insisted was in the Pentecostal faith. I had no idea about Pentecostals and I was suspicious of the whole thing as I only knew that they were a sort of cult who babbled and did not cut their hair as it is the woman's glory as written in the Holy Bible. My friend's hair was shoulder-length, however and she was an intelligent and educated woman, so I was pretty curious about her denomination.

She explained to me the fundamental doctrines of the Assemblies of God faith and as I listened to her going through the basic fundamental truths which anchor the denomination in the Scriptures, I found myself being torn to and fro. I liked and could accept all the principles, but this speaking in tongues really made me uneasy as I had been taught in the Lutheran tradition that this was of the devil. But there was one sentence she said that absolutely convinced me in a split-second that this was the truth. She said that the Holy Spirit was working today just as it had been since Christ's death and resurrection and that the operation of the Holy Spirit was at the very center of the Pentecostal faith. I kept on mulling this over, although deep inside I already knew the next step I had to take. I went with her to her church in Raleigh and I must admit I found an atmosphere of humble, sweet and kind and friendly human fellowship that was distinctly different from the Lutheran gatherings. I can only surmise that the difference was the almost palpable presence of the Holy Spirit. After my visit there I asked my husband to join me and we went together. This, too, was a godsend. Considering that much of his criticism of my church was not rooted in a careful examination of doctrine and tradition but rather that he was considered there as my husband, more like an appendage rather than the Man. His male ego caused the trouble and going to another church together, from the beginning, circumvented this serious problem. We went there to Sunday school because my friend's husband Russel was teaching it and we felt welcome. It gave my husband a chance to voice his opinion. We went to worship at the Lutheran church because I did not want to abandon the two older children who were still living at home. I invited them to come with us, which they did, but they were up in arms about the whole concept, particularly the speaking in tongues. This lasted only a very short time because I no longer got anything out of the worship, as I knew that my husband hated it. I reasoned that I had to concentrate my effort to teach my little ones the ways of the Lord with the assistance of their father, which was more than my older children's father did. Besides, they were fast approaching adulthood and I had already done all I could for them as far as their faith was concerned. Their salvation was now their responsibility.

Although I was trying hard to do all I could to make my relationship with my husband more pleasant and had the blessing of God in that effort, it was still a very stressful situation as there was always another mine I could step on that would result in huge explosions from which we would wear the scars. The best way to proceed was to be very careful and tender and loving, above all, to lessen the impact. While I was forever trying to avoid the built-in traps in a relationship such as ours, with children from previous marriages on both sides, struggling day to day attempting to cope in a way that would engender peace for all the involved parties, my mind was in overdrive just keeping up with everything, when the thought of that dream with Priscilla popped into my head. I repeated to myself what she had said so accusingly, "You could have helped him!" and the answer I gave her in that dream, but was not allowed to hear. I asked myself out loud, "Why was I not allowed to hear my answer?" It would surely have been helpful explaining a lot of things for which I had tried and tried to make any kind of sense of. I kept on repeating in my mind, "Why indeed was I not allowed to help Elvis?" over and over, as I was taking care of the little ones. They were playing in the den and watching Nickelodeon on TV. Everything was quiet and I could hear my son and daughter talking softly. I was in the kitchen and on my way into the dining room when, all of a sudden the answer came into my brain as out of nowhere and I was "told": "You have to continue what Elvis has started!"

I thought, quite indignantly, that this must be a bad joke as I was the premier critic of Elvis, whom I loved so much and lost, and the instructions continued, recognizing my confusion, "You must reverse that which he caused." I was getting increasingly agitated at this as I had enough trouble already without the additional duties that were obviously being hung around my neck so I said in my mind, hoping that this would end this "conversation," "Well if this is so, then I want to see where it says that in the Bible, because if it is not there I am not going to do it, so you are going to have to show me where it says that there. I am going into the sitting-room where my German Bible is on the accent table. I will walk over there and sit down and wait for the direction coming as I will be closing my eyes and open the Bible and you show me where while my eyes are closed!" I went very slowly and very deliberately to the table, sat down, closed my eyes and ever so slowly opened the book. When I opened my eyes and looked to see where it was supposed to say what I needed to know, I saw that the Bible was in Revelation, the twelfth chapter. I read it in German and I was stunned, as I did not understand one thing. I was more confused than ever but one thing stuck in my mind as I was reading, that I had to have a son whose name would have to be an Old Testament name at once. I mulled all this over and while I could not understand anything else, I knew what I had to do about this child and I felt very much at ease with the whole idea, as crazy as it appeared to be in my natural mind. And it was crazy!

Here I was, having more trouble than I knew how to deal with and planning to have another child. I had heard all the snide comments when I had the fourth child: "Don't you know what causes this?" and later on when I had my fifth child, people asked whether I did not concern myself with the overpopulation of the world and whether I did not know when to stop as I was expecting the sixth child. I could just hear the tongues wagging when I was going to have a seventh child! But nothing could keep me from doing what I knew I had to do and a few months later I was pregnant with what I knew deep within me was a male child.

When I told my husband that we were going to have another son, to whom we had to give an Old Testament name, he said, halfway jokingly, that I'd better jump off the refrigerator. Surprisingly enough, he was not as mad as I feared he would be after I explained to him that I would once again go to the clinic which was really his main concern. He was actually unusually nice to me and unusually caring and I was once and for all, in one sweep, so to speak, tied to him for the long haul. It was a very good thing for me as it banished my death wish. It was a very powerful distraction indeed and it made my life so much easier since I was no longer in a state of indecision but rather firmly committed to whatever was to come my way as I could feel so clearly that this was the will of God.

I was now forty-four years old and would have had to have an amnio if I had been under an insurance plan. In this case it was working again in my interest to have had a stingy husband and I did not have to argue with a doctor about not wanting an amnio. I put the power of God ahead of the experience of the medical establishment anytime. It saved me from that upsetting experience.

I was very uncomfortable as I got farther along in the pregnancy and I was private about my condition, so much so that I did not go anywhere if I did not absolutely have to. I always viewed the condition of being with child a very special one and I feared it being diminished in its sanctity by parading around in the world which violated the special relationship I had with my God, who designed it to be this way. Special and holy. I kept these kinds of thoughts entirely to myself and cherished them in secret. I was happy in my physical discomfort. Of course there was never a hint of anything unusual when I found myself in this condition outside the house. I acted quite normal for the times we lived in.

I went for one of my weekly checkups and I mentioned in passing, as I was getting dressed, that I did not feel the baby kick in the last two days. The doctor looked at me and said, "You cannot go home! You have to check into the hospital at once as we must determine what is going on!" Within no time it had been diagnosed that the baby had the umbilical cord wrapped around his neck and that the delivery had to be as soon as possible. I was to have the baby undergo a stress test to see if I could deliver normally or if I would have to have a C-section. The entire afternoon was spent trying to find out if the baby was strong enough to fight his or her way (they did not know what I knew) out into the world. It was determined that there was strength enough and labor was induced. The male child was born that evening and as I had an epidural (only in problem cases at this clinic) I was able to see him being born. They showed him to me and said, "You have a son!" I thought he was ever so cute and they took him away to be examined. We were told that he had a broken clavicle and he had low bilirubin which made it necessary for him to remain in an incubator. I was stuck in the hospital too because I was attempting to breast-feed this child, which I had not been able to do with any of my other children for one reason or the other and I was adamant about doing it this time. It was not to be. All I got from this attempt was a lot of pain for which I have a very low tolerance level.

The nuns who were running this hospital for charity cases were so very nice to me and when they were trying to counsel me in the spiritual nurture that this new earthling of mine deserved, I was probably the most receptive patient they ever had since faith in God and my obligation to my children was always the most important part of who I was and am.

My husband came to visit and it was a little awkward as he still sported the suntan he had acquired in Hawaii. I hope nobody noticed the discrepancy between that tan and my charity status. My husband had earned a trip to Hawaii with this company he brokered business through and he had taken his mother with him, since I did not feel like going. I hated to have to go on trips as I would hate being away from my children and this time I got out of going with a legitimate excuse. They had a marvelous time from all accounts and the pictures they had taken. My mother-in-law had never been out of the continental United States and it was a real treat for her.

To my surprise and, with enormous relief on my part, my husband took it upon himself to buy all the items needed for the care of an infant. Even the baby bed was purchased brand-spanking-new. I thought I had died and gone to heaven. After our daughter was born we did not want any more children as we had one of each and so I had returned the borrowed items and given the other things away to the Salvation Army. It was such a relief. The fact that he was earning more money for himself and he had this regional supervisor stop by to see what it looked like on the home front made him unusually willing to spend some money on other things than those he deemed worthy for himself as he and only he was making that money and I was just this irritating tag-along that he saw fit to trot out in commensurate (with his position) garb, and his lovely children, to prove to the company that he was what they expected from their brokers. It did not matter to me why he did anything right, just as long as he did it and spared me some portion of hell.

But this did not go on with any regularity. He was caught in a trap and he did not like to have to spend his money on things which he considered my problem, so he made me suffer doubly whenever there was an opportunity. He berated me on everything from spending too much money to spoiling Jeremy, to letting the little ones make a mess in the front rooms, saying that I was too old to have good sense about anything, etc., etc. And all this, while he was going to Sunday school and worship service every Sunday. While I noticed the hypocrisy, I did not let that embitter my way of dealing with him in kindness and loving ways. I never returned his insults with insults but instead I turned the other cheek and praised him for every little thing that he did fairly well. I did not feel resentful and I never felt like retaliating and to me it felt like there was a buffer between the things he did or said that, under normal circumstances (without that God-given divine love) would have deeply hurt me and I would have responded in kind.

Jeremy surrounded himself with people I did not approve of and I warned him that this would lead to difficulties but he always assured me that he was aware of the pitfalls and I believed him. I had brought him up in the admonitions of the Lord and I was convinced that my son would not do anything that would disappoint or hurt his mommy. After all, I thought, he loved his mother and you just don't hurt the one you love. I was so wrong in this assumption, however. He was always hanging around with questionable characters, in school as well as at home. He was going to his father's trailer, where he spent time with his father and that third wife and their two girls. When he would come back home he was belligerent toward all of us and he showed a minimum of respect, only enough to get by. I warned him over and over that I would not tolerate disrespect and that I would rather see him dead than disrespecting his mother and I meant it. Of course I would not kill him but if he were to die being this mean, disrespectful son, I simply could not deal with that and if he were to die as a result of some of the activities that he was involved in, so be it.

I just hate disrespect.

On one evening he and my husband had a verbal exchange and later on in the evening Jeremy came with some of his hooligan friends and threatened to beat up my husband. I was so angry with him that I called the police, but not before I told him but good, that he would be in a heap of trouble if he did not get rid of his buddies who were wearing the leather bands on their wrists and the spiked vests and leather pants and the crazy hair of the ZZ Top and AC/DC bums I so despised. I was defending my husband at that point and these ruffians went into their cars and drove off. Things were never the same again between my son and me.

As Jeremy had shown no interest in going to college and he made no motion to find a job after he got out of school, I had given him an ultimatum. He had two months to find a job or he had to get out of the house. He was bumming around, telling me that he was going to be a mechanic, which was fine with me. Keeping company with his father had put him on that track, because my ex-husband always belittled educated people, including his own daughter, who was attending college in an effort to make something of herself. While I do not think that everybody should go to college, I do think that those who have the ability and the drive should have the opportunity to go there. This son of mine had the ability but he did not want to go or do the hard stuff it takes to go to college. So be it. He was going to be a mechanic. Fine. He did not think, however, that I meant what I said in the ultimatum and he lived carefree through these days, coming home after curfew and generally doing just as he pleased while we were providing a roof over his head, food in his stomach and clothes on his back. I prayed and prayed for God to give me the strength to follow through with the threat of throwing him out if he did not comply, as I could feel my motherly softness creeping in and making me uncertain in my resolve. When the time came I was unmoved and explained to my son that I had packed all his things and if he did not find himself his own domicile, which would require him going to work, that I would put them out on the sidewalk. He was surprised that I was not bluffing, which is what he had thought. He took his things and disappeared. We did not hear from him for one week. Then he called and said that he was at his best friend's house, who was as drifting and ugly as my son. I asked him if he had a job and he said that he was looking. He drove my old car as I now was driving a new one. This went on for a month and a half as it was summertime and those two did what they have always done, bummed around. Of course the friend's parents got an earful of lies when my son was painting himself as this nice boy whose mother just threw him out because she had a house full of other children. I sent money to the parents for his upkeep and advised them not to tell him that his accommodations were paid for as this would then be no different than him remaining with us. He needed to be made to feel uncomfortable enough by thinking that he was eating someone else's food and feel obligated to seek employment to pay his own way.

The monies came from Marvin's child-support arrearage which he was still having to pay—even though child support for Jeremy, now eighteen, had stopped.

He eventually moved in with his sister who was living with a man. He did get a job and he learned that you don't get a free lunch. I did not like him living with his rebellious sister as she was no example to follow. It was this rebellion that has proven to be that tie that binds to this very day.

All of these developments with my children added additional stress to my already stressful situation with my husband.

I took full responsibility for having had this baby, whose name is Samuel, and therefore I felt obligated to make this baby's presence as unnoticeable as possible. At night I would sleep with the baby in the front room and practically stayed glued to him because he would cry as soon as he could not feel me beside him. He was most comfortable when he could feel my face on his cheek and that is how I ended up many a night, crouched on the floor beside him on the daybed, to keep him from crying and making my husband irate and then cruel at this imposition that I had visited upon him. Sometimes I lost track of time or got times mixed up. One day I got confused about picking up the older boy from kindergarten. I just could not get it straight when I looked at the clock. I literally lived separately from the rest of the family and ran my legs off trying to keep them all happy at the same time. I was overloaded, to be sure, but I kept up with all my obligations and I never complained as I was convinced that I was doing God's Will and that was the most rewarding feeling of all. It was during that time that I did lose track of things and my husband's sexual appetite remained high and I knew very well from experience how to keep him happy in this way and having no cause to complain, at least about this, I made sure I was available for him. Very much to my surprise I discovered that I was with child again. There simply was no way that my body could go through another pregnancy, which is a trauma for a forty-six-year-old woman.

I told my husband about this and we decided that I was going to have an abortion. The moral dilemma simply did not register in my mind because I was completely panic-stricken at the mere thought of any more stress of any kind on my already complicated life. I could not see how I could cope with another thing. We never mentioned any of this to anyone. For the record it was another boy.

It is worth noting that it is easy indeed to be indignant at my obvious moral failure but it may also be easy to understand when you are backed against the wall, so to speak and it is your life that is affected. Although I am against abortion and oppose it as a form of birth control, I can understand desperation. I asked God for forgiveness and confessed to a deaconess at church and I was forgiven.

I was still being harassed and shortchanged by my husband in the way of finances and I had given up trying to figure out why he was so stingy with the money when it was normal to want to take care of your family. But I was really hurt when he came to me one fine day and explained to me that we had to build a house because he was making too much money and he did not have enough deductions which means that the government was going to get too big a slice of his income. Here I was, being forced to scrimp and save and worry about how to keep him from finding out how much I have to buy on credit and how to eke out the minimum payment for that each month and he had too much money, so much in fact that we had to build a house! No matter how hurt I was I had no choice but to agree to everything as I could clearly see that I was lucky just to subsist, but I could take care of my children at our home such as it was.

He went looking for property and he made me look at it and even though I did not care to move at all, I put that smile on my face and complimented him on his excellent selection of the property on which we were going to build this house. I was being truthful.

He was very good at a lot of things and this piece of land was beautiful indeed and in the right price range and just a good purchase. I could even share his dream of where he would put what and it was enjoyable to see him happy about himself and his accomplishments. Ever-present was this nagging trepidation deep inside. It was my coming in touch with God Himself through this love I was now capable of feeling that I could deal with things in a God-pleasing manner and I knew that I could tap into this fountain of love by hearing Elvis's love songs for me. I had an inexhaustible supply of that love which makes us gloriously human in the way God had designed us from the beginning. This, of course was in stark contrast to the conditions in which I lived, the people I had to deal with and the things I had to agree to just to get along. I often wondered how it was that I was put smack-dab in the middle of what I could recognize as wrong but could do nothing to change any of it. When I caught myself wondering about this and for the lack of being able to do anything else but to go along for the sake of peace and enjoying it as well as anyone else involved, I said to God, "Only You can understand it and in time I will know too." One thing I was sure of was that God was in control and I could trust Him implicitly to do what He promises us in Scripture. What a blessing that is I cannot overstate!

It still fills me with sadness when I recall the degree of inconsideration my husband displayed toward me. He absolutely did not give a thought to how any of his decisions would affect me. Making my life harder was simply not enough to deter him from fulfilling what he wanted when he wanted it. Even though we were (it was really only he) in the thought process of a custom-built house, he decided that we needed to have the den outfitted with a wooden floor which was underneath the carpeting. The resulting inconvenience for me for a week-and-a-half to two weeks was mindboggling. The furniture had to be completely moved out of that room, which was a headache, not to mention that we had to balance on a plank put on blocks diagonally from the front entry into the hallway to the bedroom and bathroom area. I had to tote the baby and hope I did not fall off. To be in a hurry was out of the question. The floor was covered with some kind of resin and it was imperative that nothing would touch it until it was good and dry. That process had to be repeated to make it scratch-resistant. It was crazy. The following year we moved out and could not even enjoy the pretty floor. What sense any of this made is beyond me!

I was very busy being a mother to my children, trying to keep hubby happy even if this meant that the children and I lived in the front and he had the TV for himself where he could watch one football game after another nonstop and drink one beer after another, but at least he was at home. I worked puzzles with the little ones and we read books together and made pretty pictures or they played with their toys while I ironed or cooked or did something that needed my attention. I thought it was a pretty good family life. Men's ideas of fun are definitely different from women's. Or so it used to be anyway.

The time came where I actually had to go with Jack to look at houses, something I dreaded having to do because I did not want to move in the first place. I liked our neighborhood and I knew where everything I needed was. The thought of all the trouble a move represented filled me with opposition to the whole idea, and I did not want to leave my children even though their now seventeen-year-old half-sister was taking care of them and they were plenty familiar with her. Any time away from my children was a bad time for me!

We went into areas where real-estate companies presented model-homes by certain architects and builders. If ever anybody has looked for a house they like, they know that there are houses that are built in such a way that they make you feel so uncomfortable as to almost chase you out of there. This happened to me many times and we would come home and not have found anything I liked. For some reason it was important for my husband that I liked the floor plan and I was getting pretty nervous as this pressure of finding something I liked began to get to me! Finally, after quite a few excursions we walked into this house and I absolutely liked the whole flow of the house and the soft colors. It was open and had vaulted ceilings and lots of windows to let the light in. I even got excited about building this house which made the eventual move only half as bad as it had seemed before. Jack was an absentee-husband. When he was not working, he was negotiating, inspecting, and organizing everything he could to bring about the construction of that house that I really liked. He was so preoccupied with this project that he even skipped watching ballgames on TV, which had rendered him just as absent with the exception of the frequent, "Honey, can you get me another beer?" and the cigarette smoke which told us that he was home. Though his absence and his mental pre-occupation had their advantages, I regretted it as the children did not get to interact on any meaningful level with their father.

There was one exception I can remember. It was raining and he could not do anything on the lot he had bought, measuring it, cutting the grass, or having it surveyed to determine where which part of the property had to be leveled for the house. So he asked his cousin to our house for company which irked me but there was little I could do to prevent it. My husband was in good form and their conversation was about their respective greatness, each bragging about this and that. They drank enough beer to last them at least three days and smoked enough cigarettes that our house, the front part at least, smelled like a beer-joint. While I was willing to have this cousin of his to be a guest for a while, even though he was a borderline alcoholic, I was not prepared to suffer through beer-stench and smoke for an entire day which it was going to turn into if I did not intervene. By then I was already plenty aggravated at this cousin's blatant inconsideration to stay this long and the apparent unwillingness of my husband to gently nudge him out because it was only me who had suggested it several times to him. I went straight into their smelly room and flatly said to his cousin, "It is time for you to go home. Our house is not a beer-joint!" I think he sobered up right then and there and my husband was so shocked at my bluntness that he could not say anything. They whispered something and the cousin left and I was very afraid I would catch Jack's anger, which I was already plenty afraid of, which only shows that I was desperate to reclaim my house as it was just not a good environment for my children and I hated it in principle. But to my surprise my husband did not browbeat me and threaten me as was his normal reaction to my exerting this kind of interference with his business and taking control in such a visible manner. I was so grateful for that and knew instantly that I was mysteriously protected in this instance. I never brought up this incident and he did not either. This did not mean that he forgot about it. He would just get back at me at a later date. No matter, it was quiet on the home front then and the children did not have to smell the stench of beer and smoke because I could open the window. It did not matter to me one iota that it was raining!

I used these situations to enforce his claim that he was a Christian now, and that required changes in his behavior. He played along as he could not defend this conduct and not be recognized as an impostor.

It was important to him to please me to some degree because it was congruent with his general desire to deceive the company whose contract made it possible for him to do that which was of the utmost importance to him and that was making money. Of course I was in favor of this as it gave me the opportunity to do my part, which was to have a fairly happy stable home for the children and then I carried myself with the hope that my husband would eventually realize for himself that to live in compliance with what the Bible teaches makes for a better life for everyone. He would indeed take the role as the leader of his family. He would be right there in church attendance and he encouraged the children in their faith-based education work. He was showing all the signs of someone who was learning to bring his life in line with what he professed (or pretended) to believe. However, there were these serious lapses that put everything I hoped for into question.

He had two brothers who were no paragons of virtue by any stretch of the imagination. I kept my distance as much as I could without coming off as being either stuck-up or complicit in their various dallyings of the unacceptable kind.

The older brother had a checkered past with many females and he was always in dire straits moneywise. At this time he and his wife were trying to go to church and do the right thing by their six sons (a blended situation) and I even went with my husband to some kind of church function for one of their sons, to be there for them and show support.

It was barely a wisp of time after this when I heard that the brother had a girlfriend in addition to his wife. I was disgusted. But when he came to our house and brought his girlfriend with him and acted as though this was the most normal thing, I just could not stand it. He barely sat himself down and the girlfriend had just been introduced to me when I could not refrain from saying that he and his girlfriend were not welcome in our house as my faith as a Christian does not permit such conduct and that I would rather that they did not stay under those circumstances. My husband had to agree to this and said that he as a Christian husband must support me in this. They both left in a huff and I carried myself with the hope that I would not have to deal with this brother again ever, which was a pipe dream, as he was in constant trouble of one sort or another and his misery was entirely of his own making.

It has always confused me when people who said they were Christians failed to see that their actions made them fools for thinking they deserve the respect due to the real Christians and they even act as though they have been wronged when one takes a stand against their unacceptable conduct or stands up for one's faith in Christ. I could not understand it being this way. Something was seriously wrong but I had too many things to worry about so I did not spend time to find the answer to this problem.

Having been brought up in Germany where there was this strict adherence to rules and regulations for personal conduct which had its basis in the fundamentals of the Christian faith and where it was the norm to expect compliance with the requirements of society at large with said rules made me wonder where all this disobedience and lawlessness in this country came from. It made it easier for me to adhere and comply because this was what I was used to but it made it more difficult to deal with people who did not as I did. I was definitely different.

But was it not wonderful that my husband was on the same page as I was in matters of our faith? I truly felt blessed and I was a husband-pleasing wife and it was easy.

12

Only the Strong Survive

There were many instances in the conduct of my husband that made it a pleasure to be married to him as he took hold of the concept of being the head of his home and I was that much more devoted to him and the thought of there being a higher purpose at work was entering my mind. As humans go, there had to be an explanation why I had to marry such a man, as unsuitable for me as he was. I reasoned that it was entirely Christian to assume that I was with this man in this relationship to help him to see that it was far better to live a God-pleasing life here on earth as it brought its own reward and at the same time prepared one for the Life Eternal as promised in the Scriptures. This kind of thinking made it possible for me to endure all the misery.

It was these positive thoughts which kept me trying to hang in there, fully counting on God's promise that the faithful shall be rewarded and I was so sure that I had to be rewarded just for having had to go through this ill-fated love-affair with Elvis which had brought me to the brink of madness and left me utterly confused as I could not explain anything that made any sense to my rational mind—if for nothing else. As far as I was concerned I was due a reward and the conversion of my husband to a true, Bible-believing, born-again Christian in word and deed must be the expected reward. It was a lofty goal and surely it was reason enough to tread where no one had trod before if that was what was called for. Alone, I could never have had the courage but I knew that I was never without help—it was truly always only a prayer away. But there were those times that the suffering was too much and the goal obscured by such dismal circumstances and atrocious conditions that I could not do anything but cry on the inside, in seemingly bottomless anguish and no prayer was in me. It was these times, as I look back, that I realize that God was the closest as he was carrying me through all the way.

Even though it was a worthy goal to have my husband turn to the God of the Scriptures and so fashion his conduct accordingly, there was this very practical consequence of such a change which extended beyond just one person, as important as this was. It affected my life and, most important to me, my, our children's lives. It had been the most singular endeavor of my childbearing years to pursue the ideal, as put forth by Jesus Himself, of the nuclear family—a mother and father together in one household taking care of their children. I had taken for granted, in my boundless ignorance, that this was a very normal thing to expect when I married a man. It was beyond my ability to contemplate anything else. Utterly devastated by the reality of the dismal outcome for my children that came from an Elvis-imitator, which is what my first husband really was, I resolved that I now had an opportunity to prove God right. The children, who had their mother and father together in the same place, teaching them the Lord's way, will result in grounded individuals, capable to deal with life in a God-pleasing manner.

I held on to this dream for dear life. It would also exonerate me from the crushing realization of the wayward ways of the older children as I was trying to make up for past sins of disobedience to God's laws. I reasoned that it was impossible to maintain a marriage with an unfaithful husband and the divorce in these circumstances was inevitable and so the poor children did not have their father and mother together in the same house to take care of them and that it was because of this circumstance that the teachings of the Bible fell on undernourished soil and so could not grow the spiritual seeds that had been sown since their early childhood. I cannot describe how responsible for this failure I felt I was. It caused me sleepless nights and endless agonizing recriminations during the days. It is not surprising to me that I would make it my chief goal to do better by far this time around even if it had to be with such a horrible man, as Rachel, Judy, Jeremy, and Susan saw him as time went by and he revealed himself to be. And I had no way to defend him other than to say that he was my husband and the father of my children. It rang very hollow to them and me.

I was in this strange situation for the duration and as much emphasis as I put on the positive things my husband provided, there were these completely inexplicable devious machinations, which I feared as they were plentiful. My children were definitely worth the effort to me.

I had a very busy life—it is a busy life for any stay-at-home mom who strives to be a good mother and housekeeper and cook and nurse and counselor and taxi-driver and . . . and. . . .

We finally moved into our new house and I made sure that there was very little difference between the setting of the old house and the setting in the new one. I made sure that my children had a minimum of disturbance in the coming weeks of adjusting to the new surroundings. I maintained the same schedule and put their things in similar, that is, accustomed, proximity and I did not notice any signs of upset in their conduct.

Three days after we moved, our six-year-old, Richard, had his birthday and I made cupcakes for his class. Not being familiar with a self-cleaning oven I found my cupcakes locked in the oven and I had no idea what was going on and how to get them out. I was getting panicky. I was going to deliver them to the school at the party time and from the way things looked the oven was not giving up the cupcakes. I called this person and that person and my husband but nobody could help. I gave it one more try and violà!, the oven opened and I could take the treats to school for the birthday celebration and all was well. Much later I found the instructions to the oven and I had to laugh at this snafu, just because I did not know of the latest inventions!

Needless to say, Samuel was like an appendage to me. He was with me wherever I had to go. He was in his infant car seat as snug as a bug in a rug and I would not have had it any other way! He was so precious to me and I truly was his slave.

I loved living in the new house. It was a pretty house and even though we had our old furniture, which we had bought when we moved from my ex-mother-in-law's house into the bigger house and it was showing wear and tear, I still made do and did not really care as long as my children were happy and they were a happy bunch as far as I could tell. When it became embarrassingly obvious to my husband that we were in a spiffy home with crummy furniture, he surprised us all with a couch and a chair and a non-matching loveseat, which he said he bought from some guy off of the back of his truck. I really did not want to know the details as I had learned that in the case of my husband, the less you knew the better off you were. If it made him happy it was all right with me and he seemed inordinately satisfied with this purchase. It certainly was not commensurate with the style of the house and I would not have purchased it.

I was happy to see my husband satisfied for whatever reason and freely and sincerely complimented him on his selection, allowing for the difference in taste and it was definitely an improvement over the torn-up furniture from the old house.

Soon after we had moved in I saw that the bill for heating the house was much higher than at the smaller house. I alerted him to this fact and I expected him to increase the amount for the monthly budget. It also took more gasoline to go anywhere from where we now lived and that needed to be addressed. However instead of adjusting the amount accordingly, he threw a fit and angrily called me derogatory names and, as usual, accused me of mismanagement of funds and that my children from the previous marriage were the real reason for the shortfall, which was simply not true. He completely avoided discussing the issue, let alone remedying it. It was truly as horrifying as it was at its worst at the old domicile. I was a nervous wreck, worrying from one month to the next how to manage everything and keep everybody happy at the same time. It was a hell that I was consenting to live in if only I could pretend to be happily taking care of my family, including my husband.

He bought a paddleboat, as we lived on a lake property with at least a quarter of an acre under water, leaving one-and-three-quarter acres of land, which had a small pond on it as well. It looked snake-filled to me. My husband took to caring for his possessions like a duck to water. He was a very good caretaker of the grounds and the house as it pertained to them retaining or increasing their value. Other than that he could not care less. If something needed fixing in the house and it was inconveniencing me he was as slow as a turtle in getting it fixed. I was just not that important. He expected total cooperation in the bedroom and I do mean total cooperation and it was a good thing that I was blessed with an exaggerated libido and it therefore served me well to accommodate him this way which cemented our relationship just as it is supposed to do for two people in a marriage, according to the Scriptures. It was crucial that I let his very well-targeted injurious comments run over me rather than into me because I had to train myself to play the part of the happy wife and mother to the very tiniest detail or it would not have been an overall positive experience. This was no small feat.

I always wondered how it was possible for me to do this and I can only surmise that this over-arching, all-encompassing feeling of limitless love that had overcome me when it was set free by the love I heard coming from Elvis in his love songs to me, brimming with passion and pain in every line, which made the words, written mostly by someone else, exclusively his alone.

It seemed like no time at all that all the activities to acclimate to all the new things and to put everything into a daily routine slowed down for my husband and, being a restless person by nature, he discovered his interest in horses. We had a neighbor down the street, who had a sixteen-year-old, well-endowed, pretty blonde daughter, who just loved horses and owned one. He spent a lot of time at their house and before I knew it, he shyly approached me, saying that he had this burr under his saddle and he just had to have his own horses. I could hardly believe what I was hearing and I cautioned him about spending too much money, saying that he just could not have everything at once. He had no time for his motorcycle—his interest had changed to horses. He sold the motorcycle.

The pond had to be drained and filled in to accommodate two horses and a fence had to be erected around the entire back portion of the property and a dividing fence to keep the animals away from the house. Money did not seem to be an issue at all but he had absolutely no money for my piddly needs for our household. I was certainly accustomed to this attitude toward me and my financial needs and I did the best I could without letting my disapproval show in an angry fashion. If I would bring it up in a matter-of-fact sort of way, he simply did not respond. He'd just give me one of his habitual nasty mangy dog looks and change the subject. This was enough for me to drop the issue as this look always preceded an outburst of unsavory language and a tirade of accusations of the worst kind which were always only a step away from a physical altercation. Our baby boy was getting old enough to start walking and had always wanted to climb the stairs to the loft. I asked Jack to please get a safety door and he launched into a screaming fit, complaining of my unreasonable demands, and when I did not back down and insisted that it was an important safety concern, he just hit me so hard that I fell a long way and ended up on the couch. I was furious and hit him back and yelled at the top of my lungs and called him a few things I had thought of him. He fought back and I kept on fighting him until I was too exhausted. But I did get that gate for my baby boy. Such was my life. I had to risk life and limb to get what I needed. I was determined to salvage a tender feeling for Jack and I always took consolation in the good things he did and there were many. In order for me to make this problematic relationship work, I had to be able to love him and I did. I loved him because he was the father of my wonderful and precious children, he shielded me from the world, he was a good businessman and a good organizer. He was a man, a perfect match to me, a woman.

He'd still drink his beer and smoke his pot, and on those occasions he would wear that silly grin on his face and things that he normally would not like, he tolerated with glee, which was really confusing the children and had been a serious problem earlier on when my children from my previous marriage were exposed to this. It was difficult for me to know how to handle it and I often did the wrong thing and caused a whole new set of problems which usually ended up with him accusing me of pampering my children and not letting him be the father they needed. It was hard to know what to do and an angel I was not.

As we were faithfully going to church and we did family devotions in the evening, I expressed my thought that we should have the house dedicated by the church. I had talked about this from the very beginning of the building process and he agreed. We had a window-treatment specialist come and look at the windows and explain what kind of drapes and shades we could possibly use to accentuate the beauty of the house. We got three estimates and we went with the least expensive one, which still went into the thousands. I had my heart set on it and so we had it done but Jack absolutely resented having to spend that much money on what he called curtains. I confess that I know little about the latest things and what was in or out. That never applied to me as I could never afford keeping up with such things and it just was not important to me. Forever after, he would call the drapes derogatory names, even though they were quite elegant and fitting for the house. Everybody else thought so too. He was basically of the opinion that modern shade treatment would have been better and certainly cheaper. Another strike against me. There was no way to satisfy this man. Even if you went along with him on everything, he'd go looking for something to come up with to criticize and malign. I figured that I would always be in trouble with him, regardless, so I might as well get what I wanted on occasion. These window treatments were what I wanted. In retrospect I am still amazed that I had the courage to follow through but I guess I was still living in some sort of la-la-land and it seemed all right and important enough.

On the day of the dedication, which was on the twenty-ninth of March, we had light refreshments for our invited guests, who consisted of friends and family and church members. At the time of the arrival of the people, it was so weird, as it snowed furiously for just a short time. The snowflakes blew into the house when we opened the door to let them in and it seemed like it was all over after all the guests had shown up. It was definitely weird and for just a split-second I thought that this dedication was not going to do what I had prayed for, which was to protect us all from evil and bless us all in everything we did with God in mind. But I fully trusted God.

The horses had been bought and they were boarded at some farm nearby. At that time this subdivision was in the first phase of the development plan and farms were still a good part of the general surroundings. My husband would be gone a lot to acquaint himself with everything pertaining to horses and I am very sure he spent a great deal of money on this latest acquisition while I was still stealing from Peter to pay Paul, so to speak. I used the credit cards when I had to and did so more than I care to admit, only to circumvent a confrontation with my husband over money matters as they did nothing to solve the problem and only added my husband's deep resentment toward me because I did not work outside the home to take care of the items in dispute. I dreaded nothing more than his almost irrational hatred and the consequent, highly injurious accusations expressed in the most offensive way possible. It was just like a beating, only worse, I think. From one month to the next I was sweating bullets when I had to see the monthly minimum payment go up.

Surprisingly enough, at times he would be uncharacteristically generous to all kinds of people. He liked to play the big man and he spent his money (which was really ours) any way he pleased and it was always so that his reputation was that of a good and generous man. Contrast that with the defiant attitude with which he stingily appropriated a measly amount on the tithe for the church. He hated the concept of tithing, Scriptural though it is. He had to pay child support and I made sure that my stepdaughter's mother got the payment on time, as I had been through the misery of not getting child support from my ex because of his wife who he said used the money for other bills. Jack nickled and dimed that poor woman and took all kinds of trouble to see that she was not going to get a dime more than the minimum required by law.

I took the children on the pontoon boat outing that we all enjoyed very much, crisscrossing the lake, slowly and quietly entering the lagoon and watching birds, turtles, frogs and snakes. When the heat set in it was mentioned that we should have a swimming pool and before I knew it the people came out and measured and planned the excavation and it seemed like no time at all that we had a beautiful pool. It was an octagon-shaped pool and it beckoned you to jump in on a hot summer day. Susan, my husband's used-to-be favorite, was living with us and she liked the pool too and we all enjoyed watching the children jumping in and diving from the diving board. We were practically living in a vacation home. I considered myself blessed indeed.

My husband was a good insurance broker for this very reputable big insurance company and they always rewarded their top producers with these trips to all kinds of places all over the globe for a tax write-off.

Naturally my capable husband always qualified for these trips. Sometimes we would go but there was one time, I remember, he did not want to participate. He said that he did not care to go to London. I have no idea if that was the real reason or if he had something else going on that made this ten-day junket undesirable for him. It certainly did not bother me since I hated to have to go on these junkets and leave my beloved children behind. There was one time when the whole family was allowed to come along. We went to Orlando Kissimmee to be exact. It was such a treat. My stepdaughter came as well and we had the best time there. Our baby son was just a year old and we put him in the stroller and had a great time just watching the children having fun. That's the kind of trip I preferred. In fact my husband took all the family, his mother and the youngest daughter of mine to Panacea, Florida and we enjoyed that too. There was always this glitch—my husband's bad behavior.

Jack always had to drink beer and it is only by the sheer grace of God that we did not get either killed on the highway or murdered by this madman. Ever since I had known him he was so ugly to his mother, which really bothered me and she and I bantered our way humorously through the potentially explosive situations and made him end up laughing with us. It was strenuous but worth the effort as we all returned home with all our limbs intact. Over time I was able to convince him that it just was not right for him to treat his mother so disrespectfully and he gradually changed and became kinder to his mother and when she asked him for money, I told him to give it to her. She was his mother, for goodness sake. One fine day he informed me that he was buying his mother a new car, which she needed, and I was to pay the monthly note since he was going to increase my monthly budget accordingly. I was happy to do this, of course but I could not help but wonder why he could not throw me a few bucks to make my life a little easier. I did not use the dryer and hung the clothes out on the wrought-iron fence which we had to have around the pool, as clotheslines were a no-no in the neighborhood covenant. I used the dishwasher only when we had big holidays and all the family was at our house. I bought day-old bread and marked-down vegetables and inexpensive cuts of meat. I still used cloth diapers and rubber pants for the baby, because I could not afford to buy diapers that I then would have to throw out. This was way too expensive for someone in my position. I bought virtually everything at a discount store of one sort or another. It was so ridiculous to live in a fancy house with a swimming pool and fairly expensive window-treatments, which included Roman shades for the floor-to-ceiling windows with the view on the pool, the sloping meadow beyond it and down to the lake which sparkled like rhinestones in the sunshine, but have to shop as any poor woman living on food stamps with her children and disabled husband. But there was nothing I could change. I could not understand it. Why was he so mean and cruel to me while at the same time insisting that he loved me? I did think that he mistook desire for love and that made it understandable. He considered me to be like one of his possessions and used and abused me just like any other thing he desired and eventually got tired of and lost interest in and then ultimately dropped or abandoned it. But I just was not an It and there was nothing he could do about that and so we lived together to take care of our children as the church admonishes and as he was willing to do, if for no other reason than to enhance his reputation as a generous and kind person who took good care of his family. He was very protective of appearances in this regard and never missed an opportunity if he was in his right mind. I helped him with this as I played the part of the happy housewife and mother who was as happy as could be in this lovely home, etc. It was certainly a boon for his ever-improving standing with this insurance company, which had this regional representative coming unannounced to our house after she had business dealings at my husband's office, which she also inspected. I was a good housekeeper and the children were always contentedly playing with their toys which were strewn throughout the big great room and that's the way I liked it. Pretty as my house was, and it was that, it was foremost where we lived and did not just sit there as in a museum. She particularly liked the window-treatments and she asked my husband what that strange seam was, going quite visibly from the entry hall on the curved stairs to the loft. I had wondered that myself, but I was afraid to criticize anything since my husband was involved in every stage of the laying and of course the selection of the carpet. My only input was the color. He obviously went the cheapest route, in the quality of the carpet as well as the installation of it, for which he had probably hired one of his cronies with a drinking problem and to him this seam looked just fine. It wasn't long after this incident that we had new, much better-quality carpet installed. It was really nice carpet. It was so luxurious and beautiful. There was no seam out of place or visible. It suited me.

I was very instrumental in his rise to the respected, successful, insurance broker that he had become and it was in his interest to do everything that was expected of him as such to continue to reap the financial gains that must have been considerable. He never discussed anything financial with me. We had separate accounts with different banks and I had no clue how much money he was earning or what he did with it. I remember only one time when he was bragging to me about the big money he was making and, sort of as an aside, indicated that he was not going to let the government have their money, which unsettled me but I really did not understand what there was available for him to do. The only thing I could come up with was that he was not going to declare his total gross income. This was a very unpleasant and scary thought for me and since I had no control whatever in this matter, I chose not to say anything. Besides, his mind was made up and he took a sadistic sort of pleasure to be able to do this. When the time came for me to sign the joint tax return, he was anxiously standing beside me and it felt to me like he was holding his breath in fear that I would notice the low amount and would refuse to sign it. I signed it posthaste and thought to myself that this is all way too big and problematic for me to tackle and sincerely asked the Lord to take care of this as I simply could not deal with this. He and his CPA, like many people, found ways to hide money in some creatively constructed smoke-and-mirror scheme to get around the tax laws. He was very relieved when I signed the form, though he tried to hide it. This also kept him from having to increase the child-support payments accordingly to his ex. The correlation of this dawned on me much later. When it came to his money and how to protect it, he was practically a genius in my eyes. He was very scary to me because this greed was so foreign to my personality and I found it to be part of the basis for his continued harassment of me.

Rachel was in grad school, Judy had moved in with her boyfriend and Jeremy, her brother moved into their apartment with them and shared expenses. Soon she was expecting my grandson but the father did not want to marry her. He hated to have to be forced into something he really did not want.

As these things go, they eventually married but I had a problem with her coming to my house, pregnant and not married. I had young children in the house and I really did not like the whole situation. In fact, I hated it.

Susan, my husband's favorite, lived with us in the room over the garage, which had its separate entrance. However, now that she was older, ready to make a decision whether to pursue higher learning or not, she became persona non grata in our household which complicated everything even more for me. First of all I had no idea why Jack turned so ugly to her and she certainly did not understand; and it took her sister and brother to figure this out. She may have been his favorite when all that was required were little fun things, but nice though they were, and much appreciated, he was certainly not using any of his money to help her in higher education, since he was not even her father! We spent much time discussing the shortcomings of my husband and it was a terrible situation for me as I had to agree with my children about my husband's meanness, his selfishness, his cruelty but at the same time not get my mind and heart poisoned against him. Looking back it seems as though I had a sort of "protective covering" over my mind and the poisoned darts simply could not penetrate. One of the younger children, both of whom were then in elementary school, would saunter by and I would always shush the conversation about their father as I wanted them to have a positive impression of their father and to love him as such.

It was Susan who helped taking care of our baby boy when my husband and I went to Brazil. Little Samuel chose to sleep with her as he was missing his mommy. I was none too happy to have to leave my children and I would have gladly done without seeing Rio de Janeiro and Sugarloaf Mountain or any other attraction on the globe, for that matter, but my husband demanded that I fulfill my obligation as his wife as this trip was for the big producers and their wives. By that time we had the horses on our property and my mother-in-law was taking care of the children and their going to school as my daughter was working and going to school and was about to graduate from high school. She would get phone calls from Grandma who was frantic as the horses got out and went on their way into some neighbor's yard. Thank goodness there were understanding men around who brought the horses back.

The time in Brazil was fun but I missed my children far too much and I was counting the days, until I could come back. On these trips I never had a dime to my name. Jack got the money changed but never ever gave me a Brazilian penny. I never ventured anywhere. I was always with my husband and I never dared to ask him for any money as I was only too acquainted with his horrifying threatening attitude when it came to me and his money. He bought me some earrings I said I liked, so I was only too grateful to have gotten that. He determined what was to be given to whom but he always got me into the deliberations and then decided if the price was right for him, and in the end the decision was his alone, but he made me think it was a joint decision. If I knew what was good for me and the family I'd better play his game and play it very well and so I did. I was long past getting anything my way—only if there was some advantage for him would I get what I wanted. In spite of all the downsides to my husband's personality I still was devoted to the cause of having this family that I had always dreamed of and I was bound and determined to follow that dream as Jesus had outlined it completely for us in the Bible, the holy Word of God.

It was my comfort zone, even if most of my life was troublesome. There were workmen at our house of one sort or another as one thing or another was not done right the first time. I remember one fellow in particular whom my husband had insured since his early days in the insurance business; he was an older man and kindly looking and as it was not unusual for me to be scared out of my wits at something my husband had threatened me with which always involved the children's welfare, I felt compelled to confide in this man that I thought that my husband was the devil. For some reason I did not stop to think that this man was an old friend of my husband's and he would surely tell him what I said, which he did; but my husband waited a very long time to let me know it. He waited for a time when we had a fairly good spell as everything appeared to go his way. I could barely breathe and I had nothing to say when he said to me, "It's a fine thing to hear from other people that my wife thinks I am the devil!" I did not retract anything and managed to smile weakly as it did sound sort of amusing on the face of it and left it at that. He did not mention it again. Thank the good Lord. He could have demanded all sorts of devious things from me to make me pay—ah, what am I saying? He did, as I was his slave and I knew it and obediently did his bidding if only he would let me continue to make believe that we had a functioning family unit, consisting of a mother and a father in the same house taking care of our children.

My husband had a friend whom he had known on some type of personal level that included something secret that only the two of them shared. This man seemed to be nice and he behaved himself around me and my children in a pleasant fashion. They would decide that they would spend some time together which included an overnight stay by my husband at this man's house. I was told that they would reminisce and play music from their past. I thought that it would be far better at this guy's house than at ours. He was not married and lived alone, so this way I would not have to listen to that horrid music which did nothing but glorify everything demonic as far as I was concerned. My husband would come home the next day, early in the morning, all dragged out and spent-looking. He'd go to bed and sleep till noon. I would pleasantly ask him if he had a good time and he'd look at me somewhat confused, probably thinking that I did indeed have a high tolerance level for his mind games. How wrong he was! I always had to decide that I could not afford the luxury of pride and self-respect as any preference for my hurt self-image would always include putting my family at risk in some way.

I was still thinking of that song that I could not remember from that dream that started to resurrect Elvis for me and still kept looking for songs of Elvis's and to my astonishment found many, many songs I had never even heard before, ever. I had found some cassette tapes of songs I was familiar with and played them on my long driving time to school and back which made the children quite informed on Elvis. My stepdaughter had her spring break at a different time and so could come to our house for a short visit and she would come with me to pick up the children from school and sing along and I would tell them about my times with Elvis. I have no idea if they believed anything I said. It was not important to me. I was just glad to be able to talk to somebody about this very important part of my life. Since they were children, I did not have to fear disbelief, ridicule, or rejection. I could not get over how much I enjoyed talking about my times and thoughts about Elvis and the children were indeed a captive audience in the car.

They seemed to enjoy my stories and I must admit that my brushes with Elvis were funny, if not hilarious, when I think about how it all went down. Of course I did not burden them with the multitude of tragic occurrences that lay beneath all the joviality as I myself could not understand much, my serious contemplations always coming way short of any rational explanation. I understood deep inside that this whole Elvis thing would ultimately be as clear as a bell in its own time which was out of my control.

But the children and I had a lot of fun listening to Elvis sing "Indescribably Blue," "Do You Know Who I Am?" "Just a Little Bit of Green," "She's Not You," "I'll Hold You in My Heart Till I Can Hold You in My Arms," "It's Now or Never," "Make Me Know It," "Surrender," and many, many, more. Those love songs of Elvis were like soothing ointment on an open wound to me and I was ever so thankful that I had come to find out about this "soothing balm"—even if it had to be brought to me in a dream.

I had far too little time to agonize much about the meaning behind the mysterious happenings in my life but when it forced itself to the surface I had to respond in some way. It was so when I went looking for this elusive song that I did not seem to be able to find, though I was sure that I would recognize it instantly upon hearing it. I found *From Elvis Presley Boulevard* and I could hardly contain my curiosity to find out what he was singing about on this tape. As I was driving along, listening to his words that were disturbingly depressing, I heard Elvis saying to me in a very audible voice, "Say something, woman!" I was so stunned and I immediately reversed the song I had just been listening to and thought to myself that I had not heard this before. I switched it back and forth, this way and that, and after I had listened to the tape in its entirety and had found nothing that resembled this direct order,

I concluded that Elvis talked to me and was quite adamant about this command. I hated the whole idea from the onset and complained aloud, "That's easy for you to say. You've got the ear of the whole world. What am I supposed to do?" But I knew that this was a serious command and that I had to yield. How that was going to happen I had no idea and it was much too scary for me to dwell on. I am by nature a private person and somewhat shy in unfamiliar surroundings and the idea that I had to publicly speak anywhere was just too much. I put it out of my mind as I had more pressing things to deal with but I felt confident that "what will be, will be."

One fine sunny day, on the way to run errands with my now-walking youngest son, I was at the gas station when I ran into good old Red West, Elvis's friend and confidant for all those years. We said hello and he had that amused sort of look in his eyes. He told me that he had bought fourteen acres of land on St. Elmo and I told him where we were living and just as in the now-distant past, I was gone. I was actually somewhat scared of him because he was the reality and I was in no way ready to confront the huge implications of my time with Elvis and I clearly felt that less was enough at that juncture. But I was ever so curious to find out whether it was Elvis who sent him after me to offer me a ride home that time at The Memphian when I announced that I was leaving because I did not like the movie. I seemed to remember seeing, in my mind's eye, Elvis leaning over and telling Red something, after which Red came running after me and stopped me in the lobby where I was trying to call a cab to go home. That night my mother-in-law offered to watch the children as my husband at the time was working the late shift and I did not have a car. I could not risk being unduly influenced one way or the other. Somehow I always knew to preserve my sanity and I knew the source of that ability as it was God-given.

I still feel silly enough about having said then to Red that I was going to tell Elvis on him because I thought he was making a pass at me. Talk about ignorant! But I could not at the time face the reality which was that it was Elvis who set the tone at his house or houses, wherever they were, in Memphis or in California, and these men he had around him followed suit and that was just the way it was. I did not want to accept that, because in my way of thinking there just was no way that I could love such a man as much as I did. My husband at the time would gloss over the sad state of affairs as he, too mimicked Elvis's lifestyle (unbeknownst to me for the longest time until it was revealed to me in a dream) and I felt even sillier at the idea that it was because of Elvis that I assumed that Red had made a pass at me and that I called him on the carpet for nothing. There is a song I found much later that actually refers to this incident and it is called "My Babe." It was definitely better to let sleeping dogs lie.

At that time Charlie Hodge had finished his book and he was busy promoting it. Albert Goldman, too, wrote a searingly negative treatise on Elvis. I could hardly stand to read it as it was complete conjecture on Mr. Goldman's part. Charlie's book I never read. I glanced through it and decided that Charlie's obvious intention was not to say anything negative outright about Elvis which was the exact opposite of Goldman's aim, and for this reason unacceptable to me. However when I read in the paper that Charlie was going to be at the Peabody Library, on Peabody Avenue, which was the main library in Memphis at the time, to give a talk and a question-and-answer session to promote the sale of his book, I made plans to attend.

My husband had gone to the airport to pick up his daughter, who was scheduled to come with us and Grandma to the Grand Canyon. I never mentioned any of my plans to anyone and I drove to the library and it was so good to see Charlie after all these years. It had been thirteen years since I last saw him at the Howard Johnson's motel in June 1975. Charlie was happy too and exclaimed, "Hello, Ilona!" and he even pronounced it correctly, which I had never heard him do before. The emphasis is on the first syllable and only very few people are aware of this. None of my friends and acquaintances knew it, let alone abided by it when I tried to correct their pronunciation, as my mother taught me to do. There were thirty or forty people in attendance. Charlie was talking about benign things, always making sure that Elvis was this revered, wonderful demi-god. I realized that Charlie, like everybody else who had worked for Elvis or was near Elvis, either as a relative, friend or whatever, tried to make money off Elvis in whatever way they could and the opportunities were certainly there. I cringed at the thought that someone would think that of me also when I revealed that

I also knew Elvis and had a lot to tell. It was such an unpleasant thought as I loathed each and every one who sold the secrets to the highest bidder. It seriously discouraged me from coming out about Elvis, so to speak. I brought up Albert Goldman's book at that meeting and everybody was looking at me because of my accent. Charlie introduced me to the people as a very good friend to himself and Elvis since their time in Germany. I cannot recall anything else. When the meeting was over the people rushed toward me and asked me all sorts of things about Elvis. I tried to tell them that I did not get along with Elvis and that I had never kissed him but to no avail. I had to leave at once because I had to beat my husband home, so he would not interrogate me on my whereabouts, which would have opened up a whole new can of worms for me that I would find unpleasant to have to deal with, as I disliked telling lies. Before I left, Charlie asked me if I wanted back the pictures that I had sent him some years earlier when my attention was drawn to him during my initial attempts to find that song of Elvis's to which I had only a sliver of the melody. The subsequent power of love rolled over my soul like a tidal wave and the desire to die, as the constant vacillation between utter euphoria and abject depression was taking its toll. I could not eat, I could not sleep, and I had lost sixteen pounds throughout this ordeal until I perceived that I had to have this boy of mine. I got Charlie's post office box number in Decatur, Alabama, where he was from. I wanted him to have something of me from my younger years in Germany, just in case I would die. Charlie said that he had them in his truck. I had to leave so abruptly I had no time to buy his book either—poor Charlie—and I had no time to explain.

My family and I went on our trip and had a great time. We returned in the very early afternoon and everybody was busy getting things situated after a trip. Our washing machine had stopped working, so I decided that I could get the last load washed at a laundry mart on the way to the pizza parlor where everybody was looking forward to going, when my husband informed me that he was going to go fishing with the brother of this voluptuous coquettish sister of his who spent too much time with my husband indulging in their love for horses. This did not suit me at all but I figured that he had been doing all that driving, cooped up with all of us in a big van, which he had rented for the occasion. Beth disliked it even more than I, and she sat in the car with disgust written all over her face. I know I could have never done all that he had done to take us on that trip and bring us back and I tried my best to make her understand that he needed some relief, even though I could have done with some relief myself, considering that a trip with my husband is a severe threat to my health. So there she sat in the back of the car with total dislike of me flashing in her eyes. This irritated me and I warned her that I had a hard enough time as it was and that I was not going to look at her miserable face and have her ruin the fun for everybody else. As if she had turned on a switch, she changed her demeanor instantly and she was the fun and entertainment for the entire evening. I was perplexed for a moment and marveled at her ability to be such an accomplished actress as she was very convincingly a happy girl. In and of itself this meant next to nothing to me at the time, but it definitely figured prominently into future events, which I could have never conceived of in my wildest imagination.

I had always had a good relationship with Beth and I treated her as if she were my very own. Richard, who was three years her junior, absolutely adored her and imitated her every chance he got. She was smart, self-reliant and full of good (though sometimes not) ideas to keep our children entertained and having fun at the same time. We always hated to see her leave and she always cried very much and appeared to be just heartbroken to leave her daddy and it was a sad time for all of us. I always took the opportunity to emphasize how destructive and hurtful divorce is, especially for the children. She loved her mother and her mother loved her, there was no question, but she also loved her father and that put her into an emotional meat grinder, particularly after her mother divorced the father of Beth's half-brother and all three of them now lived in an apartment while the mother waited for the settlement, which took a long time as the ex-husband was contesting everything. It was a very stressful time for the poor girl and I felt heartily sorry for her. Although she appeared to like me, she also disliked me now that her mother was going to be free again and if it were not for me, her parents could be together again. All children dream of their parents being together. I wonder why that is so and why the social engineers choose to overlook this when they make changes that are bound to complicate things for the ones who cannot fend or speak for themselves, just so the adults can do whatever they want in order to fashion their lives according to their whims. What a crock this concept of self-actualization is!

I got several thank-you notes from my stepdaughter's mother, in which she expounded on the good care her daughter received when she came to visit and how her daughter always looked forward to going to our house.

On one occasion we went to meet Beth's new family because her mother did not want her to fly alone just yet. We met in St. Louis, Missouri, and we went sightseeing and went up in the Arch, which was exciting for all of us.

Personally I am as much against divorce as ever and it grieves me to no end to see people get divorced over the least little things. It is alarming because I feel that too many children from divorced parents, without the structured belief of religion, become uprooted and are subject to all kinds of negative influences.

I had to be sensitive to this child's dilemma—oh, just one more thing—as if I did not have enough to deal with already.

Not any time at all after Judy married the father of my grandson, she wanted to get divorced from him because he was this and that and she just did not love him. Rachel got married to a professor at the grad school she was attending, a man who was more than twice her age and older than I was. Susan moved into her boyfriend's house with his mother and sister because she no longer felt welcome at our house. After graduation this young man went to UT Knoxville and she moved back with us. Soon he managed to convince her that she should move to Knoxville and live with him because they loved each other. I warned him that he was responsible for her now, because he was the reason for her moving and that he therefore forfeited a home for her. I made my daughter aware of this also and I could barely hide my disappointment at her decision to do things the same way her siblings did and I was so hoping she would be the one who actually arranged her life with God in mind. Sometimes I wondered myself which planet I was living on. I sure could not understand what was happening here. My hopes and dreams now centered on teaching my little children the ways of the

Lord, and since they had their father participating with me trying to impress upon them the importance of God being at the center of one's life, I had every reason for hope.

We went to attend the wedding of this UT student in Knoxville and my daughter, and it seemed a good thing. We had hardly gotten back from the trip, maybe a month or two, when she called and said that her husband had been cheating on her, even before they were married, and he continued to cheat during their marriage. It was a mess! Although I felt very sorry for my daughter, I would have let her sort things out for herself, but my husband took over and talked her into coming back to Memphis. So she came back to live with us. It was a short while before she returned to Knoxville because she was going out with a former co-worker who was working with her at a pharmacy and he was a full-time student at UT Knoxville, getting his bachelor's degree in business.

Well, by writing about all these goings-on, and some more which were too undeveloped but clearly discernible on the horizon, I did not need another complication which my stepdaughter presented.

It was never more apparent to me how very uncertain my future really was than when he, my husband, for one flimsy reason or another decided that he was tired of playing by the rules and that he really did not have to if he did not want to. He would complain about this or that and act the injured party and then tell me that he simply was not going to remain a cooperating husband. He would completely remove himself from me. He would sleep in the rec room on the other side of the house and he would only interact with the children and completely ignore me. He would go to work and do whatever was required but at home he was unbelievable. He then would pack some clothes and spend the night who knows where. When he'd return, he'd continue to live separate from me. There are no words to describe the emotional trauma this engendered in me, as I was once again made painfully aware that I had absolutely no control over him. One thing was sure, I could not continue to live this way and be the mother I wanted and needed to be for my children. For that it takes two, the mother and the father, working together. I was so furious at the very notion that I was a victim of my husband and there was nothing I could do about it. Whether he was seriously entertaining the idea of getting a divorce, I could not tell, but I got panic-stricken at this very thought. Knowing him to have absolutely no scruples when it came to lying to get what he thought he deserved or even just wanted, I could not let it get that far and I blew my anger at this unfair situation and my injured pride into the wind, swallowed hard and started to beg and grovel. I would implore him to please think of the children, that I really loved him and I was telling the truth when I said that I missed him. I did, even though he was a monster of a man to me most of the time, but I felt more secure if we were husband and wife in a sanctioned union. It simply was a foundational necessity without which I felt I could not find the strength within me to provide the support and emotional care to my children. When he had satisfied his sadistic desire to see me humiliated, he would then, ever so sweetly, albeit hesitatingly, as if holding out for more groveling, agree to try to work with me.

There simply was no end to the things I was agreeing to tolerate by my throwing myself at his mercy. It was beyond my ability to understand his glaring hypocrisy when he would go with us to Sunday school and very earnestly discuss spiritual issues, worship with me in church and by all accounts give the impression that he was a man of God. I know that I had to have had divine protection, not to be consumed with disgust and hatred. It would surely have driven me to drinking or drugging or promiscuity if I had not had the advantage of my faith in a just God, who had made it perfectly clear that as a believer, though we are not spared trouble and pain, He is there with us helping us through it all. There was nothing more comforting to my soul when I was in utter distress.

Concurrent with these relationship issues, the continuing money problems, the various personal problems of my adult children, the onset of serious accusations made against me by my stepdaughter and the overwhelming physically strenuous day-to-day running of the household, the cooking and cleaning, the responsibilities as the mother of school-age children and the extracurricular activities to promote a healthy attitude toward school by my children, I was informed via documents sent by a law firm in Germany that the property my late father had been left in some sort of legal limbo as to what should be done with it and who had the right to do it. The central issue was whether the daughters of my late father could sell the property, which is what they wanted to do, or keep it in the family which is what my cousin wanted.

While I was caught between these two opposing factions, I was trying to the best of my ability to side with the one my conscience permitted me to side with. Apparently it was I who had the deciding voting power since both my sister and brother had thrown their support on the side of the would-be sellers of the property in question. Having been so swamped with problems on all sides I had no patience with the bellyaching that followed the initial contact from this law firm and then my relatives. After some phone conversations and correspondence I could fairly easily decide whom I would vote for.

I knew my cousin as a decent, ambitious person who loved that piece of land and he had cared for it and used it with permission from my father, his uncle. I had my own sentimental reasons for wanting to keep it in the family. After all, it was home to me when I had nowhere else to go and I loved the time I had spent there and I still love to recall the fond memories of a charmed time gone by. It was there when God kept me from killing myself, telling me that time would tell, and when I was given this indescribable feeling of divine peace which was in me when I "met" with Elvis a short time later at school (spiritually).

My half-sisters on the other hand I hardly knew. I met the younger one on our last trip to Germany and I never even saw the older one on that occasion. Since it had been the first time that I made it back home in twenty years at that time I had thought it to be a very important occasion indeed and that this sister of mine should have made an effort to meet me but this did not happen and I did feel a twinge of rejection. The point being that I knew nothing about her, good or bad, but one thing I could determine long-distance was that she did not love the land and it was only of use to her to sell it and get the money. My stepmother had turned all the legal wrangling to her eldest and as she was up in years I could not blame her. I had enough trouble with the American legal terminology—trying to understand the German legalese was something else. I wrote a lengthy letter, explaining in detail how and why I voted as I did. I made photocopies of the original, mailed them to all concerned and waited for another kind of hell to begin. And it did. I now had my sister, my brother, and my late father's whole family on the warpath. Not that any one of them had ever shown any interest in me before. I became important only when I was a needed means to an end. I hated this situation, and it always hurts when somebody treats me shabbily. For the sake of peace I'd go the extra mile if I could, but there was nothing I could do since they all cloaked themselves in silence. It was deafening particularly after the barrage of calls and letters and more documents. It was sad, but I could not spend much time to dwell on these developments as I had enough to deal with on the home front.

My husband thought nothing of having a few beers and then going off riding with this teenager who was a pretty sight on a horse. No doubt my husband was showing off his prowess as a horseman and he was taking risks jumping over gullies and ditches; he was unaware that on the other side, hidden by leaves and underbrush, lurked a deeper drop-off than he had anticipated. The result was a fall from the horse and he had to come home limping. He needed medical attention. Nothing was broken but this injury, though not visible, contributed to his back problems, which plagued him years down the road. I personally had limited interaction with the horses. I enjoyed giving them their treats and talking to them and stroking their lovely faces. They were beautiful creatures but I had no desire to ride them. Nonetheless, I enjoyed watching people ride them. My husband taught the two older children to ride and there was many a time when he had too much to drink and took one or the other child on a horseback ride through the neighborhood and beyond. There was nothing I could do to keep him from taking the children as they did not understand that they could be in danger. I prayed a prayer of protection for them and I was ever so relieved when they came back unhurt.

Richard wanted to ride with an English saddle, which he got for Christmas. but I sensed that my husband did not like this "sissy" kind of saddle. He preferred the Western kind. It was just one more thing to try my husband's patience, since he held the opinion that a real man just had to play football, drive a truck and ride a Western saddle, none of which our very opinionated and self-assured son cared for. He preferred gymnastics and liked to play the violin instead. It was a constant balancing act to keep these two on an even keel. By the sheer interests of this child we were drawn together. I had always loved classical music and I was delighted when he decided to learn to play the violin. His half-sister learned to play the guitar, so he had to choose an instrument too. When she got a cat he had to have one too. They were pretty chummy and I was a little uncomfortable but really had no reason to support this feeling that crept in whenever they were together.

As far as that was concerned, I had never any intention of having a cat in the house. When the horses moved to their barn which my husband had built himself, with the help of one of his buddies, he brought with him a yellow Lab and two little kittens, but they had to stay outside. I had enough trouble keeping the house from going to the dogs, as there always was mud and hay to combat. I was annoyed to no end that I was living in this beautiful house with pastel interiors and natural light everywhere and then it was covered with all the stuff that is fit only for a log-cabin with a dirt floor!

But what did it matter? What I thought or felt or wanted simply did not rise to the level of importance to even be considered. The only thing which gave me joy in all this was the fact that the children loved the animals and had a lot of fun with them and it was good for them to love God's creatures and care for them. As these animals were strays I thought it only proper to take them in, so to speak, and I enjoyed them too. The Lab did not want to stay inside the fenced-in area and we got numerous calls from neighbors who spotted the dog. The houses popped up like mushrooms as the second and third phase of the development of this former farmland progressed. Our little pond had been drained and all the snakes had slithered into the lake, save one, which was dead and swollen from the deterioration process and hence was a disgusting sight, the image of which is still in my memory.

Aghhh! here we go again! We made plans to go to Monaco. Since we were going to be on the European continent and so close to Germany, my husband decided that we could use that opportunity to visit with my people again. He got permission from headquarters and I am sure he felt very important and caring to lobby so passionately for his dear wife's wish to see her family.

I wrote to the Kreuzfelders whom I had been the house daughter for until I emigrated to the U.S. I also wrote to my mother and to my cousin, all of whom responded with delight at the prospect of a reunion.

Rachel was going to be in Germany at that time because she was doing research at the university in Regensburg for her grad school requirement that prepared her for teaching German at a university and put her on the tenure track. I must admit that I was actually looking forward to this trip and it seemed to please my husband as well. Arrangements were made that we would meet up with the group in Cannes, on the French Riviera. We were scheduled to spend four days in Germany visiting with various members of my family and friends.

It was a welcome change from the difficulties everything at home presented. No let-up of the complaints about my husband from my adult children who would never miss a chance to berate him, and add to this that his secretaries came and went at a pretty steady clip. Some of them I had to contact more often than others, but whenever I did and they felt more or less comfortable, they complained about my husband. I would always assure them that if I knew how to explain my husband I would and then we could both find a more peaceful co-existence with him and I reminded them that, after all I was married to him. They inevitably would ask me how on earth I could stand it. "It is not easy!" I always replied, when the real fact was that to be married to him was cruel and inhuman punishment, but what good purpose would that have served?

Beth, although she was always demonstrative in her affection toward me, delivered a blow I never saw coming. After her visit over the summer and the fun we all had at our house, from swimming to paddle-boat riding to horseback riding with her father and so on, she had left a note for her father in the car. It was important for me to come with her and my husband to take her to her grandfather, from where she was going to be picked up by her mother to return home to Chicago; I sat in the car and waited on my husband. When I spied that pink paper, I thought nothing of reading it because she was an avid writer of love notes to her daddy. I could hardly believe what I was reading. She complained to her father about me all the way through the letter, saying that I was a hypocrite because I pretended to be a good Christian, yet I would call my children dogs and treat them as such and that she no longer wanted to come visit and that she was so sorry that she felt this way and that she really loved her daddy. I was stunned. She knew very well that I joke around a lot and I called the children hound dogs, in keeping with Elvis's song "Hound Dog," which she liked to hum or sing and I never treated anybody, let alone my beloved children, like dogs. Yes, they were required to do certain things and I held them to their given responsibilities that were all reasonable and age-appropriate. I have no idea what she was accustomed to at home but I understood that she knew when she was at our house she did as we did and that included attending church, which she increasingly resented having to do. She would never say anything but her demeanor showed it clearly. I pretended not to notice. Just before she penned this letter she and I were sitting on the glider-bench on the back porch, when she put her head on my shoulder and said ever so sweetly, "I love you, Ilona!"

I was so hurt and I felt so betrayed by her but more than that she became a serious threat to what had already been a highly troubled relationship between her father and myself. When Jack got into the car I told him that I read this note to him from Beth and I cautioned him that she was playing a potentially dangerous game with our lives and to let her get away with this subterfuge would be catastrophic when all was said and done. I told him that he needed to do some explaining to his daughter and point out that I was his wife and that I had been nothing but good to her, which was the truth. I took her side on several occasions when she made him mad about something, but the main thing in this situation was that he firmly took his position in support of me, his wife. He never did anything and by doing nothing he invited what was coming next. I was trying to figure out where this sudden animosity was coming from and then I remembered a conversation I had with her in which she asked me if she could move in with us. I was so shocked because she always talked of her love for her mother. She always had a pretty picture of her mother by her bedside when she was visiting with us.

I was really perturbed. She then asked me if I thought that her father would want to re-marry her mother, probably because she knew the difficulties we had—there was no way that she could not know how problematic her father's behavior was on all the trips she took with us. I told her that I have been told by her father that he would never marry her mother again if she were the last woman on earth and I tried to gently indicate that her father is just not what he wants us to think he is. After having had the advantage of having witnessed this whole thing play itself out and after having seen the fallout, I am certain that she had set me up to respond exactly as I did. She took my reaction to her wanting to move in with us and twisted it here a little and tweaked it there a little and the result was that Jack received a letter of complaints from Beth's mother in which she accused me of being a bad influence on her (their) daughter and that I was berating her father and she as a result had to contact the school counselor because the girl showed signs of disturbance. She included the phone number of the guidance counselor. My husband handed the letter to me and I was absolutely aghast, though not really surprised. My husband chose not to do anything and since she was complaining about me, I took it upon myself to try to explain the change in their daughter's attitude toward me. She replied and urged me to talk to the counselor, which I did, and the consensus was that she, their daughter, could be manipulative and was pursuing a goal only she knew and would not admit to. We all agreed that this girl was an excellent actress and could cry on cue for effect. The mother indicated that this type of behavior was common in girls their daughter's age. However, I was contacted by her grandmother, who was divorced from the grandfather on the mother's side, and she told me of a similar scenario and a letter of complaints about the grandmother's conduct and together we assumed that this girl simply did not want to come to Memphis and so would try to force her father to have to travel to Chicago if he wanted to see his daughter. I put my foot down on that after the first and only time he did this and took Richard with him. I cited court rules for the custodial and non-custodial parent and their respective obligations regarding visitation. Whew!—that settled it. After all that, I was only too glad to get away and maybe even enjoy myself with my family in Germany.

13

Because of Love

Still having a bitter taste in my mouth about the dismal affair with the problems of my stepdaughter and the possible, very real unpleasantness that was looming in the future, having to deal with her on her forced visits with us, I was determined to put all these concerns out of my mind and to enjoy this welcome respite from all the depressing conditions that would still be there when I got back home.

On the fourteenth of April we went with the now-elderly couple, the Kreuzfelds, to Bad Nauheim, where I had met with Elvis Presley in 1958. They lived in Frankfurt which made it so convenient to get off the plane there to start our stay in Germany. The rest of the group changed planes and continued the scheduled trip to France.

Dr. and Mrs. Kreuzfeld (we agreed to call each other by our first names) were ever so accommodating, and it appeared to me that Jack was perfectly willing to be nice about indulging me in my trip down memory lane, even though it concerned Elvis. I had told him only some things, for him to be able to understand me a little bit better. As it was drizzling and cold and we had to walk under an umbrella and my husband's good humor disappeared fast but my sweet former employers carried on with enthusiasm as I think that they were genuinely happy to see me after twenty-eight years and did not mind putting themselves out to please me. They traipsed around with us, going down the street, around the corner and through the park to the Grunewald Hotel which stood there in its patrician splendor of days long gone. Elegant, almost regal. I was beside myself with excitement. I went to the side entrance, just as I had done thirty-two years ago, and knocked on the door after no one responded to the doorbell ringing. After some persistent knocking an older, distinguished-looking lady opened the door and she informed me that she did not let anyone in without an appointment and that people were constantly coming to see where Elvis had lived all those years ago. I explained to her, in German no less, of my desperation to see the place again that so had changed my life (and Elvis's too, but I did not say that to her, I just thought it, and it was certainly true!) and she took pity on me. The elderly couple and Jack had remained on the sidewalk, waiting to see if we could go in and my husband probably wishing that we would not be able to get inside. The lady invited them all inside and she explained that nothing had been changed on the second floor since Elvis left.

There was this hall and there still was a couch, just as so long ago, and there were the stairs leading to the landing on the second floor! It was breathtaking for me. I cannot describe it but it was the most thrilling feeling to see all these things that had been etched in my memory. There was the bed, the chair behind the door, the table and chairs which were somewhat hidden behind all these men that had gathered around as that fifteen-year-old had flung herself on Elvis who was slouched in that very chair! With an ottoman!

The lady told me that she could never understand why Elvis surrounded himself with these people as she found Elvis himself as being such a nice and decent human being.

She said that they had to ask him to leave the hotel because his odd life-style interfered with the other guests and their comfort. She said that Elvis's grandmother had to have chickens in their backyard which she wanted to feed every day and that she made biscuits for her own crew and for the hotel staff that tended to the Presleys and that amounted to fifty or so biscuits. Not only did she insist on making biscuits every day but she also fixed the greens she made everybody eat because it was good for them. The lady was getting caught up in the moment and somewhat enjoying telling her stories, almost forgetting that she had just laid down to rest. I was sincerely sorry that I had ruined that for her, but she continued to show us where Red and who knows who slept, the secretary, the grandmother and Elvis's father Vernon. We ended up passing the bedroom again where I took a last peek and recognized the Victorian-style couch that Charlie laid on when this fifteen-year-old and I did not know what to do with ourselves as Elvis excused himself to freshen up since he had just gotten up from his nap. She once again expressed her disappointment with Elvis's choice of companions and emphasized that it was absolutely incomprehensible to her (she had a look in her eyes that made me think that she knew that there was more to this man than met the eye) how someone so genuinely nice could tolerate such crass, often disrespectful, immoral and downright nasty people around him. She insisted that Elvis was so kind and gentle, so polite and that he seemed so sensitive, and she reiterated over and over how puzzled she was about this Elvis Presley who garnered so much attention from so many people. For the lack of evidence to the contrary at the time he and I met, I had to draw the conclusion that the old adage, "Tell me who your friends are and I tell you who you are!" applied here. She agreed to my assessment but left a measure of doubt. I guess she was like the legions of fans who were simply in denial.

These companions of Elvis's had made paper balls and set them on fire, the lady continued, and rolled them under the closed doors, almost setting the hotel on fire. This was simply the last straw and Elvis was ordered to leave. What became apparent was that Elvis was actually telling that fifteen-year-old the truth when he told her that he could not come to her house for Christmas as her parents had her invite him to do, when he told her that his family was coming from America to join him. But I did not call him a liar for that, I called him a liar when I heard him say to her, "I'll remember you!" There was the railing against which I was leaning when I called him so coolly a liar, when Elvis whisked around and demanded a repeat of what I had said, which I promptly did. And there stood the wardrobe to put hats and umbrellas in and on and the mirror in the middle, the place we sat on and commiserated about his mother's death and how this had affected me, my tears at the memory of this event, his gentleness and comforting ways with which he was stroking my hair. All of this came rushing back in a most exhilaratingly, albeit painful, way. It was as if the circle was somehow beginning to close. It was such a marvelous experience that only I could appreciate. I was so thankful to all concerned who had made possible this trip down memory lane with Elvis.

I was on cloud nine. We then went to see my ex-fiancé, Max, who was living in the same place as all those long years ago. I felt that I had to apologize for my dismal behavior that I still couldn't explain even to that day. It was as if I had been living in a perpetual state of confusion, being pulled here and there, wanting to leave and yet also wanting to stay. Personally, and I could not share this with my ex-fiancé's friends, who were just sitting down for dinner, or my former employers, but I remembered very well the pain it caused me when Elvis was all the way across the ocean and I was still on the European continent and I gave God the last chance to make this thing about loving Elvis into a real and very happy union when I decided to go to Memphis one more time on my way back to Germany. (I was always battling with the reality of things and what I intuitively knew.)

Max was polite and cool, as was his wife. They had added on to the old bed-and-breakfast his parents had been running just as he had explained to me many times when we were going together in late 1959 and early 1960 when I broke it off after hearing "Are You Lonesome Tonight?" We talked mostly about our respective families and pleasantly chatted about pleasant things. I was content that I took the time to apologize because it has always bugged me.

We went on back to Frankfurt and spent the night there. We rented a car and drove to Wuerzburg to visit with my mother and go to the old haunts, and this was another thrilling experience that I was not prepared for. It was so wonderful.

When we got to Wuerzburg we went to my old familiar apartment house, which was home to me from 1949 until I moved to my father's in Nürnberg.

My mother was not home and my sister did not want to speak to me because I had not sided with them in supporting the sale of that property. My husband and I went sightseeing while waiting for my mother to get back. We went here and there and down the familiar streets and so many memories of my childhood came flooding in and it was just too much fun. There was the Pestalozzi-School, still at the top of the hill. I was looking for the pastry shop our mother got the goodies from that were only for herself—only rarely would we get to taste a morsel. It was not there anymore. I saw the big hospital my mother frequented in her relentless pursuit to snag a Jewish doctor. We were good and hungry, so we went into a *gaststätte* and ordered typical German fare. My taste buds became alive! The tastes and smells just blew me away and I had a feeling of well-being I cannot recall ever having had to such a high degree. I savored each and every bite and the glass of wine was just perfect. It is standard fare in Germany to have wine or beer with the meal, as water is not of good drinking quality. It was great!

We went to my mother's apartment again and this time she was home. It was so funny how small everything looked. I could have sworn the whole place had shrunk. My mother was so amusing. She spoke fluent American English and my husband thought she was hilarious and she had me in stitches too. Everything was just so enjoyable, I could hardly believe it.

Rachel, who was doing research in Regensburg, joined us and we continued some sightseeing the following day. We went to the cemetery and looked at the graves of my mother's mother and my grandfather. I had no trouble finding them. We went to see the chapel in which I spent a lot of time praying and crying over my plight with my mother's boyfriend. We went to see the makeshift church where I had this vision and we were wondering whether to ask my sister for a way to get in there as she lived with her husband in the adjoining apartment building. But I was too scared of the certain rejection since she had told me via a letter that she did not want to see me. The Residenz was our next goal. It is a fabulously ornate, opulent structure inside and out. It was great.

What was so thrilling was the fact that I could retrace steps I took out in the manicured gardens, where my sister and I posed for pictures we took turns taking of each other in one of our mother's fancy gowns! It was too much! So many memories!

We returned to my mother's apartment and had dinner there and some more laughing and recalling funny events. She was still the same disorganized person of yesteryear and she told us that my sister came now and then to help her with the housekeeping.

All at once, and for no apparent reason, my husband and I got into a tiff. It was over a pair of earrings which my cousin had given to me when he had visited us in the States in 1981. As I understood it then, they were from my aunt, and I had not given it another thought. I had no reason to be secretive about them and I showed them to Jack because I wanted to wear them for my aunt when we visited with them. He insisted that I had been concealing them from him because they were really from my cousin and he accused me of doing everything imaginable with my cousin. He would get into these rants whenever he felt sadistic, which was often. I found his baseless accusations extremely insulting, not to mention the hurt he inflicted on me thinking me capable of such despicable conduct! As usual in these instances, he acted like the injured party and went off to bed sulking. I was vacillating between anger and fear. An uneasiness settled over me but I tried not to let it show for the sake of my mother and daughter. The next morning he acted a little distant which was only noticeable to me. This was really his MO, from "I love you!" to the worst words uttered by a civilized man. It was this seemingly irrational switching from one extreme to another that kept me on pins and needles.

We had gotten word that my aunt was in bad health and had been so for a while and then some time later that she had died. We went sightseeing some more. My husband tried to make arrangements with the coordinator of the insurance company to figure out whether we could remain in Germany to attend the funeral. While waiting to hear back from him, we went to Heidingsfeld and visited the house where we lived when we were bombed out in Wuerzburg, the fence on the cement base where I sat on when I connected with God, and the Reichenberg Castle, where my older sister and I spent time to get out of our mother's hair because we got on her nerves. We saw the train station where I was injured by the candy machine. We went back to Wuerzburg and I saw the figures of the disciples, which had been returned to their place of origin, which is the Johanneskirche. It too had been bombed during the war. We were at the war memorial park where somebody told us of the transfer of these figures back to the church. They, too seemed to have shrunk and it was somewhat disappointing to see them, appearing way too small for my taste. They were so overwhelming and impressive when I was fourteen and filled with love and adoration and devotion for God.

We left after that to go to Nürnberg to visit with my cousin and his second wife and my brother Paul. Needless to say, none of my late father's family wanted to see me. So we had only my cousin to go to.

It was no easy task to find our way to this country estate and I am using this term loosely. It was way fancier than when I lived there and it had a fantastic swimming pool and houses and stables here and there.

I saw the house my grandmother used to live in with my brother, and the old building that contained my room from so long ago. It was barely standing. The wash-house was still there. All the suitable dwellings were rented out.

We had dinner at my cousin's fabulous home. It was just unbelievably beautiful and luxurious. It was an A-shaped structure with an enormous open fireplace-cooking oven with a chimney to match, that were built of fieldstone and went all the way up to the second floor, opening up another fireplace up there. There was access from the bedroom down a spiral staircase to an indoor pool where he or she would take their morning swim. There was a balcony on the second floor and a picturesque terrace on the ground floor with big planters everywhere.

We spent a pleasant time talking. My cousin and I discussed the situation with the property and he tried to explain the legal angles that I simply could not understand and I had to let Rachel do the translating most of the time. My German was too limited for the torrent of German legal terminology that was coming at me so fast. My smart daughter is much better at speaking and understanding German than I am after all these years of English only. I am sure that Jack could feel left out but there was a way to keep up with it if he really wanted to because my daughter was translating into English what my cousin said and then I told her what to tell him in reply. Things appeared to be just as smooth as silk. We had some wine and cheese and we chatted and laughed and we took some pictures with my brother. It was nice.

In the late evening, after everybody retired for bed, going downstairs, my husband made that ugly dog-face of his that he puts on when he is about to construct one of his devious plans and trying to put it into action. This time he complained that I spent time only with my cousin which simply was a blatant lie. Certainly I had to discuss the property matter with him, since he was the one in charge, but my brother, my daughter, and my cousin's wife also contributed to the conversation.

This time it was too much for me to put up with. I could clearly see a pattern of malevolence developing and I was in no mood to play along. Instead I screamed at him and I yelled and I chewed him out but good with righteous indignation at his flimsy grievances. He apologized profusely and he spent the next two hours swearing to me his undying true love. Of course, I gladly believed him, fooling myself into thinking that he was just cantankerous and he would soon forget.

The next day we had a lovely breakfast, lovely because our hostess was the best. Nobody mentioned my screaming, though I am sure we were heard, but at the time I was too furious to worry about who heard me. As far as I was concerned nothing happened and my husband followed suit. We all drove to Nürnberg, which took us about twenty minutes, and we arrived at my cousin's business. He made tailored shirts and blouses for the rich and famous and his atelier dripped with class. Elegant. He looked things over and then he showed us where they lived during the week in town. They had an apartment over their business and a restaurant next door. It was all very convenient. We had lunch at "their" restaurant and spent more nice times together. We found out that travel arrangements could not be changed for us to attend my aunt's funeral. We ordered some flowers to be delivered for the occasion and after lots of regrets at my aunt's passing we decided to meet with the rest of the group, who by now were already in Cannes, France.

As my daughter had come by train to Wuerzburg we decided to let her return the rented car after we got to the train station in Munich and she could continue on to Regensburg where she lived.

Thanks to my smart daughter and the expert directions given by my cousin we had no trouble getting to where we needed to be. My daughter knew her way around some and it came in handy. The drive from Nürnberg to Munich was pretty run-of-the-mill autobahn driving. It gets you where you are going, fast.

We had all our luggage and ended up at the train station. We said our good-byes to my daughter and thanked her for her willingness to help us and off she went on to Regensburg and we finally got on the train to Milan, where we had to change trains for Cannes.

It was a fairly long ride to Milan and when we got off the train we realized that nobody was speaking English and we could not speak a word of Italian except "O Sole Mio!" and "Arrivederci."

The trip to Milan may have been very long but it was definitely not boring. We had to change trains in Verona and we zipped through Innsbruck, which is right between Germany and Austria. When we crossed over from Germany to Italy one could not help but notice that the houses and the scenery in general had been so much cleaner and brighter than the ones in Italy. It certainly validated the general perception that the Germans are a clean people. They love everything scrubbed and tidy. It is true as I am guilty of the same traits of order and cleanliness.

In Milan we found ourselves in a time squeeze, which was made worse by our inability to speak or read Italian. Add to this that we had to haul our luggage from here to there and back again because we were on the wrong track. It was terrible. I carried two shoulder bags and one big suitcase. The shoulder bags would slip off my shoulders and slip onto the suitcase that I was trying to pull at the same time and then there was my purse, too. Nobody offered to help me. My husband carried one smaller suitcase in which he'd put the dishes he bought from the owners of the restaurant "Erholung" in Würzburg where we had such a splendid lunch. I had commented on and lovingly admired the plates, on which they served the food, which had pictures of various beautiful, ever so picturesque castles, bridges and cathedrals of the immediate surroundings, which were so familiar to me. He had a clothes bag, too, and he left everything else for me to carry. We barely found out which way to go. We were the only ones going to Milan. Nobody made an effort to understand us. We listened to the announcement over the PA system and looked for "MILAN" and tried to figure it out ourselves but with the time constraint it was nerve-wracking as we had only this one opportunity to remain on schedule. Somehow we made it onto the right train. We had just settled in and I was so exhausted when the conductor came by and asked us, "Milan?" We nodded yes and he motioned that we had to move to the front cars as they were going to

Milan and the rest would be disconnected. So we had to get ourselves together and I had to lug all this luggage and move through six cars to reach the two front cars. I was more dead than alive at this point and vowed to myself that I would never again be caught on a train in Italy with this much luggage!

We were starving by now and it was just the best idea ever for my cousin's wife to insist to take along some sandwiches which she prepared for us. To this day she does not know that I thanked God for her foresight. Those sandwiches were so good!

My husband looked out the window as the train snaked its way through the most beautiful winter scenery I had ever seen! We were making our way through the lower Alps and the pine trees were covered with snow and growing on the ever-rising mountainside. It was grandiose, but I was much too tired to be able to enjoy all this magnificent beauty to the fullest. My husband was so excited and constantly telling me to look at this or that for which I simply did not have the strength and I asked him to leave me be as I was just too tired. I do think that if Jesus Himself would have come, I would not have had enough stamina to welcome Him. I fell dead asleep. My husband was forever making fun of me after that, saying that I just slept through a once-in-a-lifetime opportunity to see such splendor. I can only say that I was too exhausted to stay awake. I was somewhat rankled because he made me carry so much and, besides, wasn't he the one keeping me up the night before with his two-hour-long vows of eternal true love after his ridiculous accusations and my following fury. We had no food or drink since those sandwiches and I just did not have the strength. Sorry.

Finally, after five hours on one train or another we made it to Cannes. We took a taxi to the Carlton Hotel and changed clothes and we were able to join the rest of the group at a party, where there was lots of food and wine and dancing. We said hello to some and waved to others we recognized at a distance. Since the room was full and the party already under way, we ended up sitting with strangers. I was mainly interested in the food and I was so happy to get something to eat as those sandwiches from hours ago were but a faint memory to my stomach. The man next to me had too much to drink and he asked me if he could touch my leg. I thought he was kidding and asked him jokingly what he wanted to that for. He said, "You dummy you, don't you know?" His wife, who had been to the ladies' room, returned to her chair beside him, which cooled him off a bit. He continued to make innuendos, most of which I could not understand and really did not care to understand and he just rambled on. He was clearly incoherent and out of control. My husband and I excused ourselves saying that we were in dire need of sleep.

My husband and I were chatting pleasantly as we were climbing up the stairs to our room and we agreed that this man was quite lit. We were both amused at this and I thought nothing of telling him in this spirit of harmony of this man's hilarious attempts of to flirt with me. To my total horror my husband went completely crazy. He was ranting and raving that he was going to punch this man out and he was going to tell his wife about this! I tried to reason with him, telling him that the man was intoxicated. But he would not listen to me and instead tried to hatch a plan as to how to proceed to teach this fellow that he could not do this to his wife. He was being plumb ridiculous and I explained to him that there was no harm done and I certainly did not feel any animosity toward this man. I could not even remember what he looked like! I was entirely too hungry and thirsty to worry about anything else other than to quiet my grumbling innards. Besides, I reminded him that nothing can happen unless two parties agree and without my cooperation there could be no transgression and that the man was so drunk he probably would not be able to remember tomorrow what he had said and done today. I reminded him that this is too small a thing to make a federal case out of and that this must be handled very diplomatically, if at all, because the welfare of all the people could be affected if this was not handled right. He was still fuming but thank goodness he was too tired to feed his anger and certainly way too tired to do something about it.

In the morning he went downstairs to exchange some money and when he returned he said proudly that he handled this situation well, that he saw the man, that he called him over, he was alone too and that he told the man that he was stepping out of bounds by having done this last evening. The man apologized and said, "If this did indeed happen last evening I am so very sorry and will see to it that it does not happen again." One would think that was the end of it. Not so. My husband would tell that story *ad nauseum* to everybody we met in the course of going on tours, lunch and dinner. It was awful. Of course he went into excruciating detail about his valiant effort to be the defender and protector of his wife's honor. I did not even know that he was familiar with the concept! His over-reaction was inappropriate, to say the least. In spite of this embarrassing situation I was trying to have a good time, feeling somewhat like a marked woman. At every turn however, I could see that ugly husband of mine in the prime of his ugliness re-emerge full force and it made me literally physically ill because there was nothing I could do to prevent this from happening as I could not conceive the origin of it.

Even if I had known where this diabolical aspect in his personality came from, there was no way that I could successfully deal with it because it was so outside my sphere of knowledge and certainly experience. It was because it was so foreign to me that it was so scary. I did not know what he was trying to accomplish and why. I had to let whatever it was happen and hope I survived the whole thing with some semblance of composure and dignity.

I was so nervous that I had broken out in a rash and I felt awful. If this had been developing at home with this palpable animosity coming from him, I would have retreated and avoided going near him but here in a foreign country with no money of my own, totally dependent on him, and with no place to go to, I was forced to suffer the full force of his antagonistic feelings toward me and I was, to top it all off, obligated to make him look good. On the second evening Jack and I went with some acquaintances of his to lunch at Café de Paris, where my husband was monopolizing the conversation, telling the most unlikely tales. Whenever he tried to get me to go along with what I knew very well was wrong, he would so meanly and vilely whistle through his teeth, directing the air flow in an emphasized sneer out of the corner of his mouth at me, which I interpreted as a threat of some kind. The hair began to stand up on the back of my neck and I became filled with panic, which from the years of living with him, as his wife and the mother of his children was a sensation I was accustomed to. I thought at that instant that he was a dangerous, ugly man and I thoroughly hated him.

In spite of all these complications I tried to make light of it to myself as I had done many, many times before and eke out some fun; drinking wine at every turn helped this greatly. He told me that he thought a certain female was so cute and we ended up spending time with her and, by necessity, her husband, who did not appear to be bothered by the attention my husband almost exclusively showered on her—but then he drank wine too! It was nothing new that my husband had an acute lack of respect for me. He enjoyed parading in front of me with that sixteen-year old and being so flirtatious with her, which she returned in kind. I called his attention to the fact that this was not the conduct of a decent man and it certainly was not a good example for the children, who at that time did include a teenage daughter of mine, and I did not like it because it was personally hurtful. At that time he exclaimed, amused, "Ilona, don't tell me you are jealous!" He kept on repeating how he was taken with this man's wife, and I could not afford to react negatively. They made plans for this and that but I was just sick of the whole thing. They decided to go to the Monte Carlo Casino. I had my husband make my apologies as I could hardly wait to bring distance between my husband and myself.

After an hour or an hour-and-a-half, or it could have been two hours, I got worried because we had to get up early the next day as we were going into Monaco to view the Alpine region there and visit the tourist traps along the way, so I went looking for him. He was in the lobby having drinks with his favorite female and her husband. Oh well. Then we ran into another couple and I knew them superficially but well enough to have a dislike for the man because he seemed to have the same predilection as my husband, only that his wolf-eyes were on me and I considered him to be two-timing, double-dealing, and smarmy fellow. I had told my husband this at the time, but nothing seemed to matter even though he had had his own misgivings having worked for the man briefly some eight years ago.

My husband made it clear to me that there were misunderstandings between this agent and himself at the time, but that he was going to let bygones be bygones. I was under the impression that he would be glad to meet with this man and his very nice wife, so I was friendly when they spotted us. My husband happily talked them into joining us for dinner. I was trying to be entertaining, loosening things up a bit to put everybody at ease even, though I did feel some trepidation. I was going to overlook this agent's smarmy ways and it seemed that everybody was having a good time. I had a very enjoyable conversation with this agent's wife, but before long the conversation between my husband and this agent went wrong somewhere and he told me that so-and-so was a crook, and he did not like him and that I should come with him to speak to his regional representative who was entering the establishment with her husband.

I did not feel much like doing that as I was still eating and enjoying some girl talk so I stayed and finished my dinner.

Before I knew it my husband and this "crook" decided that we were going to a nightclub. The "crook" had to have a jacket, so we had to go to their hotel where said "crook" made a phone call to Memphis and off we went to the Follies Russe. Everybody was in good spirits, joking and laughing and I said, all in fun, to the smarmy man, "Hey, you remind me of Rhett Butler—you know, crafty (laugh, laugh) hey, and I am Scarlett O'Hara!" Everybody thought that was funny, I know I did, and everybody laughed. I was pleased with myself. I cannot recall one single thing about the show but it seemed to entertain all the patrons in attendance. My husband was complaining about the high prices. He was griping that he was the one who spent the most money. Another couple joined us and they were considering buying a bottle of champagne but they reconsidered and ended up buying one mixed drink and one beer while my husband had already ordered the bottle of champagne as he did not want to be outdone by anyone.

We ended up with half a bottle of champagne left over and it steamed him up but good. We shared the rest with the others and left, took our baths and went to bed dog-tired. Those vacations were too strenuous for me!

The next morning, bright and early, we went on the tour to Èze, a quaint French village perched precariously on the side of a mountain. To get there we had to take a bus on the most treacherous ride in my lifetime. On one side was the high rocky mountain and on the other side was the straight descent off a cliff. Going around the corner was very tricky. We saw the bus in front of us maneuvering slowly into the curve, with the back end of the bus hanging over the cliff. It was too scary and we were very glad when we arrived at our destination. We shopped, and my husband decided which present to get for whom, and we had lunch here and a beer over there with who knows who and on the way back I made sure that I did not look how we got off this dangerous mountain. We got to our hotel early because there was to be a clown party. Prince Rainier's favorite thing: clowns. We all needed a bit of rest before having to have some more fun! It was grueling!

We had been informed of this party ahead of time but my husband made no preparations for it and I personally disliked clowns and costume parties and I was perfectly comfortable going as one of the spectators. All at once it became so important to my husband that he went in some kind of costume. He decided that he was going as a French *artiste* with big eyebrows, muttonchops and a moustache, with one of my scarves as a bandanna around his neck.

Before we had to get ready for the party, my husband wanted to have a beer with a Charlie and a Ben. He did not return on time to get ready, so I went looking for him. He was again with his favorite female and her husband. They were having drinks and asked me join them. I immediately turned on the party-mood and sat down and I had a glass of wine and we had a good time chatting about this and that and, of course my husband was a sight to behold, trying to impress this female, and I must confess it was a rather tasteless display of interest in somebody else's wife in the presence of his own wife. He did not give that a thought because it was always about him and what he wanted. Only if he had an ulterior motive would he pretend that he thought of me or of how I felt. But I was always fooling myself into thinking that it was still possible that he loved me. After all, I carried myself with the idea that it was possibly my job—to lead him to Jesus Christ—and I just had to go through all this misery to get to the goal which, in the end, only God could accomplish. There is always hope as long as there is breath in us and as we all know, hope springs eternal.

We went downstairs into the ballroom that had been decorated in the style of a circus tent. There were lots of funny costumes. My husband's regional representative and her husband came as Raggedy Ann and Andy and looked funny together and elicited smiles wherever they went. We ran into the big boss and his wife who chose not to dress up either, so I did not feel too bad. My husband was looking for a particular couple, for reasons I did not know. Finally he had found them, and asked them to come sit with us at a big round table where others were seated already. We said hello and introduced ourselves and sat down. Everything seemed bright and friendly. Once my husband had this couple corralled, he was up and down, dancing with this man's wife. I struck up a conversation with a chubby lady from northern Florida who was dressed up as a clown and really looked good enough in her costume to have pleased Prince Rainier of Monaco. My husband was a dancing dervish and I was glad he was having such a good time, which he made sure that I was aware of as he was strutting his stuff, so to speak, when dancing with this woman. I had to dance with her husband as he was sitting there, wondering what to do about my husband, and since he was a diminutive, soft-spoken, somewhat shy individual, I felt I had to lighten his load a bit but neither one of us could really mask our displeasure with my husband's performance. It was quite embarrassing for me but I was hoping that after a few drinks no one would notice and surely not remember much the next day.

I excused myself to go to the ladies room and on the way I saw the smarmy man and his nice wife standing alone and looking forsaken. I just knew how they felt, so I took pity on them and asked them to join us. I explained to my husband that they looked so pitiful and he did not seem to mind at all and he joked and laughed and just had himself a good time. He cajoled and teased and joked and laughed and between dances, out of nowhere he called me over to him where he was standing with "the crook" and I was busy talking and joking around in the spirit of the circus atmosphere with the remaining people at our table—and he said to me, "Honey, I want you to kiss so-and-so on the cheek, he made a bet with me that you would not do this and I intend to win this bet!" My husband pushed this man in my direction and I was still sidetracked in a conversation with his wife, who was laughing at this proposition. "Hey, why the cheek?" I said, and I laughingly kissed Mr. Smarmy quickly on the mouth in a plain, no-frills-no-thrills fashion, much like you would kiss your grandmother, and my husband laughed and laughed. I could scarcely see what he thought so funny.

I went back to my conversation and danced with the clown-lady and we had a lot of fun, albeit make-believe fun.

My husband wanted to stay, even though the crowd got thinner and thinner. They finally turned off the lights and it was time to go. My husband went on his way with not even so much as a word.

I was not at all sure I could find my way back to our room. I never paid much attention to the directions we were going in because I was always with my husband. To my surprise I actually did find my way back to our hotel room where my husband was waiting since I had the key card.

There was this eerie silence. I washed out the scarf my husband had been wearing and sweated through and my anklets. I hung them up to dry, brushed my teeth, washed my face, put my nightgown on and went to bed. Not a word was spoken and I surely did not want to set him off so I laid there quietly, panic-stricken as usual, as I could feel the storm that was brewing and sure to follow that calm. My insides were quivering in the most horrible fear. I prayed, "Oh my God, I can't take this anymore—help me, please help me!" I could scarcely breathe, I was so upset.

My husband turned on the shower and started to scream the most horrible vile things I had ever heard anybody say all during his shower and he got louder during the drying-off process. I remained quiet but my heart was beating so loudly in the most horrific fear. I was so scared that I think had I even tried to say anything, my voice would have failed me.

He was through with his shower (I had decided earlier to take a bath in the morning because I was just too tired) and came to my side of the bed, close to the window, and accused me of kissing Mr. Smarmy in the mouth. He said "in" the mouth and I tried to correct him calmly and said, "Not 'in' but 'on' the mouth!" There is a big difference and I wanted to clarify from the beginning that I was aware that he was building a case against me with shoddy material. He then demanded his money, which he had given to me for safekeeping since I carried my purse. I was so upset I could not think of where I had put my purse and that was enough for him to accuse me of stealing his money and I'd better not be keeping his money from him since he worked his butt off and that it is his and only his and I'd better give it to him. I tried to be calm and told him in a subservient way that I would find it for him, when he leapt from one side of the bed to where I was and pushed me on the bed and savagely beat my face with his fists time and time again, then he would move away, all the while screaming obscenities and accusing me of everything under the sun. He screamed that he was going to tell our children that their mother kissed this man "in" the mouth and that their mother was a no-good whore and that those children were his and I could go to hell. The phone rang and he answered it. He told me that it was the front desk and that they had gotten complaints about the noise. He told me to keep quiet and that we could do this quietly. Then he punched me again with his fists on the face, left and right, then he grabbed my hair and pulled me by the hair up from the bed, pushed me down again and bent my left fingers so far back I thought they would break. I pleaded with him not to break them, that I had to work with them when we got back home. He then yanked me up, pulling my nightgown up as he was lifting me up with his knuckles under my chin. At that point I begged him to just kill me, that I had known for eleven years that he hated me and that I had no desire to continue living with him anymore. He then threw me down again, punched me all over my shoulders, neck and face, forcing me to say certain things and when I said them he beat me again. He then sat on me and put my upper lip between his teeth and bit it and pulled it at the same time and I thought he had bitten it off but I could not feel anything as the swelling started and my face was burning like on fire. He reminded himself that we had to be quiet and said, with satisfaction in his voice, "We are through!" He went to bed and turned over to get comfortable and went to sleep.

I could barely hold myself up as I dragged myself to the sink to put some water on my burning face. When I came up from splashing cooling water on my face, I saw my face in the mirror and I could hardly believe what I saw. My whole face was swollen,

My nose was huge and my lips were a swollen mass of bleeding tissue. It was horrible. I put some more water on my face and I resolved quietly that this time I was holding him to account for this attack. Once

I had made that decision, I got enough strength together to get my robe which matched the nightgown that I had gotten at K-mart just for this trip. I looked at my husband, who was sleeping soundly, and I went to the front desk and asked the concierge for help. He asked me whom he could call but I could not remember anything. I told him the name of the company I was part of and he took it from there. He called the police and the ambulance and in no time the hotel lobby was buzzing with activity.

I was seated in the lobby waiting for the ambulance. The bosses of the company were there. They told me that we had to get an interpreter as this was a French-speaking populace and we did not speak French. A very nice lady came and told me what was going to have to be done. I told her that I did not want to go back into the room where my husband was and she said that they were going to get my things out and put them into another room on a different floor. Meanwhile they had awakened my husband, who had to come downstairs as I was going to be taken to the emergency room. He was, of course, very sorry and he asked me if I needed any money and he handed me three hundred dollars in front of everybody. The interpreter had already gotten my purse. I took the money and put it into my purse, from which I had taken it just forty-five minutes earlier when my husband demanded it from me and got wound up to do all this.

The ambulance came and the interpreter and I went off. I was put in a hot dark room, then I was wheeled down dark corridors to the X-ray machine. Nothing was broken, and they informed me that I had to go to the library on Prince Albert and Princess Caroline Street and get two forms that I needed to fill out, and to bring my passport, otherwise the doctor would not be able to talk to me.

I had thought that if I had to stay Monday and Tuesday, which were the remaining days in Monaco, I would not want to be around my husband. After the judge would decide, after the consultation with the doctor, that my husband had to go to jail, that would then take care of it.

After we had gotten back from the hospital, the big bosses explained to me that it would be in my best interest and that of the company if I were to get out of Monaco early in the morning, fly via helicopter to

Nice and from there to the U.S. to settle any legalities there, because in a foreign country things were much more complicated, particularly because of the language barrier.

I had to agree that this was a good solution, just as long as I did not have to be with my husband.

The interpreter got me pain pills and anti-inflammatory meds for the bruising and swelling of my face and my upper body, which was turning black-and-blue.

I went to my room and I was ready to leave at 9 a.m. I was told that the bosses had talked with my husband and they said that my husband cried like a baby and that he was very, very sorry.

I hated his tears. They mean nothing. He cried the night he swore his love for me. He cries when he gets himself into more trouble than he knows how to get out of. I hate his ugly crocodile tears I had learned over the years that he uses them much as his power of persuasion—his well-honed skill of trickery.

Such were my thoughts at that time. I flew to Nice in the helicopter and boarded a plane for the States. I was left alone to dwell on the pieces of my life that remained. There was a layover somewhere but I cannot remember where it was and I was put into the VIP lounge. There was always somebody who had been informed from one place to the next to take care of me since I simply could not focus on such things at the time.

I had a long flying time to reflect on all this hell and I just could not believe it. It must have been a nightmare! But no! It was my reality. I had a scarf draped over my face and when that reality sank in I could not help but cry and cry. I was sitting by myself and people would be passing by and pay me no mind. I kept looking out of the window and just cry and moan softly. The saltiness of tears made my face burn, just to keep reminding me of the hopelessness of my situation. Where, oh where, was I going to go from here? I had no idea.

At the airport in Memphis I called Jeremy and told him what happened and to please pick me up and take me home. He assumed, as did everybody else, that I was surely going to divorce this man now. I was inclined to agree as I was still reeling from the impact of the assault. My husband's mother was at home, but she did not have much to say other than that that was not right of her son to do this. I did not expect anything else from her because she was deaf and blind when it came to the serious shortcomings of her children. Susan came with her girlfriend, who brought her camera, and they took pictures of my black-and-blue face, neck, arms, and shoulders. They both said I needed them for evidence in the divorce proceedings. I called the wife-abuse hotline and they told me to go to my doctor who told me that I needed to get away from this man, who was also a patient of his, and that it was going to be merely a matter of time before he would kill me. I went to my pastor at the time who displayed no sympathy of any kind and could not give me any advice. He just listened as I heard myself talk. That was all.

I was glad to be home and the company of my young children normalized my life and I became grounded again in that which had always been with me, my faith, and I felt calmer and to some degree ready to deal with my husband who was due to arrive the following day. He came through the door and he looked so pitiful and guilty and downtrodden and he told the children that Daddy did a very bad thing to Mommy and that he would never ever do that again and that he would be the best husband and the best daddy that he could be.

It sounded so good and so sincere and I was willing right then and there to forgive and forget and pretend this never happened.

But I was far too afraid of him and I surely did not trust him to keep his promises.

I can only imagine the embarrassment he had to endure during the time he had to interact with the company. It was no walk in the park for me either on that score. Who in her right mind would want to be seen looking like a rotten potato, after having been used as a punching bag by the one who promised to love, honor and protect?

I explained to him that we were going to live separately until my fear of him could subside and that I would not rush into making a decision that had not been well thought through.

It was a very trying time because I was so indecisive, thinking one moment that this was the perfect chance to free myself from this extremely difficult-to-live-with man, and the courts would not quibble much about who was going to get how much. From that standpoint it was a slam-dunk. A win-win situation. Had it only been about me

I would have jumped at the chance. But it was not. I had three young children who needed both their mother and their father, giving them the emotional and spiritual stability necessary to prepare them for a God-pleasing, and therefore happy, life. In my conviction I was and am certain that it is vitally important to have these lovely children nurtured by both their parents living together in the same dwelling and be role models for the young to learn what to do as a man or woman respectively. Such was and is my dream for every child today. I have faith that people in time will do right by their children and start to think of their welfare first even before they decide to get married. No one woman should have to go through what I had to go through because I married a totally unsuitable man. But I did and I had also vowed that I would not put another child through what I had to put my first set of children through. Here again it was because the man did not have the same goals as I had regarding the having and caring for children. If only he had turned his life in faith over to God and aspired to a God-pleasing life rather than a self-pleasing life....

As time went on, and my husband was exemplary in his conduct toward me and the children, he was pressing me for reconciliation, but I could not bring myself to view this attack on me as anything else but a very serious matter that needed to be dealt with slowly and deliberately. I put him under an order of protection. He, or rather we, were summoned to court and appeared before a judge where my husband had to promise the judge that he was not going to raise his hand against me, which my husband promised, and the judge informed me that if there was another incident I could call the police and my husband would go straight to jail where he would have to stay. My husband told the judge that he had too much to drink and he promised me that he would not drink beer anymore or smoke pot. He told me that he became aware how wrong it was for him to drink so much when even our youngest asked him if he could get him a beer. While I am all for him not drinking alcohol anymore, I resented the notion that it was the alcohol that made him do it. I have a long history of his aggression toward me and alcohol was not in the equation.

After six months of being under this order of protection it had run out; I informed my husband that I was going to extend it another six months. We had to do the whole procedure again. I insisted we go to some kind of counseling, which we did. He found the chaplain at the VA Hospital, where we went for counseling for several weeks. During those sessions it became clear to me that men will stick together and they had gotten on a path that laid the blame on my doorstep. I knew my husband and his shenanigans way too well and I realized that he was never going to be honest with himself. We stopped going as I saw no reason to continue. The only real recourse I had was with God, even though I was so confused when the attack happened because there just was no reason for me to have to go through this too. I thought He was against divorce just as I was, so what gives? I cringed in discomfort, just thinking of having to send any of my children to some kind of daycare facility. I had worked in one for years and I had seen the sadness in the children's eyes and their sometimes inconsolable crying to have to separate from their mothers, way before they were ready.

I could not bring myself to do this to my children. I just could not do it. No matter how hard I tried, I could never be a father and I certainly was incapable to be an effective, emotionally grounded woman, grounded in being bound in an intimate relationship with the children's father that enables the woman to be that nurturer she was intended to be for the sake of the whole family, including herself. I might get killed in the process, so be it, but I was not going to betray my faith and, if indeed it would require my life, I would have lost it in the line of duty. I would still come out winning!

From that point forward I took a new lease on life and told my husband of my decision and he seemed to be happy about it. We had a sort of celebration of our new commitment to our family and it was nice, very nice.

Needless to say, I got a lukewarm reaction from my adult children. My husband was for the most part a good husband and he decided that he needed to be more involved in the children's religious upbringing and he made himself liberally available for coaching the various ball teams at the children's school and he was more faithful about attending church and staying there without leaving early to catch some game from the beginning on TV. I appreciated his effort and his mother did too. She'd come more often and enjoyed herself immensely and we had many a good time. My husband even went out and bought me nice clothes. He would not give me the money to buy the clothes myself but I did not care because he had very good taste and he bought things that he thought I would like and that would look good on me. Sometimes I was wondering when the other shoe was going to drop but I did not waste any time on borrowing trouble. Today was good. Tomorrow I will deal with tomorrow and as I knew that the good Lord was there with me every inch of the way, I felt blessed indeed.

Samuel wanted to take karate lessons and so we signed him up to attend classes. Tracy discovered basketball and she abandoned the gym classes I took her to in preparation for ballet classes in the future. She was enamored of ball games and she loved competition, which is something I have always disliked. She became a daddy's girl sure enough, as those two could converse about any ball game going, it was all Greek to me.

Our older son played the violin in the orchestra at church and I was well pleased with the way things were going. I guess I should keep on talking about the good times.

We went on many trips and my stepdaughter opted to come along. I figured I had made our position clear and her father and I remained together in spite of her subterfuge and the attack in Monaco.

She was not happy with that but she had no choice but to play pleasantly along. I never let it show that she had hurt my feelings and that I thought that she had a lot of growing up to do. I was just as fair with her as with the other children and we had a good time together. We went to Yellowstone Park, to Dollywood, and the surrounding tourist destinations which included Music Row in Nashville. On one occasion she did not come along, which really made it more enjoyable for me as I did not have to suffer through her putting those earphones on to insulate herself from us. She would only converse with Richard for any length and they whispered together too much for my taste. I warned her that if she had to whisper to him it most likely did not have to be said. She knew I was onto her. I said it casually and I was always nice when talking to her because I viewed her as a victim of her circumstances and those were exactly what I wanted to keep my children from.

14

Follow That Dream

Things were manageable and I thought I was coping well with the situations as they were presenting themselves. I could have enjoyed the fairly normal life but there was always and forever the indefinable compulsion from within that kept me tied to the underlying, unfinished business of Elvis Presley. I kept agonizing over the meaning of it all and why it ended as it did, all these whys and the apparent disconnection of it all to my life.

But this ever-present compulsion kept me searching and ultimately relying on God to lead me to an understanding. I went to the senior pastor of First A/G where my children went to school and it was the church of Elvis's after their settling in the housing projects when they had moved from Tupelo, Mississippi. Somehow I thought he had some idea of the possible connection between what was known about Elvis at that time (1989) and the spiritual value of it as it was tied to me. However, although he was respectful, he warned me if I were to go public with what I thought I suspected, I would surely regret it because the papers and other publishing venues would decimate the entire story and misconstrue every unguarded utterance to make it sound like whatever they want it to sound like, as their goal was not to be the purveyor of truth but to make as much money as they could. This meant that they would assign it every tawdry aspect by digging into every last nook and cranny to shovel as much dirt as they could find, and that this would not only affect me but my whole family and for that reason I should be very careful when deciding to take that step. He was a very wise man indeed and familiar with the way this world works. This took the wind out of my sails. I'd put the whole thing on the back burner and focused on my life with my family. At least I was following the very audible order from Elvis to say something and now I could forget it for a while, which was always a welcome break from this dwelling on the supernatural.

After the decision to remain in this marriage in spite of everything and after having had a respite from the burden to do something with what I knew, I decided that I was going to write a book. For the life of me I cannot remember what I expected to accomplish with this. There was nothing I could write and prove with certainty to anyone. I was hoping that those who knew something about this and who had dealings with Elvis during the time when he met me until his death would come forward and help me to put a face on all this, so to speak.

I wrote a letter to the editor of the *Commercial Appeal*, the local paper, and it remained in their archives of possible future articles, if the need presented itself.

Some years later I did some banking business, which consisted of buying a savings bond for my grandson, and I came across an article in *Memphis*, a monthly magazine mostly filled with advertisements for the important businesses and all the movers and shakers in the community, and occasionally an insightful article on something or someone important to the financial and cultural aspects of Memphis and the suburbs surrounding Memphis, which were ever-expanding and constantly incorporated. This article was on Elvis and as I sat there waiting for my turn to be helped, I read the most in depth albeit highly intuitive and speculative article. I was nonplussed and confused, as I had never heard, let alone read, anything, anywhere, at any time before that focused so much on the things unseen when talking about, or explaining Elvis.

Quite a long time later I realized that the author sounded much like me when I was describing in spiritual terms the life and times of Elvis, that only I had real knowledge of.

As the commercial value had never been, is not, and will never be a consideration, I concluded that this writer of this article must have had access to the information I provided and he filled in his astute observations and ideas and did not want to be found even though I tried. I just wanted to get some cooperation from somebody, if for no other reason than to share my intuitive knowledge, which was a nagging constant companion. He had his own reasons for not wanting to be found. He probably assumed that I wanted to be compensated financially.

My attention was diverted from my pre-occupation with the meaning of Elvis's life and mine by my husband's continuing goal to make my life unnecessarily difficult. I had the same old trouble trying to make ends meet and, after one of my stepdaughter's visits, which put an additional strain on my budget, I gathered up my courage and threatened him with a visit to a family lawyer, who would set the amount of money I was to be given commensurate with his income. Actually I gave him a choice, which was that he'd sit down with me and calmly and thoroughly go through the monthly bills that I must pay every month and what I think I am entitled to on top of that, just because I am his wife. He was so shocked and I emphasized that I did not leave with half of our money after the beating but that I was no longer willing to worry needlessly about finances when this could be so easily remedied by him giving me what is due. The incidentals, which he absolutely did not want to consider, ever, were central to the whole discussion. He was speechless and after some ranting of mine, fueled by repressed anger that was finally spilling over freely, he said nothing in response for a while. Then he cussed and cursed and agreed that he'd rather sit down with me and work something out than have a lawyer knowing about his business and telling him what to do.

I was so relieved at the thought of having some help but I was also afraid because I never could figure out his schemes. He would surely trick me in some way and I'd end up as I was before.

We took pen and paper and went to work. I was very modest in my request for myself but I did want a small amount of money, just for me, so I could help my children if they needed help, and grown children need help now and then and as I did not have any of my own to give, I always had to ask my husband for money for one or the other child, which would always cause him to go into a tirade about my children.

I drew up a contract that also stipulated that any bill that would be paid off, that the assigned amount for that bill would remain in my account and be used for the household. He quite pleasantly agreed to this signed and dated it and I did too. This was definitely one of those occasions where I would wonder how I ever thought he was an unreasonable, mean, vengeful tightwad and it was cause for the confusion on my part as to what to expect.

It was a normal day when my husband called me from work and urged me to come to a furniture store and look at the beautiful furniture there and that he was thinking that we should have better furniture and he was even going to get a new bed for us and that I had to come right away. I was somewhat taken aback because he had not mentioned any interest in buying new furniture before even though I had muttered occasionally about the mattress on our bed which he had from his second marriage and used during his divorced father-of-one time, and that I did not like the stains on it from who-knows-who or what. So I met him at that store and he acted all excited. I could hardly not cooperate. We looked at real nice couches chairs, tables etc. After a lot of back and forth he decided on the style and color and I liked it too as it would look just right in the great room. He bought a love-seat for the loft and a big chair to match with an ottoman and a new bedroom set. It was nice. I could hardly believe it. Soon I would discover that this furniture purchase was conveniently coinciding with the paid-off date of the car he had bought for his mother! It was just too much to ask of his narcissistic, greedy self to let me have that freed-up amount of money. However, since he bought something that had been overdue for quite a while and it was for the benefit for everybody, I never mentioned this amazing coincidence. I had learned to keep my mouth shut.

I knew that our house was in no way like anyone else's house where there was an independent businessman with a very good income. We had things from way back and to some it may have been tacky but that was what I had and it never bothered me. I had my children at home with me and their daddy came home every evening and took an interest in our children's school and extracurricular activities. We went to church and Sunday school and participated in special church events at the church in Raleigh and the First A/G in Memphis and we shared the school programs and that was just more important to me. It had almost been normal for me to live in an environment that was more in line with the residents of a lower-income group as I personally lived as a poor person, only that I lived in a fancy house.

When the teachers at the children's church school were installed after summer vacations we went to the church service there and I was immediately persuaded to change from the Assembly of God church in Raleigh to the First Assembly of God church on Highland in Memphis where the children's school was. I mentioned my impression to my husband after the service and when he found out that we could get a discount as members of the church, he agreed. It only made sense.

We had spent some time having our loyalties divided, as we liked the Sunday school at the old church because Russel, the husband of the lovely Christian lady, who had helped me to stay in the marriage when I just wanted to get away from my ugly husband, was teaching our class and we did so like it. But we liked the worship service at First A/G better and so we would leave after Sunday school to attend church service across town. It was crazy until we finally decided that we could consolidate our driving time and just go to one place and it was a good move and I felt at peace with that development. Everything was coming nicely together.

The children blossomed, each in their own way. I had trouble with my youngest and his deficient reading skills. I took time with him to master the homework assignments but I just could not accomplish anything. I had no experience with this kind of inability and I had very little patience, which evaporated after trying and trying for him to catch on but without any improvements. We enrolled him in remedial reading class because I was getting so frustrated with him and it just was not good for him to sense my impatience. I dreaded those daily torture sessions, which is what they were for him and me. How thankful I was that there was help available for him and the remedial reading classes helped him to master what was required of him and it was certainly for the best thing.

One summer we had the third grade at our swimming pool for a morning of swimming and outdoor cooking. Some moms and dads helped with the running of this event. My husband was the head cook and he was his most charming self and ever-so-well suited for this role, as he was the proud proprietor of all this outdoor beauty.

On another occasion we had an Easter-egg hunt on our property, as it included wooded areas and lots of safe places to hide the eggs. The children would have their friends over for an afternoon of play and outside-fun and the pool was a favorite among all concerned as many children did not have a pool available to just jump in when the mood struck them. It was a very good time in the lives of our children and I thought that surely my husband felt as gratified as I felt and I was confident that all my putting up with my husband's irrational ways were worth all the ill feelings his treatment of me always engendered. I thanked God from the bottom of my heart and I did everything I could on a daily basis to make sure that my family was the God-pleasing family I had always dreamed of having.

The time came when we joined some members of First Assembly of God church in a social at their home. It was an opportunity for new members to be introduced to the important members as well as to establish their comfort level. I personally prefer the modest, median-income folks or even the downtrodden and poor because I am just more comfortable around them. Too much high society made me miserable because there was no way for me to keep up appearances as I just did not have the necessary funds and I had an acute lack of interest. So there we were, giving a convincing appearance of being equal with these affluent and established, very nice people. The conversation was going well and my husband dove into a description of how he had singlehandedly and without any help from anyone got himself into the great position he is in today. He dropped a few hints about new cars and building a house, his first one no less. I tried to inject that none of this could have been possible without the blessing of God and I was quite unsettled over this display of arrogance by my husband, as he always acknowledged in our prayers at home with the children that it is God who is responsible for having blessed my husband's efforts and hard work which I respected greatly. It stuck in my mind and I could not help but be only cautiously optimistic about my husband becoming a true born-again Christian.

We quickly discovered that we were not comfortable with the so-called "high-society." I particularly felt out of place because these ladies had known each other for a long time and in some cases shared hairdressers and manicurists which was way outside my experience. I had no interest in going to a beauty parlor every week to get my hair done and I have never had a manicure and I did not want one and I certainly did not mind that at all but these were the things that these ladies talked about and I just had nothing to contribute. If I had told them of my daily life and the absence of what they took for granted I would surely have turned them all against me and I would have been forced to discontinue associating with them for the feeling of sheer discomfort at the inequity of our living standards. I was most comfortable, with the downtrodden who thought I was well-to-do. As far as they could see, I was.

I have found that in the so-called high society the same miserable things happen that happen to me when it comes to our children, but they deal with it differently. They hide everything and pretend that they have no disobedient rebellious children, and when they do it's their business only and it remains under wraps. I cannot and will not do this. It goes against my intrinsic open and honest character and I bristle at the idea of keeping everything hush-hush and acting as though nothing was or is wrong. I just had no talent for it and I was not about to learn a new skill to please people who cannot help me.

It was the new pastor whom I approached with my now ever-more urgent need to confide in someone who is familiar with the supernatural. The pastor I talked to before he went to Russia with his wife as some kind of coordinator of the Assemblies of God churches in Moscow, where they stayed for a long time. The new pastor did just as I had asked him when he agreed to see me in his office. I had asked him for someone to join us as I did not want to put him in jeopardy, but he had a very good secretary who was on her toes, so to speak. So he explained to me that there was no one available to join him and he agreed that he would not say anything and just let me talk. There simply is no telling what was going through this pastor's mind. He said that he had a tape recorder going and that would make up for the absence of another person.

I cannot emphasize it enough but it took a great deal of fortitude on my part to go this far. I had taken a great risk of being viewed as some kind of a deranged person in dire need of psychoanalysis. However, I felt compelled to do this, come what may. The pastor listened to my strange (to say the least) story. He handled it with diplomacy and sensitivity. Even though I had insisted on no response from him, I was desperate to hear him say something positive, but he did not and he only repeated, "You said that I should not say anything?" I so regretted having said this but in the end it was the only thing to do. I could not have dealt with any criticism at all. As it stood, I felt I was making headway following Elvis's order to "say something" and let God take care of it.

It seemed that by talking about my Elvis story I had to remind myself that all this did indeed happen to me and that I should be able to talk about it. The complication always reared its ugly head when reality got in the way and by that I mean the droning on TV, in the papers and the magazines, which squeezed the last bit of money out of everything Elvis, from Priscilla to whoever, and the twisted truth (which is a lie) was promoted and fed on a constant basis. I grant Priscilla that she was rather candid about her troubled relationship with Elvis in her book and she did a very good job in turning their former home into what Graceland is today, like it or not.

I never told anyone of this talk. I could not afford making myself sound like some kind of nut.

We were now full-fledged members of First A/G Church and it never bothered me in the slightest when I had to come in contact with the good pastor. That good secretary I mentioned earlier was a former girlfriend of Elvis, when they were in high school. I told her in passing that I had met Elvis in Germany and that he was a bad boy. I think she did not like what I said because I always had the feeling that she tried to avoid me.

On the home front things were busy, busy, with activities of the children and their various tournaments and all the practices that preceded those tourneys. Our older son was now in gymnastics and Jack was forever taking one child or the other to something. He was supportive of our son's love of gymnastics as he could possibly get a scholarship to a university later on and he was preoccupied with the state of his health. He went to the doctor more than anyone I had ever seen except his mother who I think was a hypochondriac and he, like her, believed in taking pills for every little thing. I believe that since he no longer drank alcohol and he did not smoke pot (and I do prefer to think that he kept his promise) he did not know how to deal with life without their numbing effects. He now was gobbling prescription medication and all kinds of OTC pills and herbal supplements and he turned out to be just as insufferable, if not more so, than when he was drinking beer and smoking the now-illegal substance. He became unreasonable and totally paranoid and argumentative and the children had a hard time with him when they did not agree with him on something and he was surely very cruel to Richard who had already garnered his ire by being different (not a macho-man).

I would see our son coming in from helping his dad with something outside and the tears were streaming down his face and he would say to me that he really hated Daddy. This, of course, was very upsetting to me and there was no way that I could let my husband know that I thought he was not treating this boy right. He was way too unreasonable and he was always right. At least one time, I remember my stepdaughter was witness to this cruel treatment of her half-brother and she must have been shocked by this. I think that it was quite natural that she was sympathetic as far as her brother was concerned and she was an important source of support for him. I reminded our son that we all knew that there was something wrong with his daddy and that he should find it within himself not to hold it against his father, as it would surely make things worse for himself and everybody else.

Richard was a devout Christian as far as I could tell, and he went on a mission-trip with the church to Mexico and he came back a happy young man, having had fun while sharing the gospel with some children in Mexico. I was so pleased.

That very year we had gotten a computer for him for Christmas which is what he wanted, as Beth had already had one for quite some time. I thought nothing of it, as it was still just another new gadget. We put it upstairs in the rec room and he spent a good amount of time on it. Of course the whole idea was that he could chat with his sister in

Chicago and as neither my husband nor I had any idea as to how to operate the thing, he was safe as could be from prying eyes. I trusted our son and as far as I was concerned he would never do anything to hurt me or make any kind of trouble for anyone.

However, shortly after Christmas he was scheduled to go to China with the church on a missions-trip, which he had been looking forward to, when he all at once urged me not to sign him up as he was not sure if that is what he wanted to do. I was a little confused because it was just not like the son I knew to change his mind.

I must mention here that I had taken him to an endocrinologist which we were instructed to do by the geneticist. It was very important to have his hormonal levels checked out. His testosterone level was normal and the physical measurements all seemed normal as well.

One day when I drove him to school/church for practice with the orchestra, he appeared to be agitated and I cannot remember what I said but I always made sure that he knew I was his ally, no matter what. I cannot recall what made me return to the church after I dropped him off, but when I did, I saw him leaving the church and walking briskly down the street toward the shopping mall. I was so shocked and I caught up with him and asked him what he was doing. He said that he had to do this and for me not to worry and he would call me when he was ready to be picked up. I thought that this must really be important and that it could not really be too bad and that he would tell me all about it when I picked him up, which is something he had always done, I thought.

That call never came. Our son was gone. There are hardly any words that can describe the desperation that set in unless one has been in that situation, under those circumstances. We were caught completely off guard and we did not know who to call or what to do.

We realized that we could get that information from the computer but we did not know how to access it. My husband called somebody his cousin knew who was familiar with computers. Until he came the next day we scoured all the phone numbers he had put into our family phonebook of friends, and we called all of them. Most of them had no clue and those who knew something were not forthcoming with any helpful information. At the time raves were all the rage and we went to those horrifying places where I would never ever think any one of my children would dare to go, but seeing that I also thought that none of my children would ever disappear like this, made it only sensible to look there too. After twenty-four hours we notified the police and we continued to search high and low for this son of ours. We then got a phone call from one of his friends who told us that he was going to go to Chicago to his half-sister's house.

My husband called there and sure enough he was there, I was relieved and angry at the same time, angry at myself for not having followed my gut instinct that this stepdaughter of mine had more than one way to skin a cat to accomplish what she had set out to do.

She was going to cause as much havoc as possible while looking completely innocent. I have to hand it to her, she was one smart cookie. A plan was made as to how to get him back to our house which I did not look forward to. The whole remaining family planned to travel to Chicago and pick him up. Meanwhile this computer-guy got all the information and when we followed the trail there, very prominently, was his sister in Chicago with benign writings and a name of a local student at the then MSU, and another from a boy somewhere in the middle west. We could not make heads nor tails from this and we had no choice but to wait and let the boy explain his strange behavior.

On the way back I was trying hard to act as I normally do and I wanted him to remember all the good times we had spent together. We certainly did not want the younger siblings involved in the problems of our son, so we all pretended we were on a vacation.

I was so upset though, as I could clearly sense that this was a troubled child, and that I could in no wise deal with yet another problem, certainly not one so obviously life-changing. I hated change anyway but when it involves only unpleasantness, who wants it? It was so important that my husband and I were a solidly united front as far as this boy was concerned and we talked about how to proceed and discuss any change in strategy beforehand. We were really trying hard to show our son that we were there for him, even though somebody had obviously convinced him that his father did not love him and that his mother was too preoccupied with everything in the family to pay enough attention to him and his needs. Somebody had really done a number on him and someone as impressionable as this child could easily fall into a trap somebody set for him. It was now up to us to change his mind.

My husband decided that we should have a policeman come to our house and explain the law concerning juvenile runaways and all the dangers that are lurking out there. The boy was dutifully listening but did not appear to be interested in this information.

The next morning he told us that he was a homosexual and that there was nothing we could or should do about it. It really did not come as a total surprise since there were signs all along the way. How does one deal with this? I had no idea. Laboring under the impression that it was something to have treated as an illness, we sent him to a Christian psychiatrist with a well-known Christian group that primarily deals with homosexuals and has had success, not exactly in curing homosexuals from homosexuality but in convincing them not to act on their feelings, as they always change, but to actively pursue the God-pleasing way.

That, of course, can only work if the person wants this changeover, which our son simply did not want. We had to suspend the sessions because he refused to participate in the conversation and he got very snappy with me and said that he wanted to be a homosexual and that's that. Well, I felt like killing him right there and getting it over with, but I knew only too well that my stepdaughter would have been dancing a victory dance because she would have been proven right—that I was but a hypocrite, parading as a Christian but hating my own son enough to kill him for what she had always been taught, at the ultra-liberal Adlai Stevenson High School in Chicago, which she attended, is just an alternative lifestyle.

As a Christian who sincerely believes that homosexuality is a sin, it is completely unacceptable for me to view it as an alternative lifestyle. However, I must admit that the stigmatization of one group to such a degree that it would invite and oftentimes be incited to hate them and to hurt them in any way, is an outrage and cannot be tolerated particularly by the Church. To be Christ-like excludes violence and hatred. Love is the only right response.

I had no choice but to live that which I preached and it was not easy. We had to change him from the church-school to a public school in our district which meant that I had to go in one direction to get him to school and in the opposite direction to get the other children to their school. He then was booted out of there and we had to enroll him at an alternative school for one year. He was caught with pot in his schoolsatchel. I was just disgusted with this boy.

We did not want him around the other children and as he was getting old enough to have his own room we put him upstairs into the rec room. The computer was moved downstairs to a central location. I must say I saw this once-beautiful boy full of promise turn into something I loathed and yet—this was my son! I loved him. I loved him more than I hated homosexuality. God loves him too, but He too hates homosexuality. Love the sinner—hate the sin. It is difficult to do but perhaps somewhat easier when the sinner is your own child.

He had admitted to us that he had been involved with a twenty-eight-year-old whom he had contacted via the computer—he was the MSU student. We went crazy and told him then that we are going to have this man arrested for contributing to the delinquency of a minor but our son pleaded with us not to do this because he loved this man and if we did this he would surely kill himself. I was beside myself and gathered information from all kinds of health professionals and they advised me without exception not to push for jailing the perpetrator as no one can predict with any certainty that the boy was only bluffing.

By then I had a very modest goal for this child and that was to keep him in town long enough to finish high school. At one time—and it was not that long ago—he was planning on becoming a heart surgeon, and he had to have *Grey's Book of Anatomy!* He was working part-time and I had to drive him everywhere at all hours and he was seeing this man and there was nothing I could do because he would just run away again and this time to someplace we would not be able to find him.

My husband stayed largely out of dealing with him. He became disinterested in the day-to-day goings-on and left it entirely up to me to see to it that I provided everything for everybody at all times, which included nightly excursions to downtown Memphis in the sleet and snow where this boyfriend of my son's had an apartment.

Our son wanted—no, he insisted—that he needed to divorce us which means he wanted to be emancipated. Under the guidance of this friend of his he got a lawyer who was a lesbian to represent his interests and it was a cut-and-dried deal after we had some sessions with a progressive psychologist, at which time my son complained at length about his father and I had to agree with everything the boy said because it was the truth. The lady asked me what it was that made me marry such a man. I said, in dead earnest, "God told me to marry him." Even as I was saying these words, it was clear to me that she and I were operating on different frequencies and she promptly said, seriously albeit with a tinge of amusement at such simplemindedness or even backwardness, that if God tells me to do something, not to listen, that I could see what happens when I do.

After this son of ours graduated from high school, he and this lover of his moved to Phoenix, Arizona, and I was glad to be rid of him. At this stage he did not fit into our lives. He was doing as he pleased and since he had his own car he came and went as he pleased too, and his room was a pigsty and we no longer could enjoy the room at all. Wherever you looked there were reminders of his rebellion against what he had been taught from early childhood and it was too painful to have to witness this disintegration, knowing there was nothing I could change. I loved him still, to be sure, and it was comforting to know where he would be and how he was getting along but it was more bitter than sweet sorrow at this parting.

Now it was five children down and two to go. I was trying hard to continue to do everything the Bible tells us to do to raise the children up in the admonition of the Lord and even though my track record on that was dismal when you consider the result, maybe with the remaining children it would be different!

Our daughter, Tracy, was a wonderful girl. She never caused us any trouble and she never needed to be reminded to fulfill her responsibilities. It seemed to me that she and I were operating on different frequencies too, because I never could really understand her. Oddly enough, she was the only one who adhered to all the do's and don'ts she was being taught but I just could not figure her out. There was something missing but what that was I did not know. She was not a demonstrative person and I never got the feeling that she loved me and we certainly were not like the average mother and daughter because her interests were in another direction from mine. She had no capacity for those girly-things mothers and daughters usually share, and I found dealing with her somewhat challenging. Her father had by far a better relationship with her and I had to leave it at that. She was going her way no matter what and as she seemingly upheld the teachings of her youth in every way, I could not complain. After all, I loved her unconditionally, as she was my angel since she was born. She was going to college for sure and she did work hard to be able to get a scholarship to finance her education as she opted for a car when she was sixteen if she was on track with her grades. She always was and there was no reason to withhold any reward for academic excellence.

My husband, meanwhile, discovered that he did not have to put himself under the pressure of having to work for this very good company and that he could represent several companies with whom he could land a contract—or maybe that very good company gave him the boot after that fiasco in Monaco—he never told me and I am not certain about the circumstances to this very day. He had only so much time to roll the business over from one company to the other which was a lengthy and tedious job and he found himself without a secretary again when Judy decided to work for him. I was astonished that she would even consider this because she knew how difficult a man he is and she knew of the constant turnover of secretaries who surely did not quit because they were so happy working for him, but she needed to change careers and this was a step in the right direction for her. She was a very capable and intelligent woman who could deal with anything she put her mind to.

Now I not only had to listen to him blowing off steam about the other secretaries who were strangers to me but it was no time it seemed until I started hearing endless complaints about my daughter. I knew that she had to have time to learn things and the whole concept of insurance was foreign to her but I also knew that she was a quick study and she was pretty too which is always a plus when dealing with the public. If I defended her this way he would get even angrier, so I just listened and let his cutting remarks about my child run off me like water off a duck.

There were too many times when my subconscious stored all the unguarded remarks he made when reacting to something and each time I got increasingly uneasy about his conversion. He lied, he cheated, he stole, he bore false witness if it secured him another buck for his god, which was money. There was simply nothing he would not do to make that money and still appear to be a decent guy to the people he needed for one reason or another.

It has been obvious to any half-witted observer if he or she would have been able to watch Jack in his day to day conduct that he was wavering back and forth to devise a maneuver to rid himself of me and at the same time maintain his carefully constructed image or to improve it and even elicit sympathy for himself as the poor mistreated husband who, as he prefers to think of it and re-tells it, married this unfortunate mother of four children to help her heal from the very painful treatment by her first husband.

I was out of the house, having left my husband with the children and our youngest son's friend from across the street. It was early 1996. I do believe I was at some function of the karate-studio.

When I came home I found my husband in an interrogative mood, asking what kind of cereal I was buying for him. He always wanted Kellogg's Raisin Bran for his breakfast. I have to insert here that I had switched the contents of the generic brand and put into the Kellogg's box. I had checked the ingredients and realized that I was paying two or three dollars more for the brand with the name Kellogg and I decided that there was no harm in substituting. It has long been a reason for humor among us housewives that men simply do not know the difference as long as they can see the box they are used to seeing. So why not save some money, which was in short supply. All the rest of the family was eating like this.

Well, do not underestimate a person with a specific goal in mind. They will not leave a stone unturned or in my case, the contents of the trash-compactor unexamined! He found the generic cereal box and came to the conclusion that I was deceiving him and that he is certain now that I do not think him worth an extra two or three dollars! He screamed and yelled in a most atrocious way in front of Samuel's friend who was looking scared to death. I reminded my husband of the child's presence but he did not care and screamed even louder and declared that this was truly the end of this marriage and that he was going to file for divorce.

I was scared to death and so incredulous. I asked him if he was serious about getting a divorce because of a box of cereal, pointing out that this makes it quite obvious that he has no regard whatever for our children's welfare, not to mention his lack of concern for me or my feelings and they were being trampled on on a regular basis. I literally talked and pleaded ourselves into an albeit still glimmering dangerously, ceasefire.

But this way of living where he would think nothing of it to come up out of the blue and accuse me of anything at all continued literally for years. It did not matter what it was, he pursued it doggedly—on the flimsiest evidence he would decide that he was going to get a divorce. Another time, I remember as if it had been yesterday when he was walking upstairs into the loft and saying with finality that he could not remain in this marriage. I was stunned as always and for the first time I realized with such painful clarity that I had absolutely nothing to show for myself, personally, that he just could arbitrarily decide to dump me for any reason and there was nothing I could do about it. It was then as if a veil was removed from my eyes and I saw things as they really were. It seemed to me that whatever it was that put a sort of a protective cover over me had now been removed. All the things he had ever hurt me with came into my memory and I could not get over how I did not see things for what they were! It was very scary.

There was really no point in protracting this untenable situation which it now was. He had never taken a stand with me when it came to my stepdaughter whom I held partly responsible for our son's development as she was a bad influence. He always took his daughter's side. She was no longer in the picture as she only used her father to get to me.

Once the smoke had cleared I had no choice but to admit to myself that this relationship simply could not survive, that I was literally at the mercy of this treacherous man and that the only way out was a divorce, which I then initiated by hiring a female lawyer to whom I paid a retainer fee.

I secured a female lawyer and filed for divorce. He was stunned but tried to act as if it did not bother him in the least. It was at that point that things changed in my daughter's favor at work. He was trying his best to bring her over on his side by telling her that I did not love her and since she had been such a rebel against my authority from early on, I said plenty to vent my anger at all the stunts she pulled. She believed him, of course, and with getting bonuses left and right, she was not going to help me to secure information on his financial holdings that my lawyer told me she needed. When I asked Judy for help in this regard she told me that she could not do this as he was her employer. I felt strange asking her for help as this was distasteful to me, too, but I did not mind that she did not comply.

The lawyer had to just work for her money and do it the way they have to do it to get the necessary information to represent the interests of their clients. Some untoward things occurred between my husband and my daughter which I can just imagine.

My eldest daughter wanted to go to Germany and wanted me to come with her but I did not have the money as I had to pay a retainer fee from my measly scraped-up savings. My husband, who had been served, offered to pay for it. I counseled with the pastor and he, of course worked on a reconciliation of which I would not have any part. One thing was certain though, I would never put myself through the hell I suffered through after my first divorce. There was never going to be another man! No way. That part of my life as I had known it was over. The pastor kept on saying that I should make sure that this was what I wanted. Since I was leaving for Germany I did not want to be so definite and allowed for God to let me know which way to go upon my return from Germany.

My daughter and I had a wonderful time in Germany. My mother had been moved in with my half-sister as she had become unable to take care of herself. My older sister and my brother-in-law came to Erlangen, where our mother now lived, and we all had a nice visit. When our mother went to bed we went down memory lane and we, her children, could not believe that we survived. We went to see my cousin and his wife. My brother had died two years earlier. I enjoyed going the way I went to school so long ago with my daughter, down through the meadow to the train station, the restaurant from way back which was still where it had been and we had a delicious lunch there. We went to Nürnberg and I showed her the student home where I lived for almost two years. I wanted to go inside and check on any mail that may have come, hoping that this fifteen-year-old had sent me the picture of herself with Elvis and myself when I was hiding that letter I had retrieved from Elvis's boxes of fan mail. It was closed. I was very disappointed.

On the way back to the States we had a delay of eight hours which we spent at the airport as the plane was going to be fixed early in the morning and ready for takeoff.

Being so seriously inconvenienced, I felt so indescribably uncertain about the divorce. Having been away from everything that gave me a sense of belonging, a sense of security, I was just glad to be home and the thought of messing all this up and having to deal with a lawyer on top of this, which really scared me as I knew my husband's ability to sell ice to the Eskimos and make you believe that white is black and green is red, I got cold feet. Not only that but when I went into the loft, where I had been sleeping for a long time by then, primarily because of his snoring, there was a letter waiting for me from my husband. Being so uncertain and downright scared, I was willing to believe every word of his confession of true love.

The next day I announced that I was remaining in the marriage. At that point I was just as determined to put up with everything as I had always done to be able to live with him. I reminded myself of the fact that I was reliving the same scenario I lived through with my ex-husband's mother. In fact I was just like one of those intimidated women I met on my debit and whom I always pitied but I now knew how one can get into this situation and I finally understood.

A lousy tyrant was still better than no protector at all.

As a celebration of sorts my husband took us to the Bahamas and Tracy and Samuel were happy as clams that the storm clouds had passed over.

Susan graduated from UT where she had studied to be an occupational therapist in December. The graduation ceremonies were at the Peabody with a luncheon and special mentions, of which my daughter was a recipient. This made me so proud of her hard work and excellence. Everything was going well. I had bought a dress for the occasion and my husband seemed to share my joy.

We went from the Audubon Botanical Gardens to the Peabody Hotel, and all at once, from out of nowhere and for no apparent reason, my husband took on the same mannerisms as he did in Monaco. He did not care if I found my way to the right entrance from where we were parked and when he talked to me it was with that same kind of dismissiveness and annoyance at my presence. For a moment I was very alarmed but he seemed to catch himself. But as the degrees were handed out he was making such a scene with one of the parents of one of the other students and he acted as if I was not even there and when my daughter came to join us, he took it upon himself to introduce Susan to these people he had befriended for the sole purpose of offending me, which I was, and plenty at that! He continued to be belligerent toward me and snarled whenever I dared to say anything. I was getting madder by the minute and I was murmuring under my breath for him to just bring it on and I had resolved to stand my ground this time, come what may. Susan and her second husband went to their hotel room as they did not like to be around my husband anymore than they needed to be and we were supposed to meet them with our children at some restaurant.

We got to our car and he was already winding up to launch into this horrid barrage of cussing and cursing and hurling accusations of all kinds at me that were nothing but lies. At first I tried to be reasonable but he knew very well that I was completely innocent of all the charges but that he needed to do this for one of his diabolical schemes that were but a mystery to me. I let him rant and rave, scream and yell and insult me every which way and my mind was so made up to leave him it was not even funny. I resolved right then and there that I would not ask a thing from him but my freedom. We stopped by the school and picked up the children and his ravings stopped and we play-acted "normal" for the children. But that did not get me around being devastated. I had so completely lost everything I tried to accomplish over all these hard years of marriage. I cried and cried and cried when we got home. When it was time to meet my daughter I was in no condition to go anywhere in public. My eyes were red and swollen, but it was my daughter's day of honor. I put cool compresses on my eyes and I put on a face and a smile and joined in the fun that the children had with their favorite older sister. Jack and I did not speak to each other unless there was no way around it. At night I cried and prayed for God to help me through this and it was as if there was peace in my soul that affirmed the need for this rupture in this relationship. I wrote my husband a request for divorce, outlining that he could have everything, that I would claim nothing that we had accumulated during the marriage, that I wanted him to stay in the house with us and that the only difference would be that there would be no intimacy ever again. I would be running things much the same as I had always done. I would require a small stipend as I no longer expected him to pay for my personal things, but I needed to be compensated for my services, much like an au pair. I handed this request to him on his birthday. He read it and threateningly said, "I will teach you." I also left it up to him to get the lawyer and file against me. It simply did not matter at this point as long as I got rid of him. He did not let any grass grow under his feet and the next day he asked me to sign off on the house by agreeing to put it into his name only, which I did.

I was so through with him I would have rather slept in a sandbox with an umbrella for a roof than have to have sex with him. I found this to be the most important feature in this whole process. I realized that it was through sex that my emotional attachment was secured, which was fine when it was to the benefit of the children but they were growing up fast and I do not think that they really cared all that much as long as their needs were being met. I tried to make sure of that by asking their father to live with us.

As much as I loathed him from the bottom of my heart as my husband, I had to protect myself from him and his advances which I found embarrassing, to say the least as he was primitive enough to think so little of women, that these inferior creatures, that he thought we could be controlled by a roll in the hay, that everything that ailed women could be cured with sex. For this reason alone, a legal separation was out of the question, as Jack would undoubtedly recite the Bible to remind me of my wifely duty.

I also am certain that this way was the best way, as a lengthy court battle over possessions would have done so much collateral damage. It would have put the children in the middle and I know that my husband would have put them under undue pressure to take his side and they would surely have been harmed, just as I would have been. It was extremely difficult for me to take this step, as I had always been on my soapbox, touting the sanctity of marriage and the serious commitment that is required to live up to God's standard. How irrelevant all this spouting now sounded. It was painful.

In no time, my daughter left his employment, insisting that he was the most horrible jerk she had ever known, when he hired some woman who was married and they became quite friendly and she got a divorce from her husband and before I knew it, my husband was building himself another house about a ten-minute drive from our house and after our divorce had become final and the house was finished he moved out from our house into his new house with this secretary.

There are no words to describe how hurtful all this was to me. Tracy did not seem to mind to visit her father there and she would describe all the pretty things there in glowing terms. She resented my having caused all this confusion and she let me know it. Not overtly, but I got the message loud and clear.

I had to pay rent to him to continue living in the only home these children had ever known, as it was necessary for him to get some sort of tax advantage. He made it so very hard for me to live.

I had started working for our church as a nursery attendant in Mother's Day Out (MDO—a time for mothers to get a break from their children) and during church services and Sunday school and I made a paltry amount of money but I enjoyed working with little children and it kept me near my own as they were on the premises whenever I was there.

Things did not go well with this secretary for long. He threatened her and she called the police on him. After this Jack came and tested the waters to see whether I would let him move back in and he was jokingly asking, looking at Samuel, who would like for him to move back, to which Samuel lowered his eyes and said nothing. Did we not we would all agree, often, that it was better to be at home when Jack was not there and we dreaded his coming home? I am sure that my children were embarrassed by their mother working at such a lowly job. More and more did I understand the hypocrisy that is inherent in the organized church and I had always had an instinctual dislike for becoming too close to the inner workings of the church and the school. I had always accepted the status quo and did not bother to ask the right questions just so my little world would not be turned upside down. Slowly but surely I became aware that all was not well with the church, not only my own but with the Christian Church in general. The more I was exposed to the dealings of church folks with church folks I became disillusioned. I questioned their conduct and I concluded that we church people were completely off track as far as the teachings of Jesus was concerned. Oh yes, we gave the impression that we were following Jesus' example but we were at the same time serving that insatiable beast within us and participated in all kinds of things that our culture, particularly after Elvis had left his mark on it, throws at us from every corner and in every known medium. They encourage us to do this and buy that and use this and we would be better, feel better, look better and we all accepted it as a matter of course and we would have been aghast if someone had come along and told us that this was not a Christian's way to act but to be a separate people every day in our conduct and not only on Sunday when the so-called Christians would be separate only because they were in church and the non-Christians were not. It was indeed a mess.

It is important that I mention here that simultaneously with all the downturn of everything that was my life, there was an upturn.

Very unexpectedly, there was a moment when I was minding my own business, wiping the countertop and thinking of nothing in particular when I saw—yes, saw—Elvis flitting through the breakfast room into the hall of the separate part of the house that led to the laundry room, the half-bath, the rec room and the garage. He was wearing a gray shirt and black trousers.

I had secured Charlie Hodge's new address. My daughter, who lived in Knoxville at the time, had told me that they had gone to some theater where Charlie Hodge was introducing himself and his Elvis impersonator and his band. She could not tell me anything specific. I had read that Red's wife was teaching acting at a studio at their home and it listed their phone number. I contacted her and asked if she knew Charlie's address and she said that it was the Memories Theater in Pigeon Forge. It was at that time when she and I got to talking about the years going to the Memphian and how we simply had better things to do, as we were mothers and had to be awake in the daytime. She had only one son but I am sure that going to the movies in the middle of the night was no thrill for her, as she was around Elvis all the time.

I did write to Charlie and told him of Elvis's appearance and many other things, as they happened at a fast clip and all dealt with Elvis. There was a very vivid dream that heralded my future in a succinct way.

In this dream I had entered into what appeared to be a house, maybe Elvis's. Charlie was talking to me telling me something important. I was listening intently and while he was still talking I ran down some stairs, where I knew I would be finding who I was so desperately searching for: Elvis. He was lying on a gurney, his legs were broken at the knees, and his head was wrapped in bandages, but when he saw me, the happiest smile came over his face. I smiled in return and rushed to his side, grasped his hand and looked him in the eyes. We were all smiles and full of happiness when I abruptly woke up. I sat on the edge of my bed recalling what I had just experienced in a dream and I noticed that I was still smiling. I gently felt that smile with my fingers, and I knew that I would soon understand everything that had happened to me with regards to Elvis and also my husband and that these seemingly unconnected features were really part and parcel of the same thing. The timing was intriguing as it was but three days before my divorce from my husband was final, which was on September 23, 1998. After this dream I felt the need to travel to meet with Charlie. I took the bus to Knoxville and from there a taxi to Pigeon Forge. He entered the theater with his girlfriend on his arm and when he saw me he smiled broadly and introduced me to his fiancée. It was almost showtime and he urged me to stay till after the show. It was so very strange because it was like déjà vu, except that he was the celebrity this time around. I was standing in the lobby at the concession stand, just like at the Memphian—it was positively weird. After the show I purchased his book, which was the least I could do to help him earn a living. He autographed it and I absolutely did not see any purpose to stay until all this merchandising was over, as it really put me in a bad mood. I returned to my hotel room and returned home the same way I came, but I could not understand any of this visit. I hated to have to bow and scrape to gain favor and that seemed to be expected from people in show business. At any rate, I was at a loss what to make of Charlie, but I did peruse his book and I discovered one thing he wrote in there which alluded to me—it's on page 168. He said that on those lonely nights, all the boys could do was let him (meaning Elvis) talk and they listened and gave him all he needed but the single most important thing of all was that special kind of love that comes from a woman (and not just any woman). And this they could not provide.

Charlie has already been dead for some years at this writing, so suffice it to say that Charlie was a likable guy who could put you at ease and he could talk and talk. He was nice to me and did whatever I asked of him, not that I think he understood much. It was Elvis's understanding I was after. His book gives you a glimpse of the life that was Elvis's and it must have been busy, sure enough. The only way poor rich Elvis could cope was to become stark raving mad. He suffered more than we can even imagine and for a long time he was able to hide his grief over his dismal personal life as it concerns the love he had for me ever since we had met at the Grunewald Hotel, Charlie says it was the Park Hotel, but it is just as well, since these German words were difficult to remember and impossible to spell.

But from then on I wrote to Charlie on a frequent basis, as if writing into a diary, as he never even acknowledged that he got my letters. For some reason I had to write to him.

For better or for worse I had to do what I had to do even if it did not make any sense to my rational mind. The only way that I could escape from this track I was on was with a lobotomy and since I was careful not to sound too crazy, I had no one to chase me down and confine me to the insane asylum or put me under the care of a psychiatrist who would give me some psychotropic drugs, which I sometimes thought might be the only way to get away from all this mysterious stuff that put a serious, ongoing, crimp in my life. Even though I was under the impression that the answers to my questions and wondering would come soon, I am still here now writing a book trying to explain the unexplainable, twelve years after my meeting up with Elvis in this happy dream in 1998.

Tracy was getting ready to prepare herself for college and she had been accepted with a full scholarship to UT-Knoxville. She had brought some friends from school over to watch a movie on the VCR in the loft and I stayed downstairs to do something but I could listen to the dialog in that movie. It was unacceptable to me to have to listen to that raunchy talk and I chided the whole lot of them that I had expected better of them since they all went to a Christian school and most of them were our church members. It did exemplify what I had found to be true, that they had no clue as to what it really means to be a Christian They were all ashamed and uncomfortable and my daughter gave me a disapproving glance and they all left in a huff. I did not mean to spoil their fun, but if I did not let my first set of children watch Sonny and Cher because of the revealing outfits Cher wore, I was surely not going to let this go unaddressed. And yet, I was doing things that were not in keeping with my Christian ideal, but I just could not see it, just as they could not see their shortfalls. It must be very confusing to children to grow up being taught one thing but then the everyday life was dominated by everything that came down the pike labeled progress and progressive and it came straight into your living room. It was unsettling to me, I must say, and it seemed to me that the beloved Elvis was the epitome of that duality and helped to propagate this notion of having it both ways and so changing the devout Christian into a notional Christian, which is what we were all becoming and most of us are, even in the ranks of the clergy. We have lost our moral moorings and we are free-falling and God better help us see the error of our ways. It is a dangerous place to find ourselves in.

The fact that I had no longer any dealings with any man, on any personal level, freed me to contemplate the things that interested me most and that was my relationship to Elvis and its meaning which undoubtedly had everything to do with Jesus Christ as I had loved Him way before I had to fall in love with Elvis. I remember thinking when I tried to find out who this man I loved was, as Elvis was still enjoying his early success in the U.S., and the things I discovered were such that I could not help but wonder if God knew what he was doing, as I thought I could have found someone more fitting for me in my own neighborhood. I was and liked everything he was not and did not like. We were total opposites and yet we were also identical in our weaknesses and spiritual strengths. It is hard to explain, indeed. Some things cannot be explained. Just believe that they are what they are for a purpose only the God of the Scripture knows.

I had never been inside Graceland when Elvis was alive, as I was of the opinion that it was the pit of hell, and now, twenty-three years after his death, I had to pay good money to get a look at the place where he lived and died in such a desperate move to get away from this world that kept him caught in a trap.

I must say I was pleased at the comfort level Presley Enterprises provided for their paying customers. I enjoyed the ride on the bus and I could see all the familiar things I remember from hanging around at the gate with my husband way back in 1963. The surrounding area had changed drastically since then, as the Estate bought all the lots around Graceland. It was strange because it looked so odd to me, just like any other tourist-destination anywhere in this country that must accommodate hundreds and hundreds of people per day. This was just that well-run and the personnel were friendly and helpful. When we got inside I stayed pretty much with the group I came in with and I could not get over how small the place really was. When we got to the hallway leading up to Elvis's bedroom after we had seen the jungle room, I was standing there listening to the information on the recorder and as I was looking up in the direction of the bedroom I was suffocating and I had to worm my way out of that group of people and walk hurriedly through the dark kitchen to the backdoor and outside into the sunshine. I took a deep breath and was glad to be out of there. Then there was Vernon's office and then off to what used to be the racket-ball facility, then recording studio, which was now housing all the awards that Elvis garnered during his lifetime. It absolutely floored me. I had no idea—no idea. It was most astonishing to me, as it only proves my point, that the world held him captive for its own gain and rewarded him handsomely for services rendered with the things of this world (as opposed the things from above). Then came this barn-like structure where everything Elvis was on display. This was utterly boring to me with one exception and that was a navy-blue three-piece suit, very conservative, and just what I liked a man of importance to wear. That was it. How much Elvis hoopla can one take? We went on to the meditation garden and I have to admit I found all these colorful flowers just as garish as Elvis's costumes in Las Vegas. I always thought of him, the show person, as a clown who was hired to sexually excite women as well as men which brought in the crowds who brought him the money or should I say brought the money to pay Tom Parker, the carny-man turned into the all-time best promoter of his golden boy. Together they formed a mutually beneficial alliance and although it seemed unfair to many for Tom Parker being in control, Elvis knew instinctively that it was good for what both of them were after. But when the devil has your soul, for a person like Elvis it was torture and he could not get out of his commitment even if he wanted to, as many people had jobs because of him and many people depended on Elvis doing what he did so well so they could provide for their families. I really would not want to have traded my lifestyle for Elvis's—it was harder than mine and mine was hard enough for me. At the very least I could suffer through my hell in private and without the sting of criticism from people who had no idea what he was going through. That came his way at each and every misstep somebody found out about and sold it to the tabloids so they could make money, as people were forever fascinated by anything and everything Elvis did or did not do, did say or did not say. I always told my husband then, who kept up with all things Elvis, that they would buy poop if they knew it was Elvis's. Please do not ask me to explain the influence this man had over the people—he was extraordinarily charismatic, but I suggest that this love that found him just as it had me enabled him to transmit this powerful emotion in his music which secured the second rise in his standing as a phenomenon on the world stage. It is sad indeed that all these hordes of admirers forgot that he was only human and that he had the same needs and longings as any human with one very important difference: he also knew of the God of the Scriptures as he was taught the Lord's way by his mother who took him to church with her, First Assembly of God church there in

Tupelo, where he spent his formative years and beyond, singing lovely hymns and believing in God the father, God the Son, and God the Holy Spirit. He roamed the very hills where I now live, which I was not aware of when I moved here. It was this knowledge that he was privileged to have become intimate with that ultimately caused his misery. The constant admiration and the constant expectation from his admirers to titillate forced him to play with the fire of temptation, which he was then destroyed by. It was a very sad case of reaching the pinnacle of what the world calls success and losing that which is more precious than anything the world has to offer and that is a thriving intimate relationship with our Lord Jesus Christ.

So I have had my work cut out for me as far as my Elvis story goes but I had yet to learn what it was all about from the very beginning.

Meanwhile I was trying to take care of a big house, the landscaping around it, and the whole property as my husband had it put into the final decree of divorce. I tried to get the children to help me but it was very difficult because our lovely daughter had absolutely no pity whatever for me. In fact she so much as said this when I was complaining about all the things I was expected to do with no money to boot. I settled for the smallest amount of money that he could get away with, as the courts would not have granted the divorce after twenty years of marriage and three children unless I was independently wealthy in my own right but I did not even have a marketable skill that could enable me to support myself. My daughter let me know in no uncertain terms: "You agreed to it, now live with it." Whatever attitude this girl displayed influenced my youngest son and so I had two unwilling children waiting on me to do everything. At first I enjoyed doing yard work but I was no spring chicken and some things I simply could not do by myself. My ex would come by and notice what needed to be done and said that he would come over and take care of it but he never did. I would have to clean the pool while my daughter sat inside the cool house with her boyfriend and they both watched me working in the broiling sun. It was really hurtful and I was really beginning to wonder what kind of Christian conduct this was. Apparently they had no idea, even with her boyfriend having been the son of a pastor. I think my daughter told him just as she had told me—she wanted it, she got it!

Before Tracy had to move to UT Knoxville, she searched on the computer in the kitchen/breakfast room for songs which she had pulled down from Napster.

I was busy doing my household chores when I heard Elvis sing "Please Don't Stop Loving Me" which stopped me in my tracks. I instantly recognized this song to be the one of which I was permitted to hear only a snippet of in one of my dreams in the eighties.

This snippet of a melody long forgotten had so captivated my attention and had so monopolized my spiritual life as to start me on this quest to find the answers to my persistently nagging questions pertaining to the meaning of all the strange occurrences in my life.

The lyrics to this song are so poignantly affirming of this overwhelming love that had found us. Elvis sings so hauntingly mournful, revealing his utter helplessness and deepest devotion.

However, when she moved to Knoxville it was a shock to my system, as I saw my children leaving one by one to conquer the world, so to speak, and everything I had counted on to be there to give me that wonderful feeling of closeness of one's family was disappearing faster than I could get adjusted to. It was a very upsetting reality for me to have to come to terms with the children literally growing away from me and I had to let them go. I had no power to hold them back. They grew into these products of the society that is unavoidable thanks to the technological advances in mass communication. We did not recognize the destructive potential it carried and it led us far away from the ideals of our forefathers, who could not have had the ability to imagine the kind of folly we were capable of, trading right for wrong and good for evil, and we have so deceived ourselves over at least fifty-plus years (Elvis-time—a coincidence?) that we no longer could recognize the truth if it bit us on the nose!

I had no way to combat this effectively in my children as any attempt was met with, "Oh Mommy, you are so silly!" Considering my children's blindness, I resolved that it was probably a good thing that they were becoming independent. I was truly too tired to fight the same old fights the same old way with the results being the same. It came into my mind, seemingly out of nowhere, that I had to move away from this big house which I had to pay a hefty sum to be able to live in and keep up with. I pondered going here, going there, but nothing felt right. I was still puzzling over where to move to when Judy called me in a panic, saying that the people she had rented a house to up and left suddenly and she was in a financial bind. She was now married for the fourth time and had added two girls to her son who was now entering his teenage years. They lived close to her husband's parents where they bought a bigger house. Eureka! I knew where I had to move to and I suggested to my daughter that I needed to move away from this big house which had become like a noose around my neck and that I could possibly rent that cute little house from her and so help her and myself at the same time. I talked to my ex about my plans and suggested for him to move back in the old homestead He was now married to yet another woman with whom he lived at his new house that he occupied once with that secretary of his. Our youngest son would have to live with them there as I would not want to force my poverty on him as he was used to getting everything he wanted within reason. Besides, I was forever being accused of having had too much to say about the rearing of the boys and spoiling them, so I figured that maybe when my ex-husband was the father-figure, in complete charge, things might turn out better for Samuel. My oldest son, Jeremy, changed from a drug user to a responsible married man and apparently lived the good life, working hard for his wife's grandfather who owned a car dealership, among many other things, including an impressive house that he and his wife called home. He had a daughter with this woman, who was also a former drug-user, and a graduate of a school for problem girls. This marriage was over after a very short time and my son descended into alcoholism and drug use of which I was not aware until some time much later and after I had lost a significant amount of money from my puny settlement to keep him from going bankrupt, which he ended up being regardless. Being like any mother under those circumstances, I asked myself the universal, albeit rhetorical, question: "What did I do wrong? What could I have done to prevent this?" It was a reasonable decision to try something different and my ex-husband agreed to move back to his (and only his) old house.

While I was busy preparing to move to my daughter's little house, carload by carload, I was too busy to think much about anything else but when all the intense moving process was completed and things put in place there was quiet-time to fully realize the enormity of this change for me, I was devastated. I was in such serious pain of separation from my home, my son, my family, I thought that I would die. It was truly a time of great sorrow and yet I could not let anyone know it because that would have made me vulnerable and I could become tempted by certain individuals to cancel everything I had changed so drastically, and I was very sure that there could never be a turning back, no matter the pain.

For a long time after our divorce I did not share this fact with anyone, but this pretending that I was what I really was not was an intolerable situation for me. I had not consulted with my pastor before I took this step to divorce, as I was certain that this was what I had to do and there was nothing he could do to help me.

Once I told the ladies of my secret at one of our Women's Ministries meetings there was a unified response of shock. But I was so relieved and things did change for me in my church and the children's school and not for the better I might add.

I continued to work for the church that had now moved to Cordova, a Memphis suburb. The people I worked with were nice to me. There was no telling what they said behind my back, but what I did not know could not hurt me!

At this point my ex-husband and I had a mutual interest in seeing to it that we had as little outward animosity toward each other as possible and we tended to the needs of our progeny in a pleasant and sometimes even enjoyable manner and our children's lives were the better for it.

As it stood we each had what we valued most. He had his money and other earthly possessions and I had my inner peace of knowing that I had rid myself of an antagonist who willfully withheld whatever he needed to in order to put me in my place, over and over again, and I had to accept it just so I could get out of it what I needed most to bring our children up in accordance with God's Word. I left it all behind and took a vow of celibacy and poverty to safeguard my soul for eternity. So why could we not deal with each other in a civilized fashion?

When I had to go shopping for groceries, I continued to shop at the same Walmart we used to go to after dinner as a family and the children would always find something they thought they wanted. Daddy bought it for them and we would all go home happy. It was a ritual I enjoyed so much because the children then did not require much to be happy. Here I was, all alone, my children were here, there and yonder, and I would stand there and remember, particularly our youngest son who was just such a happy cutie pie. I had to force myself not to burst into tears and I hurriedly purchased what I went for and got into the car and sat there and cried and I looked back at the store with longing in my heart so strong that I could even see my beloved youngest son, whom I hovered over with care because I had him for the Lord.

On Sundays it was another agonizing confrontation with the enormity of that which I had initiated. Sometimes Samuel and I would arrive at the same time, get out of our respective cars and he would come over to me and say, "Hi, Mom!" He'd sit with the youth group and I would sit in my usual place and after church he'd go to his home and I'd go to mine. It nearly killed me to be away from him but I could not let anyone know that I was hurting like crazy and that I spent a lot of time crying in my little house.

Undoubtedly the Lord protected me and gave me the strength to do what I had to do.

My older children had no understanding for my settling for so little and they, too, thought I was just pitiful, working at the church for peanuts. They had no idea how important it was for me to be near my children during school hours and they did not understand that I loved little children, the babies in particular, as I loved to interact with them and make them smile with glee at my antics. These were mostly children whose mothers stayed at home with them but needed some time for themselves.

I thought it strange for a mother to leave her child with someone she did not know. I would never let my children get away from me, as I missed them far too much. I still do not understand it.

My new place was a pretty house and I really liked living there. It had three bedrooms and in one of the two rather small bedrooms I had pictures of my children all around the room. In the other I had books and a map of the world on the wall and some plants. Each of these rooms had a bunk bed in it—yes, the very bunks our sons used as they grew up. I had a lot of reminders of my former life even as far back as my life with my first husband.

I retained the living room furniture, which my husband selected on the spur of the moment and then decided that he did not like.

He also let me have the secretary desk which he bought for me after the trip to the Bahamas. Everything else was very old and dear to me as it held great sentimental value. I used all the closets for my clothes and other storage and if I forgot about the negative and concentrated on the positive, which was my solitude and inner tranquility, then I actually enjoyed this little house. It was something for me to get used to though as the space between my bed and the next thing in the room was only inches away and I ran into things simply because they were all so packed together in a much smaller space. It felt as though I was living in an oversized closet.

Since people knew that I was divorced, the ladies would ask if I was lonely. I never really was because it was in my aloneness that much closer to God with whom I stayed in constant contact. The men would ask me if I thought of marrying again to which I politely and honestly replied, "No—it was entirely too hard and I will never marry again." I am sure I was confusing to a lot of people. Add to this the fact that I no longer colored my hair. I was so surprised to discover that I was solid gray. I like my gray hair. To me it means I have matured and I am at a new stage of life that primarily is devoted to reflection and contemplation, trying to make sense of life and its purpose. I loved going to church and worshipping God, and it always lifted my spirits—that is if nothing major put a cloud over my spirit, but I could always count on my children or my ex-husband to do this for me.

Jack was forever trying to shortchange his nemesis, the government. One year, it was the year he had moved out, he said on the way out that he was going to switch the amount of money between child support and alimony as that would give him an advantage. I did not concern myself with it because this was his idea and it probably would not matter much. Wrong! The IRS informed me that I had been cheating as I declared the correct amount of alimony and the correct amount of child support when I had the tax people file my income tax. They levied a hefty fine and I had to pay it. I told my ex about it and asked him to help me pay this fine—it was close to a thousand dollars. He flat-out said no to me. How unfair can it get? I pestered the IRS and complained about my ex and his and only his culpability in this and said that I should not have to pay this as I could ill afford it. They refunded me the money after I submitted proof. Boy, was I surprised. They are human after all! But all the trouble this caused and the notion that I would cheat on top of it, made me feel miserable for a long time and I already had plenty to make me feel miserable.

I had lived peacefully for about six months when I was told that my ex-husband had a girlfriend on the side. I was livid. No doubt Samuel was living in a bad environment and his father was an example of moral turpitude and I just could not believe that he would think so little of his son as to set such a bad example.

It was always to my detriment to give my ex-husband credit where none was due. It was just inconceivable to me that anyone would do this, let alone the father of my children. It was during that time that my son became enamored of a girl at school who had a bad reputation. I warned him about this girl but she had him under her thumb. Having been the baby in the family all his young life, I venture to say that he was emotionally behind boys his own age. So here comes this street-wise girl who had taken it into her head that she was going to make this boy hers. I cautioned my son and when I brought up her background, which was drugs and truancy and other things that had gotten her expelled from several schools, he assured me that she had changed her life around since she started at First A/G school, where my son had been since kindergarten

Jeremy had moved in with me and I seriously thought that I could help him if he were living in an orderly home. His girlfriends all had thrown him out and he had no place to go. I explained to him that he could not smoke in the house, that I could not tolerate drunkenness and bad language. He told me that he could do this and it lasted five days. He obviously was an out-of-control alcoholic and drug-user, and when he would talk to one or the other girlfriend he would use language like my ex-husband used when he was on a tear. I was not going to have any of this and I showed him the door and said that I could not help him, that he needed to admit he had a problem which he adamantly denied having. He said as he was leaving that I would not see him again and I very seriously replied, in a questioning sort of way, "Is that a promise?"

I must admit, my children have repelled me plenty and there was a sincere wish I would never have to see them again in those repulsive conditions.

I opened every window and scrubbed every trace of this child out of my house, which was my sanctuary, and I prayed over the purged house after I had removed all the beer bottles.

Barely a month had passed when my homosexual son called and asked me to pick him and his friend up at the Greyhound bus station late at night. I did and I almost died from horror when I saw Richard. He looked gaunt and sick and thin and his friend looked even worse. This twenty-eight-year-old from the past was no longer in the picture even though he had moved with my son to Pittsburgh. These two, Richard and Delbert stayed with me, as Jack's wife did not like homosexuals. What else could I do, as they had no money and all their belongings were in their duffle bags, which were big enough to stash a body in. We had bought our son's duffle bag on his request when he was supposed to be going to China on that missions-trip some years ago.

It was something else to see two gay people interact. They slept in different rooms! I must say I was so repulsed I could not stand it. I asked my ex to please help find these two an apartment and he did. He paid for it and we all collected stuff for them to set up housekeeping in mid-town. There again, I could not change them, as they were proud to be the way they were, discussing whether to wear eye shadow and lipstick when they had one of my son's longtime friends pick them up. She was the one who had tipped us off as to my son's whereabouts after he had run away from home. It was something else I do not want to have to experience again. Gruesome, that was. I cannot for the life of me understand how anyone could think that this is just another way to live—it is so unnatural! My son explained to me that straights to them are unnatural. How twisted can you get in your thinking? I was thoroughly disgusted.

This friend of my son's, Delbert, received a monthly unemployment check and they gave my address as the forwarding address and every month I had to drive to their apartment and bring them this check. Then I had to take them to get it cashed. They were not an oddity where they lived. They arranged things to their liking and got themselves jobs eventually and were self-supporting. It is worth noting here that my son assumed that my past performance of accepting the fact that he was a homosexual and my support of him as such also meant that I accept homosexuality in principle, but nothing is further from the truth. I just could not agree to mistreat or harm them because of it which I think is un-Christian, hence my dealing with him as an equal in our shared humanity.

It then became a fact of life that these two were also heroin addicts for which I had zero tolerance. That explained the haggard look when they arrived in Memphis. I even had to be thankful that he was not dying of AIDS, which was my first thought upon seeing him. He assured me that he would clean up his act and get off the heroin. According to him he had been in rehab at least two times. What a sorry state of affairs! Never would I have been able to imagine such degradation in any of my children but there it was!

I got barely out of that mess when my youngest son wanted to move in with me and I thought it was because of moral outrage over his father's immoral lifestyle, so I was pleased as that indicated to me that not all was lost and he could still be bothered by immorality. He moved in with me and I was so happy. I had to put up with him bringing this girl over but then he was soon to be seventeen and this was perfectly reasonable. Two months into the year two thousand and three and, one month into his stay at my house, I was contacted by the police. They said that my son and his girlfriend were having sex in the car at some park and she had a pregnancy-kit that showed that she was pregnant. I was aghast! What next?

The police brought him home, or rather, they escorted him home and drove his girlfriend home to her parents. I loathed my son (his behavior). Soon a meeting was set up at my house with the parents of this girl. There we were, her parents, the girl, my son and my ex-husband and I. My son said that the girl told him that she could not get pregnant because of some health issue. The mother of the girl said that this was not true and that their daughter was on birth-control pills as she had been sexually active for some time. I looked the girl in the eye and asked her if she deliberately stopped taking birth-control to get pregnant and, without a hint of shame, she answered cockily, "Yes, I did." I had to control myself not to jump off my chair and kill that girl, or at least give her a serious dusting of the derriere, which she probably never got growing up. The parents were both working and the children just had to fit in as best they could. Some children simply need more supervision and discipline than others. It was suggested that they take their daughter out of school before she started to show, which meant not too long down the road, and that my son could then continue finishing high school at the school he attended since kindergarten and graduate with his class the following year. I was far too upset to think clearly about anything because the whole disaster was just too distasteful.

After calming down I thought the girl could have an abortion as she appeared not to bothered much about anything, but I forgot that it was my son whom she wanted at the moment. Trying to secure my son's bright future I was willing to do almost anything. Then I thought that he should have known better and since he did not he needed to pay the price for disobedience. I took him out of the school, disclosing the reason, and making babies is definitely cause for dismissal in a Christian school. He did not want to go to another high school and he did not want to go to night school. He decided to do the Gateway school program with his girlfriend and it ended up that the girl's mother did all the checking and submitting of test scores or whatever it was that she had to do. I hated the whole darn thing, and as I had no control over anything this son of mine did, I did not want to deal with this. It was an unpleasant fallout of this primary transgression of one of the important laws of the God of the Scriptures, the living God, and this was not the only one.

One day before I withdrew Samuel from the Christian School the secretary of the school called and said that Samuel was not in school and asked whether he was sick. I did not know what to say as I had seen him leaving for school that morning, which is what I told her. I was so upset and I called my daughter, in whose house I was living, and she said right away that he was with that girlfriend of his at her house. So I got into my car and drove to her house and sure enough there was his car. I rang the doorbell many times and got no response. I let myself through the gate to the backyard where there was this big barking dog. I told that dog to shut up and get out of my way and I went straight to the backdoor and let myself in what looked like a cyclone had hit the place. Everything was strewn everywhere—it was a sight! My son had told me that they were getting paid to clean the house and if that was their idea of cleaning and getting paid for it, somebody needed to talk to those parents of hers. I looked around and kept advancing, calling my son's name all the while. I had made it to the stairs and stood there calling her name and I was getting madder by the minute. Finally she appeared at the top of the stairs and looked down at me, saying calmly, "You know that you are trespassing?" I said that if she had answered the door I would have had no need for it and where was my son? She motioned that he was over there, hiding in the closet. By then I was upstairs, ready to escort my son out of there and commandeer him home. He finally appeared and I chewed him out for skipping school, which he had never ever done before. He said that he did not feel well and so they came home to her house, because she was not feeling well either, and I told him that there was no excuse for this conduct, that there were rules in place to deal with not feeling well and school attendance. I told him to come with me when this girl told him, "No, you are not!" Turning to him, she continued, "You know what we have talked about and what we have to do!" That was like waving a red flag before a bull in Spain at the bullfights and I lunged at her and tried to strangle the girl, all the while screaming that I sure would not like her to be the mother of my grandchild, that she was nothing but bad news. She fought back and we wrestled and I ended up pinning her against the wall. I did not take karate lessons for nothing, and since I had earned my black belt after four years of training, I was letting loose, observing no rules of engagement. I do believe I was mad enough to kill the kid and if my son had not have come between us I probably would have thrown her down the stairs which were only two or three feet away.

As it stood, I had to leave as she was threatening to call the police and have me arrested for trespass and assault. She was simply not worth that much trouble to me.

However, her father called me that night and said that he was pressing charges of illegal trespass and simple assault and for me to be ready to expect the police. I told him that this was fine and that I would be ever so happy to tell the police about their no-good daughter. And I was. I had to alert my co-workers the next day that I might be picked up by the police but they never showed. After this I withdrew Samuel from his school.

The months dragged by and this girl was getting bigger and bigger and she paraded around me as if she had accomplished something to be proud of. She hung around my house like a stray cat. I guess when things got hairy for her at home, she came to my house. Through their conversations I could sense that my son's decision to stay with me was not because of moral outrage over his father's immorality but because he was unhappy there because he was told to rake the leaves. Did I say five down and two to go? It was now six down and one to go and my daughter looked like she was going to avoid that down-turn. Thank goodness there was at least one who did what she had been taught!

Rachel came to town with her new fiancé to show him off while introducing him to her crazy family. She had divorced the professor after ten years of marriage and she had been single for several years. They asked me what I would like to do or was there any place I would like to go to when I remembered that it had come into my mind out of nowhere that I needed to find out what Tupelo, Mississippi was all about. Until then I had always thought of Tupelo as the place where Elvis was born and that they were probably doing the same thing everybody has done, which was to cash in on his name, and I shrugged it off as one of those holes in the wall. I surely had never thought of going there by myself because I am positively scared to death of driving on the highway unless somebody drives in front of me and shows me the way. My daughter and her fiancé were nice enough to take me there, and they were kind of curious themselves. It was June 5, 2003, a beautiful sunny day. We got there around lunchtime and we were kind of looking around, trying to figure out where everything was. We oriented ourselves and headed for the Birthplace of Elvis Presley and as I got out of the car I had the distinct, almost overwhelming, feeling that I belonged there and I immediately announced with the utmost certainty that I was going to move here. My daughter and her fiancé looked at me as if I had lost my mind and I could just hear my daughter thinking, "Oh no, here she goes again with this Elvis-insanity and in front of my fiancé!"

I did not comment on it further but I knew that this was where I needed to be. The time was uncertain but I was sure I would know when the time was right.

As far as Tupelo was concerned we were all pleasantly surprised as the people were ever so nice and helpful, kind and accommodating. The Birthplace itself was just wonderful, the lay of the land was perfect for this use and it was very well maintained. We took the whole tour and I enjoyed going into the shotgun house where the beginning of this Elvis-magic was spawned. Of course we had to suffer through the inevitable peddling of Elvis-trinkets. I know that I did not buy anything but that my daughter's fiancé did, as he is a seasoned souvenir collector. It was very pleasant and I was ever so excited as I could sense that I was getting closer to fulfilling my destiny. We ended up in a place called Starting Over. We had one of the proprietor's good muffins and a cup of coffee and, as business was slow, she told us all about how she ended up in Tupelo and it was not about Elvis. Her story was interesting and as people came in who seemed to feel right at home there, we got the feeling that this was a gathering place for gays and lesbians. It was a nice place to sit and relax on the love-seat and the comfortable chairs—it was like a living room. Of course there were tables, too, for those who liked to stand while they had their refreshment and were in a hurry. She offered us a map of Tupelo and she pointed out some places of interest but I have completely forgotten whether or not we went to any of them as I was totally preoccupied with this new direction I had to go in. Nothing else registered.

When I returned to work at the church I announced, with a made-up mind that surprised even me, that I was going to move to Tupelo. They were stunned. When, why, and how were the following questions, to which I answered that I did not know the time and that I would retire there and I had always been joking about running away from home, so I added, to get away from my children. They, of course had to suffer through my stories of endless trouble with children and ex-husband and they had seen me cry as I was being put through the wringer with one miserable thing after another with hardly a let-up to recover in between. Was there a conspiracy afoot to make my life as hard as possible to see if I would break? But my faith in Jesus Christ was on solid footing, and though I was being sorely tried on all sides I knew where my help was coming from and it protected me. It is almost like good old Job in the Old Testament. In fact I had always had the feeling that God and the devil had entered into that same kind of deal as far as my life was concerned.

I often said to God, "Aren't you overdoing it?" when I thought that I would die from the exaggerated intensity of mental anguish. It was a hard row to hoe indeed, but anything worth having has to be earned with sweat and tears. I had already weathered so many storms I was not about to give in now that it was almost over.

One thing is for sure—none of my co-workers blamed me for wanting to get away and wanting to have a measure of peace.

It was a short time before Thanksgiving that same year that I had a dream in which I must have had some sort of cardiac episode—it could have been real, because I was asleep so I do not know. In this dream I was being picked up by somebody and carried away. Up-up-up we went. I saw the earth, and the houses getting smaller and smaller. In this person's arms I was being cradled and comforted and it was the most intense feeling of utter euphoria, far, far better than that wonderful feeling those Placidyl capsules provided all those years ago in the last trimester of my pregnancy with my second child. I was let go and completely against my will I was pulled back by something as if I had been tethered to a rubber band and I snapped back. I was baffled, sure enough. The very next night we went through the same ceremony in my dream and as we were going up I kept thinking to hurry up and get this over with already, as I thought in my dream that I was crossing over for the last time when instead I found myself somewhere in the clouds and I was very angry as invisible hands were trying to grip my hands but in my fury I shook them loose when some other invisible hands were grabbing at me everywhere when I woke up.

I had very little time to ponder the meaning of these dreams as Susan came into town with her two children and I was busy getting things ready for her.

It was the Saturday after Thanksgiving. Susan came and my grandchildren were eager to play with the toys I had kept from my younger children's childhood for just that purpose. They were playing and my daughter and I talked a bit and discussed what to put on which pizza to suit the preferences of the children, as we could eat anything, when the younger child, my granddaughter, started to whine about this and that and really nothing. She wanted to be picked up and her mother had to lug her around until lunch was ready and the child agreed to sit at the counter when she started to kick the wall under it which I had just repainted, she would look at me to see what I would do. I told her to stop doing that and explained to her why, not that that was really necessary but I was trying to be patient, when she looked at her mother who said nothing, so she started it again. Rather than making a big deal about struggling who is her boss, I just took her shoes off. That spoiled her fun and she went back to whining. Then Judy called and invited herself over which I really did not want as I never get a chance to get a word in edgewise when those two get together and she could have done this on her own time. But I could not tell her not to come either as she had already had one child with her sister-in-law and she was just bringing the younger one with her. Everything was going well as the two little girls played together and the boy sort of played with the both of them. We went into the living room and sat down and talked about this and that when the one who I was renting from, Judy, started to complain about my having married an awful man and that I could not have been much of a Christian to have put my children, meaning herself specifically, into such a situation, as they all had been exposed to some horrible scenes. What kind of a mother would do that to her children and still consider herself a Christian? I tried to defend myself by saying that I was following God's orders which was the wrong thing to say to her. She lambasted me from every angle and criticized me for everything under the sun because it made her life a living hell, "So thanks, Mom, for nothing." I looked at Susan who said that surely I knew that this was true. They were getting louder and louder as they were making fun of me, saying that I had some nerve to blame God for this, and they were laughing. The boy was just enjoying this as nobody was paying any attention to him, so he took the opportunity and threw the toys up in the air and sent them flying all over the place, onto things that could break, and I was trying to retrieve or protect them as the little girls were screaming that he was taking their toys away from them. In all this I was still trying to explain that I in no wise blame God to shirk my own responsibility but that made them even angrier. It was chaos when all at once they decided that they were not going to listen to me any longer, grabbed their purses, picked up their children and dragged the boy out by the hand, plopped him in the car and the boy said, as I was still trying to be pleasant, "You give me a headache!" His mother heard this and said nothing to the boy. And then they were gone. Just like that. I went inside and slowly closed the door and I was talking to myself as I picked up the toys and cleaned up the mess they had made, telling myself that I cannot believe that they would say such things to me as I had always been there for them and always helped them the best I could and I certainly never set out to marry a man who I knew would make them unhappy. I was just as horrified as they were, more so, and my life was surely a living hell . . . when all at once I stood up and stomped my foot as if to kill a nasty critter. I screamed at the top of my lungs and boxed the air as if there were somebody there to box, and my heart was beating so hard I thought it would jump right out of me. I got lightheaded and flung myself on my bed and cried and cried until there were no more tears left to cry. After I had calmed down I was trying to grasp what had happened, and why, when I realized that I had gone through this once already—in my dream! I was astonished, to say the least, but it gave me a sense of peace as I knew that this was another piece of that puzzle I was working to finish.

 I took a bath and got things ready for church the next day, then I called my eldest daughter and told her what had happened and I also told her about those dreams. She always brushes them aside, because she does not know what to make of that kind of thing. It was dark already when I lay on my bed, facing the picture showing the broken body of Jesus on Mary's lap by Michelangelo that we had brought back from Èze, and I was just lying there. The TV was on, Elvis was singing softly on my CD player, Samuel was spending the night at a friend's house. My head was where my feet should have been and my feet were where the head belonged and I had not even pulled back the covers. I woke up and it was five o'clock in the morning and I tried to remember what I last heard on the TV—it was before the ten-o'clock news. I could not believe that I had slept seven hours at least, which is unheard of for me, so I went into the living room to check the clock there, and indeed it was five o'clock. I was in the exact same position which made me think I had just drifted off. It was highly unusual.

I went to Sunday school as usual and then to the worship service as usual. When the altar-call was made I went up front to pray with someone, hopefully, as I was in extreme distress at the performance my children had given the day before at my house. I was just so hurt by this and I could not understand why this even happened. Did my children think so little of their mother or did they not even love me? I was one confused mother who loved her children. I was standing there alone for quite a while when some ladies saw that I was in dire straits. They came rushing to my aid and did their best to console me after I had told them my story of my ungrateful children. They prayed with me and I got control of myself. I cannot recall whether my son was there. As things settled down I was sort of numb and did not know how to deal with these girls after this. One thing was for sure—when this daughter of mine, who was the instigator to this debacle, did not get what she wanted from me, and I was in a vulnerable position as I no longer had Mr. Moneybags for protection, she let me have it. She had borrowed some money from me and we had agreed on a payment schedule and she wanted to change things around which I did not want to do as one thing was connected to another in my financial structure and she was spending money she did not have and looked to me to get her out of the hole. I refused and she just could not stand it. She called me and gave me an earful, only this time she took me to task over Elvis, saying that I must be some kind of crazy to have this interest for a dead man (that sounded like my husband when he went through the motions to get some counseling before the divorce, which was really an attempt to undermine my integrity and character with the judge as this was my first try to divorce Jack by reciting that the counselor said that there was hardly anything that he could do as he was competing with a dead man) and that it was my fault that her half-brother was gay because I continued to stay with Jack even though I could have gotten a divorce. Then she said that she should raise my rent, as she needed more money anyway and she did not charge me enough from the get-go. I could not believe my ears! She would not let me say anything and when she was finished she just hung up. I was so mad I saw stars and without another thought I decided right then and there that I was moving to Tupelo and that was that. Let her figure out what to do from there. I called her and told her of my decision and I gave her a month's notice and told her to find somebody in the meantime to rent the house.

My grandson had been born then, just shortly before that fateful Thanksgiving. My son moved back with his father and I had taken another trip to Tupelo with a co-worker to familiarize myself with the way down there so I would not end up in Birmingham. Rachel and Tracy came to town for a visit and I went with them to look at some property, as I thought I might buy something suitable and keep working somewhere. I had made an appointment with somebody who had advertised in the local paper. I checked things out on the map of Tupelo and so we went to keep that appointment. We were a little early so we looked around on our own. I did not like it and I left a note on the garbage can to let this person know that I was not interested. We looked at this property and that, and judging by what I saw that was available for the amount of money I had to spend on this, I decided to abandon the buying idea and concentrated on finding an apartment. There were some nice ones, but they were too expensive, and others looked pitiful and run down. I got discouraged but for some reason I remembered a street that I liked on the map and neither of my daughters wanted to be bothered with anything anymore but since I was their mommy and I begged them, they relented and we drove to it. We went to the office and inquired about a vacancy. The woman said that they had several and she gave us the keys to one apartment. I looked it over and I did not like it. She could not give us another key, but she told us where this apartment was and that she thought that it would be something I could like. We went there and it did not look too good but I could see the possibilities. It was a former single-family home which had been modernized and converted into a duplex. It had a storage room and we peeked inside. We could not go in as the person was not moved out completely, but it had paneling halfway up the wall in the kitchen and it looked rather dark and my daughters convinced me that I would be miserable there because I liked light, lots of light—daylight that is—and so we returned the key and thanked the lady.

After we had gotten home and my daughters went somewhere, I phoned the lady and told her that I would be there Tuesday to look at the place as I wanted to rent it. She said that would be fine, that the person had moved out and she told me that this unit was slated to have new linoleum put in before I move in. I went at the appointed time, saw the place, rolled up the blinds and violà—it was light—and I put down the necessary amount to hold it for me till I figured out when moving day was going to be.

In no time at all everything was lined up. At the church I took a two-week vacation—it was Christmas and Mother's Day Out was cancelled for two weeks—after which I told my supervisor I would not return. On January 6, 2004 I moved in.

15

Bridge Over Troubled Water

I was literally running away from home. My home had become a dangerous place for me and I felt almost forced to flee to save myself

I must confess that it is with utter astonishment that I have to concede that God Himself had to have been with me every step of the way to enable me to do what was necessary to facilitate this move to Tupelo, as there were seemingly endless details that had to be done for an orderly, successful move. I had never moved a whole household from one place to another and if anyone would have told me that I would be doing this, I would have recoiled in fear of the unknown and would have thought it completely impossible. But here I was, doing things as if I had done this before and I was actually deriving a fairly high degree of satisfaction from my apparent skill to pull this off and, in true human fashion, I gave myself credit for being so smart and capable. I remember having felt this exhilarating rush of, "*I am WOMAN, hear me roar!*" when I adjusted to the divorce from my habitually unfaithful first husband. I understood the desire of women to want control over their lives and follow their dreams; and we too have dreams and they do not necessarily include or require a man.

But, as it is with every upside there is inevitably a downside. I eagerly drove back and forth to Memphis as I missed all the familiar places and faces and yet I felt pulled back to Tupelo, this strange and unfamiliar place with strangers all around.

It was very, very unsettling because I felt as though I were hanging suspended in the air, between heaven and earth, and belonging nowhere. It was ever so frightening and I had to force myself to concentrate on the tangible reasons for my having made this move and, even beyond that, sending my second husband packing, so to speak. This was an exercise in misery. For one thing, I had only myself to talk to—nobody could disagree with anything I brought up and then, just to prove to myself that I knew what I was doing (the roaring-woman syndrome!) I tortured myself with the unpleasant forays into detailed accounts of transgressions against me heaped on me by my husband and my children.

Did my husband not torment me in a thousand ways to impose his imagined superiority on me? An exercise the whole of civilization had given to the man since Adam and Eve to unleash on woman? Did I not feel the sting of humiliation at his deliberate attempts to hurt me by not fixing something that needed repair by a professional, because it was just something that inconvenienced me, made my life harder. Like the time before a Thanksgiving dinner that was for all my children and grandchildren at our house. I loved to prepare for it and I thoroughly enjoyed the anticipation of this nice event. However, over time the burners on the stove stopped functioning, one after the other, and I was left with just one working burner. I had told my husband repeatedly that we needed to get this attended to, but he did nothing and I surely could not do anything since I did not have the money to hire a repairman nor did I have any idea why these burners were on the blink. It was terrible, as I had to schedule when to fix what on that one burner to make everything work. But I managed. I always did. The microwave and oven helped.

Or the time we did have a broken icemaker. That thing was in a nonworking condition for the longest time and he knew that it bothered me as I detest things not working as they were designed to work. But just as soon as he made our home available to our Sunday-school class for a Wednesday evening meeting, he made sure that everything was in working order. All at once there simply was no problem. He was just that obvious with his disdain for me, a mere lowly woman, too helpless and weak to do anything about it. These incidents left a very deep impression on my psyche and the effects of these kinds of things were cumulative. I chose not to react to his assaults on my human dignity, my self-worth, for the sake of peace and harmony in the family and as my top priority was to provide a stable home for our children. He showed himself to be ever-so-kind, sweet and generous, often entirely unexpectedly, not because he was kind and sweet and generous but rather to confuse and disorient me in his diabolical scheme to keep me off-balance and it worked perfectly for the longest time. I remember distinctly the time we were discussing something while I was sitting in the straight-backed chair by the phone in the great room and he was going upstairs into the loft. While he was climbing the stairs it was as if I had a glimpse as clear and concise as a laser beam into his soul. He was—maybe unwittingly, maybe deliberately—giving himself away by the things he was saying, which were so utterly inconsistent with what he had up until then carefully concealed, in an effort to convince me that he was becoming this true believer in the Triune God of the Bible as he had promised to become if only I would not divorce him after the attack in Monaco.

It was this moment of truth that kept haunting me and in effect constituted the beginning of the end of this marriage. I could not get around the realization that this husband of mine was an unregenerate hater, not only of me, but womankind in general. He derived pleasure from tormenting the so-called weaker sex and while he did not want me to divorce him, he had no problem with divorcing me if and when it suited him. I had to face this fact and accept that there was no security in that relationship as it was not founded on spiritual principles of love, honor, and respect. There was nothing I could do to change anything. I used to be willing to believe him when he tried to convince me that he loved me, because this is what every true woman craves, but it simply was not real, as he was incapable of love.

After taking myself to task in these painful excursions into the past, trying to justify my actions, I did not necessarily feel better as it was a sad reality indeed to have to admit that I had yoked myself to such a man for almost twenty years, and that now that I was getting on up in years, had nothing to show for it in the way of financial security. It was dismal and yet it was also good and liberating and therefore right to turn my life upside-down for the sake of an inviolate principle which comes into play here in a larger sense: Good and evil cannot peacefully co-exist unless one decides to accept the superiority of the other and compromises, which is the nature of this world-system.

To round out the tangible reasons to buttress my assertion I should not omit the incident with the windshield on my car. It remained visibly cracked for years for no reason other than to drive home the message that I was just not worth anything and therefore did not qualify for a nicely maintained car. The crack started out with a pebble dinging the windshield, and I guess my husband held me responsible for that in his dark little heart and so he made no effort whatsoever to have it fixed. He was the insurance man, he knew what to do, but he chose to do nothing and I did not say a word of complaint. It was a little embarrassing to have one lady or the other from church saying matter-of-factly, upon seeing the crack, which was becoming larger and larger, "You should get that fixed!" He had bought himself a new car and his interest was focused on keeping it in pristine condition, no matter the cost. Needless to say, when he graciously let me have the car when he filed for divorce after months of dragging his feet, in hopes I would change my mind, the first thing I did was to get this crack fixed. I saw no reason to continue to drive around in a luxury car that looked like it was owned by a slob. I was not a slob and I did not like to appear as one. It made me feel better about myself and I think it was this neglectful conduct on my husband's part to foster just that kind of feeling of worthlessness he tried to superimpose on me. Did I ever mention that my husband was very smart? Never let it be said that an evil man is dumb. He knows exactly what he is doing and why and I can only say that I feel sorry for any decent woman who falls for my ex-husband's lies when he charms his way into her dreams of happiness with him. He never lacks the company of women as he has money aplenty. He inevitably picks women who are vulnerable for whatever reason and he exploits that with all the gusto he can muster but sooner or later they all run away from him. He prides himself in the fact that he obviously is capable to remain in a relationship for twenty years, which he wears like a medal of sorts, never admitting that the credit for this accidental (for him) longevity of our marriage was mine, not his, because my focus was on the welfare of our children.

Then there is this spiritual aspect in the relationship with my husband that ideally finds its most rooting, elevating, and intensely pleasurable expression in the act of sexual intercourse. I had always been acutely aware that the union of a man and a woman is designed not only for the melding of two bodies into one but also the intermeshing of two spiritual beings uniting on that very level. It is this fact that distinguishes a "marriage made in heaven" from all others and it is for this reason that one is well-advised to be very selective in choosing one's mate for life. Falling into a marriage by transgressing God's law, as I had done the first time does not make for a good marriage, although it can become a workable relationship that can endure if both parties realize and accept the responsibility to live according to the Biblical principles and take the focus off oneself and shift it onto the other person and the children who deserve a mother and a father in the same home, with their joined commitment to work toward the same goal: the welfare of the children. It is superfluous to say that none of these elements were present in my relationship with my husband. However, I took what I had and tried to do the best I could to live up to what God expected of me and it provided a fairly happy childhood for the children and to me it was worth every injury I received psychologically and physically.

It was this spiritual element that my husband trampled on and so eventually made it wholly unbearable for me to consent to any sexual relationship and it was for this very reason that only a legal and full divorce could assure me protection from his "trampling" my spirit where I was most vulnerable and therefore extremely sensitive. This kind of injury could, over time, have caused me to lose my mind and either be driven to suicide or to abusing drugs or alcohol in an effort to deaden the pain, which was inescapable under those conditions. It is a disservice of the secular progressives to insist, without any proof, may I add, that we are nothing more than animals driven by compulsions that have been present in our gene-pool since primitive man evolved into what we have become today, still compelled by primitive urges to assure the continuation of the human race. What a sad conclusion on the "nature" of man. I can only respond with palpable anguish by saying, or rather asking, "Is that all there is?" to borrow a line from a song written by somebody in the sixties. We are obviously finding ourselves in a battle between the ideologues on the left and the "dreamers" on the right, which is nothing more or less than this epic conflict between good and evil spoken of in the Scriptures. Therefore it is well for us to consider a statement made by Aldous Huxley, which goes like this, "The triumph of humanism is the defeat of humanity." Having experienced myself this very real spiritual me that does co-exist with the physical me leads me to conclude that we are indeed made in the image of God, just as it is written in the holy text of the Bible, the living Word of the living God. I consider it therefore our duty to live up to this divine image we were created to be from the beginning.

The first few months here in Tupelo were nothing less than grueling, vacillating between a deep depression and this inexplicable feeling of joy way down deep at the mere thought that I had taken a very important step toward what I perceive is the end of my earthly journey and therefore that much closer to being where I truly belong. Heaven is my destination or paradise.

It was my connection to the spiritual that my love for Elvis provided that was always there, in the form of his many love songs to me. Elvis' song "The Girl I never loved" came to my attention in 2009 for some inexplicable reason and provided the quote "The Girl I never loved" under my name on the cover-page. These and my fervent pleadings to God to help me and the reassurance I received on a continuous basis were and still are the cornerstone of my existence.

The contact with my children, however was torturous because I am their mother and I love them dearly and yet I could not afford being near them as I would have continued to be drawn into the neverending position of enabling them to remain as they are by constantly helping them with the messes they got themselves into by living as they pleased but not as they were taught from childhood.

I did not like the comment made by my pastor long ago that children will make mistakes and you do damage control and hope for the best. Since everybody was doing just that, I grudgingly did the same thing, telling myself that it is because I love them when in fact the reality was that I was too weak and too afraid about what people would say if I had done anything different from the common practice at the time.

As parents who have taught their children the Lord's Way we can and must expect a better conduct from our children and if they do not deliver, tell them kindly but firmly that they are on their own to solve the problems they made for themselves. Tough love is a sign of true love as it requires inner strength and a sturdy faith in the author of LIFE.

As my children showed themselves to be impervious to anything I said to them about their choices, I had to conclude that they loved me only if I was in their service, helping to facilitate their happiness, and I was surely persona non grata if I did not act in accordance with their expectations in this regard. If I have heard it said by parents, and in most cases by grandparents, once, that their children did the most unacceptable things with dismal consequences but that there was nothing one could do about it and one could surely not afford to criticize anything because then the would cut themselves off or would not let one see the grandchildren, I have heard it a hundred times during my time as a nursery-attendant at "Mother's Day Out" at my church. I recognized that for myself this was a different proposition than it was for everybody else. I resolved that I was not going to be used by my children in this fashion any longer as it truly violated a basic principle I believed in which is the Fifth Commandment. By "honor" I understand "demonstrate respect and obedience," and my children obviously had neither. For me this was unacceptable at this particular stage of my life and it was the other tangible reason for my escape from Memphis.

As I have experienced time and time again, it is most certainly true that God does not put more on you than you can bear even though I would have argued many, many times that that just cannot be true because my life was way too harsh for me to survive, He came through for me each and every time when I was on the brink of madness and the ensuing acts of sheer desperation. He was there, always.

After I had moved to Tupelo and had left Samuel in the care of his father, I got a frantic phone call from my son, tearfully explaining that his father had threatened to beat him up and that he did not know what he should do as he did not want to beat his father back. I was so outraged I could have easily killed that father of his had I been there! I do not know the reason behind this altercation and I did not care, so I told my son to defend himself if his father would indeed beat him up. Maybe he could kill his father in his own defense. Saves me the trouble! I also told him to never aggravate him unless it simply could not be avoided and to be very careful not to respond in kind, no matter how unfair, hurtful and cruel he treated him, always try to make him think he is right even when you know very well that he is not. By the time we got off the phone my son had calmed down and I felt, with a newly gained perspective, he was able to face the next days.

Needless to say, this incident upset me to no end. Having been scared to death by this man for years, I could only imagine what our son had to go through. This affected me physically, which I was not aware of until my face started hurting. My right upper jaw, to be exact, kept on hurting so that I found myself forced to consider that I might have a dental problem. The dentist could not find anything wrong and suggested for me to go to an ear, nose, and throat specialist if the pain continued. The pain continued.

I went to the ear, nose, and throat specialist who took my blood pressure, looked at the gauge and then took it again, looked and then told me that my BP was 210 over 115. I almost fell out of the chair. I had never heard of such a high BP before and certainly not me being the one having it! The doctor said that this was way too high and referred me to an internist. I went to the internist and got a prescription for some pills.

My blood pressure went down but I was still agonizing over the whole situation with my being in Tupelo and not in Memphis where I could have prevented this violence against our son when I had a dream:

There we were, Elvis and I, lying on the ground, an ever-so-green, lush meadow which was very expansive, and way, way, away there were throngs of people, many, many people, all looking in our direction. Elvis and I were dressed in white and we were having a good time, cracking jokes and laughing. We were happy as clams and waiting on something. Then I woke up.

Believe it or not, this dream gave me the needed reassurance that I was in the right place at the right time and it ended my fretfulness over my son's dilemma with his father.

After a while in Tupelo, shortly after that happy dream I was compelled to think seriously about writing that book but I felt utterly helpless and inexperienced and full of doubt. I had given my word processor to the Goodwill in Memphis as I was preparing to "go home" (a spiritual home which requires a physical death).

Trying to figure out who could help me with this I thought of my pastor in Memphis. I called him and he was glad to hear from me and upon his inquiring how I was doing, I answered: "Thank you I am very well, actually I am as happy as a clam—and I have no idea how happy clams are." He responded with a detailed account of where this saying originated.

During that conversation I completely forgot why I called him in the first place which I confessed to him.

If I had ever doubted the ever-present help that is available for every true believer, I had proof-positive once again here in Tupelo where Elvis was born. Having been a hands-on mother for forty years it would have been a much more painful separation from my children than it was. The Lord provided me with a neighbor who was an amputee who had just recuperated from a heart attack a year before my arrival. This lovely lady was truly a Godsend as she was so nice to me and so patient and helpful in my trying to acclimate myself to the ins and outs of living here. She also told me of her being related to Elvis's father, who hailed from Itawamba County, and her best friend, Corinne, was best friends with Elvis's mother Gladys. I got to hear of all the goings-on in this poverty-stricken family that was Elvis's.

This wonderful woman, Vivian, became my stand-in mother, as I had always been wondering what it would be like to have a mother since I had had no experience in that area. The only time I felt loved as by a mother I ended up getting deeply hurt in the end. So this was such a blessing. We did lots of things together and I could take care of her without being burdened too much as her own daughter was very attentive. She lived and worked about thirty minutes away, so it was a good thing that there was this distance as this made me feel needed by this woman who was confined to a wheelchair.

She loved flowers and we'd make plans on where to plant what and then go to the nursery where she had always been shopping before the heart attack that had made it impossible for her to drive on her own. She was very happy to be able to get out of the house and meet with people she had known for years and years but had not seen in a long time. It was a source of happiness for me to see her happy and without realizing it I was absorbed in the daily concern for her welfare and I scheduled my life with her schedule. I never noticed that I was usurping much of her time but she never complained. I was always looking forward to our days out. It was just so pleasant and rewarding. She died in March of 2008 and I was struck by how much a part of my life she had become. It was a difficult time adjusting to living without her. But God is good and He comforts the bereaved and hurting who willingly choose to obey His commandments and trust Him completely.

If I was distraught over my ex-husband and my children I must also add that I was very disenchanted about the function of the organized church, as it had become something other than what Jesus had in mind when He walked here on Earth and taught the principles of godly living and the founding of His church, the bride He is coming to receive for Himself at His second coming.

I had told myself that I was going to give myself time to recuperate from the unpleasant and ungodly shenanigans perpetrated by the Church. Little did I know that I had ended up next door to the very church Elvis attended as a little boy and I felt literally pushed to go there on the very first Sunday of my stay here in town.

It was a pleasant enough outfit. The pastor was such a nice man of God, dedicating himself to serve God by preaching and teaching from the Scriptures and adhering to the Word even if it was unpleasant. The members were so sweet and kind and they welcomed me, strange, and foreign though I was, and they did their best not to take issue with my idiosyncrasies. Well, I returned that favor. I felt as part of the small congregation and this has been a source of comfort and support for me and I am thankful for the continual grace and mercy the good Lord shows me each and every day. For me it is always a very good thing to be in the house of the Lord, to praise and worship Him.

As I became more and more a citizen of Tupelo in every respect, which included changing my driver's license and registering to vote and so firmly establishing this separation from Memphis, I felt more at home in my new abode. My apartment, ironically, is almost the same kind I occupied with my first husband and our one, two, then three and four children on 2299 Elzey Avenue. It is a duplex apartment and it became my sanctuary over the years and I have enjoyed living here and I hope to live here as long as it is God's will.

The early months were hard as I tried to settle into this emotional separation that will never be complete as I will always love my children but the physical distance between us did shield me from the direct exposure to things I had an aversion to and was loath to have to deal with.

I'd go to Memphis for something that needed to be attended to and I would be excited to see my children but it was always a letdown, because it seemed that they were clueless as to my reasons for leaving, even resentful, as they thought it selfish of me to remove my help from them. So on the way back to Tupelo I could not help but cry and cry as it was ever-so-painful for me to have to realize that there was a big gulf between us which I could not bridge by myself.

I'd go to my lovely neighbor and tell her some of my story, my trials and tribulations, and she always had something biblical ready to help me with and before I knew it we were talking about how much everything in this country has changed and in some very real ways not for the better. As she was telling me of her life growing up on a farm, where she had lost her leg when she was twelve in an accident involving farm equipment of some sort, and my own experiences growing up in post-war Germany, we discovered that our upbringings were strikingly similar. This brought to my mind a letter I once wrote to the *Commercial Appeal* in response to something about Dwight Eisenhower, "Ike," in which I opined, "As wonderful as you made Ike sound in retrospect—how elegant, unobtrusive, capable—and I am sure he was all that, for after all I liked him too; let us not forget that he was the product of a more 'elegant' time! A time when youngsters respected their elders because their elders were worthy of their respect, when the adherence to a moral standard, even in school, was expected and therefore taught, which also was the norm of everyday life. Wonderful Ike almost could not help but be what he was." We would try to identify the reasons for the drastic changes we had undergone here in this country (and in Germany also). There were these iconic occurrences like television, the Pill, the Vietnam War, Woodstock, the "God is dead" movement, the sexual revolution and there are many more, all symptoms of an underlying illness which is the result of a systematic attempt to annihilate everything spiritual from our memory by a well-organized force.

It was a very good thing to have had this sweet dear lady for my confidante. She could not understand some of the problems I had with my children, as she had no direct knowledge of such things, as her life was on a much simpler level and I would not tax her system with the distasteful happenings in my family. Some I divulged and all she could do was shake her head in disbelief. These are things one read about in magazines, never recognizing that these things have become part of everyday life in this country today and it is getting worse by the minute. Sometimes we would depress ourselves and we had to simply switch gears to lift our spirits and we'd make plans to go somewhere out for lunch. We both loved to eat good food. She'd pay for the meals and I would pay the tip. She had more money than I had. Only on special occasions would I take care of the whole thing—as a treat.

On Thursdays I would take her to the store with me and she'd be ever so happy to be able to get out of her house. Her daughter was happy too, as it made it more pleasant for her mother without her having to take off from work to take care of this herself. We just had a good time together and it certainly filled a need I did not even know I had but God knew and He provided. At Walmart I had her hold on to the shopping cart and then wrap the handles of the purses around her wrists and she'd put her one foot on the cart and I would pull her in her wheelchair like that through the aisles of the store. We got plenty of amused looks at our little train going along and sometimes positive remarks which always made us happy. Afterward she'd treat us to lunch, after which we both went home exhausted and ready for a nap after putting up the groceries. It was very difficult for my friend to get accustomed to being housebound, as she was a very independent lady who did what she wanted when she wanted as she had always managed with a prosthesis. She worked all her life and she had enjoyed her retirement years doing things for and with her church which enriched her life until she had this heart attack at eighty-four, and from then on was unable to wear her prosthesis, which made her so unhappy. This relationship of ours was as beneficial for her as it was for me and that does make for a good relationship, when each can bring something constructive to the table.

I am a faithful student of the Bible and I do consider it to be the source of infinite wisdom which is why I had told my friend, who was a smart woman, that it is true that escapism plays a part in the lives of the faithful on the low rung of the socio-economic ladder—the poor. This fact makes it obvious that a very important element of a happy life is missing, the spiritual element which does indeed set us apart from the animals.

As everyone who reads the paper or watches television knows, our secular-progressive government goes all out to fight outright against anything that barely hints at anything spiritual or religious (i.e., Christian).

Those who believe in the living God, no matter how poor, they who love God with all their hearts though they may find themselves on the very low rung of the socio-economic ladder, fashion their lives according to the tenets of their faith. They will strive to live a God-pleasing life, which includes treating one's body as a holy temple (no drug-abuse, promiscuity, etc.).

It is the indifference of our government to seriously consider the welfare of our churches and to support the individual by making believer-friendly laws that has so profoundly altered our daily life for the worse. We would do well to remember that man does not live by bread alone.

It was these kinds of talks that made me realize how much the God of the universe is part of my daily life, and how sad it is that we as a nation founded on the basic principles of the Judeo-Christian faith have lost this vibrant connection to the One who was there with this nation from the very beginning and through all the struggles. Where did it go?

This question has been on my mind for a long time now and as I go on my mulling-sessions, which consist by thinking of nothing in particular, yet, being fully mentally and spiritually engaged on a deeper level, I can sense the infusion of a higher knowledge to which my conscious self has no access. I take what is being revealed to me and then search for the validation in the Holy Bible which is a must, as I am convinced that there can be no true wisdom without God being the author of it.

It may seem like a pretty organized way of life, controlled by the Omnipotent One and so it was, if only I was not subject to that human self which is by its very nature contrary to the things of the spirit and it is therefore a daily struggle to subdue that carnal self that comes with all kinds of tricks to trip one up. Doubt is probably the most persistent problem, with double-mindedness running a close second. Add to this the influence of this enormous spiritual power that has been unleashed to trap, kill, and destroy. It is tough to be tough and yet nothing else will do. Remain standing and if you fall, which I often do, get back up and stand your ground, and when I am reminded by reading God's Word that I am not alone in this fight, I can make it another hour or so, sometimes even a whole day!

So it was that after maybe a few months into my stay here in Tupelo, I woke up one morning and got out of bed and walked to the back door and peeked through the Venetian blinds when I simply could not figure out where I was or why I was here. It was as if in my sleep I had a lobotomy and I could in no way connect emotionally to what had brought me here. It was so frightening that I have actually no words to describe it other than to confess that at that point I did not care one iota about the whys and wherefores; all I wanted to do was to go back to Memphis and see my children. I was completely unhinged and I made preparations at once to drive to Memphis, come what may. However, I called my dear pastor, who was putting things into perspective for me, and I gained some semblance of balance, enough to where I could function as a quasi-normal person.

I arrived at the house of my ex-husband, who was living in Summerdale with his then-fourth ex, after his divorce from the fifth who was the girlfriend of his in this extra-marital dalliance of old. Samuel was living with the mother of my grandson (not married, of course). I was so disgusted and hurt all over again to realize what I seemed to have completely forgotten and that was that they did not care a whit about how I felt about their lifestyles, as this was now the accepted norm and they could in no wise fathom that I would consider their conduct as anything but a minor issue, and their having had a child the way they did just a minor mistake, not enough to lose any sleep over.

It was a good thing that I went to Memphis to watch, up close and personal and in Technicolor, why I had no place there with my children. Once again I was devastated and even though I had a neutral place to go to, there was no joy as I was living in exile of sorts, cut off from everybody that had constituted the reason for every major decision in my adult life, namely my children, albeit a voluntary flight forced on me by circumstances and conditions. I simply had no choice. This constant collision of ideology, mine from the faith of our fathers and theirs of the post-modern, secular-progressive kind of thinking that was shaping their lives and those of their children.

If I could do as anybody else does and just adjust to the changing ways I would have no problems but this is where I am so very different from the rest and that is why I am breaking rank with the average mother of today. I believe that there is an absolute right and an absolute wrong and I will defend this reality unto death. It is written in God's Word and that is the way it is.

I remember many an evening when I would walk home from a church service and scan my surroundings and feeling utterly confused and very unhappy, so unhappy in fact that it was normal for me to cry and pray for death to come and set me free from this torment. I had to go so low that I really thought I would die from pain when my faithful Friend and Savior would come to my rescue and lift me up and comfort me. I would then be on the highest high and the world was bearable to me and I could in all honesty agree when my dear Friend would reassure me that life is good. Never could I let anyone know of the intense despair that would take hold of me a if I were just a rag, twist me and turn me upside down and wring me out to where it seemed, no spark of life (spiritual) was left in me, so deep and bottomless that it sapped every bit of strength from my body and made me feel as though I weighed a ton and I could barely move and I would just lie there on the floor, too tired to lift myself up on to the bed, too tired to eat or drink, too tired to think. My little apartment, which on a good day I considered my sanctuary, my refuge, became like a tube which surrounded me and became tighter and tighter, ever more constricting and squeezing the breath out of me. It was truly horrifying and yet I could not let anyone know of this as I would then have become of interest to every health authority in this town, not to mention my children and my ex-husband and be committed to a treatment center for the severely depressed and I would have had to take all kinds of psychotropic drugs to alleviate the symptoms of depression.

Did I not know the reason for my depression? I did. Until the reason for my depression was removed, no pill of any kind could help me. It would only camouflage the real culprit and make me prone to fall in line with the prevailing thought of today—that there is a pill for everything that ails you. I have discovered, though, that for me this way of dealing with an unpleasant feeling was just to do what I was doing and to rely on this enormous self-healing power within me to come to the fore through suffering, and it would then enable me to rise above my circumstances and to pay homage to the Provider of this innate divine power and sing His praises. Granted, I would not have been able to do any of this if I had had to go to work every day and I knew this which is why I opted to take early retirement as I was truly in no condition to work.

There are times when medicine is necessary, like antibiotics for an infection, but as with antibiotics, they should be used very sparingly.

I have come to the conclusion that with all the knowledge we as human beings have been able to acquire, we have taken it upon our arrogant selves to surmise that we no longer need a God who expects us to conform to His image as we were intended to do from the beginning and so we cut ourselves off from that which connects us with Him which is this spiritual element within us that elevates us above the animals. It is this denial of this very essential quality in us humans that causes almost all the problems we have. We have starved it almost to death in this country and the results of it attest to its validity.

My biggest fear in even talking about my depression came from the regular folks. They would not and could not understand why I took everything so seriously, why I couldn't just live and let live and concede that I could not deal with my situation as it is, so I should go back to where I came from and be where they thought I should be, which is with my family.

But that is exactly where the rubber meets the road. I could not do that and live with myself. I was accountable to my conscience, which is so sensitive and picks up on the slightest deviance from the proverbial straight and narrow, and I knew this deep within since I read the book *Intuition versus Intellect* all those many, many years ago, where Paul Maslow describes the conscience thusly:

"A superior conscience or morality raised to an emotion creates a sense of honor far above the average. On this level behavior is governed by intractable laws of conscience. The individual cannot live in any other way than that revealed by his moral-ethical code. Honesty is axiomatic because the individual is honest to the core with himself and others. His word is his bond, better than a legal contract. Keeping his word is more than a mere matter of self-respect: it has now grown into a philosophy of life. Abiding by the higher tribunal within himself makes the world rational and the individual true and just in his own eyes. This unbending type is incapable of harboring thoughts or behaving contrary to his exaggerated code of honor. Such a person is forthright to the extreme, above deceiving others about his intentions, saying what he means and meaning what he says. This individual is neither detracted from moral obligations by opportunities for personal gain nor is he a passive bystander in the presence of an outrage. Honesty to himself and others is placed before the need for personal success, security and mental complacency. He also remains very much concerned with what he must do and what he has left undone. Such a type can be trusted to risk life and limb (in exceptional circumstances) to sacrifice biological demands and social necessities, rather than break his moral code."

I have deleted a tiny bit there at the end for easier understanding in terms of my Christian faith and to end on a positive note for that reason.

This passage in this book has evidently buried itself in my memory and I can retrieve it when things become so confusing in trying to make sense of the way the world works and how it differs from the world God has in mind for us in the future.

I would be desperately unhappy if I had to work in an environment that disparages true Christians. Since it is now considered a violation to speak of matters of faith in public, this land has indeed become a foreign country to me and I do feel discriminated against. How strange is it to have to practically be forced by the powers that be to go underground in the very nation that is composed of the refugees from other nations that oppressed them and their religious beliefs, and who founded this very special nation on the principles of their faith? Very strange, but not unexpected, as one can read in the book of Matthew and the book of Revelation and others.

As anyone can readily see, it was by divine providence that my next-door neighbor was the person that she was, because she kept me grounded in the real world and gave me a much-needed diversion from these strenuous mental, emotional, and spiritual pursuits by immersing myself in everyday, ordinary, mundane tasks and yakking about them at length. It was on her account that I had to force myself to put make-up on every day just as I had always done for my husband and my children (no reason to scare them to death seeing me *au naturel!*). She would always compliment me on my good appearance and it was so easy a thing to please her. I always tried to be positive and cheerful, even if I was in the grip of a deep depression. After my quick morning hello I would leave, get her paper, telling her that I must be intruding but I had to know how she was doing and then I would retreat back into my private hell.

Sometimes I'd divulge that I was depressed and I needed to be alone and she would promise that she would pray for me which I am confident that she did. She was that kind of person, a real treasure. We were sharing our troubles and our joys and it was so nice to know that God does indeed provide what is needed for the true believer in need. If that knowledge does not make me happy then there is no happiness!

I loved "my" church and I still do and it has been the single most important, steadying, influence on my life here in Tupelo. Our pastor is a kind and friendly man who loves God and lives to teach the tenets of our faith in the Triune God of the Bible and I am always looking forward to go to Sunday school and talk to the sweet and kind members there who have taken me into their midst and have been able to tolerate me for as long as they have. I love to hear about things of our faith and I love to study the Bible under the direction of a very able Sunday school teacher. I will continue to look forward to my growing in the Spirit into a mature Christian along with all the members there.

I often hear it said that one can follow Jesus Christ without the church attendance, which I think is true, but why deny yourself the friendship and support of like-minded people? Why not do as Jesus Christ commanded, to get together and worship as a congregation praying one for the other? It is that much closer to a walk with Jesus if one is really serious about it.

We must acknowledge that many Christians often do not know details about their particular denomination and many accept the religion of their parents and grandparents as their own for a multiplicity of reasons. Add to this the enormous increase in knowledge in virtually all fields and the unprecedented material wealth this has spawned worldwide which requires more and more higher education to be able just to keep it going and (hopefully?) growing.

This combination of developments has proven to be a prescription for the spiritual vacuum which the average human being tries to fill with just about anything that relieves this "empty feeling" way down. Hence this relentless "pursuit of happiness" which today means just about anything as long as it feels good (for a moment) and there is a provider handy everywhere for the right amount of money.

The tried and true advantage of faith in the Triune God of the Scriptures is that it provides an abiding joy deep within which remains unaffected by the surrounding circumstances (as miserable as they may be). If Love is the motivator to adhere to the rules of conduct as outlined in the Scriptures (Old Testament and New Testament), an earthly authority is simply not needed to rule things in or out of our daily life.

While I had plenty of trouble dealing with the fact that I could not be near my own children without suffering crippling damage, I also had to examine my attitude about Elvis. This was real life I was living and I just had turned it upside down, much as I did all those years ago when I had been compelled by the force of my love for Elvis to move to the United States of America. What indeed was this man who is not even alive anymore and with whom I had a quasi-relationship and it was mostly adversarial in nature here in the real world, to me? I had to put myself through the paces, much as a psychologist would, and ask the hard questions that were even harder to answer if there was a plausible explanation at all. It could only be explained in terms of FAITH. Having read extensively the writings of many great thinkers—sociologists, philosophers, theologians, mystics, psychiatrists—I had to listen to my inner self, which is connected to the divine, and take heart that I was not insane, that I had done what had to be done. But until I came to this conclusion it was sheer agony. It was not at all unusual for me to cry and cry and cry. I'd just throw myself on my bed and wail uncontrollably, wishing I could die. My eyes would be swollen and I would have to pull myself together and call the church and excuse myself from attending church. There was no easy way to explain any of what I was going through without causing more trouble for myself in the real world, which I had to keep to a minimum.

As far as the learned men are concerned I must say that I have a healthy respect for their intellectual prowess, as they explore all kinds of knowledge and it has been beneficial to the human race on the whole but with all this knowledge we have failed to bring peace and prosperity to the world. It is safe to say that the only one who made a life-altering change for the better was Jesus Christ, the Son of God. Without Him this, our planet Earth, would be a whole lot darker place.

It is this fact that I hold most dearly close to my heart which put me in direct conflict with my love for Elvis. On the face of it, here was this man who, by all accounts of people who were around him day and night, was everything I could not approve of, let alone tolerate, yet I loved him. I had to admit that there must be more to this than meets the eye and it was just a matter of time until all would have to become clear to me.

No intellectual wants to give credit to a religious figure, even though they are using precepts that have shaped the human experience for thousands of years put forth by these religious (spiritual) men of God who preceded the Son of God. We believers are viewed as ignorant and gullible and weak and we are becoming so marginalized that at the present rate, if this is allowed to continue, the Church as we have known it for so long will become extinct and be but a faint memory of some quaint, totally irrelevant creation of a "'primitive'" people. All I can say to this future development that only God can and will control is that only He has the Master Plan. In view of this I would rather be a Christian lowbrow (dummy) than an intellectual highbrow (fool)!

Even though I remembered this information on the superior conscience that Mr. Maslow wrote about, I had taken notes at that time as I was teaching myself to understand these thoughts which were oftentimes in very difficult words and foreign to me as I was still a very "new" immigrant from Germany. I had to use the dictionary a whole lot and it was important to me to be able to become fluent in the American English language. However, life was very busy then and getting more difficult by the day. I had to forego studying and I simply put these things away and I would come across the notes every now and then, usually because of a move from one place to another, and it was always a reminder that the day would surely come when these notes would become important again. And so it was. I only had the first sentence of the paragraph that I included in my ruminations as only it seemed to be relevant to me but I could not remember the title of the book. I had to call the local library and they recited three books by Paul Maslow and I recognized the title. They had to get it from some college library for me and I then got my own copy from my daughter who bought it for me on amazon.com, which was so nice of her.

But to get back to this Elvis fascination of mine. There was nothing more irritating to the children by my first marriage than Elvis Presley, because they had always heard about him growing up, as their father's life was wholly consumed by wanting to be just like Elvis. Many of our conversations would be about Elvis and what he had been doing last night, or the night before. Rachel believed at one point that Elvis was her father. She was confused! At that time it was not at all unusual for us to go to the gate, as we hangers-on all called it, and the children, there were only two then, would sit on the curb inside the gate and their father and I would chat with Harold (he was also part of Marvin's good ole boys club—they covered each others' backs in their adulterous liaisons) who was on duty in the guard shack. I'd be mostly watching out for our children but keeping tabs on the conversation. Of course we knew that Elvis was going to do that special in 1968 that sealed his phenomenal success as the consummate entertainer and showman of the century.

And then there was the music! My husband had every record of Elvis's and occasionally I would buy a single which I liked but that was rare. After Elvis's divorce, which was amply discussed backwards and forwards, and then subsequently our own divorce, the topic of conversation was still Elvis when my ex-husband would come for his weekly visits (if it fit into his busy schedule of sampling the wide variety of cuties who congregated at the gate). Since he, my ex, lived up the street from Elvis's house, he knew about everything and he always trotted the information out to me. I had a very dim view of anything Elvis did but I had to listen to all of the tawdriness that was Elvis's life.

When these children of mine became adults, I would only tell them of the strange occurrences that had happened to me as I wanted somebody to tell me if I was on the verge of going mad or if this was really real. I took it for granted that they loved me and they would be kind but that was not the case. Rachel was more lenient than Judy who simply shrugged everything off as insanity.

As years went by, and after many conversations between the two girls, the older one also tried to suggest that I could have inherited some of my mother's apparent madness. This was very disappointing to me and I had to be casual whenever the subject of Elvis came up. Any explanation I could have offered, they would have rejected simply because they absolutely hated the subject altogether.

I cannot, in clear conscience, fault them in the least for their attitude toward Elvis in conjunction with me. It is rather fantastical, if not outright pathological, and I was well aware of it. However, when I was put into the position to have to rationally, logically, make the eldest understand somewhat as she had the ability to follow me in my mental excursions, I made sure that I presented the emotional development that was anchored in the spiritual from its inception in sequence upon which she then would not be able to come up with any critique that could stand up. There was none. There is none. I am either a nut and I know very well that I am not, but then what am I?

It is this question to which I knew I had to find the answer and the proof for it. It is for that reason that I chose to be alone and solitary. Somehow I had known in advance what my future would hold, but it was nothing I wanted nor wished for and it was nothing that would make my life easier. On the contrary, from a purely human perspective there was nothing appealing or desirable to be had but it was an inescapable reality for me but would be most beneficial in the long run.

It is to this quest that I devote the major part of my daily life to and it is only fitting that I find solace in God's Word.

16

That's the Way it is

Through continuous study, and a very active prayer life, a lot of this neverending search for answers to questions that have plagued me for such a long time and the feeling that the time would surely come when the reason for this seemingly senseless and needless suffering would at long last become evident, that time had finally come.

The fact that I had to come to know Elvis in the manner that I had, back in 1958—which was so life-changing for me and I was so young and inexperienced and so devoted to God—has always been nothing less than miraculous to me. One day I was pleasantly living my life, peacefully, in a God-pleasing way, and the next day was in turmoil over somebody I had never heard of before, or ever even known of his existence! It was definitely cause for me to wonder what on earth was going on. My belief in the God of the Scriptures however, gave me the help I needed and things from then on went toward the very definite goal of which I was not aware but simply had to trust that it would be for the better—somehow. Of course having been as young and innocent and having my head full of rose-colored dreams, I was sure that a happy union between myself and my beloved would be inevitable in the end and I was full of hope and anticipation of everything good coming my way, never mind that ever-so-faint feeling way down deep that not all was well with this entirely preordained journey I had embarked on.

We are now in the year 2005. Rachel finally got married to the right man, which has been a source of pleasure and thankfulness for me.

I just had come back from a trip to Memphis, having to realize once again that I had no business there, as my four remaining children there had simply adopted the sentiment of the day and rejected the idea of SIN. Whatever they did, if it had negative consequences, they regarded it merely as a mistake which put us at odds.

To me this was very serious and I could not make them understand it.

It is certainly true that any of what I had discovered does in no wise give me any pleasure but it does give me a sense of having accomplished what had to be accomplished. So the way to adequately describe my feeling on the matter can be expressed by saying that is a horrifying relief, even though that seems a contradiction in terms. In order to understand this one must think it through. . . .

After having spent weeks trying to digest information I got in Sunday school, where we were studying contemporary Christianity in the struggle with the spiritual darkness, my mind seemed to go its own way while I was pacing back and forth, back and forth, from the back door to the front door, which is a straight shot, having that "feeling in my body" (the sentiment of the song Elvis sang, by the same title, in his LP *Promised Land*) and it was to me very much as he sings about. I sat down in my chair, which faces my bedroom window from where I can watch the birds crowding around the birdfeeder I had hung up, but I did not notice the feisty birds nor did I see anything as I was staring holes in the air, which is what I call it, as my attention was entirely monopolized inward and slowly but surely a recognizable train of thought emerged and I took a sheet of paper and started to write what came into my conscious mind: "The real reason Elvis Presley was thrust onto the world-stage has been foretold in the Bible."

Almost everybody young and impressionable was eventually mesmerized by his stunning good looks, his smoldering sexuality, hinting alluringly at the forbidden, his feel-good music with its repetitive beat, accompanied by an almost irresistibly thrilling quality of voice, combined with his freewheeling performing style, he even managed to take in the parents of the hapless youth who were trying to grow up, with his puzzled and disarming, "Aw shucks, I dunno why dem girls is actin' so crazy," country charm. He even did his stint in the army, like any patriotic American, he loved his mama and his papa and he professed to be a Christian who did not drink or smoke.

What more could you reasonably expect from such a fine young American? Most of us surrendered our reservations, telling ourselves that he could not be anything but a little fun for our restless youth, who were becoming ferocious defenders of Elvis, and we simply had no proof to the contrary, not any the public was aware of, anyway.

Add to this the enormous, mind-boggling earning power Elvis had, his ostentatious lifestyle, his legendary generosity! Very effectively, yet imperceptibly, he galvanized unwittingly the already simmering social/cultural unrest into an outright rebellion against the accepted social norms that until then were rooted in the Judeo-Christian value system.

No one noticed the change we underwent in our thinking and we embarked on a me, me, me, binge that has permeated every facet of our society to this very day.

Elvis was so incredibly appealing on so many levels, it was virtually impossible to denounce him effectively.

By 1956–57 he had all the major players in his pocket, so to speak, that is everybody who could see the dollar signs attached to his style of entertainment for the masses. His influence on every notable singer and musician is well-documented and they, in turn, carried the seed of rebellion into the following generations with a degree of lawlessness that surely would make our forefathers turn in their graves and which causes those of us who can still remember the innocent times of the past to bemoan the current conditions in "the good ole USA" with shock and disbelief.

Elvis's appeal was wide ranging and hardly anyone could remain unaffected by his influence on some level: Talk about subliminal messaging—and he did it without really trying.

Very few recognized him for who he really was and those who had an inkling, and spoke negatively about him, were quickly silenced by the overpowering, ever-growing popularity of the man.

This is how the sense-numbing party began and it has been roaring on since 1956, providing the climate for unprecedented changes in mainstream thinking, which up until then was determined by the Judeo-Christian system of values of our forefathers.

Even the Church, without much ado, succumbed to the intoxicating, disorienting influence and she was caught wholly unprepared to put up the fight necessary to effectively oppose the legislation which, over time, robbed us of our foundation. Instead, the Church simply made adjustments out of sheer survival instinct. She incorporated the wayward ways of her members right into the conducting of business, which has rendered the Church inconsequential for the most part in this day and time.

However, for the true believer the end of this world-system is near and the promise of joy unspeakable in the Holy Word of the living God of Abraham, Isaac and Jacob is "just around the corner."

What an unpleasant assertion for me to make about the man I love so deeply! But that does explain the feeling of doom that accompanied my euphoria of falling in love, or I should say that very clear sense of danger this man (and I did not know who he was then) found himself in and I could feel this imminent quality which gave it such urgency which caused me to leave nothing untried to be able to talk to him and warn him. Of course, only in retrospect and after all that I have been through, does this my ordeal make any kind of sense and it only makes sense to the spiritually attuned. To those who have not been born again it will remain a cause for ridicule, just as the Bible and what it teaches is, and has been relegated to the status of just another book of tall tales, something to ignore as it is just backward drivel from a long time ago and irrelevant in the progressive techno-world of today.

I went, on August 8, to the editor of the local newspaper and I tried to explain to him what I had discovered. It was a surreal experience for me as I had actually found myself talking about this fantastical story of mine. The kindly editor was paying attention and he was amused at some of the things I was saying and I assured him that I would now be glad just to go home and faint dead away as this visit and my talking was simply too much stress for me but that I had to do it.

I can imagine how fantastically this revelation of mine must have gone over, as this is our community paper and it is supportive of all that benefits this region and this region benefits greatly from the fact that Elvis was born here! Not only that, but when I got home and got the newspaper from my sweet neighbor, Vivian, who saved it for me every day, I discovered that it was Elvis Presley Fan Day here in Tupelo! I felt like crawling into a deep hole and pulling the cover in over me.

I am just about as welcome with my assertion as a downpour at a picnic. It does take courage to go against the current but in my case it is hardly courage but an irresistible compulsion to do what I must do. Period.

I sent the editor a copy of what I titled "Elvis, the Son of Perdition." The paper published a heavily edited version which did not please me but I must concede that many people here are either related to Elvis or they knew him or they benefit from his name's value in some way.

It is for that reason that I could not and did not discuss the very negative aspects of Elvis's fame and fortune with my neighbor. Hardly anyone wants to hear things that potentially could throw their entire belief-system into some kind of chaos or at the very least make them uncomfortable. They had never thought much about anything other than the enjoyment that Elvis brought to them with his music and, yes, also with his scandalous private life which they would acknowledge from their perch of superiority as they could easily sit in judgment of him as they themselves never did such things because they were church-going Bible-believing good folks.

That very same year I had an experience that clarified something else for me although, again, it did not make me happy. During my many years of writing to Charlie Hodge in Pigeon Forge, I had described a dream I had. This dream was the one where I felt cradled and safe and indescribably euphoric and I remember writing that it was to me as if the puzzle pieces were falling into place and I had "become this other person." I cannot recall the exact context but it had to do with the cosmic battle between good and evil. On the day that this clarification came, I was still in bed, just lying there when all at once it hit my conscious mind (and I had been plagued for quite some time by the recurring thought of this phrase "become this other person" going round and round in my head and my knowing full well that this must be significant but what was it? What did it all mean?). As I was still lying there with nothing in particular on my mind and it was so overpowering that I was unable to do anything about it, my subconscious forced this information from deep within into my consciousness. Instantly I knew that I was the person of the Holy Spirit which so shocked me into a sort of paralysis that I could not move a muscle and I could not close my mouth which was still midway to a breath. I lay there stock-still but my mind was racing, racing to connect the dots . . . and it all fit perfectly. Once I began clarifying these things to myself, I regained control over myself and finished the breath I had started and I got up and started pacing back and forth, back and forth, thinking how incredible all this was and how it was that I was stuck with this and how convenient it was that I was on my bed because if I had been standing up this revelation would surely have knocked me over. It was all too much for me to digest and I certainly had no intention to let any of this interfere with my regular, everyday life as I must live it and let whatever has to happen, happen. There was nothing else I could do. It was the same as at the time when I was guided to the twelfth chapter of Revelations I just had to go on living and doing what I was predestined to do, like it or not.

Most of the time that followed I took comfort in the fact that no one knew and I mused how utterly preposterous this must sound to the everyday person but to me it was not so unusual, as my whole life was littered with these supernatural occurrences.

For the most part I put it out of my mind and struggled on to try to deal with my children and life in general.

The youngest daughter (Tracy) had gotten married that year and the following year Charlie Hodge had died, which had put me into a tailspin of confusion and doubt about my sanity and my faith, and I was in such dire straits that I had decided to go to a Christian psychologist. I was hoping to have him refer me to a mental health clinic that could pronounce me insane and treat me with their psychotropic drugs—anything, just anything but get me out of this misery! And I was in acute meltdown mode and I needed help badly.

However, while talking to him and trying to describe what I was dealing with, the psychologist looked at me and asked, "What exactly do you want me to do?" At that simple question I realized that there was really nothing he could do for me at that moment in time and I left scheduling another session open. I went home and settled down in my mind and started to pray in all earnestness for help as I just could no longer bear any of this and, as if by a miracle, it became so clear to me that I had had a severe crisis in faith and I found the eleventh chapter of Hebrews to be a confidence-builder and I had regained my anchor which is Jesus Christ.

It is interesting to me to have had to discover that no matter how strong I feel in my faith, how devoted to the cause of faith I am—and I am that—this world we are living in and all the pressure it puts on me, still makes me vulnerable.

I remember distinctly the time I had to come face to face with having to decide the validity of "speaking in tongues" which the Pentecostals have as part of their doctrines. I had always thought this to be a rather odd practice and having been taught the Lutheran tradition, which simply dismisses this practice as the work of the devil, I was not at all sure about its validity.

It was on a Sunday evening. I was at church and we ladies were praying for a woman who had a lot of problems and had requested for us to pray for her. I was standing behind her and I was touching her shoulder and I was praying earnestly for help for this woman, when I could hear in the right part of my brain a language I had never heard before and I was thinking quickly that this must be one of the "unknown tongues" I had been hearing about and had heard people in the congregation speak in many, many times, and I continued to pray in English and I felt that God was listening and surely providing the help this woman needed.

After the service, and on my way out the door, all of a sudden, as I remembered this strange language that I had heard, I started to formulate the sound of what I had heard and as if I had just found out how to speak, I mouthed the words, first one, then another one and then there was this gusher of words and syllables I had never spoken before in my adult life and I kept on speaking, now aloud as I did not care one bit about who saw or heard me. I was on a roll! I finally knew how to speak in tongues! I was ever so thrilled and thankful to God to have blessed me with this ability.

I shared this experience with one of the ladies and she was almost as thrilled as I was.

I had really never sought to speak in tongues, as I had always thought that it was not an end in itself to be able to speak in tongues and that it is somehow a deficiency in one's faith if one does not speak in tongues but rather that it is a gift of the Holy Spirit, freely given to the believer who is sincerely seeking to please God in word and deed.

As I have said before, even with all the evidence of this higher power, this eminently creative force that is the living God of the Holy Bible, I am still vulnerable if I do not stay securely fastened to my Savior, my Friend, my everything, Jesus Christ.

In the summer of 2007, in August, the television was devoting a lot of time to Elvis Presley and the various people who had worked with him on his musical endeavors and their tearful recollections, which are moving to be sure as Elvis was a big part of their lives, but it just galls me to no end that no one seems to notice, let alone criticize, anything the man did, no matter how despicable, how low-down, how completely unacceptable. It is as if they have struck a deal with the devil and they just do not think anything is wrong here. But there is. And because there is plenty wrong which must be addressed and acknowledged and condemned as unacceptable, I cannot rest until this distasteful but necessary task is completed.

It is indeed a very difficult position to be in as I am so much in love with this man who is dead, and yet to have to acknowledge that I absolutely hate the things he ended up doing. It felt to me as if I was compressed between two polar opposites which is not a good place to find yourself in. At some point I had to decide which polar pull I was going to give dominance to. Without realizing what was transpiring I got so unbelievably angry with myself for letting this continue for no apparent good reason and I was getting so very aggravated with Elvis for putting me into this untenable position that I irrevocably cut my emotional attachment to Elvis.

There are no words to describe the relief I felt. It was as if the whole world had been sitting on my shoulders and kept on weighing me down. I was free, free at last. I had made my decision and it dawned on me that I now also knew the identity of the person I was looking for in that dream and the identity of the apparition after this something or someone breathed on my right cheek. It was and is Jesus Christ Himself.

To get to this point of exasperation I must confess that my children helped me a lot as they continued to do just whatever they wanted without any thought of, "What would Jesus do?"

One was in jail, the other was having an affair with a married man who had two children and she was married and had two children too. One son had gotten married and then divorced in short order because he found his wife in their bed with another man. Another daughter declared bankruptcy because she overspent and then she got divorced for the fourth time, and another son was still battling his heroin addiction.

It is true that the distance between my children and myself was a godsend. However it did not keep me from being directly affected by everything that was going on in Memphis that they were sharing with me. I was going ballistic over one thing or the other, having barely enough time to recuperate from one blow when the other came. I was stressed to the limit by the time this Elvis-adoration time started and I simply was primed to do something, anything, turn the world upside down—whatever it took—but DO something! And so I did.

After having been so emotionally tied to Elvis for so long, it was very strange, to say the least, to be cut off from him and yet I felt so good about it; more than that, I experienced a sense of peace, a tranquil pleasant sort of nothingness which told me that this was the right thing to do.

I now felt free and unencumbered to do whatever had to be done and I no longer felt sidetracked by anything the people who have known Elvis personally and are making their living trying to keep him alive for the future generations might do. Whether they know it or not, they are indeed rendering a good service, and that is ever so true for Priscilla, who dealt with the problems that fell in her lap, so to speak, in a most astute way by summoning the experts who gave her good advice, and also Lisa Marie, who supports her daddy in her own way.

Here in Tupelo a lot of shakin' is going on, as everything now focuses on the expansion of the Elvis Presley Birthplace. Elvis had bought eleven acres, I am told, and the city is securing monies as I am writing this to forge ahead and compete with Memphis for the tourist dollars. As the love of money makes the world go 'round, it is no surprise to me that they are doggedly pursuing this. I wonder what made them wait this long.

The area I am living in is now called "Presley Heights" and I suggested to my fellow congregants to change the name of our church from East Heights A/G to Presley Heights A/G but they do not seem enchanted about the idea. I can hardly blame them as they probably think to themselves, "Who does she think she is, coming all the way from Germany of all places, where they murdered all those Jews, and telling us what we should do?" To me it makes perfect sense on several levels. Elvis's spiritual home was here and I am here to make sure that the emphasis is placed only on Jesus Christ and it is of practical benefit as it brings much needed attention to the church and what it stands for and what is being taught there. It is surely no accident that we are studying The Prophecies of Daniel in Sunday school. We had been working our way through this book very slowly, as if going through it with a fine-tooth comb, digging up every conceivable spiritual nugget, stretching our poor minds in lengthy speculations, suppositions and conjectures. Behind the Sunday-school teacher's back we promised ourselves that we would throw ourselves a party in celebration of finally having completed this very detailed, slow-moving study. We found out at the yearly business meeting that we had accumulated a good amount of money by giving an offering faithfully every Sunday and so we could afford it, like a graduation of sorts. It is something to look forward to!

When we were in Daniel, chapter five, where the finger of God wrote on the wall when Belshazzar, just like his predecessor Nebuchadnezzar, in his debauchery and blasphemy, was having one of the customary orgies, filled with wine and women and song and loose speech, it coincided with the emergence of this push for more money from the state coffers that it hit me—that precisely as God had used the worst of the bad to bring about the ever-ongoing Plan of Redemption, He can certainly use Elvis in the same way. This recognition brought the name-change to my mind and I felt confident that it was a nudge from Heaven and that the proposal was a good one.

As an aside, this very detailed account of the Book of Daniel would give me all kinds of trouble because I have no faculty for thinking logically and keeping the necessary information of years and times and epochs and kingdoms in a memory bank. It would bore me to tears to have to listen to these long, drawn-out, descriptions and view diagrams of important information, and I had to laugh to myself when I was reading one of the following chapters at home, where the author used the following statement to describe "the sum of the matter" as "the essential features were culled out of the great variety of details so as not to present a bewildering array of detail"! And what does he think he was doing with the whole book? It reminded me of the time I served on jury duty and we jurors had to listen to an endless description of detail over and over again as this was a malpractice proceeding. I noticed the presiding judge checking every now and then to see if we were still awake or if our eyes were glazed over! I felt sorry for the judge because he has to do this every day! I could not anymore do this than I could fly. But my goodness, all this minutiae—it was positively maddening but I guess it was necessary to hear the same thing said by various witnesses for the plaintiff and the defense. All in all it was very interesting at its core and the defendant was cleared of all charges of negligence.

Ah, such can be the toil required to a better understanding of the matter at hand and sometimes it is not easy or pleasant but we must put ourselves through it regardless as this teaches us a valuable lesson of one sort or another. But I will be glad when we finally get to the last page of The Prophecies of Daniel.

As any student of the Scriptures knows, Daniel foresaw the future of the human race, and as he describes conditions in his own time it is quite obvious that there are parallels to this day and our own times and conditions. It is remarkable to have to realize that humankind on the whole does not change when it comes to good and evil. The fight between those two forces still goes on much the same as it has for thousands of years. Even with Jesus Christ appearing as the sacrifice for our sinful nature, which is inborn, and the marvelous message of hope and redemption He brought to us, thereby giving us a way to choose a better way to live which made this blue planet a much brighter place, we still stubbornly insist on doing things our own way.

Our spiritual nature has been all but denied in the last fifty-plus years (Elvis-time coincidentally?), making "the pursuit of happiness" in our constitution out to be an endless pursuit of carnal pleasures. To this end we have embraced the "if it feels good do it and if you can make money doing it, sell it" philosophy, which we practice outright and openly with all the passion we can muster. After countless victims find themselves in the throes of the aftermath of living as though God were dead, we are confronted with a multitude of problems, which are, for the most part spiritual in nature; but rather than go seek help where help is available, namely in the Church, we have now become way too smart for that and choose rather to go to a psychiatrist who does very little else than to widen the distance between God and man. Very few people (comparatively speaking) regard the Church as a vital part of their happiness. When all else fails they remember that help is available there for their ailing souls. But it is simply senseless to passionately insist on living contrary to God's Will and then turn to the Church and demand that it change according to societal whims so as not to offend anyone. God never changes, neither do His laws.

The average American churchgoer today indulges liberally in everything that pleases the senses, which is fundamentally un-Christian. They think nothing of it, see nothing wrong and even go to their worship-centers and "play church." There the pastor gives them a feel-good, pablum sermon or the bitter truth couched in feel-good homilies or otherwise cleverly camouflaged.

This spells trouble for the Church, as the bitter truth, which is the changing of our carnal nature into a spiritually aware nature is the central goal. To give it less than the required attention with all seriousness has brought on a decline in the quality of the Church as a whole.

This decline in the Church, and therefore the nation, began, in part, in 1963 when the U.S. Supreme Court ruled it unconstitutional to teach about God in public schools. Every ruling involving the worship of God since then has brought this country a step closer to what we are today: a nation not only without God but a nation vehemently against God.

What has actually transpired while we were busy following every conceivable self-indulging desire and its immediate gratification is that we have lost sight of our destiny. It is the unholy trinity of I, me, and myself which we have placed at the center of the universe and we have essentially elevated everything that is human to a status of a god whom we have dedicated our lives to by slavishly serving "self" and in so doing worship ourselves.

Any force driven or generated by this unnatural exaggeration of self is unholy and so very much in opposition to the Holy Trinity of Father, Son, and Holy Spirit.

It appears that this unholy force has made itself at home here and we are perfectly comfortable with it, since we have found euphemisms for selfishness, lack of love, sin and flagrant disobedience to God's Word (law) and we are effortlessly speeding headlong to our ruin.

It has always been true that "'following Jesus" is no cakewalk. Following Jesus, taken very seriously, is a very hard row to hoe indeed, but the reward is immeasurable and everlasting.

The fact that church membership is in serious decline has prompted many churches to resort to unconventional approaches to try to reach people, to spread the still-good news, which has a watering-down effect on the message itself. The idea that "the truth" can be told by pandering to the prurient interests of the lost to save them is nothing but a mixing of the profane with the holy and the outcome is fairly predictable.

It is indeed a very good practice to go to Sunday school and the worship service. If one pays close attention to what is being said, one can certainly find out what all this life-bringing, regenerating, incomparable, living Word of God can do for that which is divine within us and which longs to be nurtured.

I am simply going nowhere with this fact with my children and I am doing good by not commenting on the condition of their souls as I have given complete responsibility to God as I have been a failure to show them God's Way. But I have done what the Bible teaches, which is to teach them the ways of the Lord. They were growing up in a time when the television took away the influence of the parents and shifted it to the messages coming into our living rooms via entertainment and advertising. The colorful images on the tube and the pleasant sounds accompanying the images were much more powerful than any Bible lesson could ever be. Surely one can recognize the uncanny accuracy in that dream where Elvis plummeted out of my reach into some buildings that looked like Manhattan! This onslaught of ideas contrasted sharply over the years with the Judeo-Christian doctrine and has changed mainstream thinking by neutralizing what the children have been taught at home and in church and, in my children's case, also at school. It is my consolation to know that I have fulfilled my responsibility and that their future is of their own making and their responsibility which as we can clearly see, has left us as a society wholly in a lurch as personal responsibility has been replaced by an attitude of victimhood.

It is of never-ending consternation to me how unaware we were of what was really happening. It was just so unrecognizable and so unexpected, but now that we can look back we can clearly see that with the ever-increasing technological knowledge and the inevitable mass-communication came the wholesale abandonment of virtually everything we were taught and believed in, going back to the founding of this "Nation Under God" and beyond and in conjunction with the meteoric rise of Elvis Presley, a phenomenon like no other in the last century (and he is most certainly dead) but he is also still very much alive through his influence, he has attained the status of a god and is being worshipped by many worldwide.

The young Elvis, growing up here in East Tupelo, roaming the hills (where I now live), going to church with his mother, singing lovely hymns of faith and wholly believing in God's Holy Word, was an innocent. However, in his youthful innocence and bruising, abject, poverty, he opened himself up to materialism, which carried him at breakneck speed into the clutches of this world system, which is ruled by the evil forces, with God having set the parameters. This warped and perverted the "real" Elvis beyond recognition. No wonder that I was unable to connect with him when we first met! With his music and the life he was living he deceived the whole world into believing the lies—every lie of the unholy one. It is well for us to remember that this can happen to us as well on a smaller scale and in private but potentially just as destructive.

This brings to mind Michael Jackson's life and times. What an embarrassing spectacle this misplaced adulation of Michael Jackson had become at the occasion of his death. It is indeed a sad day when a people celebrate, admire and worship a person who, by all accounts, is to the sane, unquestionably a disgrace to the human race. He obviously fashioned his life after his idol, Elvis Presley, and he became the flag-bearer for the depraved and debauched, who passionately practice the "if it feels good, do it and if you can make money doing it, sell it" syndrome of this post-modern era and then have the audacity to call it art, and worse yet, musical genius!

Surely the love of money (materialism) has made everybody spiritually bankrupt and this is indicative of where we are headed as a nation. Like a self-indulging child we know no limits.

17

It's Now or Never

This emotional break from Elvis that I had tried so hard to accomplish in my younger years and which would have made my life much easier, was so profoundly life-changing but astonishingly easy. No more feeling as though he would take my heart and just disappear with it if I did not stay "in touch" via his music. No panic, no terror anymore that I would be inextricably stuck in this no-man's land, so to speak, where you feel you are neither here nor there. All this unsettledness was gone. In place of it is this quiet and sure knowledge that I had reached a very important goal—finally—and that what comes next will not be as long-lasting or as intense.

It was almost a relief not to have to listen to Elvis talking to me in his music and I cannot get over how pleasant this freedom actually was and is.

It is for all these reasons that I was ever-so-amazed and puzzled when I had a very vivid dream in which I was "visiting with Elvis."

The scene was a noisy, milling crowd of people, talking, talking, much as was the case whenever Elvis would appear anywhere in public in Memphis. I could not see him, as we were in different spheres, but somehow I was made aware that I had an appointment with him.

The next scene was the old sanctuary of Christ the King Lutheran Church on Park Avenue in Memphis, which was my spiritual way station while Elvis was alive.

I entered the sanctuary and it was empty, with the exception of some ancillary people tending to some things that needed to be done in the church who paid absolutely no attention to me whatsoever. I saw Elvis sitting in the pew on the left side of the sanctuary, probably two seats away from the middle aisle, on the second to last row.

I went over to him and I noticed that we were wearing the same kind of clothes. Oddly enough it was the identical material of an ensemble I had bought, maybe in 1996 or so. It is made of light material, made to be worn in very hot weather. The color would be light gray as it is a weaving together of white and medium gray. Elvis was looking straight ahead with the same forlorn look in his eyes that he had the last time I saw him in Germany when he was complaining of an upset stomach.

I sat down beside him as I was saying, "We have the same clothes on, which must mean that we belong together!" He kept on staring straight ahead and said monotonously, "But it isn't over yet!" to which I replied, "At least we are together." He said again, this time with resignation in his voice, "But it isn't over yet!" at which point I woke up. I was pondering the meaning of this dream and it was amusing to me that we were wearing those clothes as I still love to wear that ensemble. I took it to mean that something was coming my way that I needed to be warned about.

This happened shortly after I had cut the emotional ties with him, which was in the middle of August, as the observance of his death was in full swing. It was the early part of September.

While I did not dwell on the meaning of that dream, I did like to replay it in my mind and enjoy the feeling of partnership which we were obviously sharing and it was calming to have seen him if only in a dream!

I went to Memphis for a visit with my granddaughters as they were having fall break and their mother, Judy, had to work so I stayed for two or three days that year, which was 2007.

Samuel came over with my grandson and I remember that I was having fun with the children. The adults were having their problems: one was trying to chase down the fifth husband and the other was living with a girl who had a child by some boy who up and left her high and dry when the boy was born.

There are no words to describe how miserable all this made me feel as I could clearly see that the trouble they were in was of their own making and it always pained me to have to come face to face with the fact that they did not, and do not, put any value on God's Word. They give lip service but they cannot see the correlation between their respective miseries and their disobedience of God's laws.

The one was complaining that she was having trouble with her boyfriend of two years and after the many stunts he pulled it was obvious to me that he was only after a good time, which he got, since it lasted two years.

The other was complaining about an insufferable ex-wife who had given birth to a girl so prematurely that extraordinary preemie care had to be administered, which meant that the child had a very lengthy stay in the N-ICU, and he wanted to get out of town with his new girlfriend. Depressing.

As it is in these circumstances, I do the best I can to be attentive to their stories of trouble and I have learned that one never eats the soup as hot as it is cooked, meaning that my son would see the fallacy of trying to run away.

I wrote him a lengthy letter explaining a few vital things to him, and telling him to ask himself a few questions pertaining to his girlfriend, to whose child he was playing daddy. My heart still aches for him as he had to go through so much pain, even though it was his fault all the way down the line because be ignores the guidelines of good living that are explained in the Bible backwards and forwards. I suffer with my children and wish I could take their pain away but this I cannot do but I can do the best thing for them that I know of and that is to pray for them.

My daughter, with her two girls in school and her teenage son staying with her fourth ex-husband, has bought hook, line and sinker into the lie that women can have it all.

Ever since the court ruled in favor of the "no-fault divorce," the stampede by women heading to the divorce court had begun.

We encouraged our daughters to become independent and self-reliant (career-minded) which is a good thing in and of itself. It is good to be educated and trained to be able to support yourself. It also increases the option for the choice of a better-suited spouse but as it is with any basically good thing there are these unintended consequences that no one can see in advance.

And so it is that the woman of today is simply in no mood to put up with much of anything. She often outperforms her husband. If she is married—and that has become a big IF!—and if it gets too hard, off she goes and gets a divorce. Of course, she only considers her needs and wants and wishes, primarily since that is what she has become accustomed to doing for a long time already—well, since her growing-up years. But where does that leave the children? Exactly where we find them today—in jeopardy—and we as a society must all pay the price.

It is high time that we shift the focus away from the equal rights for women, though I am supportive of this, and put it on the welfare of the children. Regardless of the social experiments and the assertions from liberal thinkers that it does not matter if the children have no daddy or no mommy in the home, it is still best for a child to grow up in a home with both biological parents who are in a joint commitment to the nurture of their child.

Why, oh why, is it so difficult in this post-modern day for us to acknowledge that we were wrong? Why? Because we are a stubborn and rebellious lot, completely consumed by our self-importance, so preoccupied with progressive thinking that we send our children into a state of uprootedness and confusion that inevitably lands them in trouble for which all of us as a society must pay—financially and otherwise.

It is therefore high time that we elevate the status of the stay-at-home mom, the wife of one husband, as the most desirable position for a woman, which it truly is. An entire society depends on her.

It is for this reason that a woman today must realize that she is very important in the shaping of a nation. What a demeaning, absolutely destructive conduct has emerged by the female in this day and time!

Today it is a sought-after goal to look like I remember the naked models on *Playboy* magazine looked (40 years ago!): like brainless sex-kittens. Have we women fought for equal rights to be now forced into thinking by the sheer onslaught of this endless and unacceptable sexualization of everything to see nothing wrong in having young girls sexualized at ever-earlier ages in their development to womanhood?

I feel very strongly that we women are the "keepers of the flame" and as such it behooves us to consider that a man is more sexual (scientific research has concluded that a man thinks of sex much more often than a woman) and is therefore more susceptible to this rampant peddling of almost pornographic images everywhere, which renders any clear-thinking, self-respecting, responsible woman obligated to shun the exhibitionistic parading around in revealing and provocative clothes and to be coquettish, forever luring and tempting the men.

The joys of sex are present in a loving tenderness of caring for the spouse and usually do not require handbooks and potions and prodding by a sex therapist or the viewing of pornography.

These kinds of observations come into my mind as I think about my children and their conduct and how all these influences have been and are affecting their thinking and consequently the things they do to fit in with their peers, who are equally mesmerized by the follies of the secular progressives who seem to run things in an effort to make money.

Can I make my children understand any of this? If I could refrain from referring to the Holy Bible I could probably be heard. But that is just impossible for me. Hence, as soon as the word "God" or "Bible" is spoken, they all turn deaf or argumentative and hostile.

I find dealing with my children rather strenuous for this reason and I have not been in Memphis for almost two years. I just hate to go there. It feels to me like I am going to the scene of a crime in which I was the victim!

In my earlier years here in Tupelo, I would always ask the people in my church to pray for me when I had plans to go to Memphis. Since I am not too good at navigating on the highway and my car is pretty old and the destination is unpleasant, I surely needed prayer.

My children do love me, I know, and they come to see me. With seven of them there's enough contact to last me quite a while.

I had barely adjusted to the fact that Susan was now in the process of being divorced by her husband of twelve years for adultery when my ex-husband called me and asked me if I was sitting down. I could feel my knees getting weaker and I got more upset by the second when he finally told me that our youngest and only daughter, Tracy, had left her husband of two-and-a-half years, and had moved in with a woman, and that she had told him that she was a lesbian.

Had I not had that warning of sorts from Elvis in that dream, I am sure I would have suffered a stroke or a heart attack. Instead I talked to my ex-husband quite rationally about this turn of events and whether there were any signs that we missed when she was growing up. She was a daddy's-girl and she loved all kinds of sports but this was no sign of lesbianism as society accepts girls being tomboys. Unfortunately this does not hold true for the boy. If they prefer activities girls primarily engage in, they are called disparaging names. I think my ex was more upset than I was and he is the one that deep down is a fervent adherent of the "if it feels good, do it" crowd.

When I got off the phone I must admit I was stunned. Was she not the only one who would live her life as the Bible urges to do? Was she not the only one who read her daily devotions without my having to remind her? Was she not the one who dated a pastor's son whom she fell in love with and married? Was she not the one who was absolutely no trouble at all? I really was stunned. I simply could not understand a thing about it and I still don't.

That makes seven down!

One thing was perfectly clear: I loved her just the same as before, and when she then called me to tell me herself, she said that none of this was my fault, that she had the best upbringing, but she is a lesbian just the same. When I asked her at what point she realized that she was in love with a woman she told me it was in early September at work where she had met this woman. (It was the same time I had this warning from Elvis in the dream!)

I barely got all that squared away when I then called Judy to let her know of this development. She said, "Here goes another one whose life you have ruined, just like you ruined mine," and when I told her that I had been exonerated by the lesbian herself, she accused me of having been a bad mother, and she said that if I had given her the support she needed, she would not be where she is to day—four times divorced. I cannot explain it but this accusation coming from her made me so upset that my heart started to beat ninety miles an hour and I could hardly breathe; I screamed into the phone that she was a witch

(I had the b-word in mind!) and I hung up on her. My heart was still pounding and I lay down to recuperate and the thought of her calling me again filled me with dread. I called my pastor and explained to him what had happened and I asked him if he would be willing to take care of things should I indeed become incapacitated by another phone call from my daughter, and so could not do it myself. He agreed and assured me that whatever this daughter accused me of was not true. I was furious beyond belief. I had always had all kinds of trouble with her and the choices she made and her stubborn rebellion, in which she cut off her nose to spite her face, so to speak. I was always there for her and I regretted that I had let her sweet-talk me into a relationship with her in spite of the fact that it was my anger at her behavior and the accompanying accusations that prompted me to move to Tupelo when I did in the first place. I was mad, mad, mad.

I was fresh out of patience with her and I resolved to cut all ties with her. To show her how serious I was about this, I had her siblings tell her that I would put her under a peace-bond if need be to shield myself from her. At this point she was a threat to my health and I had to protect myself.

I wrote her a note, explaining my position, telling her that I could not afford a relationship with her or her children because I cannot be this horrible mother on one hand and this wonderful, fun grandmother on the other. She could not have it both ways and neither could I. If I wanted a relationship with her children then I had to deal with her also, which I cannot afford, so I have to sacrifice my relationship with them. She had mentioned once before when we were talking on the phone that I had "ruined all my sons' lives" to which I strongly objected. I had gotten very upset then, too, and my heart had started pounding hard and I could barely speak when she asked what the matter was. I recuperated as the subject of the conversation changed, but it left an indelible impression on me and contributed to the quick resolve to cut ties completely with her.

There was nothing to be gained by continuing a relationship under those conditions. Nothing. I simply cut my losses. Was this what loomed on the horizon when I had that dream with Elvis saying "But it is not over yet"? It upset me more than Tracy's lesbianism. Or both?

I felt at peace with this decision I had made, having asked God to help me with this, as it was not going to be easy in the long run. It was not easy because I had the constant criticisms of her siblings who tried to convince me that I was heartless and mean, that the poor girls won't understand any of this. This, I told them, is their mother's problem. She can tell them that I am a horrible mother and therefore they can't see me anymore. Besides, I went to see them very rarely and they were doing just fine without me. To now make it sound like it would seriously affect them negatively is just not true. I explained to them that my granddaughters' lives are like an ice-cream sundae with a cherry on top. I am the cherry. Remove the cherry and you still have all the other goodies!

It was trying, though, and I made sure I kept any unpleasantness to a minimum. It goes without saying that cut off meant cut off and they were omitted from my list. It would be a problem when I had to collaborate with Susan, mother of a boy and a girl who expected her sister and her girls, to make sure there were no unnecessary hurt feelings. I regretted the whole affair but I am not going to play the blame-game. Period. It hurts but this is actually love in action. Real love is strong and therefore tough when called for. It is not that namby-pamby fuzzy, feel-good, sentimental kind that plagues people these days and keeps them from doing the hard stuff, like saying "NO," like setting limits, like expecting respect and insisting on it. We have lulled ourselves into this mode where it is cruel to expose children to real life—it is so harsh, so unfair! True, and the sooner the youngsters find out that this is the reality, that they can and must learn the skills to cope successfully and that simply cannot be accomplished by keeping them shielded from every adversity and crying and feeling sorry for them and heaping all the sympathy on them and spoiling them rotten. (Even though we often cry in secret over all the cruelties!)

It is this same kind of thinking that fashioned Jesus into some weak, ineffectual, milquetoast martyr we must feel sorry for when the exact opposite is true. He is strong and decisive and tough enough to do the hard stuff—it is ourselves we need to bemoan as we have a lot to learn, but learn we must to enjoy the abundant life here on earth with the certainty of paradise in our eternal future. Today Jesus Christ had been changed into this inconsequential good person from long ago. With hardly anyone taking the time to discover who this Jesus really is, is it any wonder that most Christians do not even know why they believe and what they believe? Anyone can come along and convince them of something else.

Christianity has become a commodity to be traded for political advantage and it is regrettable that there are far too few true believers in politics, but the people running for the various positions will use their Christian faith, weak as it may be, for all it's worth, never realizing that it is detrimental to do so, as these types put themselves up as these Christian paragons of virtue who are then being tripped up by not meeting the required standards of conduct. When it comes to Christian values we must remind ourselves that it is absolutely essential to think live and breathe Jesus' teachings every day. It is sheer folly to try to package those into some catch-all phrase or logo ("armband religion") when these lack substance. The ongoing struggle within each of us and the seemingly endless anguish just cannot be expressed in anything appealing to the human vanity. There simply is no place for feeling superior to anyone as we are all finding ourselves in the same boat, trying and striving to the best of our ability to live up to what is expected of us as true believers, and nothing less will suffice.

How the Scriptures have been interpreted to suit one group or another would really be somewhat amusing, if it were not so deadly serious. We are in a nation which keeps religion and government politics separate. Can anyone remember when it was Christian men only who had made laws for everyone to live by, which put women in the category of possessions, chattel, second-class citizens, who had no rights or voice other than what men allowed them to have? And this had been going on for thousands of years, having its origin in Genesis 3, verses 13–16 of the Old Testament. Nobody wanted to acknowledge that Jesus Christ Himself had leveled the playing field when He was here on Earth and dealt with everyday situations involving women and there was never a hint of discrimination against them or a gesture indicating a woman's lesser worth.

Ephesians 5, verses 21–33, outlines exactly the inherent equal value of women with men. This passage has been twisted and tweaked by men who were the rulers to suit their own selfish inclinations (Ephes. 5:22) which forced women into the streets to demand the right to vote at the turn of the twentieth century and later on to have equal rights in the 1960s.

It was not an easy thing to change centuries-old attitudes through the political process, I am sure.

There is this lingering fear in women that some superior-feeling men would try to turn back the hands of time and recommend that for the good of this nation women should all stay home and tend to the children (which they should—but not exclusively) and preferably voluntarily.

It was primarily because men did not, and do not, live up to their responsibilities that women found themselves forced to change their lot. It is because men have abrogated their duties as heads of their households—their families—let alone met the criteria to lead a nation. It is instead a dangerous situation to have a Bible-toting imposter of any stripe make laws of any kind.

Only equality between the sexes can foster the kind of mutual respect conducive to a reciprocally beneficial union in the marriage relationship. Women have so much to contribute to the fabric of society, as they possess an array of abilities that men just do not have and vice versa. It only makes sense to utilize both sets of abilities in a complementary way to create a well-run society. It is a known fact that goodness and morality cannot be legislated with any kind of lasting success.

Only if a people agree to have the faith in the loving God at their center can laws be passed accommodating the rules of that belief.

And that has ceased to be the case here in this country where everybody insists on their legal right to be whatever they choose. We also know that just because something is legal does not mean it is good. As Christians we have the choice to pursue a quality of life commensurate with our faith, which is what is expected of us, but sadly the average Christian loses sight of that and so has become as worldly as their worldly counterparts and all they do is give lip service, oftentimes led by ministers who are as confused and misinformed as the sheep they shepherd.

There is a positive side to the institution of the Church and that is that it is still here for now and I am confident that we are going to see a great revival and continuing spiritual revolution taking place because this is going to be the last push against this almost unstoppable, destructive, mighty force of evil.

So many, many devoted Christians have over the centuries prepared the way for us by providing the witness of their faith by leaving their testimonies behind. The availability of help in the search for a relationship with God through faith in His only begotten son Jesus Christ is divinely providential and designed to lead multitudes to Christ in these last days. I am grateful for all the help I have received from countless saints working for the Lord and there are many. I remember when I was a young girl, another girl shared a room with me and two others at the student-home in Nürnberg. She caught my attention by being what God had planned for us to be, lovely, sweet and completely devoted to doing God's will. I saw her doing her devotions in the mornings and in the evenings and her whole demeanor was so other-worldly. While I was a believer too and did many of the same things, there was a quality about her I did not possess. She was already where it took me fifty-some years to get to and I am astonished to realize that some people are spiritually predisposed to reach a maturity way beyond their years. I think they are angels, really—beneficial to everyone, wherever they go, at all times. It would take them as much effort to do something wicked as it takes a normal person to refrain from doing something wicked.

I have often thought about her and could not understand much at the time but her mere presence impressed me and today I understand.

Before my lovely neighbor and friend, Vivian, passed away I had a lot of things to think about as I watched her health steadily decline. I often wondered what keeps people who profess to believe in the saving grace of God and who by all accounts lived a good life, yet are hanging on for dear life to the last moment, fighting, with all they have, to stay alive.

If we take seriously the claim of the Scriptures that there is life after death, that Jesus indeed had come as predicted in the Old Testament and as it is clearly witnessed to in the New Testament, to defeat sin (evil) and to remove the sting of death, would it not be a reasonable expectation for the true believer to have faith to help him/her to do just as Jesus has modeled for us; to pull ourselves out of this physical, material world by living to the fullest in this life only as it prepares us to enter into the other world where we will be truly alive? This would enable us to face the end of this life matter-of-factly, if not with anticipation. There would be no more desperate pursuit to artificially squeeze one more minute out of the physical.

My dear friend, Vivian, put herself through so much unnecessary misery and she was determined, as if it were some sort of law, to avail herself of every conceivable method to stay alive, which left her exhausted and increasingly diminished in mental capacity. It was hard to watch her suffer and yet there was nothing else anyone could do but keep watching and praying. She was just under eighty-nine years old and she had lived a good life. I still miss her and I can still hear her saying, "Ilona! Are you coming?" and that was three or so days after she had passed away, which was on a Sunday morning.

I am sure that things are going according to a plan and that is in line with what the Bible teaches, that everything happens for a purpose, as I have come to know the importance of having had this dear lady as my neighbor and friend and that I must now go on without her and that is really a good thing as I can now concentrate on things that remained undone and I simply did not have what it takes to flesh out the continuing story of God and I and Elvis! I came across bits and pieces here and there but I did not have the time or the understanding to give it the meaning, as it was there from the beginning. I just could not put it into perspective. For that I needed uninterrupted silence and prayer, no trips to the stores, having fun going out to eat or anything else in the way of spending time with friends and most of all, I had to sever ties with Elvis. This emotional attachment, though extremely important for such a long time, became a serious liability that kept me stationary in my spiritual development.

I am so gratified that I have a "pilot" in my life who steers me every inch of the way and I am confident that He will lead me home where I belong.

To touch briefly on the speaking-in-tongues phenomenon, I have to say that I have felt myself moved by the Holy Spirit to speak in tongues aloud during a worship-service, which I had thought impossible for me as I am quite shy, and one time I even gave the interpretation. I can hardly believe it myself, but I did. I also was moved by the Holy Spirit to sing, in front of everybody, The Lord's Prayer, which I was really happy to do as this is my favorite prayer of all time. But I cannot do any of these things on my own I must confess.

Contemplating writing this book I was naturally preoccupied with having to decide what to put into the book and what to leave out. I was struggling to decide whether I should include the notes from that trip home from Monaco on the plane and an irrational fear of my ex-husband plagued me and I just could not come to a decision when I had a dream in which I saw my ex-husband going up some stairs that resembled the stairs in the lovely home we shared. I was at the foot of the staircase and he was wearing jeans and a black shirt. The light around him was muted, much as it was when the wall lamp was on. I was talking to him and as he was reaching the top of the stairs, he turned around and he had that same hideous grimace on his face that he had way back in Monaco when he was coming towards me threatening "to give me what I deserve." I was positively paralyzed with fright and I could not breathe, my heart started to beat furiously and as I tried to catch my breath in my dream, I woke myself up with my heart still beating so hard I thought I was going to have a heart attack right then in my bed.

I pondered the meaning of this dream and I decided that I did not have to fear anything, that I have gone through hell and back many times and the Lord has seen me through all of it and He is going to be with me all the way home but my ex was walking away from me. Not toward me!

I do not know if it makes a difference that the stairs in my dream were free-standing, with darkness all around but I could hear my children, the older ones from the previous marriage and my son and daughter and youngest son, who was still in his walker, scooting around somewhere.

It is worth noting that my children were present in some form but I just could not see them, which points to the importance of my being a very caring mother, not unlike millions upon millions of mothers in this country alone. A mother's love is the nearest thing on earth to God's love. The wisdom of God is exhibited in motherhood. We are not a by-product of some biological process. We were not made on an assembly line by the combination of chemicals. Our mothers nurtured us and formed an intimate relationship with us before we were born. She jeopardized her life for us. A woman's greatest, most fulfilling and far-reaching role is expressed in motherhood.

The aforementioned mothers' day message comes from the Harvester gospel tract and exhorts children to remember Proverbs, first chapter, eighth verse . . . "forsake not the law of your mother . . . unwritten but indelibly stamped upon your mind! It is the law of love, kindness, of selflessness and giving."

As this underscores the importance of mothers it implies the importance of good fathers, for without them we mothers have a much harder time living up to our responsibilities.

Elvis loved his mother very much and she had indeed fulfilled her responsibility and taught Elvis the things of God that he remembered throughout his life. He was truly lost after her death, I am sure. He knew very well that without her keeping him straight he'd be vulnerable to all sorts of things, which were already evident when he was in the army and stationed in Texas. It is fairly safe to say that he knew even before then the many pitfalls that were appearing left and right as his popularity grew so fast and furious and the temptations pulled him from what he had been taught and what he believed. It must have been extremely difficult for him to find balance. I have often wondered how well I would have fared if that had happened to me and I know I would not have done any better. The reason most of us do not do the things Elvis did is mostly because we do not have the opportunity, I can only be thankful that I was not put into poor Elvis's position.

It is with this in mind that I assert that Elvis was a highly spiritual man and he had a role to play on the stage which is the world, a stage where high drama is playing itself out.

In conclusion, may I add that Elvis sang a song called, "Words":

> Smile an everlasting smile,
> A smile will bring you near to me.

> Talk in everlasting words,
> and dedicate them all to me.

... and that is what I have done with this book. It is a labor of LOVE and it is ultimately LOVE that will set things straight in keeping with the message of Christ.

AFTERWORD

Inasmuch as I have told my side of the story, it behooves me to delve a little bit into the life of Elvis to show the spiritual connection he and I share.

If you recall on Elvis's return from Germany in 1960 he gave an interview that showed him to be melancholy and answering pensively when asked if he left someone special behind. It seemed to me that he was remembering the moment he met with his true love. No, it was not Priscilla even though she became the focus of all speculations. Priscilla was merely a stand-in as she reminded him of me in her fourteen-year-old innocence. I saw this interview for the first time in 1998 and I was nonplussed as I would have liked to have known earlier on in order to have circumvented the doubts and fears that kept me as indifferent as I must have appeared to him. It was just like this for him, which he clearly addresses in the "Moody Blue" on his last LP, released shortly before his death. Most of the songs on this effort of his were recorded at Graceland as he was already feeling the coming end. He also sings "Unchained Melody," a true testament of his feelings of an all-consuming love. He sang it before an audience in June of 1977, profusely sweating and bloated and barely able to finish, asking Charlie to help him. This too I did not get to see until 1999, and it was excruciatingly painful for me to have to see him in such a state.

After his stint in Germany his whole demeanor changed. One could argue that having been in the army, away from home, the death of his mother, or just growing up were the cause for this change but I beg to differ. Please consider his musical output in the following years. He preferred the more classical ballads and he had an orchestra accompanying his vocals which reveal a very deep emotional dimension, so deep where no one has any control and that had not been before in any of his songs. There are many references to this in various accounts by people who surrounded him.

Elvis was a shy, private introvert by nature; he was very insecure and he feared rejection. His fragile ego had to be protected at all times and at all costs—and it was. Confused about the position he was now holding on the world stage, he felt pressure from all sides and he had to pay to provide a cocoon for himself to retreat to which also isolated him. In this protected environment his ego was fanned and coddled and he had a base from which to be able to handle his show-business career which is by all accounts a cutthroat business. However, Elvis was also very smart and his astute observations he had to keep to himself as he knew better than anyone the ugliness of show business which no one talked about in those days.

It was sort of a life-saver for him to have the opportunity to express his emotions of this deep, lost love in the beautiful love songs he loved to sing. This made his relationship with the Colonel a reciprocal one and one he maintained for just that reason. Otherwise he would have changed it as he was shrewd and he could have taken the reins and fashioned his life his own way but he was accountable to a higher power.

After we saw each other again after six years, I could clearly discern that he was talking to me in his songs made in 1964, 1965 and 1966 as he was singing about what was transpiring between us, or it is better to say what did not transpire between us. It was a source of consternation for both of us.

I must conclude in retrospect that the dreams I had in 1958 in Germany defined the blueprint for our lives, which are rooted in the supernatural. The "Time will tell!" re-assurance in my meeting with God provided the "Golden Thread" which weaved itself through my entire life which I assert is my faith in the living Triune God of the Bible.

Whenever I felt compelled to make an attempt to bring about a harmonious "meeting of the minds" by calling Charlie and to get things going, which poor Charlie really tried to do, I made a royal mess of things, saying things I had never even thought of before instead. Strange as it seems the outcomes of these attempts were a guide of sorts which I had to follow and it was a "no-go" each time for any kind of earthly togetherness.

As hope springs eternal, Elvis and I kept hoping and dreaming and he managed to convey the depth of his longing, his joy, his passion and his pain with such eloquence, it is clearly audible in the ever-so-nuanced complexity of his emotions in his delivery in "I'll Hold You In My Heart (Till I Can Hold You In My Arms)" and "Now After Loving You," just to name two, as I really do not want to give an RCA masters list. There are many though.

Our spiritual connectedness gave him support that he sang about in "The Wonder of You," and "Come What May," again just to name two, but there are many more with similar sentiments. There is something so poignantly sweet, almost achingly emotional and therefore revelatory in Elvis' rendition of "That's Someone You Never Forget" penned and arranged by Elvis Presley and Red West in 1972.

After his death and the revelation of Elvis's perversion, debauchery, drug abuse and narcissistic way of life, I simply tried to forget him and consequently missed vital information that could have shed light on the mystery that was Elvis for me, but it was revealed to me in such precise timing where it would accomplish what had to be accomplished—it is truly amazing!

Even his contribution in the gospel genre I dismissed as a crass attempt to avail himself of the commercial opportunity, a calculated pandering to the legions of older females who were brought up in the Judeo-Christian tradition, never mind the exquisite sincerity in his delivery of the gospel songs, in which he seems to transcend into the supernatural, thoroughly encompassing deeply held love for God in every believer's heart. It was on a PBS fund-raiser on TV when I first heard of his abiding love for gospel songs and hymns from his Pentecostal upbringing, which his mother provided him by taking him to the First Assembly of God church on Adam Street in Tupelo, Mississippi. The original building has been sitting on the grounds of the Birthplace here in town since last year. However, the congregation, of which I am happy to be a member, worships at 1921 Briar Ridge Road.

It was never about the happiness of two lowly people here on this planet, in this dimension and Elvis "knew" as much or as little to be able to do what he had to do in keeping with our assignment as it required both of us and this holds true for me as well—I "knew" as much or as little to function just as needed. Only God can and will choose the time when He will disclose the fulfillment of His Plan of Redemption that He devised and put into motion at the dawn of time and the spiritual man.